Latin American Social Movements and Progressive Governments

LATIN AMERICAN PERSPECTIVES
IN THE CLASSROOM

Series Editor: Ronald H. Chilcote

Titles in Series

Urban Latin America edited by Tom Angotti

Rereading Women in Latin America and the Caribbean: The Political Economy of Gender edited by Jennifer Abbassi and Sheryl L. Lutjens

Contemporary Latin American Revolutions, Second Edition by Marc Becker

Development in Theory and Practice: Latin American Perspectives edited by Ronald H. Chilcote

Latin American Studies and the Cold War edited by Ronald H. Chilcote

Latin American Extractivism: Dependency, Resource Nationalism and Resistance in Broad Perspective edited by Steve Ellner

Latin America's Pink Tide: Breakthroughs and Shortcomings edited by Steve Ellner

Latin America's Radical Left: Challenges and Complexities of Political Power in the Twenty-first Century edited by Steve Ellner

Latin American Social Movements and Progressive Governments: Creative Tensions between Resistance and Convergence edited by Steve Ellner, Ronaldo Munck, and Kyla Sankey

Venezuela: Hugo Chávez and the Decline of an "Exceptional Democracy" edited by Steve Ellner and Miguel Tinker Salas

Contemporary Latin American Social and Political Thought: An Anthology edited by Iván Márquez

Mayan Lives, Mayan Utopias: The Indigenous Peoples of Chiapas and the Zapatista Rebellion edited by Jan Rus, Rosalva Aída Hernández, and Shannan L. Mattiace

The United States and Cuba: From Closest Enemies to Distant Friends by Francisco López Segrera

Rethinking Latin American Social Movements: Radical Action from Below edited by Richard Stahler-Sholk, Harry E. Vanden, and Marc Becker

Memory, Truth, and Justice in Contemporary Latin America edited by Roberta Villalón

Latin American Social Movements in the Twenty-first Century: Resistance, Power, and Democracy edited by Richard Stahler-Sholk, Harry E. Vanden, and Glen David Kuecker

Transnational Latina/o Communities: Politics, Processes, and
  Cultures edited by Carlos G. Vélez-Ibáñez and Anna Sampaio, with
  Manolo González-Estay

Latin American Social Movements and Progressive Governments

Creative Tensions between Resistance and Convergence

Edited by Steve Ellner, Ronaldo Munck, and Kyla Sankey

ROWMAN & LITTLEFIELD
Lanham • Boulder • New York • London

Published by Rowman & Littlefield
An imprint of The Rowman & Littlefield Publishing Group, Inc.
4501 Forbes Boulevard, Suite 200, Lanham, Maryland 20706
www.rowman.com

86-90 Paul Street, London EC2A 4NE

British Library Cataloguing in Publication Information Available

Library of Congress Cataloging-in-Publication Data

Names: Ellner, Steve, editor. | Munck, Ronaldo, editor. | Sankey, Kyla, editor.
Title: Latin American social movements and progressive governments : creative tensions between resistance and convergence / edited by Steve Ellner, Ronaldo Munck, and Kyla Sankey.
Description: Lanham : Rowman & Littlefield, [2022] | Series: Latin American perspectives in the classroom | Includes bibliographical references and index.
Identifiers: LCCN 2022026280 (print) | LCCN 2022026281 (ebook) | ISBN 9781538163948 (cloth) | ISBN 9781538163955 (paperback) | ISBN 9781538163962 (epub)
Subjects: LCSH: Social movements--Latin America. | Social problems--Latin America. | Latin America--Politics and government.
Classification: LCC JL960 .L373 2022 (print) | LCC JL960 (ebook) | DDC 361.2/4098–dc23/eng/20220801
LC record available at https://lccn.loc.gov/2022026280
LC ebook record available at https://lccn.loc.gov/2022026281

Contents

Foreword

Susan Eckstein

Latin American countries share both common colonial heritages and exposure to similar contemporary global economic, political, social, and cultural processes that have contributed to the region's having the most inequitable distribution of wealth and income in the world. The neoliberal restructuring that took the region by storm beginning in the mid-1980s deepened the inequities, despite countries' having transitioned by then from military rule to electoral democracies. The new democracies did little immediately to reduce the long-standing inequities or to advance the rights of women, indigenous peoples, and other minorities. Against this backdrop, around the turn of this century disillusioned citizens in many countries in the region voted into office so-called Pink Tide progressive governments, distinct both from Soviet-era Communist-dominated "red" and right-wing military and civilian regimes.

The Pink Tide governments owe their origin not merely to voters who supported political parties of the left but also to dissatisfied folk who mobilized to make new demands on the state. The seeds of many of the demand-making movements that proliferated under the new democracies lay in the mass movements that had helped bring the military governments to heel, having convinced previously powerless people of the "art of the possible." As a consequence, women, indigenous peoples, and blacks, among others, separately and in new "intersectional" combinations, came to feel empowered to make social, cultural, and economic demands on their governments through extrainstitutional channels.

The social movements and the protests they organized brought into the political arena new as well as previously active Latin Americans pressing for both new and long-sought changes. In the process, the Latin American social movement repertoire expanded. Some of the movements addressed rights for abortion and same-sex marriage, which the Catholic Church, allied with ruling elites, had historically opposed. Women who had courageously protested against the military governments that murdered their children and grandchildren went on to mobilize for specific gendered concerns, such as reproductive rights, but also LGBT rights and a stop to violence against women. The essays in this book by Eduardo Moreira da Silva and Clarisse Goulart Paradis and by Daniel Burridge highlight relations between feminists and governments in Bolivia, Argentina, Chile, Brazil, and El Salvador.

Indigenous peoples, in turn, have mobilized for land and cultural rights, including the right to education in their native languages, after centuries of forced acculturation and social exclusion. They and others have also called for national ownership of natural resources and for a halt to environmental destruction by foreign-owned companies that have aggressively been extracting nonrenewable resources for export to take advantage of high international commodity prices. Still other social movements have been pressing for the affordable food, transportation, and education to which they feel entitled.

Many of the movements have been referred to as "new social movements" because of the new people they have mobilized and the new demands on the state they have made. In contrast, during the heyday of import substitution, in the 1950s and 1960s, the most vibrant and effective mobilizations were class-based, by workers demanding better wages, better working conditions, and better health and other social benefits. The military governments of the 1970s that promoted the interests of local and foreign capital repressed the labor movements so that they lost their earlier vitality. Then, the new democracies that had sent the military back to the barracks instituted neoliberal reforms that further weakened workers' bargaining power by subjecting them to unfettered global market competition so as to attract foreign capital.

Nonetheless, even when labor's collective bargaining power weakened, labor won rights, as illustrated by Fabricio Carneiro, Guillermo Fuentes, and Carmen Midaglia in their essay on the relationship between progressive parties and union movements in the Southern Cone. Moreover, workers took their class-based concerns and collective organizing experiences with them when they moved into new work settings. In Bolivia, militant miners who lost their jobs with the closure of inefficient mines resettled in regions of the country well-suited to coca growing for the ever-expanding global market for cocaine. Unionizing to defend their economic interests against U.S.-financed efforts to destroy their livelihoods, coca growers, along with teachers and other lower-middle-class urban groups and poor migrants (as detailed in John Brown's essay), mobilized to help elect Evo Morales Latin America's first self-identified indigenous president in 2006. Morales campaigned on an anti-neoliberal platform that called for raising taxes on the hydrocarbon industry to finance social spending on projects to combat illiteracy, poverty, racism, and sexism for the benefit of the majority of Bolivians whom neoliberal and earlier governments had either ignored or discriminated against.

While in no other Latin American country did social movements play so central a role in ushering in a Pink Tide government as in Bolivia, broad-based social movements in other Latin American countries also contributed to the Pink Tide. As early as 1998, after the Carlos Andrés Pérez administration introduced International Monetary Fund (IMF)–backed neoliberal policies that raised gasoline and transportation prices, angry Venezuelans turned to the streets en masse in what came to be known as the Caracazo. Building on the discontent, Hugo Chávez won the presidency on the promise to fight disease, illiteracy, malnutrition, and poverty. In Ecuador Rafael Correa won the presidency the same year as Morales in Bolivia on a similar platform: critiquing the established political elites and the neoliberal model they promoted and calling for policies to reduce poverty and income inequality and raise the minimum wage. Newly politicized indigenous groups were important to his electoral victory.

Brazil is the one country where labor, well organized in unions and with a political party dedicated to it, withstood the neoliberal onslaught. In 2002, the main worker-based political party successfully won the presidency. Under the savvy leadership of Luiz Inácio Lula da Silva, the Partido dos Trabalhadores (Workers' Party) implemented antipoverty programs that both lifted millions of Brazilians from poverty and improved the distribution of wealth. However, amid accusations of corruption in Lula's and his successor's administration and mounting crime, Brazilians went on to elect a conservative, Jair Bolsonaro, president in 2018. Bolsonaro turned on labor, increasing unemployment and poverty. In so doing, he fueled resentment that contributed to a build-up of support for Lula's running again for the presidency. The labor movement remained an important political force in Brazil even when not officially in power.

The country case studies in this book address, in turn, the impact social movements have had on the evolution of left-leaning Pink Tide governments and the impact of such governments on social movements in the region. In a theoretically informed and historically grounded analysis, the essay by Kyla Sankey and Aaron Tauss on state–social-movement relations elucidates the dialectic relationship between governments and social movements in various countries of the region over the years. Because there is an inherent tension between social movements, with their specific concerns, and governments, with their wide range of economic and political responsibilities, governments try to co-opt social movements in order to contain their demands.

Yet, social movements themselves are inherently unstable. Their leaders are likely to prioritize maintaining and expanding their base of power, which often conflicts with rank-and-file member interests. The German political sociologist Robert Michels brilliantly illustrated this in his study of the German Socialist Party, which led him to postulate his well-known "iron law of oligarchy"—that even the leadership of a political party committed to egalitarian precepts prioritizes its own interests. The iron law gives reason to expect leaders of social movements who played a central role in the coming to power of progressive Pink Tide governments to be co-opted and, in losing their autonomy, come to prioritize the state over their social bases' concerns. In Nicaragua the broad-based Sandinista movement that overthrew the repressive, corrupt Anastasio Somoza government allied with the United States returned to power in 2007 after losing two elections, at which point Daniel Ortega, as president, turned on the very social movements that had brought him and the Sandinista party to power in 1979. Similarly, in El Salvador the Frente Farabundo Martí para la Liberación Nacional (Farabundo Martí National Liberation Front—FMLN), a key Marxist guerrilla group in the country's 1980s civil war, in the 1990s laid down its arms and regrouped as a political party. In 2009 its candidate, Mauricio Funes, won the presidential election but then, amid allegations of money laundering, fled the country. When governing, the FMLN turned on the once-autonomous progressive social movements that had helped it get elected.

The case studies, in turn, point to the fragility and vulnerability of Pink Tide governments, especially when macroeconomic conditions such as a downturn in international commodity prices reduced fiscal resources for financing antipoverty and other social programs on which their support rested. A plunge in world market commodity prices after the 2008 financial crisis contributed to new electoral victories by conservative political parties committed to neoliberalism, for example, in Chile, Brazil, Argentina, Bolivia, and El Salvador, where candidates promised to crack down on crime and corruption but also promoted fiscal austerity involving cutbacks in antipoverty programs and spending on education that had helped reduce ethnic, racial, and class disparities. As detailed in the essays by Lucas Koerner and Emelio Betances, respectively, Venezuela and Mexico, under the presidencies of Nicolás Maduro and Andrés Manuel López Obrador, were among the only countries in Latin America that maintained Pink Tide governments amid the region's neoliberal "backsliding."

At the same time, the new neoliberal turn generated its own contradictions, fueling new mobilizations to return to office Pink Tide governments that prioritized ordinary citizens' concerns. In Chile the neoliberal policies of President Sebastián Piñera brought Chileans to the streets to bury the remaining vestiges of Augusto Pinochet's brutal military government of the 1970s and 1980s, calling for a new constitution that would not only formalize rights for women and indigenous peoples but also revoke military privileges. Chileans also rallied to put a stop to neoliberal policies they considered unjust, such as Piñera's increase in user fees for public education and public transportation. The protests persuaded voters to elect Gabriel Boric, a 35-year-old former student leader, president. In his victory speech he addressed indigenous rights and gender equality and took aim at mining projects that hurt the environment.

With a much slimmer majority, in Peru the leftist Pedro Castillo, a former teacher and union organizer who had led teacher strikes against the former neoliberal Pedro Pablo Kuczynski administration, won the presidency (Kuczynski having resigned following corruption charges to avoid impeachment). Building his campaign on the massive protests that had rocked the country in 2019, he vowed to overhaul the political and economic system that favored the elite, reduce poverty, inequality, and social injustice, and equalize access of all Peruvians to quality education. He campaigned against the backdrop of the highest documented per capita COVID death toll in the world and the new impoverishment of some 10 percent of the population. To finance his proposed reforms, he called for nationalizing ownership of the country's natural resources and imposing tax increases on the superrich.

The Pink Tide governments speak to the strengths and weaknesses of the new Latin American democracies. They are far more inclusionary than previous governments in the region, but they are rooted in the breakdown of the traditional political party system, which over the years ignored the yearnings of the electorate. The 2021 Chilean and Peruvian elections, for example, were won by candidates associated with newly formed political parties. Boric founded his own political party in 2016, and Castillo won the presidency despite never having held political office and being affiliated with a political party formed in 2016 that won its first seat in Congress in 2021. Whether their political parties will stand the test of time remains to be seen.

Thus, after centuries of entrenched inequalities between rich and poor, between men and women, and between light-and dark-skinned peoples, social movements and Pink Tide governments have tried to make Latin America more just and equitable. While they have made inroads, they leave much work to be done.

Introduction

Progressive Governments and Social Movements in Latin America: An Alternative Line of Thinking

Steve Ellner

In country after country in Latin America, social movements and mass protests at the turn of the century undermined the legitimacy of neoliberal governments and in doing so paved the way for the Pink Tide phenomenon—leftist and center-leftist governments.[1] Widely different scenarios played out depending on the case. In Bolivia, Pink Tide president Evo Morales and his Movimiento al Socialismo (Movement toward Socialism—MAS) emerged as a result of social struggles involving the coca growers dating back to the early 1980s. In Venezuela the nationwide disturbances against neoliberal policies of the week of February 27, 1989, initiated a wave of protests that led into the February 4, 1992, coup led by Hugo Chávez and then the ouster of President Carlos Andrés Pérez, which in turn set the stage for Chávez's election as president in 1998 (López Maya, 2002: 18–21). In Ecuador and Argentina, social movement protests toppled governments that preceded the Pink Tide's triumph in presidential elections. In Mexico, mobilizations that discredited governments prior to Andrés Manuel López Obrador's election as president ranged from protests against the brutal disappearance in 2014 of 43 students in the city of Iguala to those in opposition to multiparty agreements leading to the privatization of the oil industry, as discussed by Emelio Betances in this volume.

Similarly, two decades prior to the Pink Tide, social movements facilitated the Latin American transition from military rule to democracy. In Argentina, for instance, protests carried out by the Madres y Abuelas de Plaza de Mayo did much to discredit and disgrace the military rulers. Mass mobilizations ended up voicing the slogan "Direct Elections Now!" in Brazil and calling on people to vote no in the referendum in 1988 on Pinochet's continuation in office in Chile. However, once momentum for democracy was achieved in the 1980s, elite actors called on social movements to play a subordinate role to moderate politicians and in some cases military ones. Indeed, many prominent scholars, including Samuel Huntington, Daniel Levine, Robert Kaufman, Adam Przeworski, and Samuel Valenzuela, argued that militant popular mobilization and leftist parties only held back the process of democratization, while some claimed that "the general citizenry may not have the values a sustainable democracy requires" (see discussion by Bermeo, 1997: 306). Other writers argued the contrary on the basis of Latin American experiences in the 1980s and faulted the literature for playing down the contribution of social movements and highlighting "the salience of elite actors and political pacts" (Foweraker, 1995: 102: Bermeo, 1997: 305, 312). The sequence of events leading up to regime change in the 1980s contrasted with the lead-up to the Pink Tide in Bolivia, Ecuador, Venezuela, and Argentina, where protests that brought governments to their knees tended to be more massive, violent, and focused on socioeconomic demands, specifically anti-neoliberalism.

During the period of democratic transition in the 1980s, a number of scholars embraced the "new social movement" paradigm associated with the French sociologist Alain Touraine, which focused on the transformational impact of social movements on their members and the cultural change it produced. For these writers, the newness of new social movements was manifested in their determination to maintain complete independence from the state (absolute autonomy). Writers on new social movements also lauded the recently formed social movements for raising principled nonclass demands related to indigenous and women's rights that were nonnegotiable. In the 1980s and much of the 1990s, the concept of new social movements (in contrast to the more statist political opportunity theory)[2] attracted many writers in Latin America, where antistatist sentiment was especially pronounced (Davis, 1999: 586–587). In their apprehension of state intrusion, the defenders of the concept of new social movements converged with advocates of neoliberalism in spite of occupying the opposite end of the political spectrum.[3] Two implications of the approach are especially relevant to the study of Latin American social movements in the twenty-first century. First, its champions argued that the absolute autonomy of social movements vis-à-vis both political parties and the state needed to be safeguarded at all costs. Second, they defended social movement demands as a matter of principle rather than watering them down for pragmatic purposes, adopting an all-or-nothing approach as opposed to negotiating with politicians and state bureaucrats.

By the 1990s, activists and scholars put forward a critique of this line of thinking on the basis of social movement experiences in the age of democracy and neoliberalism. Joe Foweraker best articulated it in his *Theorizing Social*

Movements (1995), which argued that engaging with the state and political parties in order to achieve concrete objectives did not necessarily hamstring social movements. He pointed out that, far from fitting the mold of new social movements, social movements in the 1990s were unlikely to "escape the pressures of partisan politics in a more open political society" and more likely to operate in an institutional framework, seek allies, and negotiate than those of the period of military rule (Foweraker, 2001: 848–849). He argued that advocates of new social movements acted "as if the continent ha[d] suddenly become postmodern and postmaterial" (Foweraker, 1995: 35)—terms that were Touraine's point of reference.

The issues framed by writers on Latin American social movements in the twenty-first century recalled the debate between Foweraker's line of thinking and that of the advocates of new social movements in the latter years of the twentieth century. Timothy Wickham-Crowley and Susan Eckstein (2015) and Eduardo Silva (2015: 28) considered the idea of new social movements inapplicable to Latin American social movements in the twenty-first century. Wickham-Crowley and Eckstein examined social movements in Brazil and Bolivia and concluded that twenty-first-century social movements in the continent were not particularly novel and were more class-and economic-oriented and more closely related to the state than was claimed by new social movement theory (see also Silva, 2015: 29; Munck, 2020: 59, 85). Wickham-Crowley and Eckstein (2015: 16) summarized their discussion of Brazil by saying that "an NSM [new social movement] frame privileging issues of culture and identity . . . provides no analytic tools for understanding the most important aspects of the MST [Landless Workers' Movement]."

Among the writers on twenty-first-century social movements, John Holloway most resembles the twentieth-century advocates of new social movements. He argues that transforming society through social movements rather than the state is what the revolution is all about. His libertarian thinking is influenced by the autonomism associated with Antonio Negri, which championed the absolute autonomy of social movements without any input from political parties or the state. Holloway has lived and taught in Mexico since 1991 and has heaped praise on the Zapatistas since their initial actions in 1994. Accepting the same assumptions as the new social movement paradigm, he writes that the Zapatistas broke with the politics of the past, as represented by the guerrilla movement and other Leninist organizations that had their eyes on state power. Thus, from the outset the Zapatistas indicated that they would not accept support from or "negotiate" with the state and would "take part in a dialogue" with it only in order to reach out to civil society and the world in general, where allegedly it enjoyed considerable influence (Holloway and Peláez, 1998: 1–18; Holloway, 2019: 103, 235,

238). Holloway's thesis on the need to bypass the state and political parties and the emergence of a new type of social movement has had limited influence among twenty-first-century scholars (for one example, see Motta, 2009: 44; 2013: 6–7, 11). The Zapatistas, for their part, in spite of their original ambition of impacting Mexican politics at the national level (Stahler-Sholk, Vanden, and Kuecker, 2007: 13), have had a limited following and negligible political impact. This weakness was demonstrated in 2018, when they were unable to collect the required number of signatures to run their candidate in that year's presidential elections. For the twenty-first-century defenders of the new social movement thesis, the fact that the Zapatistas have been politically marginalized is not of particular significance (Motta, 2009: 43).

A much larger group of writers of a leftist orientation, while not defending the absolute autonomy of social movements in principle or antipolitics rhetoric, views twenty-first-century Latin American social movements as in permanent conflict with governments over irreconcilable differences. Although some of them explicitly reject social movement autonomism as defined by Negri and Holloway (Gonzalez, 2019: 19, 154, 169–170, 255–256), they all stress the importance of autonomy. Furthermore, although they are not antistatist in principle, they condemn all twenty-first-century Latin American governments. They identify with a variety of schools of thought including Trotskyism (Gonzalez, 2019), radical environmentalism (Acosta, 2017), postcolonial theory (Lander, 2014), social movement–poststructuralism (Raúl Zibechi [see Cruz Rodríguez, 2019]), libertarianism-anarchism, and democratic socialism or do not have a well-defined ideological orientation (Svampa, 2018; 2019).

The fundamental issue on which these writers focus is the failure of all governments in the region to reduce their dependence on global capitalism and their commitment to extractive industry for increasing state revenue. The resultant policies allegedly enter into conflict with the essence of the various social movements in that extractivism undermines democracy, intensifies gender injustices and ecological devastation, and denies communities, especially indigenous ones, their rights, such as the right of previous consultation (Lander, 2014: 11; 2019: 94–98; Svampa, 2018: 21–22; 2019: 32).[4] The same writers reject the "statist" or "Stalinist" model followed by Pink Tide governments in their relations with social movements, specifically the violation of social movement autonomy (Lander, 2017). They are also highly critical of the Pink Tide's stormy relations with some social movements and its tendency to co-opt their activists, the end result being the weakening of social movements in general (Zibechi, 2019b; 2008: 84; Cruz Rodríguez, 2019: 191).

The views of these writers are influenced by two social movements that they hold in high regard, both of them hostile to the Pink Tide governments in their respective nations, the Zapatistas and the Confederación de Nacionalidades

Indigenas del Ecuador (Confederation of Indigenous Nationalities of Ecuador—CONAIE). It is thus not surprising that they minimize or deny the existence of important differences among twenty-first-century Latin American governments, all of which are sometimes alleged to be representatives of new elites and neoliberal in orientation (Zibechi, 2019a; Zibechi and Machado, 2017: 128; Svampa, 2018: 23–25; Webber, 2011: 234). Just as in the case of the Zapatistas as well as many of the champions of new social movements, they tend to adopt an all-or-nothing position with regard to conflicts over extractive projects (Svampa, 2018: 22–23; see also Ellner, 2021: 15).

On the positive side, the works of these writers serve as a point of departure for critically analyzing social movement struggles beyond an exclusively political focus on the clash between progressive governments and a radicalized pro-neoliberal opposition. The staunch defenders of the Pink Tide tend to brush aside the specificity of social movement demands and strategies and instead center their analysis on political imperatives—the threats posed by powerful and intransigent adversaries supported by the United States (see Munck, 2020: 118). Certainly, these challenges to Pink Tide governments cannot be overestimated, and they have had a direct bearing on government–social-movement relations, as Lucas Koerner demonstrates in this volume. Nevertheless, even in the context of intense political hostility there were opportunities for Pink Tide leaders to deepen democracy and promote the symbiotic relationship with social movements that they had committed themselves to from the outset (Ellner, 2020c: 12–14; 2020a: 184–185). The works of many of the Pink Tide critics on the left raise the need for an examination of the options available to progressive governments and social movements and the feasibility of concessions on the part of both. As some scholars have pointed out (Stahler-Sholk, Vanden, and Kuecker 2007: 14; Bacallao-Pino, 2016: 109),[5] the uniqueness of the Pink Tide in Latin America, which involved more governments that lasted longer in power than those of previous democratic and leftist waves, makes such an examination of relations with social movements especially compelling.

A starting point is the rejection of the binary view (Sankey and Munck, 2020: 4; Munck, 2020: 116) put forward by many analysts and some activists of social movements as either completely autonomist or dominated by the state or the party, generalizations that belie what is happening on the ground. As Wickham-Crowley and Eckstein (2015: 8) point out, few Latin American social movements in the twenty-first century conform to the model of autonomy envisioned by new social movement advocates. At the other extreme, left-leaning political parties are sometimes viewed, even by writers on the left end of the political spectrum, as intent on dominating social movements and organizations and subordinating issues of gender and ethnicity to class (Bacallao-Pino, 2016: 107).

The chapters in this book present a balanced view of the relations between Pink Tide governments and social movements. On the one hand, Pink Tide governments sometimes overreacted to the critiques and assertions of autonomy of social movements and held back from engaging in dialogue with them. On the other hand, they promoted the creation of social organizations and movements by marginalized and semimarginalized sectors of the population, thus facilitating their sense of empowerment and their incorporation into the political life of the nation. The rest of this introductory essay will first examine the actions of social movements in the years immediately prior to the onset of the Pink Tide, which prefigured the types of relations between the state and social movements that prevailed under Pink Tide rule. Next it will explore the areas of convergence and conflict between Pink Tide governments and social movements. The last section will deal with the resistance of social movements to the neoliberal policies of conservative and right-wing governments that broke out in 2019—protests that demonstrated that anti-neoliberalism was a common thread linking (or potentially linking) social movements with progressive political parties, some associated with the Pink Tide.

SOCIAL MOVEMENTS IN THE LEAD-UP TO THE PINK TIDE: PAVING THE WAY FOR CHANGE

The 1990s were the heyday of neoliberalism, which envisioned a divorce between the state and civil society. They were also a period of disillusionment with the democratic wave that had swept the region in the previous decade. The disenchantment triggered the politics of antipolitics best expressed in the slogan associated with the mass mobilizations that forced the Argentine President Fernando de la Rúa out of office in 2001: "Out with them all!" Both developments—neoliberalism and disillusionment with the performance of post-transition governments—contributed in their own ways to the sentiment in favor of the separation of social movements from political society.

Nevertheless, many of the most important social movements of these years were hardly apolitical. In Ecuador, for instance, CONAIE abandoned its position of electoral abstention in 1995 to help found the political organization Pachakutik, which months later ran a candidate in the presidential elections who received 21 percent of the vote. Another outstanding example of the nexus between social movements and political society was the role played by MAS in the protest movements in Bolivia that achieved major concessions from various governments and the ouster of president Gonzalo Sánchez de

Lozada. In the first place, MAS and its standard-bearer Evo Morales emerged from one of the nation's major social movements, that of the coca growers, some of whom were former miners. In the second place, MAS in its initial years defined itself as not a party but a movement, a term that it later largely abandoned. In the third place, although MAS did not play the lead role in the major protests prior to Morales's election in 2005, it was, in the words of two political observers, "the only [one] capable of constructing a political project and an electoral program where all the unsatisfied demands of the popular sectors and the subaltern classes could find space" (quoted in Munck, 2020: 89).

The clash within the Venezuelan neighborhood movement between leaders of the Escuela de Vecinos (Neighbors' School) and the Federación de Asociaciones de Comunidades Urbanas (Federation of Urban Community Associations—FACUR) in the 1980s and 1990s sheds light on the contrast between the antipolitical point of view associated with neoliberalism and the political strategy of other social movements. The Escuela de Vecinos, which held classes for neighborhood activists, defended the position of absolute autonomy, while FACUR defended the political position. FACUR's ambivalence with regard to political involvement was typical of many social movements, which participated in politics but were also committed to maintaining their independence (Davis, 1999: 609). Throughout the period, political parties were well represented on the federation's governing board and in its presidency. At the same time, however, FACUR objected to the political party membership of alleged "nonpartisans" sitting on the executive board of the nation's electoral council and as a corrective proposed neighborhood movement representation on that body. In addition, some FACUR leaders were elected to city councils not as party members but as neighborhood leaders. One former FACUR president and nonparty member, Angel Zambrano, who ran for mayor of Baruta, a municipality of Caracas, three times and was elected once, encouraged other neighborhood leaders to run for office in the name of the neighborhood movement.

In contrast, the former FACUR president Elías Santana, who headed the Escuela de Vecinos, envisioned the neighborhood movement as basically an interest group within the political sphere and expressed fear that FACUR would be absorbed by political parties and specifically by the nation's largest party, Acción Democrática (Democratic Action). FACUR leaders lashed out at Santana, claiming that he represented a Trojan horse for business interests within the neighborhood movement (Ellner, 1999a: 80). Indeed, Santana had a column in the nation's leading newspaper, *El Nacional,* that coincided with the newspaper's editorial line critical of political parties per se in accordance with neoliberal thinking. Subsequently he became a spokesman for the social movements that were opposed to Hugo Chávez in the early years of his government.

The electoral triumphs that brought Pink Tide movements to power, far from occurring in a vacuum, were the result of conditions largely created by social movements (Webber, 2017: 284; Gonzalez, 2019: 24). Most important, social movements articulated the loss of legitimacy of the governments that preceded those of the Pink Tide. Protests called by social movements in Argentina against the de la Rúa government, in Bolivia against Gonzalo Sánchez de Lozada, and in Ecuador against Lucio Gutiérrez brought to the fore the issues of repression and neoliberalism (including privatization in Bolivia, free trade in Ecuador, and the dollarized economy in Argentina and Ecuador). The social movement victories with the ouster of governments in all three countries (as well as that of neoliberal Venezuelan President Carlos Andrés Pérez) created expectations and a sense of empowerment that were favorable to far-reaching change. Furthermore, alliances between social movements and leftist parties that were forged in the heat of battle against neoliberal governments in Bolivia, Uruguay, and Brazil were also conducive to progressive change. In Brazil, the tight relationship between the Partido dos Trabalhadores (Workers' Party—PT) and social movements dated back to the democracy movement against the military regime in the 1980s. Indeed, in all three countries (and in Chile and to some extent in El Salvador), social movements had an input into the formation of what was to be the governing party of a Pink Tide government. Finally, mass mobilizations and expressions of popular outrage were a hedge against electoral fraud that would have deprived Pink Tide presidential candidates of their electoral victories. The rejection of the electoral results of October 2019 in Bolivia that favored the presidential candidacy of Evo Morales and the resultant coup against his government demonstrated the possibility of such a scenario.

The fact that Pink Tide movements rode the wave of social protest at the turn of the century helps explain the popular thrust of Pink Tide governments, specifically their social programs. This cause-effect relationship is often lost on those who minimize the difference between progressive and conservative heads of state in Latin America (Ellner, 2021: 3, 6–7). Social mobilizations that threaten to bring down governments sometimes produce backlashes or retreats that result in the restoration or strengthening of the status quo. This is what happened, for instance, with the overwhelming electoral triumph of the party of Charles de Gaulle in the wake of the student protests in France in May 1968. Similarly, the army colonel Lucio Gutiérrez collaborated with CONAIE-led protests that in 2000 toppled an Ecuadorian president who pursued neoliberal policies but, after being elected president in 2002 on an anti-neoliberal platform with social movement support, ended up embracing neoliberal formulas. Nevertheless, more often than not, mass social protests that rock nations usher in progressive change and have an impact on governments. In the case of the Pink Tide, the close relations and in some cases organizational ties between social movements and the governing party prior to its coming to power were conducive to the Pink Tide's continued commitment to the popular sectors. In addition, the fact that social movement activists took credit for its rise to power, and felt empowered by it, contributed to the likelihood that it would be subject to considerable pressure to honor its commitments. This view of the relationship between the Pink Tide and social movements contradicts the thesis of Huntington and others on the adverse effects of social movement disruptions in the period of democratic transition in the 1980s.

The prior relations between social movements and the Pink Tide influenced their relations once it was in power. In Ecuador, for example, in contrast to elsewhere in the region, there was considerable distance between CONAIE-Pachakutik, with its distrust of reformist politicians, and President Rafael Correa, with his technocratic background and lack of ties with social movements. In the first round of the 2006 presidential elections, Pachakutik ran the CONAIE president, Luis Macas, as its candidate on the basis of an ethnic appeal and in doing so broke with leftist organizations that endorsed Correa's more broad-based candidacy. Of all the Pink Tide countries, Ecuador had the most acrimonious government–social-movement relations, and indeed Correa—in an obvious reference to CONAIE—at one point lamented that his major political challenge came from the "ultraleft" and not the oligarchy. In Venezuela and Argentina government relations with popular sector movements were not nearly as intense, even though Pink Tide leaderships in those nations had lacked ties with social movements prior to reaching power.

AREAS OF CONVERGENCE AND CONFLICT

The chapters in this book present a mixed view of the relations between social movements and Pink Tide governments. On the one hand, the progressive governments failed to live up to the expectations of popular protest activists, which were especially high because of the key role they played in the Pink Tide's coming to power. On the other hand, Pink Tide governments were more receptive to social movement demands and less repressive in their handling of social movement protests than neoliberal governments. Indeed, one of this book's basic postulates is that in order to understand the attitudes of social movement members toward the Pink Tide it is necessary to compare its performance with that of the neoliberal governments that preceded and followed it. Among other factors regarding the relations between Pink Tide governments and social movements were the following. First, social movements incorporated previously excluded sectors of the population (indigenous people in Bolivia, members of the informal economy in Venezuela) that were part of the social base of Pink Tide parties. Second, the perception by popular social movement activists that the government was friendly fostered a sense of empowerment and was conducive to movement consolidation, as Anthony Pahnke shows in his chapter on the Movimento dos Trabalhadores Rurais Sem Terra (Landless Workers' Movement—MST) in this volume. Third, Pink Tide governments relied on social movement mobilizations in response to the disruptions and threats originating from an opposition committed to regime change. These actions cemented Pink Tide–social movement ties.

Throughout the period under study, anti-neoliberalism was a common ground shared by popular social movements and Pink Tide political movements. Even the popular social movement that most clashed with the Pink Tide, CONAIE-Pachakutik, represented a shaky alliance between Amazonians who championed regional autonomy and indigenous rights and the urbanized and leftist residents of the sierra region, who staunchly opposed neoliberalism (Baud, 2007: 35–36; for a similar situation in Bolivia, see Gonzalez, 2019: 71). The latter were largely supportive of the Pink Tide government. This convergence beneath the surface is overlooked by those on the left who play down differences between Pink Tide governments and neoliberal ones and view the differences between the Pink Tide and social movements as deep-seated if not irreconcilable. Many of these writers attribute social movement support for Pink Tide governments to their strategy of co-opting social movements and their activists (Bacallao-Pino, 2016: 117–121; Zibechi and Machado, 2017; Svampa, 2018; 2019; Webber, 2011).

To their credit, these writers shed light on a major dimension of the topic—the downside of Pink Tide governments in their relations with social movements. Once in power, Pink Tide leaders perceived that the economic and political conditions they now faced required a pragmatic approach to alliance formation. To accommodate new allies and neutralize intransigent adversaries, they felt pressured into revising certain positions and abandoning others. These modifications alienated some social movement activists, who were emboldened by the instrumental role they had played in the downfall of repressive neoliberal governments.

Nevertheless, as Koerner demonstrates in this volume, Pink Tide critics often fail to contextualize the negative features of Pink Tide rule. Political exigencies and pressure varied from country to country, but the result in each case was tensions with social movements. In Brazil under Lula, the PT's minority status in Congress and at the state and municipal levels influenced its decision to form alliances with six to eight parties mainly to its right and provide them ministerial positions, in the process putting the brakes on land distribution, to the disappointment of the MST. During Lula's two terms, the

PT held only 15–16 percent of senatorial seats and controlled between three and five of the governorships (see Gabriel Funari's chapter in this volume). Similarly, in Bolivia, Evo Morales's agreement with the business elite of Santa Cruz following his reelection in 2009 and the ensuing modus vivendi put an end to the violent disruptions in that economically strategic region at the expense of social movement allies. The Sandinistas, for their part, reversed their position on women's reproductive rights largely as a result of their alliance with the Catholic Church and other conservative sectors, which was designed to calm fears that Daniel Ortega's return to power would reignite the bloody conflict of the 1980s (Cruz-Feliciano, 2020: 277). Similarly, in Venezuela, in spite of Chávez's profeminist discourse, his movement's alliance with Evangelical groups resulted in the government's disregard for the demand of feminist groups for the decriminalization of abortion.

In order to better judge the Pink Tide in light of these pragmatic calculations, government–social-movement relations need to be placed in a broader context. Many scholars and activists in Latin America and elsewhere recognize the importance for social movements of having a government that is perceived to be friendly and open to dialogue even over hotly contested issues. According to two leading social movement scholars, "the perceptions of opportunity . . . are as important as the objective conditions" (Martí i Puig and Silva, 2014: 14). The existence of such a government enhances the sense of efficacy among activists and the possibility that protests will draw large numbers of people and remain peaceful (Eisinger, 1973: 26–27). Many U.S. African-American leaders, even those highly critical of the Democratic Party, pointed to these advantages in the context of the Black Lives Matter movement as the reason to support the presidential candidacy of Joe Biden in 2020 in opposition to that of the "unfriendly" Donald Trump.[6] The friendly government thesis was upheld from the outset by political opportunity scholars, who pointed to the relationship between the growth, life span, and influence of social movements at the national level and the openness of the state. Social movement institutionalization, professionalization, and interaction with the state may eventually lead to a decline in street protests but at the same time foster other forms of mobilization and the achievement of a collective identity (Tilly, 1995; Eisinger, 1973; Pahnke, 2017: 14–21).

In the case of Latin America, the Pink Tide governments' "openness" (a term often used by political opportunity scholars [Meyer, 2004: 128–131]) toward social movements and their overall record on relevant issues in comparison with neoliberal governments need to be taken into account. Scholars have noted the correlation between governments that engage in consultation and the enhanced political influence of social movements, which, as Eduardo da Silva and Clarisse Paradis point out in their chapter in this volume, is conducive to advances in social movement agendas (Arce, Rice, and Silva,

2019: 199). In general, Pink Tide governments, in contrast to neoliberal ones, systematically consulted social movements and organizations on relevant issues. The Frente Amplio (Broad Front—FA) governments in Uruguay between 2005 to 2020, for instance, promoted national conferences, councils, and dialogues with social organization representation to make policy recommendations in the areas of education, labor, social security, and health care reform (Betancur and Busquets, 2020: 115–122). Similarly, the PT governments in Brazil set in motion a large number of public policy conferences with extensive participation on a significant number of topics. Some scholars have argued that these meetings failed to fulfill expectations (Goldfrank, 2017: 152, 155–157), but nevertheless they stood in sharp contrast to the imperviousness of governments before and after. Other scholars point to the participation of social movements in over half of the 34 councils that functioned with mixed effectiveness at the end of Lula's presidency (Rossi, 2018b: 106).

In addition, even considering the use of force by Pink Tide presidents in the Territorio Indígena y Parque Nacional Isiboro Sécure (Bolivia) and Yasuní (Ecuador) conflicts, state repression of social movements under these governments was considerably less intense than under neoliberal ones.[7] This contrast became especially evident with the wave of antineoliberal protests against conservative and right-wing governments that broke out in the region in 2019–2020. The two confrontations under Pink Tide governments that resulted in a substantial number of casualties occurred during the *guarimba* protests of 2014 and 2017 in Venezuela and the protests of April 2018 in Nicaragua. Both governments used excessive force against the antigovernment protesters, though to what degree was controversial.[8] Unlike in the case of numerous massacres under neoliberal governments (such as the gas war in Bolivia in 2003, the Eldorado do Carajás massacre in 1996 in Brazil, the disappearance of 43 students of Ayotzinapa, Mexico, in 2014, and the antineoliberal protests throughout the continent in 2019–2020), these protesters demanded regime change from the outset in Venezuela and shortly after the confrontations began in Nicaragua.

Perhaps the best example of Pink Tide government tolerance toward a militant left-wing social movement, even though its demands were far from met, is the case of the MST in Brazil. The PT government's stance toward the MST's right to dissent stood in sharp contrast with the positions assumed by the party's adversaries. The administration of Lula's predecessor Fernando Henriquez Cardoso had viewed the MST as a mob that intimidated foreign investors. In contrast, Lula refrained from enforcing the severe antioccupation measures implemented by his predecessor, and at the end of a well-publicized 500-mile march to the capital in May 2005 he met with a 50-member MST delegation in a friendly encounter. During Lula's rule, the assassination of rural leaders greatly declined, but nevertheless a congressional inquiry commission dominated by landowner-friendly members sought to criminalize the MST. The campaign against the MST included accusations of misuse of funds, ties to criminal groups, and terrorism. PT congressmen belonging to the commission fervently denounced its findings. The investigation ended in November 2005 and coincided with a decline in the organization's land invasions (Sauer and Mészáros, 2018: 399) at the same time that it served to tarnish its reputation and cut into its private funding. The anti-MST campaign was then taken up in the courts at the behest of landowning interests. The most immediate and pressing political preoccupation of MST leaders was thus not the PT's failure to live up to its pledge of mass land distribution—which the PT's leftist critics emphasize and indeed was the case (Gonzalez, 2019: 146–147)—but rather the governing party's weak position in Congress and the courts and its failure to dismantle authoritarian enclaves in the state (Stédile, 2021; Durazo Herrmann, 2014: 35–36).

The Pink Tide's incorporation of social movements and their activists, a salient feature of its governments, had mixed implications and has been interpreted differently by scholars. The harshest critics of the Pink Tide on the left view benefits such as government funding for social-movement-sponsored programs and employment opportunities for activists as part of a strategy of co-optation designed to undermine protest (Zibechi, 2019b; 2008: 84; Cruz Rodríguez, 2019: 191; Webber, 2017: 291). In recent years, however, many scholars have questioned the use of the term "co-optation" for failing to take into account agency and the complexity of relationships of this nature, as well as the fact that it may have been a natural by-product of the institutionalization of social movements with the return to democracy beginning in the 1990s (Foweraker, 2001: 865; see Ronaldo Munck's concluding chapter in this volume as well as those by Daniel Burridge and Federico Rossi). Furthermore, social movements such as Argentine *piqueteros* (unemployed workers who engaged in militant protests) and the MST have denied that these types of benefits amount to "handouts" or paternalistic relationships, considering them hard-won "rights" achieved through struggle (Wolford, 2015: 64–65; Bacallao-Pino, 2016: 114). As I observed in Venezuela following Chávez's election, leftist social movement activists who were called on to form part of the state bureaucracy stressed their eagerness to collaborate as opposed to the prospect of personal benefit.

The most controversial case of alleged co-optation was in Argentina under the Pink Tide governments of Néstor Kirchner (2003–2007) and Cristina Fernández de Kirchner (2007–2015). The Kirchners incorporated social movement activists of the 1990s through economic support for piquetero-run cooperatives, occupied factories, and food distribution programs, employment and legislative positions, and regular meetings with the nation's president. The debate stemmed from the reversal of those activists who had cried "Out with them all!" in the heady days of 2001 but then became avid supporters of both presidents. In addition, the Kirchner strategy of incorporation encouraged the abandonment of militant tactics and contributed to the fragmentation of the piquetero movement, which (in contrast to the MST) never had centralized leadership.

The argument of co-optation (which implies that activists were immobilized and neutralized) overlooks the fact that a political strategy with ideological implications was in play on the part of both the Kirchners and the newly incorporated. The Kirchnerist activists (not all of whom belonged to the presidents' Peronist party) had a sense of identity associated with their commitment to thoroughgoing change and their youth (a condition glorified by the Kirchners [Vázquez, 2018: 213; Vommaro, 2015: 43]) that contrasted with that of the union bureaucrats, the Peronist national leadership, and the mayors and governors, who belonged to more conservative currents within Peronism. The social movement activists viewed the government as "under dispute" and their role in promoting change as essential, at the same time that they identified themselves as "militants" rather than bureaucrats (Vazquez, 2018: 214–216; Vommaro, 2015: 44–45).

The Kirchners, for their part, promoted young social activists as part of a strategy to achieve a degree of independence from other power blocs within Peronism and acquire a mobilization capacity to face conservative adversaries outside the party. There was undeniably a vertical dimension to the relationship. Thus, for instance, Néstor Kirchner created the youth group La Cámpora (headed by his son) in vertical fashion in 2003, and shortly thereafter the Movimiento Evita emerged as a result of a combination of top-down and bottom-up initiatives (Rossi, 2018b: 100). Both organizations consisted largely of 1990s youth activists and were part of the alliance of incorporated groups designed to counter traditional Peronist blocs. The activists, who considered themselves the "pure Kirchnerists," felt called upon to take to the streets in defense of the government. Mobilizations of this nature took place at the outset of Cristina's first term in the face of a perceived pending coup and again at the time of her reelection in 2011, when she distanced herself from the traditional Peronists and assumed more leftist positions. The Kirchnerist activists were hardly a monolithic group (some became disillusioned when Néstor Kirchner accepted the presidency of the Peronist party, convinced that he had made his peace with party bureaucrats), but the political consistency and sense of commitment of many of their members are at odds with the co-optation explanation (as Leandro Gamallo discusses in this volume).

Some political commentators and scholars have echoed the position of those piquetero groups that continued to embrace the banner of absolute autonomy raised by their movement in the 1990s. John Holloway, among other libertarian writers, lauds the alternative structures (community kitchens, bakeries, popular education workshops, and vegetable gardens) created by the intransigent piqueteros and asserts that the state subsidies for programs received by the incorporated piquetero groups were won through struggle and are self-administered (Holloway, 2013; Sitrin, 2012). A more negative opinion was expressed by the U.S. diplomat in Buenos Aires Thomas P. Kelly, in cables released by Wikileaks (2009) that characterized Néstor Kirchner's strategy toward the piqueteros as co-optation. The harshest critics of the Kirchners claimed that their activist allies took on the appearance of "shock troops" and characterized their zeal as blind fanaticism (Palermo, 2015: 79; Bárbaro, 2014) and their relationship to the government as clientelistic (Mazzuca, 2013: 120–121).

The incorporation of social movements and organizations and their members by Pink Tide governments is particularly important because the process involved large numbers of marginalized and semimarginalized sectors of the population. Programs and policies that incorporated organizations representing excluded and semiexcluded sectors cannot be judged by the same standards as similar ones benefiting those already incorporated into the political, economic, and cultural life of the country. Marginalized sectors often (although not always) lack the organizational experience of the organized working class; providing their fledgling organizations with resources and opportunities has far-reaching implications. In addition to the piqueteros and the MST, other examples of organizations representing the marginalized and semimarginalized supported by Pink Tide governments and parties ranged from indigenous groups in Bolivia to the Ayotzinapa victims and their families in Mexico (Gravante, 2020: 89–92), worker organizations representing the participants in the hundreds of company takeovers in response to the 2002–2003 business-promoted economic shutdown in Venezuela, and the Venezuelan *comuneros* (members of agricultural units promoted by Chávez). Eduardo Silva and Federico Rossi call this process "second wave incorporation," comparing it to the first wave of the early decades of the twentieth century, when the working population achieved incorporation largely through the organization of unions and the right to vote (see Rossi's chapter in this volume). In both cases, intense conflict often characterized the relations between progressive governments and social movements, and as a consequence the latter sometimes faced internal divisions (Rossi, 2018a: 26–27). Comparisons along these lines through an examination of the broad historical context provide a different perspective from that of left–leaning analysts who emphasize the conflictive relations between Pink Tide governments and social movements while passing over important areas of convergence.

The discourse and rhetoric employed by a government have much to do with whether social movements view it as friendly, a perception whose importance is emphasized by political opportunity writers (McAdam, Tarrow, and Tilly, 2001). Certainly when discourse is completely at odds with policies and concrete actions it is of little significance, but this was generally not the case with the Pink Tide, as this introductory article attempts to show. Neoliberal governments were both in words and in action much more distant from popular social movements than Pink Tide ones, as is shown in extreme form by Bolsonaro's abrasive law-and-order rhetoric and his holding of the environmentalist movement responsible for the ecological destruction of Amazonia (Londoño and Andreoni, 2018: A-8).

For the anti–Pink Tide writers on the left, Evo Morales's assertion that MAS was a party of social movements was empty rhetoric, as were the claims of other Pink Tide leaders (Krommes-Ravnsmet, 2019: 77–78). They point out that both Morales and Correa had antagonistic relations with the indigenous social movements that were allegedly the true defenders of the official government doctrine of *buen vivir,* based on community values and respect for the environment as opposed to submission to market imperatives. Both governments are said to have turned their backs on those ideals, employing clientelism to divide indigenous movements. This thesis, however, overlooks the material basis for the divisions in the popular sectors of Pink Tide countries (Angosto-Ferrandez, 2020: 255–257) and the fact that the buen vivir concept was itself subject to distinct interpretations. Pink Tide supporters argued that economic growth was a means to achieve the goals of buen vivir rather than representing an obstacle to their attainment (Borón, 2015).

Furthermore, much of the social base of movements such as CONAIE resided in isolated regions such as Ecuador's Amazonia, even though it also had an important following in urban areas, where large numbers identified themselves as indigenous (Lucero, 2006: 34–35). Proindigenous candidates who ran against Pink Tide ones and took radical positions in favor of antidevelopmentalism and the absolute autonomy of social movements generally fared extremely poorly in presidential races. Examples included Luis Maca (with 2 percent) in 2006 and Alberto Acosta, himself a leading proponent of buen vivir (with 3 percent), in 2013, both in Ecuador, and Felipe Quispe (with 2 percent) in 2005 in Bolivia, in addition to the inability of the Zapatistas to collect the required number of signatures to be on the ballot in Mexico in 2018. The anti–Pink Tide leftist writers extol these candidates and their respective social movements in spite of their poor showing at the polls (see, for instance, Gonzalez, 2019: 3, 17, 71, 94–96). Although electoral results are not the only criterion for judging the performance of social movements, the extremely poor showing of these candidates needs to be taken into account in any evaluation of their political effectiveness. Furthermore, the selection of certain social movements as the authentic representatives of the indigenous population belies its diversity and complexity (Lucero, 2006: 32–34).

Some Pink Tide leaders relied on street mobilizations to counter the regime-change efforts of the disloyal opposition on the right. The extent to which social movement activists played a role in these conflicts varied from country to country. Nevertheless, mobilization among previously underrepresented popular sectors in the face of destabilization campaigns was significant in that it generated a sense of empowerment among sectors that represented an essential component of social movements. Thus, for example, mobilizations were instrumental in the defeat of the two-month-long economic shutdown engineered by the Federación de Cámaras y Asociaciones de Comercio y Producción de Venezuela (Federation of Chambers and Associations of Commerce and Production of Venezuela—FEDECAMARAS) to topple the Chávez government in 2002–2003. Again, during the four months of disruptive protests (known as *guarimbas*) by the middle-class-based opposition in early 2014, Maduro addressed progovernment marches consisting of specific sectors (workers, women, peasants, young people and the elderly) on different days with significant turnouts. The objective of the concentrations was to demonstrate that the Chavistas had at least as much mobilization capacity as the opposition. In both of these conflictive situations, Venezuelan social movements played an active role. The Sandinista government of Daniel Ortega also mobilized followers in the face of mass protests calling for regime change beginning in April 2018. The pro-Sandinistas engaged in prayers for peace as part of a narrative that attributed the violence to opposition insurgency.[9]

Nevertheless, in other situations of intense political instability, Pink Tide presidents opted for closed negotiations with elite actors without input from social movements or leftists. The Partido Comunista de Venezuela (Venezuelan Communist Party—PCV) criticized Maduro for displaying deference in negotiations with representatives of the parallel government of Juan Guaidó in the absence of public debate, at the same time that the party expressed concern about possible government concessions unacceptable to social movements and the left (PCV, 2019: 8; Gonzalez, 2019: 132). Lula, who at first threatened to promote mobilizations at the time of the impeachment of Dilma Rousseff and the trial leading to his own imprisonment, ended up following a similar approach of negotiations from above (Prada, 2016; Mendes Loureiro and Saad-Filho, 2020).

CONVERGENCES IN THE ANTI-NEOLIBERAL PROTESTS OF 2019–2020 AND OTHER EVENTS

The repression unleashed by conservative and right-wing governments against protests in 2019–2020 and their neoliberal policies clearly demonstrated the common ground occupied by popular social movements and Pink Tide and other parties on the left. A partial convergence occurred in Ecuador, where CONAIE and the Pink Tide's Rafael Correa had hostile relations, and in Bolivia and Brazil, where the two sides had maintained an uneasy alliance interrupted by occasional conflicts over the years. The events demonstrate that "creative tensions" between leftist parties and social movements are normal and are overcome only in moments of crisis. As Fabricio Carneiro, Guillermo Fuentes, and Carmen Midaglia point out in their chapter on organized labor in this volume, social movements and progressive governments sometimes confronted each other, but the links between them were never broken, and thus when conservatives returned to power the two blocs quickly converged in their resistance to neoliberal policies. The protest movements in various countries in the region since 2018 shed light on the importance of these areas of convergence in moments of pushback coming from the right.

Bolivia

Social movements played a pivotal role in MAS's return to power in 2020 just as they had in Evo Morales's rise to power 15 years earlier. As discussed by John Brown in his chapter in this book, the long-standing divisions within social movements and the left were set aside during the street protests that forced the right-wing government of Jeanine Añez to respect the October 18, 2020 date set for presidential elections after they had twice been delayed (see also Farthing and Becker, 2021: 177–179). The Pacto de Unidad (grouping the most important indigenous and peasant organizations) and the Central Obrera Boliviana (Bolivian Workers' Central—COB) organized roadblocks and, at first, called the decision of MAS congresspeople to accept the delayed date "treason," at the same time that Felipe Quispe demanded Añez's resignation. Nevertheless, these same radical social movement leaders endorsed MAS's presidential candidate, Luis Arce, and in early 2021 mobilized their followers in support of the decision to jail Añez and two members of her cabinet for their role in the 2019 coup.

Ecuador

Three aspects of the protests against the International Monetary Fund–imposed policies adopted by the government of Lenín Moreno in late 2019 stand out: the indigenous social movements split into two currents with regard to relations with the Pink Tide movement headed by Correa; the Moreno government followed a strategy of driving a wedge between social movements and the Pink Tide political movement by privileging the former and marginalizing and criminalizing the latter; and the social movement leaders who adopted a "plague on both your houses" position with regard to the Pink Tide versus the political right played into the hands of the latter at the same time that they declared extractivism the main enemy. During the anti-neoliberal protests that broke out in late 2019, Moreno at first successfully called on CONAIE to negotiate a solution to the conflict while placing the entire blame for the disturbances on Correa's followers (and arresting some of their leaders), a claim that was echoed by Washington, the Organization of American States, and conservative governments in the region. In the second round of the presidential elections, held in April 2021, CONAIE President Jaime Vargas's endorsement of the Pink Tide candidate, Andrés Arauz, was rejected by leading members of his movement at the same time that he was expelled from Pachakutik. Over 16 percent of the voters responded positively to Pachakutik's null vote campaign, enough to ensure the victory of the neoliberal candidate Guillermo Lasso. Those leaders within Pachakutik who favored possible talks and an alliance with Arauz's party demanded its recognition of the error of having "frequently insulted CONAIE and the indigenous people " (Iza, 2021), an obvious reference to Correa's harsh remarks and aggressive treatment of protesting indigenous groups (for more on the conflictive relations between Correa and CONAIE, see the chapter by Alejandra Santillana Ortiz and Sebastián Terán Ávalos in this volume). The two indigenous leaders who were most receptive to attempts at reconciliation with Correa's political movement—Jaime Vargas and Leonidas Iza (who succeeded Vargas as CONAIE's president)—were among the most prominent leaders of the protest movement that broke out in 2019. The party of Arauz and Correa (the Unión por la Esperanza [Union for Hope—UNES]) joined the anti-neoliberal protests that took place in late 2021 against neoliberal measures implemented by the government of Lasso, who attempted to scapegoat CONAIE president Iza personally for the ensuing disruptions.

Brazil

The impeachment of Rousseff, the jailing of Lula, and the Bolsonaro government's repressive measures against the MST, which were unmatched in the organization's history, served to strengthen its ties with the PT party, which previously had been far from solid (Stédile, 2021). In a letter delivered as he presented himself to serve a prison sentence in April 2018, Lula thanked the MST for its daily support and added, "More than anyone else, the MST knows what it is like to feel the pain of injustice and persecution and face fabricated and manipulated charges, countless arrests, and the death of comrades" (Brasil de Fato, 2018). Following the Supreme Court's decision in April 2021 allowing Lula to run for office, some moderate Brazilian leaders called for a broad-based front against Bolsonaro in which a nonleftist rather than a PT member would run for president on a unity slate. In contrast, the MST and other groups on the left were wary of including former Bolsonaro allies and other rightists in an electoral alliance and declared that only Lula had the leadership capacity to confront the president at the polls (Agencia EFE, 2020).

Argentina

In December 2020, President Alberto Fernández fulfilled a major campaign pledge by passing legislation providing free and legal abortions up to the fourteenth week of pregnancy. His firm support contrasted with the oppositional position of his predecessors, including Peronist President Carlos Menem, who in the 1990s went so far as to state that the "defense of life" was a "foreign policy priority." Up until then, the only other Latin American nations to have legalized abortion were Cuba, Guyana, and Uruguay, where the feminist movement and congresswomen belonging to the governing Pink Tide party played a central role in the legislation's passage in 2012 (Pérez, 2015: 114–115). Similarly, in Argentina, legalization represented the culmination of a half-century of struggle on the part of the nation's feminist movement. Indeed, Argentina's Vice President Cristina Fernández attributed the reversal of her stand to the "thousands and thousands of young women who have taken to the streets," a statement that her adversaries characterized as indicative of her opportunism (Radio Perfil, 2020).

Venezuela

Following Maduro's reelection in May 2018, the PCV and other leftist parties and a number of social movement leaders (Marquina and Gilbert, 2020) took an increasingly critical position toward the government, culminating in their decision to run separate slates for the legislative elections of 2020. This bloc, located to the left of the government, objected to concessions to the private sector designed to ameliorate the harsh effects of U.S.-imposed sanctions. The same leaders criticized the government for failing to consult pro-Chavista but critical organizations and characterized its attitude as sectarian. Some social leaders upheld these positions but, in contrast to the PCV, did not break with Maduro, focusing their criticism on government bureaucrats rather than the president. One of the most prominent of these leaders was Angel Prado of the nation's emblematic commune El Maizal, in the state of Lara, where he ran for mayor against the candidate of the ruling Partido Socialista Unido de Venezuela (Venezuelan United Socialist Party—PSUV) in 2017. In spite of the sharpness of his criticisms of the government, Prado stated: "We have never wavered in our support for Nicolás Maduro. . . . Because of a municipality, or the actions of a party, or because at one point the government did not pay heed to us, we are not going to lose sight of the strategic enemy" (Prado, 2018; 2020: 49).[10] The highly vocal peasant movement expressed a similar position that singled out the Instituto Nacional de Tierras (National Land Institute—INTI) for criticism. In mid-2018, peasants participated in a 200-mile march to the capital (in commemoration of the bicentenary of Simón Bolívar's legendary Admirable Campaign). The peasants made urgent demands on the INTI but applauded Maduro vigorously when he addressed the marchers. One spokesman stated that the purpose of the march was to "liberate Venezuela from the virus that is affecting its institutions" (*Correo del Orinoco*, 2018).

Chile

The mass protests against the neoliberal measures implemented by the government of Sebastián Piñera in late 2019 cemented ties between the Frente Amplio (Broad Front—FA), founded by activists of the student movement of 2011 and other struggles, and the Partido Comunista de Chile (Chilean Communist Party—PCC). Previously (as Kyla Sankey and Aaron Tauss point out in their chapter in this volume), relations between the two had been colored by the view of some activists that the PCC represented the old way of doing politics in that it supported a center-left alliance from above (the Nueva Mayoría), which ran a moderate presidential candidate in 2017 against the FA's more leftist one (Larrabure, 2019: 232–236). During the 2019 protests, the FA, which some considered the spokesperson for the protesters, and the PCC acted largely in unison (Larrabure, 2019: 237). They both insisted on the lifting of the state of siege as a condition for accepting Piñera's proposal of negotiations, brought the issue of human rights violations to international court, and acted in Congress to indict Piñera on the same grounds. As in the case of Ecuador, Piñera and his allies attempted to drive a wedge between the two parties by accusing the FA of, in the words of one congressman, "kneeling before the PCC in order to survive" (*Noticias Financieras*, 2021). In spite of these efforts, leaders of both parties ended up supporting a united candidacy for the 2021 presidential elections. Social movement leaders were well represented in the cabinet of 2011 student protest leader Gabriel Boric, elected president of Chile in 2021. The presence of PCC member and 2011 student leader Camila Vallejo was a clear example of the convergence of social movements and progressive parties that characterized the anti-neoliberal protests that took place throughout the region in 2019.

Honduras

Popular protests broke out in April 2019 and lasted half a year in opposition to legislation proposed by the government of Juan Orlando Hernández allegedly designed to pave the way for the privatization of health and education. Following an initial wave of repression, protests extended to rural areas and came to include indigenous and other social movements demanding Hernández's ouster. At this point the protesters questioned the legitimacy of the string of governments that succeeded Pink Tide President Manuel Zelaya following the coup of 2009, and indeed on June 29 they recalled the tenth anniversary of Zelaya's forced removal from office. The protests contributed to the momentum of the successful presidential candidacy for the November 2021 elections of Xiomara Castro de Zelaya, wife of the former president, who had led the resistance to the 2009 coup. Castro was endorsed by fellow party member and social movement activist Olivia Zúñiga Cáceres, daughter of the murdered environmentalist leader Berta Caceres. In an indication of the tight nexus between the president-elect and the environmental and social movements, Castro announced that her government would refrain from granting permits for open mining and the exploitation of rivers and national parks.

FINAL THOUGHTS ON THE ROLE OF SOCIAL MOVEMENTS IN THE STRUGGLE FOR RADICAL CHANGE

Ever since its emergence with Chávez's election in 1998, the Pink Tide has been attacked for attempting to suffocate social movement autonomy and replicating Lenin's metaphor of social movements as transmission belts for the party of the revolution. Writers such as Jorge Castañeda in the early years of the century painted representatives of the Pink Tide's "bad left"—Chávez, Morales, and Kirchner—as throwbacks to the alleged demagogic populism of Juan Domingo Perón (Castañeda, 2006: 33–35). The implication was that in countries where the underprivileged were entranced by ruling charismatic leaders, autonomous popular-sector social movements were largely absent.[11] The string of Pink Tide defeats beginning in Argentina with the election of conservative Mauricio Macri in 2015 appeared to confirm the validity of the all-encompassing critique of the Pink Tide put forward from a leftist perspective. These writers (who unlike Castañeda championed bottom-up politics) viewed the positions and behavior of left-wing governments in the region as consistently and inherently at odds with social movements. Their writing contained an element of reductionism even as it shed light on important negative features of Pink Tide policies. According to this viewpoint, the dependence on the export economy and global markets and capital by Pink Tide governments was the sole explanation for their alleged rejection of social movement autonomy as well as of community decision making, environmental demands, and indigenous and democratic rights.

Social movements played an important role in the Pink Tide's return to power in Bolivia and the triumph of progressive presidential candidates elsewhere, as well as in the massive protests against neoliberal governments of 2019–2020. These events displayed a convergence between anti-neoliberal social movements and Pink Tide political movements, as well as the shortcomings of the anti–Pink Tide thesis coming from the left that is poorly equipped to explain the continued popularity of the Pink Tide. Taken together, the conservative–right-wing pushback beginning in 2015 and the Pink Tide's recovery beginning in 2018 call for the balanced and critical analysis of the Pink Tide phenomenon that this book attempts to put forward.

These recent experiences point to the need to place social movements at the center of the analysis of the Pink Tide phenomenon. The later writings of Nicos Poulantzas (1978) provides a theoretical context for understanding the Pink Tide experience and the role of social movements. Poulantzas viewed the state as a social relation in which different sectors of the economy and society find expression partly in accordance with their relative strength. His theory may be more applicable in situations in which the left has gained power in a democratic setting than in a capitalist nation in which the capitalist class is fairly cohesive, the popular sectors are weak, and instrumentalist mechanisms ensure the domination of the ruling class. The basic predicament facing the left in power is that the state, which many mistakenly view as a leftist state, is really a "battleground" involving sectors with conflicting interests. The outcome, whatever the socialist commitment of top government leaders, will be determined by institutions and organizations outside of the state. For this reason, as Poulantzas points out, the left needs to have a friendly and mutually supportive relationship with fairly autonomous social movements that, in contrast to the political leaders at the helm of government, are not constrained by imperatives imposed by their place in the system (for instance, the need to ensure economic and political stability). Poulantzas adds that popular movement struggles are essential in their own right as a means for building the new society. In short, vibrant social movements and a left that respects their relative autonomy are a sine qua non for the achievement of socialism by democratic means.

This book demonstrates that Pink Tide leaders were not keenly aware of the fundamental role played by social movements and other spaces outside the direct control of the state (such as rank-and-file political party cells). If they had been, they would have been more open to dialogue with nonelite activists and their relations with social movements would have been more harmonious. In many instances, as their leftist critics point out, they failed to reach out to social movements in moments of crisis. At the same time, however, these critics overlook the fundamental difference between social movement relations with the Pink Tide and those of neoliberal governments, which were overtly distrustful of, if not hostile toward, social movements and their demands.

NOTES

1. I thank my two coeditors for having put together the articles of two issues of *Latin American Perspectives* titled "Social Movements in Latin America: The Progressive Governments and Beyond" (July and September 2020), of which seven of the chapters in this book are revised versions.

2. Political opportunity theory posits that the success of social movements depends largely on political opportunities often originating from the state.

3. An example during this period was the left-wing Causa R party in Venezuela, which called itself a "movement" and employed a strong antiparty rhetoric. The Causa R, which was a major force in the workers' movement in the industrial region of Guayana, enjoyed a degree of support in neoliberal circles (Ellner, 1999b).

4. Scholars who adhere to the "resource curse" school advance these same positions. They argue, for instance, that highly profitable resources raise the stakes for heads of state who seek to retain power and have sufficient revenue to finance repressive apparatuses. The resources are thus conducive to autocratic rule as well as sharp and at times internecine political conflict in addition to patronage politics (Venables, 2016: 174–175).

5. Another aspect of the Pink Tide that distinguished it from earlier waves in Latin America was the demonstrations of solidarity among member nations, as shown by the formation of regional organizations (such as the Comunidad de Estados Latinoamericanos y Caribeños [Community of Latin American and Caribbean States—CELAC], the Unión de Naciones Suramericanas [Union of South American Nations—UNASUR], and the Alianza Bolivariana para los Pueblos de Nuestra América [Bolivarian Alliance for the Peoples of Our America—ALBA]) designed to promote integration and resolve pressing problems (Ellner, 2020b: 41).

6. In one talk show, two leading members of the African-American community, Cornel West and the former NAACP president Ben Jealous, advocated support for Joe Biden in the presidential elections of 2020 on grounds that he could be moved in a leftist direction, even while West was staunchly critical of the Democratic Party candidate (Democracy Now, 2020). The Code Pink leader Medea Benjamin reached the same conclusion with reference to foreign policy issues.

7. Middle-class movements formed for the purpose of achieving regime change are not included in this discussion.

8. For two opposite versions of the Nicaraguan conflict, both adopting a leftist perspective, see the symposium on the topic in the November 2021 issue of *Latin*

American Perspectives. Leftist critics of the Pink Tide in general accuse it of making excessive concessions to conservative interests, but their critique of the Sandinista government is the most comprehensive.

9. The outcome of the antigovernment confrontations in both nations contrasted with that in Brazil, where popular protests, first in opposition to public transportation price hikes in São Paulo in 2013 and then at the time of the Summer Olympics in Rio in 2016, were exploited by conservatives in a successful regime change strategy.

10. Significantly, Prado was elected mayor of the same municipality on the PSUV ticket in 2021 and declared that the correct strategy for his followers was to work within the party.

11. Castañeda (2006: 38) claims that for the bad left "the despair of poor constituencies is a tool rather than a challenge." In a more extreme view, some journalists and political leaders portrayed the followers of the bad left in Latin America as "lumpen" and characterized the popular sectors as slavishly obedient to the charismatic ruler (Roosen, 2010; *Economist*, 2003; Anderson, 2013; see also Lester, 2009: 86). These descriptions of the bad left fit the pejorative mold of radical Latin American populists associated with the writing of Gino Germani, specifically with regard to the working class.

REFERENCES

Acosta, Alberto
2017 "Post-extractivism: from discourse to practice—reflections for action," pp. 77–101 in Gilles Carbonnier, Humberto Campodónico, and Sergio Tezanos Vázquez (eds.), *Alternative Pathways to Sustainable Development: Lessons from Latin America*. Geneva: Brill-Nijhoff Publishers.
Agencia EFE
2020 "Los Sin Tierra de Brasil: Lula es el único que puede plantar cara a Bolsonaro." February 21. https://www.efe.com/efe/america/destacada/los-sin-tierra-de-brasil -lula-es-el-unico-que-puede-plantar-cara-a-bolsonaro/20000065-4178890.
Anderson, Jon Lee
2013 "Slumlord: letter from Caracas." *The New Yorker* 88 (45).
Angosto-Ferrandez, Luis Fernando
2020 "Neo-extractivism, class formations, and the Pink Tide: considerations on the Venezuelan case," pp. 243–269 in Steve Ellner (ed.), *Latin America's Pink Tide: Breakthroughs and Shortcomings*. Lanham, MD: Rowman and Littlefield.
Arce, Moisés, Roberta Rice, and Eduardo Silva
2019 "Rethinking protest impacts," pp. 195–213 in Moisés Arce and Roberta Rice (eds.), *Protest and Democracy*. Calgary: University of Calgary Press.
Bacallao-Pino, Lázaro M.
2016 "Agents for change or conflict? Social movements, democratic dynamics, and development in Latin America." *Voluntas: International Journal of Voluntary and Nonprofit Organizations* 27 (1): 105–124.
Bárbaro, Julio

2014 "La secta." May 13. https://opinion.infobae.com/julio-barbaro/2014/05/13/la -secta/index.html.

Baud, Michiel

2007 "Indigenous politics and the state: the Andean highlands in the nineteenth and twentieth centuries." *Social Analysis: The International Journal of Anthropology* 51 (2): 19–42.

Bermeo, Nancy

1997 "Myths of moderation: confrontation and conflict during democratic transitions." *Comparative Politics* 29: 305–322.

Betancur, Nicolás and José Miguel Busquets

2020 "The Frente Amplio governments in Uruguay: policy strategies and results," pp. 113–135 in Steve Ellner (ed.), *Latin America's Pink Tide: Breakthroughs and Shortcomings*. Lanham, MD: Rowman and Littlefield.

Borón, Atilio

2015 "'Buen vivir' and the dilemmas of the Latin American left." August 31. https:// climateandcapitalism.com/2015/08/31/buen-vivir-and-dilemmas-of-latin-american -left/.

Brasil de Fato

2018 "Lula to Landless Workers' Movement: 'We are on the right side of history.'" April 26. https://www.brasildefato.com.br/2018/04/26/lula-to-landless-workers -party-we-are-on-the-right-side-of-history.

Castañeda, Jorge G.

2006 "Latin America's left turn." *Foreign Affairs* 85 (3): 28–43.

Correo del Orinoco

2018 "Movimiento campesino cuenta sus verdades ante el Presidente Maduro." August 2.

Cruz Rodríguez, Edwin

2019 "Pensar los movimientos sociales en y desde América Latina: una mirada crítica a la contribución de Raúl Zibechi." *Estudios Políticos* (Universidad de Antioquia) 56: 175–197.

Cruz-Feliciano, Héctor M.

2020 "The rise and fall of Sandinista alliances as a means of sociopolitical change in Nicaragua," pp. 275–294 in Steve Ellner (ed.), *Latin America's Pink Tide: Breakthroughs and Shortcomings*. Lanham, MD: Rowman and Littlefield.

Davis, Diane E.

1999 "The power of distance: re-theorizing social movements in Latin America." *Theory and Society* 28: 585–638.

Democracy Now

2020 "Cornel West and Ben Jealous on the DNC and whether progressives can push Joe Biden leftward." August 21. https://www.democracynow.org/2020/8/21/biden _dnc_cornel_west_ben_jealous.

Durazo Herrmann, Julián

2014 "Reflections on regime change and democracy in Bahia, Brazil." *Latin American Research Review* 49 (3): 23–44.

The Economist

2003 "The Bolivian revolution marches on: Venezuela's conflict." *The Economist* 366 (8310).

Eisinger, Peter K.
1973 "The conditions of protest behavior in American cities." *American Political Science Review* 67 (1): 11–28.

Ellner, Steve
1999a "Obstacles to the consolidation of the Venezuelan neighbourhood movement: national and local cleavages." *Journal of Latin American Studies* 31 (1): 75–97.
1999b "The impact of privatization on labor in Venezuela: radical reorganization or moderate adjustment?" *Political Power and Social Theory* 13: 109–145.
2020a "Class strategies in Chavista Venezuela: pragmatic and populist policies in a broader context," pp. 163–191 in Steve Ellner (ed.), *Latin America's Pink Tide: Breakthroughs and Shortcomings*. Lanham, MD: Rowman and Littlefield.
2020b "Has the Pink Tide cycle come to an end? Will it have a long-lasting impact?" pp. 39–58 in Steve Ellner (ed.), *Latin America's Pink Tide: Breakthroughs and Shortcomings*. Lanham, MD: Rowman and Littlefield.
2020c "Introduction: Latin America's Pink Tide governments: challenges, break-throughs, and setbacks," pp. 1–19 in Steve Ellner (ed.), *Latin America's Pink Tide: Breakthroughs and Shortcomings*. Lanham, MD: Rowman and Littlefield.
2021 "Introduction: Rethinking Latin American extractivism," pp. 1–28 in Steve Ellner (ed.), *Latin American Extractivism: Dependency, Resource Nationalism, and Resistance in Broad Perspective*. Lanham, MD: Rowman and Littlefield.

Farthing, Linda and Thomas Becker
2021 *Coup: A Story of Violence and Resistance in Bolivia*. Chicago: Haymarket Books.

Foweraker, Joe
1995 *Theorizing Social Movements*. London: Pluto Press.
2001 "Grassroots movements and political activism in Latin America: a critical comparison of Chile and Brazil." *Journal of Latin American Studies* 33: 819–861.

Goldfrank, Benjamin
2017 "The Latin American left's missed opportunity to deepen democracy." *Journal of International Affairs* 71 (1): 147–160.

Gonzalez, Mike
2019 *The Ebb of the Pink Tide: The Decline of the Left in Latin America*. London: Pluto Press.

Gravante, Tommaso
2020 "Forced disappearance as a collective cultural trauma in the Ayotzinapa movement." *Latin American Perspectives* 47 (6): 87–102.

Holloway, John
2013 "Zapatismo urbano." http://www.johnholloway.com.mx/2014/03/10/zapatismo -urbano/.
2019 (2002) *Change the World without Taking Power: The Meaning of Revolution Today*. London: Pluto Press.

Holloway, John and Eloína Peláez

1998 "Introduction: Reinventing revolution," pp. 1–18 in John Holloway and Eloína Peláez (eds.), *Zapatista! Reinventing Revolution in Mexico.* London: Pluto Press.

Iza, Leonidas

2020 "Leonidas Iza: No quiero ser presidente, pero. . . . " July 10. https://www.youtube.com/watch?v=--qgN56Qleg.

Krommes-Ravnsmet, Jeppe

2019 "The frustrated nationalization of hydrocarbons and the plunder of Bolivia." *Latin American Perspectives* 46 (2): 65–83.

Lander, Edgardo

2014 *El neoextractivismo como modelo de desarrollo en América Latina y sus contradicciones.* Berlin: Heinrich Böll Stiftung.

2017 "The sources of Maduro's crisis." International Socialist Organization, April 5. https://socialistworker.org/2017/04/05/the-sources-of-maduros-crisis.

2019 *Crisis civilizatoria: Experiencias de los gobiernos progresistas y debates en la izquierda latinoamericana.* Guadalajara, Mexico: CALAS.

Larrabure, Manuel

2019 "Chile's democratic road to authoritarianism." *European Review of Latin American and Caribbean Studies/Revista Europea de Estudios Latinoamericanos y del Caribe* 108: 221–243.

Lester, Jeremy

2009 "Prometheus unbound in Caracas." *Socialism and Democracy* 23 (3): 61–88.

Londoño, Ernesto and Manuela Andreoni

2018 "Brazil shifts right as voters reject old guard for law-and-order populist." *New York Times,* October 9.

López Maya, Margarita

2002 *Protesta y cultura en Venezuela: Los marcos de acción colectiva en 1999.* Buenos Aires: CLACSO.

Lucero, José Antonio

2006 "Representing 'real Indians': the challenges of indigenous authenticity and strategic constructivism in Ecuador and Bolivia." *Latin American Research Review* 41 (2): 31–56.

Marquina, Cira Pascual and Chris Gilbert (eds.)

2020 *Venezuela: The Present as Struggle—Voices from the Bolivarian Revolution.* New York: Monthly Review Press.

Martí i Puig, Salvador and Eduardo Silva

2014 "Introducción: Movilización y protesta en el mundo global e interconectado." *Revista CIDOB d'Afers Internacionals* 105: 7–18.

Mazzuca, Sebastián L.

2013 "Lessons from Latin America: the rise of rentier populism." *Journal of Democracy* 24 (2): 108–122.

McAdam, Doug, Sidney Tarrow, and Charles Tilly

2001 *The Dynamics of Contention.* Cambridge: Cambridge University Press.

Mendes Loureiro, Pedro and Alfredo Saad-Filho

2020 "The limits of pragmatism: the rise and fall of the Brazilian Workers' Party (2002–2016)," pp. 89–112 in Steve Ellner (ed.), *Latin America's Pink Tide: Breakthroughs and Shortcomings*. Lanham, MD: Rowman and Littlefield, 2020.

Meyer, David S.

2004 "Protest and political opportunities." *Annual Review of Sociology* 30: 125–145.

Motta, Sara

2009 "Old tools and new movements in Latin America: political science as gatekeeper or intellectual illuminator?" *Latin American Politics and Society* 51 (1): 31–56.

2013 "Reinventing the lefts in Latin America: critical perspectives from below." *Latin American Perspectives* 40 (4): 5–18.

Munck, Ronaldo

2020 *Social Movements in Latin America: Mapping the Mosaic*. Newcastle, UK: Agenda Publishing.

Noticias Financieras

2021 "Government rejects opposition-driven 'anti-repression agenda.'" January 6.

Pahnke, Anthony

2017 "The changing terrain of rural contention in Brazil: institutionalization and identity development in the Landless Movement's educational project." *Latin American Politics and Society* 59 (3): 3–26.

Palermo, Vicente

2015 *La alegría y la pasión: Relatos brasileños y argentinos en perspectiva comparada*. Buenos Aires: Katz Editores.

PCV (Partido Comunista de Venezuela)

2021 "Con el pacto de élites de México, el gobierno venezolano se somete al FMI." *Tribuna Popular*, no. 3025, 8.

Pérez, Verónica

2015 "Decriminalization of abortion in Uruguay: the successful end of a long road." *Femina Politica/Zeitschrift für feministische Politikwissenschaft* 24 (1): 112–116.

Poulantzas, Nicos

1978 *State, Power, Socialism*. London: Verso.

Prada, Paulo

2016 "Cargos y amenaza de prisión ponen a brasileño Lula en un papel que ya conoce, el de mártir." Reuters, March 11. https://www.reuters.com/article/idLTAKCN0WE007?edition-redirect=ca.

Prado, Angel

2018 "Interview with Angel Prado (Part I): 'The commune holds the solution to the crisis.'" Venezuelanalysis, August 16. https://venezuelanalysis.com/analysis/14005

2020 "Grapes of wrath in rural Venezuela: a conversation with Angel Prado," pp. 48–55 in Cira Pascual Marquina and Chris Gilbert (eds.), *Venezuela: The Present as Struggle—Voices from the Bolivarian Revolution*. New York: Monthly Review Press.

Radio Perfil

2020 "Jorge Lanata: 'Cristina estaba en contra del aborto pero cuando vio que le podía servir, se montó al tema.'" December 16. https://www.perfil.com/noticias/politica

/jorge-lanata-dijo-cristina-kirchner-estaba-en-contra-del-aborto-pero-cuando-vio
-que-le-podia-servir-se-monto-al-tema.phtml.

Roosen, Gustavo
2010 "El Chavelotodo." *El Nacional,* April 10.

Rossi, Federico M.
2018a "Introduction to Part I: Social movements and the second wave of (territorial) incorporation in Latin America," pp. 3–31 in Eduardo Silva and Federico M. Rossi (eds.), *Reshaping the Political Arena: From Resisting Neoliberalism to the Second Incorporation.* Pittsburgh: University of Pittsburgh Press.
2018b "Social movements, the new 'social question,' and the second incorporation of the popular sectors in Argentina and Brazil," pp. 78–112 in Eduardo Silva and Federico M. Rossi (eds.), *Reshaping the Political Arena: From Resisting Neoliberalism to the Second Incorporation.* Pittsburgh: University of Pittsburgh Press.

Sankey, Kyla and Ronaldo Munck
2020 "Introduction: Social movements, progressive governments, and the question of strategy." *Latin American Perspectives* 47 (4): 4–19.

Sauer, Sérgio and George Mészáros
2018 "La economía política de la lucha por la tierra bajo los gobiernos del Partido de los Trabajadores en Brasil," pp. 315–346 in Cristóbal Kay and Leandro Vergara-Camus (eds.), *La cuestión agraria y los gobiernos de izquierda en América Latina: Campesinos, agronegocio y neodesarrollismo.* Buenos Aires: CLACSO.

Silva, Eduardo
2015 "Social movements, protest, and policy." *European Review of Latin American and Caribbean Studies/Revista Europea de Estudios Latinoamericanos y del Caribe* 100 (December): 27–39.

Sitrin, Marina A.
2012 *Everyday Revolutions: Horizontalism and Autonomy in Argentina.* London: Zed Books.

Stahler-Sholk, Richard, Harry E. Vanden, and Glen David Kuecker
2007 "Introduction: Globalizing resistance—the new politics of social movements in Latin America." *Latin American Perspectives* 34 (2): 5–16.

Stédile, João Pedro
2021 "Personal interview with founder and ex-president of the MST." March 2. https: //www.youtube.com/watch?v=5fcuriNDOoU.

Svampa, Maristella
2018 "Latin American development: perspectives and debates," pp. 13–32 in Tulia G. Falleti and Emilio A. Parrado (eds.), *Latin America since the Left Turn.* Philadelphia: University of Pennsylvania Press.
2019 *Neo-extractivism in Latin America: Socio-environmental Conflicts, the Territorial Turn, and New Political Narratives.* Cambridge: Cambridge University Press.

Tilly, Charles
1995 *Popular Contention in Great Britain 1758–1834.* Cambridge: Harvard University Press.

Vázquez, Melina

2018 "'Ponerse la camiseta': compromiso político y trabajo en la gestión pública de jóvenes militantes kirchneristas," pp. 209–263 in Pablo Vommaro, Alejandra Barcala, and Lucía Rangel (eds.), *Derechos y políticas en infancias y juventudes: Diversidades, prácticas y perspectivas*. Buenos Aires: CLACSO.

Venables, Anthony J.

2016 "Using natural resources for development: why has it proven so difficult?" *Journal of Economic Perspectives* 30 (1): 161–183.

Vommaro, Pablo

2015 *Juventudes y políticas en la Argentina y en América Latina: Tendencias, conflictos y desafíos*. Buenos Aires: Grupo Editor Universitario/CLACSO.

Webber, Jeffery R.

2011 *From Rebellion to Reform in Bolivia: Class Struggle, Indigenous Liberation, and the Politics of Evo Morales*. Chicago: Haymarket Books.

2017 "Contemporary Latin American inequality: class struggle, decolonization, and the limits of liberal citizenship." *Latin American Research Review* 52 (2): 281–299.

Wickham-Crowley, Timothy and Susan Eckstein

2015 "The persisting relevance of political economy and political sociology in Latin American social movement studies." *Latin American Research Review* 50 (4): 3–25.

WikiLeaks

2009 "Argentina: Profiling key Kirchner-allied piquetero leaders." https://wikileaks .org/plusd/cables/09BUENOSAIRES794_a.html.

Wolford, Wendy

2015 "Rethinking the revolution: Latin American social movements and the state in the twenty-first century," pp. 53–79 in Jeffrey W. Rubin and Vivienne Bennett (eds.), *Enduring Reform: Progressive Activism and Private Sector Responses in Latin America's Democracies*. Pittsburgh: University of Pittsburgh Press.

Zibechi, Raúl

2008 *América Latina: Periferias urbanas, territorios en resistencia*. Bogotá: Desde Abajo.

2019a "Las vueltas del neoliberalismo." *La Jornada,* September 27. https://www .jornada.com.mx/2019/09/27/opinion/020a1pol.

2019b "The state of social movements in Latin America: an interview with Raúl Zibechi." Black Rose: Anarchist Federation. January 17. https://blackrosefed.org/ social-movements-latin-america-zibechi/.

Zibechi, Raúl and Decio Machado

2017 *Cambiar el mundo desde arriba: Los límites del progresismo*. Quito: Huaponi Ediciones.

PART 1

Labor, Rural, and
Feminist Movements

Much of the writing on social movements over the past half century, beginning with the works of the French sociologist Alain Touraine, has emphasized the diversity of the identities of activists. This heterogeneity characterizes Latin American social movements in the twenty-first century more than in the past. Another feature of the period that stands out is the influence that social movements exerted on progressive parties and leaders. This relationship manifested itself in the anti-neoliberal struggles that paved the way for the Pink Tide's ascent to power and those after 2015 with the return of right-wing governments. An example was the former Argentine President Cristina Fernández's reversal of her opposition to reproductive rights in 2018 after seeing (in her words) "the thousands and thousands of young women who have taken to the streets," thus contributing to the momentum in favor of the legalization of abortion two years later.

Federico Rossi puts social movements front and center in his explanation of why incorporation processes differed among Pink Tide countries. A major factor has been the vitality of social movements shown by "the expansion of the repertoire of strategies performed by movements due to the bridging-with-the-state that incorporation waves build." The diversity included the role played by social movements in the rise of Pink Tide governments, which was especially pronounced in Argentina, Bolivia, and to some extent in Brazil. Also, in Bolivia, more than elsewhere, social movements at first constituted the "constituency core" of the progressive movement party in government. Another factor that differentiated Pink Tide countries by degree was the role of social movements in "contending elite-based resistance to reforms by left-wing or populist governments." In some nations the social movements were "(generally weak) coalition members" of the progressive governments. Finally, Rossi points to nations (particularly Ecuador) where social movements acted as "opposition to left-wing or populist governments." These variations help explain why some progressive governments were "favorable to incorporating popular movements into government and others not, as well as the diversity of relationships" that emerged.

In his chapter on Brazil's Movimento dos Trabalhadores Sem Terra (Landless Workers' Movement—MST) under progressive presidents Luiz Inácio Lula da Silva and Dilma Rousseff, Anthony Pahnke helps differentiate the generally (but not always) "friendly" government–social-movement relations under Pink Tide governments from those of conservative and right-wing ones. In the face of waning public support for land occupations, the Lula and Rousseff administrations facilitated the MST's consolidation (though not growth) through schools administered by MST leaders and the "development of agroecology . . . with the Partido dos Trabalhadores [Workers' Party—PT] as the central player." These developments were conducive to the MST's professionalization but were rejected by some movement leaders, who felt that they "distracted from radical forms of engagement." Pahnke notes that the MST's consolidation prepared the movement for the challenges posed by the pushback of succeeding governments by "creating new leaders, revising movement practices, and gaining resources." Government policy after Rousseff's impeachment in 2016 "showed that the time of 'friendly' government was over," particularly under the administration of Jair Bolsonaro, who "publicly branded the MST a terrorist organization and cut resources dedicated to nonprofits affiliated with the movement."

Fabricio Carneiro, Guillermo Fuentes, and Carmen Midaglia focus on the links between progressive parties and organized labor. They argue that much of the diversity in the interactions between progressive governments and unions can be explained by "the electoral strategies associated with putting together governing coalitions and the fragmentation of the union movement at the time that those parties took office." They emphasize the importance of the convergence of but also the tensions between Pink Tide governments and certain labor movements in Uruguay, Argentina, Chile, and Brazil. In Chile, the neoliberal policies of the 1980s and 1990s so weakened labor unions that they failed to recover even after more reformist parties reached power. In Brazil, the ties between organized labor and the progressive PT weakened after Lula da Silva reached the presidency in 2003. In contrast, in Uruguay, the alliance between the Frente Amplio (Broad Front—FA) and the main labor confederation during the neoliberal period was strengthened after the FA finally came to power in 2005. In Argentina, it was the rise of Kirchnerism that actively revitalized the labor movement. The ties between progressive parties and organized labor proved crucial once Pink Tide parties left office, when they converged with labor unions in resistance to the dismantling of progressive policies and the renewal of neoliberalism.

The chapter by Eduardo Moreira da Silva and Clarisse Goulart Paradis contributes to the social movement literature by showing that the interactions between feminist movements and the state are not simply contentious but also collaborative. During the Pink Tide, they argue, feminist movements attempted to influence public policy through strategies combining participation in the state apparatus with mobilization "outside the collaborative frameworks with the state." The analysis is supported by a comparison of the collaborative interactions of feminist movements and the state in Chile, Brazil, Argentina, and Bolivia. Overall, the chapter demonstrates significant developments in the feminist movement, with the previous technocratic agenda that dominated the debate on gender in the second half of the twentieth century replaced by a more transformative program. However, subsequent conservative governments have isolated state institutions that had previously been more open to feminist participation, "at the same time that convergences between progressive parties and social movements have emerged around contentious actions."

Daniel Burridge relies on his study of various feminist groups in El Salvador and Nicaragua to go beyond the binary of co-optation and confrontation to explore the more complex relations that exist between most social movements and Pink Tide governments, located in what he calls "gray zones." The first case study is of a territorial-based feminist movement in El Salvador that developed a symbiotic relationship with state institutions during the leftist governments of the Frente Farabundo Martí para la Liberación Nacional (Farabundo Martí National Liberation Front—FMLN). Burridge describes the resultant interaction as "cogovernance" in matters related to gender politics. A second study is of a more pragmatically oriented women's cooperative in Nicaragua that abandoned issues related to reproductive rights in order to "privilege interactions with Sandinista state institutions that provide them technical and financial resources to pursue their cooperative economic initiatives." The third is of a feminist group in León, Nicaragua, that is dedicated to the self-management of women's rights and sometimes clashes with the Sandinista government's "hostility toward feminist frames of reproductive justice." All three movements, he claims, have "deepened democracy in different ways." In general, "feminist movements in Latin America have been particularly adept at negotiating their objectives with Pink Tide governments."

Chapter 1

Popular Movements—Progressive Governments Dynamics

Considerations for an Analysis of the Latin American Experience

Federico M. Rossi

The relationship of popular movements with progressive governments has been contradictory in Latin America.[1] Although generally more supportive than right-wing governments, leftist or populist governments have not always promoted constructive relationships with popular movements. While popular movements achieved positions in government to promote their agendas in Argentina during Kirchnerism, Bolivia under the Movimiento al Socialismo, and Brazil under the Partido dos Trabalhadores, this was not the case under the socialists of the Concertación in Chile and is not the case under Andrés Manuel López Obrador's government in Mexico and even less in the case of Daniel Ortega in Nicaragua. This means that there is not a unified form of interaction of popular movements with progressive governments in Latin America but that in some cases there was an increase in the number of institutional nexuses with the state, while in others there was no favoring of popular movements' agendas (Abers and Tatagiba, 2015; Hanson and Lapegna, 2018; Perelmiter, 2012; Rossi, 2017). This is a result of a dynamic that crosses the ideological distinction of governments into a different analytical category to sort out the so-called left turn or Pink Tide in Latin America. This dynamic is the long-term and cyclical expansion and contraction of the sociopolitical arena produced by the (re)incorporation and disincorporation of the organized popular sectors in Latin America from the mid-nineteenth century to the present.

I will not analyze this dynamic in detail, since the first wave of incorporation has been masterfully examined by Collier and Collier (1991) and I have extensively studied the second wave of incorporation (Rossi, 2015; 2017; 2018; 2020; Rossi and Silva, 2018). I will refer to these works to help contextualize my argument that the experiences of progressive governments are not uniform and that the most relevant explanatory factor for the type of relationship developed between popular movements and left-wing or populist governments is whether and how the sociopolitical arena was expanded. I believe that my approach can best explain why some progressive governments in the early twenty-first century were favorable to incorporating popular movements into government and others not, as well as the diversity of relationships developed during the second incorporation.

THE TWO WAVES OF INCORPORATION

The history of Latin America is characterized by two waves of incorporation (Rossi, 2017: xi):

> The waves of incorporation signal the recognition and inclusion of poor people's organized interests in the socio-political arena. The concept of popular incorporation refers to the recognition of the claims of politically active poor people's movements as well as the creation or reformulation of formal and informal rules and regulations that govern their participation in politics and their connection to the policy process.

The first wave, between the 1930s and 1950s, as described by Collier and Collier (1991: 783), was "the first sustained and at least partially successful attempt by the state to legitimate and shape an institutionalized labor movement" that "occurs in relatively well-defined policy periods, which we frequently refer to as the 'incorporation period.' These periods emerge as part of a larger program of political and economic reform." The end of the first incorporation was marked by coups and a restriction of political and social rights. As I have argued, "The aftermath of first incorporation was one of exclusion or disincorporation, as a result of the application of economic and political reforms that reduced the political power of the popular sectors and marginalized them from the sociopolitical arena" (Rossi, 2017: xxi). Since the 2000s, after decades of struggle, there was in some countries a "second major redefinition of the sociopolitical arena . . . caused by the broad and selective inclusion of the popular sectors in the polity after being excluded or disincorporated by military authoritarian regimes and democratic neoliberal reforms" (Rossi 2015: 2). This second wave was the result of the accumulation of changes in response to the struggle for reincorporation of popular sectors organized into territorialized social movements. The emergence of left-wing or populist parties in government was one of the by-products of two decades of struggle against disincorporation.

These waves of incorporation are political dynamics with strategic actors disputing models of society, and the historical period covered by the second wave includes but extends beyond the Pink Tide or left turn. My approach analyzes a long-term sociopolitical dynamic, showing how the struggles of the popular sectors are interconnected across waves and beyond governments.

INCLUSION AND INCORPORATION

Inclusion and incorporation are different processes. While the former can sometimes be pursued by individualizing means, the latter is a collective process of expansion of the polity. In this regard, "It is also important to bear in mind that waves of incorporation should be equated *not* with the constitution of a more equal society or the creation of a welfare state but rather with the reshaping of the sociopolitical arena by redefining and expanding the number of legitimate political actors" (Rossi, 2017: 12). In other words, incorporation means that the mobilized actors seeking to be recognized as the legitimate articulators of the "social question" associated with the victims of the model of development become part of the actors defining a central policy domain aimed at resolving this "social question." However, as a recursive dynamic of Latin America's capitalism, the second incorporation involved similarities and differences among countries just as had the first. The emergence of recommodification and marginalization (unemployment, impoverishment, exclusion, etc.) as a new "social question," the modification of policing techniques, and the creation of massive social programs can be seen as equivalent to the preincorporation dynamic. Although the emergence of a "social question" is a necessary condition for identifying an incorporation wave, some national processes were instances of incorporation with inclusion, while in others inclusion and incorporation were disconnected dynamics. Moreover, in the second incorporation as in the first the expansion of the sociopolitical arena started before leftists or populists achieved government power. The expansion and consolidation of ongoing dynamics and policies were a result of the sedimentation of institutions and practices produced by the elites' response to the struggles of popular movements for bridging their lives with the state. In this sense, in both waves of incorporation we can see cases of promotion of mobilization and others of demobilization (for comparative analyses of the cross-national differences, see Collier and Collier, 1991, for the first and Rossi, 2017: 251–274, and Silva and Rossi, 2018, for the second).

Discussing these topics, Kapiszewski, Levitsky, and Yashar (2021: 10–11, 17) appear to confuse different social dynamics in arguing that instead of a second incorporation there has been an "inclusionary turn" in Latin America, conflating as equivalent inclusion and incorporation. They consider inclusion just the formal attribution of individual citizenship rights, empirically sustaining their argument on counting formal reforms across Latin America without considering the sociopolitical dynamics of struggle, the change in practices, the sedimentation of transformations, and the institutionalization of norms for regulating and articulating the actors and claims attached to the struggles. They fail to distinguish the moment of the legal formulation of a new regulation or right from the antecedent conditions of ongoing social struggle that led to it (see Mahoney and Thelen, 2010; Collier and Collier, 1991: Chap. 1, for detailed discussions in theoretical and methodological terms). As a result, they conflate the transformations of the state in Latin America since the 1980s, offering no substantive criteria for distinguishing which of them can be associated with democratization and which with the neopluralization of society, the disincorporation of the popular sectors, the neoliberalization of the economy, the resistance to any of these transformations, and/or any other dynamics that may have (partially) overlapped with them during that period. In the process they neglect to perform the analysis of the mutually reinforcing influences of these processes or lack of thereof that is analytically essential for identifying the connection of each formal right with a specific sociopolitical dynamic. Thus the inclusionary turn thesis confuses the expansion of neopluralism (see Oxhorn, 1998, for an exemplary analysis) with other sociopolitical dynamics, overlooking the crucial difference between the achievement of formal legal recognition (Kapiszewski, Levitsky, and Yashar, 2021: 14–15) and the sociopolitical restructuring that (re)incorporation means for a polity (for the characteristics of struggles for recognition, see Auyero, 2003, and Lucero, 2008; for (re)incorporation, see Pérez, 2022, and Rossi, 2017: 18–19). As a result, this view disregards both the recursive dynamics of struggles for (re)incorporation that characterize the history of Latin America since the late nineteenth century and a particularity of the second incorporation that is not present in the first, its having been carried out by democratically elected progressive governments. This mixing of processes even leads them to argue that "Latin America's most recent inclusionary turn began slowly around 1989–1990" (Kapiszewski, Levitsky, and Yashar 2021: 10), a period characterized by the consequences of the debt crisis—the continentwide adoption of neoliberalism and its massive exclusionary consequences. This historically erroneous argument is a result of doing only a formal analysis of the expansion of neopluralist rights. The apparent confusion of dynamics causes them to argue that the center-right governments of Mauricio Macri in Argentina, Sebastián Piñera in Chile, and Iván Duque in

Colombia did not reduce inclusion because they did not revoke formal rights (Kapiszewski, Levitsky, and Yashar, 2021: 11). The 2019–2020 Chilean and Colombian popular revolts against disincorporation clearly disprove this thesis. Instead, the present volume offers an in-depth analysis of the role played by the progressive governments, opening up a crucial debate in the literature.

VARIETY OF MOVEMENT-GOVERNMENT RELATIONS OF THE SECOND WAVE OF INCORPORATION

Where incorporation took place, the governments were not necessarily ideologically more radical than governments not involved in these dynamics. However, what incorporation produced was the creation of institutional channels and the expansion of the repertoire of strategies performed by movements due to the bridging-with-the-state that incorporation waves build (Rossi, 2017: 32–65). This implied innovation and recursiveness in strategizing by social movement actors in response to the opportunity for transforming long-standing claims into public policy and legislation (Etchemendy, 2019; Perelmiter, 2012; Rossi, 2017). This opportunity was not always seen as such and was sometimes a demobilizing factor because of the divisions it produced among movements between groups entering a governing coalition and others that rejected that option (Hanson and Lapegna, 2018; Silva, 2018).

The relationship of movements with progressive governments has been contradictory. Briefly, seven types of roles were played by popular movements with regard to leftists or populists in government that were part of the second wave of incorporation (Anria, 2018; Conaghan, 2018; Etchemendy, 2019; García-Guadilla, 2018; Hanson and Lapegna, 2018; McNelly, 2020; Padoan, 2020; Rossi, 2017; 2018; Silva, 2018). The first is popular movements as the mobilized actor that produced the conditions for the emergence of left-wing or populist governments. This was the case of Argentina, Bolivia, and partially Brazil. The second is popular movements as the territorial (re) connection of left-wing or populist governments with the popular sectors and grassroots claims. This was the case of Argentina, Brazil, and to some extent Venezuela. The third is popular movements as the constituency core of left-wing or populist movement parties in government. This was the case of Bolivia. The fourth is popular movements as the instrument for contending elite-based resistance to reforms by left-wing or populist governments. This was the case of Argentina, Bolivia, and Venezuela. The fifth is popular movements as (generally weak) coalition members of left-wing or populist governments. This was the case of Argentina, Bolivia, Brazil, and Venezuela. The sixth is popular movements as (generally critical) external allies of left-wing or populist governments. This was the case of Argentina, Venezuela, and to some extent Bolivia. The last is popular movements as the (generally not crucial) opposition to left-wing or populist governments. This was the case of Ecuador and to some extent Venezuela. The elements that define these types of relations are a result of multiple dynamics but are intrinsic to the type of reincorporation, its antecedent conditions, and its aftermath. It is important to emphasize that these are *not* types of reincorporation but types of movement-government relations *within* the second wave of incorporation. In this sense, it is crucial to determine whether reincorporation was mainly from above or below, whether it was mainly political or technocratic, and whether the mobilized popular sectors were considered relevant by the elites in the construction of governability for these governments (Rossi and Silva, 2018).

The governability dilemma for any party with executive power transcends ideologies and (incorporation) paths, leading to the perceived gap between the promises and expectations deposited in left-wing or populist party, leader, or coalition and the actual results. In some countries, the results in terms of social policies, recognition of intersectional claims, and relative inclusion were impressive. In others, however, the redistributive dimension of these policies was short-lived, and this divided movements between those calling for inclusion and those demanding recognition. Sometimes progressive governments just gave lip service to popular movements' agendas while perpetuating old practices. In those cases, state repression was sustained and sometimes directed at new political targets (Hanson and Lapegna, 2018; McNelly, 2020; Padoan, 2020).

To understand cross-national incorporation paths, we need to observe how actors, dynamics, and processes interact: first, how the party system was reformulated (or not) during the resistance to disincorporation and the subsequent reincorporation phase and the role played by the governing party (whether a movement party, a party family, inchoated party, cartel party, personalistic party, etc.) during these periods (Anria, 2018; Roberts, 2018; 2022); second, the role of unions in relation to neoliberalism (privileged actors of the previous model of development or victims of disincorporation), and the degree of neocorporatism since first incorporation and its weakening or dissolution since then (Oxhorn, 1998; Collier, 2018; Ellner, 2018; Gindin and Cardoso, 2018; Rossi, 2020); third, the degree of organicity of social actors and vertical and spatial coordination of protest into social movements with the capacity for producing a new "social question" and creating a legitimate actor mobilizing around it that can produce and sustain a policy domain (Rossi, 2017); fourth, the degree of intersectional coordination and divisions on the left (and whether it is divided between class-based and national-populist sectors) and the elites' capacity to counterreact and coordinate the resistance to reincorporation (Ferrero, Natalucci, and Tatagiba, 2019; Gold and Peña, 2019); and, finally, the type of model of development precedent to neoliberal reforms (for example, rentier, light industrialization, import-substitution industrialization, etc.) and its economic legacies combined with the degree of territorialization of interest intermediation mechanisms (Silva, 2018; Rossi, 2019; 2022).

CONCLUSION

The second wave of incorporation and the reshaping of the sociopolitical arena that allowed for different types of incorporation is a result of the struggles of popular movements to reconnect the popular sectors with the state. Combinations of the transformations just enumerated explain and contextualize the different types of relationships of popular movements with progressive governments in a reincorporation process. Thus, the type of incorporation developed is a relevant variation among the ideologically not-so-distant governments that constituted the second wave of incorporation. This crucial difference also explains why, even though governed by leftists or populists, some countries cannot be considered part of the second wave of incorporation, with its fundamental implications for movement-government relationships.

NOTE

1. I thank Steve Ellner and Ronaldo Munck for the insightful comments that encouraged me to improve this text.

REFERENCES

Abers, Rebecca Neaera and Luciana Tatagiba
2015 "Institutional activism: mobilizing for women's health from inside the Brazilian bureaucracy," pp. 73–101 in F. M. Rossi and M. von Bülow (eds.), *Social Movement Dynamics: New Perspectives on Theory and Research from Latin America.* Farnham: Ashgate/Routledge.
Anria, Santiago
2018 *When Movements Become Parties: The Bolivian MAS in Comparative Perspective.* New York: Cambridge University Press.
Auyero, Javier
2003 *Contentious Lives: Two Argentine Women, Two Protests, and the Quest for Recognition.* Durham, NC: Duke University Press.
Collier, Ruth Berins
2018 "Labor unions in Latin America: incorporation and reincorporation under the New Left," pp. 115–128 in E. Silva and F. M. Rossi (eds.), *Reshaping the*

Political Arena in Latin America: From Resisting Neoliberalism to the Second Incorporation. Pittsburgh: University of Pittsburgh Press.

Collier, Ruth Berins and David Collier

1991 *Shaping the Political Arena: Critical Junctures, the Labor Movement, and Regime Dynamics in Latin America.* Princeton: Princeton University Press.

Conaghan, Catherine M.

2018 "From movements to governments: comparing Bolivia's MAS and Ecuador's PAIS," pp. 222–250 in E. Silva and F. M. Rossi (eds.), *Reshaping the Political Arena in Latin America: From Resisting Neoliberalism to the Second Incorporation.* Pittsburgh: University of Pittsburgh Press.

Ellner, Steve

2018 "Conflicting currents within the pro-Chávez labor movement and the dynamics of decision making," pp. 157–178 in E. Silva and F. M. Rossi (eds.), *Reshaping the Political Arena in Latin America: From Resisting Neoliberalism to the Second Incorporation.* Pittsburgh: University of Pittsburgh Press.

Etchemendy, Sebastián

2019 "The politics of popular coalitions: unions and territorial social movements in post-neoliberal Latin America (2000–15)." *Journal of Latin American Studies* 52 (1): 1–32.

Ferrero, Juan Pablo, Ana Natalucci, and Luciana Tatagiba (eds.)

2019 *Socio-political Dynamics within the Crisis of the Left: Argentina and Brazil.* Lanham, MD: Rowman and Littlefield.

García-Guadilla, María Pilar

2018 "The incorporation of popular sectors and social movements in Venezuelan twenty-first-century socialism," pp. 60–77 in E. Silva and F. M. Rossi (eds.), *Reshaping the Political Arena in Latin America: From Resisting Neoliberalism to the Second Incorporation.* Pittsburgh: University of Pittsburgh Press.

Gindin, Julián and Adalberto Cardoso

2018 "The labor movement and the erosion of neoliberal hegemony: Brazil and Argentina," pp. 179–207 in E. Silva and F. M. Rossi (eds.), *Reshaping the Political Arena in Latin America: From Resisting Neoliberalism to the Second Incorporation.* Pittsburgh: University of Pittsburgh Press.

Gold, Tomás and Alejandro M. Peña

2019 "Protests, signaling, and selections: conceptualizing opposition-movement interactions during Argentina's anti-government protests (2012–2013)." *Social Movement Studies* 18 (3): 324–345.

Hanson, Rebecca and Pablo Lapegna

2018 "Popular participation and governance in the Kirchners' Argentina and Chávez's Venezuela: recognition, incorporation and supportive mobilisation," *Journal of Latin American Studies* 50 (1): 153–182.

Kapiszewski, Diana, Steven Levitsky, and Deborah J. Yashar

2021 "Inequality, democracy, and the inclusionary turn in Latin America," pp. 1–55 in D. Kapiszewski, S. Levitsky, and D. J. Yashar (eds.), *The Inclusionary Turn in Latin American Democracies.* Cambridge: Cambridge University Press.

Lucero, José Antonio

2008 *Struggles of Voice: The Politics of Indigenous Representation in the Andes.* Pittsburgh: University of Pittsburgh Press.

Mahoney, James and Kathleen Thelen

2010 "A theory of gradual institutional change," pp. 1–37 in J. Mahon and K. Thelen (eds.), *Explaining Institutional Change: Ambiguity, Agency, and Power.* New York: Cambridge University Press.

McNelly, Angus

2020 "The incorporation of social organizations under the MAS in Bolivia." *Latin American Perspectives* 47 (4): 76–95.

Oxhorn, Philip

1998 "Is the century of corporatism over? Neoliberalism and the rise of neopluralism," pp. 195–217 in P. Oxhorn and G. Ducatenzeiler (eds.), *What Kind of Democracy? What Kind of Market? Latin America in the Age of Neoliberalism.* University Park: Pennsylvania State University Press.

Padoan, Enrico

2020 "The role of social movements in the 'second incorporation' of popular sectors in Bolivia and Argentina." *Revista Española de Sociología* 29 (3-Sup2): 155–167.

Perelmiter, Luisina

2012 "Fronteras inestables y eficaces: el ingreso de organizaciones de desocupados a la burocracia asistencial del Estado, Argentina (2003–2008)." *Estudios Sociológicos* 30 (89): 431–458.

Pérez, Marcos

2022 *Proletarian Lives: Routines, Identity and Culture in Contentious Politics.* New York: Cambridge University Press.

Roberts, Kenneth M.

2018 "Political parties in Latin America's second wave of incorporation," pp. 211–221 in E. Silva and F. M. Rossi (eds.), *Reshaping the Political Arena in Latin America: From Resisting Neoliberalism to the Second Incorporation.* Pittsburgh: University of Pittsburgh Press.

2022 "Social movements and party politics: popular mobilization and the reciprocal structuring of political representation in Latin America," in F. M. Rossi (ed.), *The Oxford Handbook of Latin American Social Movements.* Oxford: Oxford University Press.

Rossi, Federico M.

2015 "The second wave of incorporation in Latin America: a conceptualization of the quest for inclusion applied to Argentina." *Latin American Politics and Society* 57 (1): 1–28.

2017 *The Poor's Struggle for Political Incorporation: The Piquetero Movement in Argentina.* New York: Cambridge University Press.

2018 "Social movements and the second wave of (territorial) incorporation in Latin America," pp. 23–31 in E. Silva and F. M. Rossi (eds.), *Reshaping the Political Arena in Latin America: From Resisting Neoliberalism to the Second Incorporation.* Pittsburgh: University of Pittsburgh Press.

2019 "Conceptualising and tracing the increased territorialisation of politics: insights from Argentina." *Third World Quarterly* 40: 815–837.

2020 "Labor movements in Latin America," pp. 325–338 in X. Bada and L. Rivera Sánchez (eds.), *The Oxford Handbook of Sociology of Latin America.* Oxford: Oxford University Press.

2022 "Social movements and capitalist models of development in Latin America," in F. M. Rossi (ed.), *The Oxford Handbook of Latin American Social Movements.* Oxford: Oxford University Press.

Rossi, Federico M. and Eduardo Silva

2018 "Reshaping the political arena in Latin America," pp. 3–20 in E. Silva and F. M. Rossi (eds.), *Reshaping the Political Arena in Latin America: From Resisting Neoliberalism to the Second Incorporation.* Pittsburgh: University of Pittsburgh Press.

Silva, Eduardo

2018 "Reflections on the second wave of popular incorporation for a post-neoliberal era," pp. 309–324 in E. Silva and F. M. Rossi (eds.), *Reshaping the Political Arena in Latin America: From Resisting Neoliberalism to the Second Incorporation.* Pittsburgh: University of Pittsburgh Press.

Silva, Eduardo and Federico M. Rossi (eds.)

2018 *Reshaping the Political Arena in Latin America: From Resisting Neoliberalism to the Second Incorporation.* Pittsburgh: University of Pittsburgh Press.

Chapter 2

Social Movement Consolidation and Strategic Shifts

The Brazilian Landless Movement during the Lula and Dilma Administrations

Anthony Pahnke

Shortly before his successful bid to become Brazil's thirty-fifth president in 2002, Luiz Inácio Lula da Silva, whose support for the Brazilian Landless Movement dated to its emergence in the early 1980s, said that a Partido dos Trabalhadores (Workers' Party—PT) government would lead "a real agrarian reform" through "expropriating large estates" (Silva, 1999).[1] His statement carried tremendous weight for the Landless Movement—the Movimento dos Trabalhadores Rurais Sem Terra (Landless Workers' Movement—MST) and its many allies[2]—and the more than 1.5 million people who have been engaged in a multidecade struggle for agrarian reform. While it worried Brazil's economic elite, their concerns were assuaged when Lula selected the conservative businessman José Alencar Gomes da Silva of the Partido Liberal (Liberal Party—PL) as his running mate and then issued a letter to the Brazilian people emphasizing his commitment to free-market capitalism.

This ambiguity with respect to the Landless Movement and its struggle for agrarian reform continued throughout Lula's time in office. Various public policies, among them the National School Food Program and the Food Acquisition Program, which supported small rural producers, including many movement members, were allocated significant resources (Hespanhol, 2013; Peixinho, 2013). Additionally, the Instituto Nacional de Colonização e Reforma Agrária (Institute for Colonization and Agrarian Reform—INCRA) received considerably more financing and altered its strategic mission to address problems of rural development (Oliveira, 2010).

Although these policy changes appeared to indicate commitment to agrarian reform, Lula's government redistributed less land than the previous government of Fernando Henrique Cardoso (Oliveira, 2011). Dilma Rousseff similarly received critiques from the MST and its allies for her administration's seeming unwillingness to redistribute land (Nascimento, 2015). As the MST celebrated its thirtieth anniversary in 2014, the total area expropriated for redistribution was at a historic low (Arruda, 2014). Furthermore, the number of land occupations—the trademark tactic used by the movement to demand land redistribution—declined by 66 percent from 2004 to 2016.[3]

To bring these dynamics—especially the tense yet productive relationship between the center-left PT and the MST—into sharp relief, it is necessary to observe how the right-wing Bolsonaro government has confronted the struggle for agrarian reform. Since winning his bid to become Brazil's president in 2018, riding a wave of evangelical-nationalist-populist sentiment, Bolsonaro's administration has publicly branded the MST a terrorist organization and cut resources dedicated to nonprofits affiliated with the movement (Lázaro, 2019; *Brasil Econômico, 2021*). *Meanwhile, deforestation of the Amazon has increased since the years of* PT rule as environmental regulations have been relaxed and large-scale property owners have organized groups of marginalized people to assist them in opening up spaces to increase the soy frontier at the expense of national parks and indigenous people's holdings (Maisonnave and Almeida, 2020). All this, as well as the creation of new agrarian reform settlements for Brazil's rural poor, has been essentially frozen (Giovanaz, 2021).

In this chapter I argue that the ambiguity of PT governance offered the Landless Movement the opportunity to strengthen its leadership and internal organization. Seminal studies on the movement document its origins and organization (Banford and Rocha, 2002; Fernandes, 2000; Wright and Wolford, 2003), while subsequent scholarship analyzes the increase in its interaction with the Brazilian government (Carter, 2015; Pahnke, Tarlau, and Wolford, 2015; Wolford, 2010). This latter literature recognizes that interaction has not resulted in the movement's demise. In fact, it continues to lead protests and occupations despite the Bolsonaro government's repeated efforts to derail the struggle for agrarian reform. Helping to explain the movement's persistence and complementing these studies, I document how consolidation resulted from the conditions in which the movement found itself while the center-left PT was in power.

This chapter has six sections. In the first, I discuss the role of external factors in social movement theory, addressing certain matters with the concept of political opportunity structure. In building from this concept, I propose an alternative that differentiates between governmental, economic, and state conditions. The following sections employ this framework to describe the problems that the Landless Movement faced shortly before the election of Lula in 2002 and show how the Lula and Dilma governments contributed to the movement's efforts at addressing its weaknesses. The final two sections describe the movement's strategic shift to an accumulation-of-forces strategy and its agroecology.

The research for this chapter took place from 2009 to 2016 and included semistructured interviews and participatory observation conducted in 2009 and 2011. I also analyzed newspapers, movement newsletters and training manuals, and legislation. I interviewed movement members and leaders, their opponents and allies, and state functionaries and members of political parties in Brasília and in the states of Pernambuco, São Paulo, Rio Grande do Sul, and Paraná. The ethnographic section was conducted in primary, secondary, and postsecondary schools, economic production cooperatives, and informal training sites administered by the Landless Movement.

EXTERNAL CONDITIONS IN SOCIAL MOVEMENT THEORY

Exploring the influence of external factors on collective action, theorists have typically turned to the concept of the political opportunity structure to chart movement origins and the ebb and flow of protest (Almeida, 2019; Ondetti, 2008; Tarrow, 1998). The concept calls attention to the effects of the use of repression by governmental actors and the presence of allies in certain institutions. Following critiques of its mechanical application (McAdam, Tarrow, and Tilly, 2001), additional ways of thinking about external conditions have been offered. Examples include work on external factors such as networks (including relations between individuals and organizations [Diani, 2013; McAdam and Boudet, 2012] and fields, denoting broad cultural and discursive systems [Snow, 2004]). Despite these efforts, social movement scholarship remains troubled. As Goodwin and Jasper (2004) noted with respect to scholarship on contention in general, studies that have employed the political opportunity structure concept lack a clear definition of "political." This conceptual problem renders it difficult to explore the dynamics of movement resistance without a way of identifying the different contexts in which mobilization unfolds. Scholarship on fields, networks, and discourse has not solved this problem; new concepts have been introduced without adequate concern for their meaning, application, and relationship to previous frameworks.

Instead of introducing yet another concept, I propose to follow others who have noticed the narrowness of social movement theory and begun to connect it with research on revolutions (Buechler, 2016; see also Goodwin, 2013). What this scholarship emphasizes is the role of the state and the economy in the development of collective action. Skocpol (1979), emphasizing the breakdown of state power as central to the unfolding of revolutionary struggles, argues that the state is more than institutions, allies, and repression. Similarly, from Lenin's (1917) conception of dual power to Tilly's (1977) work on revolution, we find that state power is not the same as government. Analyzing sovereignty—taken as the monopoly claim to legitimately control a certain people in a particular territory—leads us to document the way authority is claimed over and through populations that reside in specific areas. Sovereignty targets certain people and makes an exception of others who are considered outside it (Agamben, 1998; Schmitt, 2004 [1922]). Furthermore, studies of sovereignty draw our attention to the way space is appropriated and divided, as in Foucault's (2007) understanding of biopolitics. Mitchell (1999), adapting Foucault's concept, details how populations are identified, controlled, and coerced through everyday forms of administrative power.

Studies of revolution lead us to consider the nature of state power, which is apparent in everything from the distribution of social security numbers and the protection of private property to the allocation of resources for public policy. Studies of revolution also draw our attention to the ways in which economic factors influence collective action. For example, Migdal (2015 [1975]) and Scott (1977) have noted that rising inequality and rural displacement offered opportunities for revolutionary mobilization. Similarly, others have recognized that the class relationships of actors impact the development of resistance (Wolf, 1969). Conceiving of economic conditions means paying attention to labor markets, employment levels, and wealth inequality. Labor, additionally, involves relationships, and this may point to the influence of wage labor or sharecropping on social movement mobilization.

Combining the approaches of revolution studies and social movement research, I propose distinguishing external conditions as governmental, state, and economic. Governmental conditions, for instance, include the presence or absence of allies, the degree of legitimacy of an administration, and the kind of regime (liberal democratic, authoritarian, etc.; see, e.g., McAdam, 2010 [1982], and McAdam, McCarthy, and Zald, 1996). State conditions are different, given that sovereignty is a form of power that works through institutions but is not reducible to them. Economics as a condition for mobilization includes the effects of inequality, class relationships, and employment on social movement efforts and practices. These distinctions provide a nuanced way to think of external factors. In what follows I present the case of the Brazilian Landless Movement's evolution during the time of PT rule to illustrate the value of this approach.

THE CRISIS OF THE LANDLESS MOVEMENT:
ECONOMIC AND GOVERNMENTAL FACTORS

When a longtime MST member said, "You know, if the cooperatives fail, so do the settlements" (interview, near Rio Bonito, Paraná, August 11, 2011), I was shocked. Another leader made a similar remark when I asked if there were any "issues" with economic production: "Oh, you mean the crisis? Yeah, there've been problems, and families have left. Some felt that what the movement promised them didn't happen" (interview, near Bagé, Rio Grande do Sul, May 13, 2011). What made these statements provocative was that they referenced movement activities in Rio Grande do Sul and Paraná, where the MST and its allies have been active for decades, and revealed a vital need for seriously addressing economic problems.

As the Lula administration was coming to power, the MST was assessing its economic problems. One internal study noted that most cooperatives were plagued by debt and mismanagement (MST, 2006). The main credit policy for agrarian reform beneficiaries between 1985 and 2001 was the Special Program for Agrarian Reform Credit. Resources dedicated to this program tripled, from R$89 to R$250 million, between 1995 and 1998. The problem was not the increase in available money but the policy's incentive structure. The Special Program incentivized the formation of groups by dividing funding opportunities into two levels (Souza and Gebara, 2010) and requiring the formation of a group for eligibility to seek credit at the higher level. The MST (1995) encouraged members to form cooperatives to receive the additional resources. Meanwhile, the movement had difficulty crafting effective economic development plans. Visiting one cooperative, I was told that in the 1990s families had intended to engage in monocultural production of commodities such as corn and soy. The goal was "to be like the big ones, you know, like the big landowners" (interview, near Pontão, Rio Grande do Sul, April 5, 2011). According to MST (2006) assessments, this sentiment was dominant in many cooperatives. It is hard to fault its members, given that their knowledge of production came from working on large-scale operations. The 1996 Agrarian Reform Census shows that the vast majority of movement members occupied nonmanagerial positions in large-scale operations (Todorov and Viero, 1997). Members who had received government credit referred to this period as a time of "easy money" because initial restrictions and requirements for obtaining credit were lax (interview, director of a milk producers' cooperative, near Pontão, Rio Grande do Sul, April 1, 2011). As a result, cooperatives debt-financed many of their assets but without the knowledge required to develop sustainable business plans.

An additional conundrum unfolded in collectivization efforts. Early movement plans for settlement development called for communal living. The idea was that property, production, responsibility, and profits would be shared equally in collectively administered production cooperatives. This arrangement, in fact, is what visitors see when they visit many of the MST cooperatives that have remained. Not every effort was a success; indebted members stopped participating in the movement's economic and political activities, and so did some who wanted to work individually (interview, MST state director, Porto Alegre, Rio Grande do Sul, April 3, 2011). Others have noted that the movement's collectivization plans led to member alienation (Diniz and Gilbert, 2013; Wolford, 2010: 188–192).

When the PT came to power, the Landless Movement was in the process of evaluating its successes and failures in economic production. Governmental and economic conditions made movement members throughout Brazil insolvent, threatening the movement's struggle for agrarian reform.

STATE AND ECONOMIC CONDITIONS
UNDER PT RULE

The Landless Movement encountered other economic challenges while the PT was in power. Income inequality was reduced during the Lula and Dilma administrations, with the Gini coefficient dropping from 59 in 2002 to 52 in 2014 (Loman, 2014). Since 2002, approximately 40 million people have become middle-class and 35 million people have been lifted out of extreme poverty. Social programs such as the Bolsa Familia (Family Fund) have been credited with removing extreme poverty from the Brazilian landscape (Pereira, 2015). While benefiting economically marginalized populations, these changes had less than positive effects on the Landless Movement. Fernandes (2008) notes that with a modicum of economic well-being throughout Brazil's rural and urban periphery, the movement's efforts at mobilizing were blunted. As recipients of assistance took on new roles as managers of resources, they had less time for and commitment to collective action (Morton, 2015). An additional change occurred with export agriculture. In 2002 it accounted for over US$25 billion in sales, while in 2010 that number was US$76 billion (ANDA, 2011). Given that export earnings were used to pay foreign debts and stabilize domestic currency, neither Lula nor Dilma sought to interfere in agribusiness.

State conditions also changed during the time the PT was in power. First, the Lula government sought to regularize territorial holdings in terms of *territorios de ciudadanía* (citizenship territories), more than 120 rural areas especially designated for production support programs and public works.

This effort imperiled the Landless Movement's mobilization because land occupations targeted irregular landholdings, notably those with multiple owners. Another change was that Lula repaid Brazil's debt to the International Monetary Fund in 2006. While this did not end deficit spending (international creditors were exchanged for domestic ones), state power was strengthened by the transfer of control over governmental affairs to Brazilian actors. Conflicts over land and resources remained constant, but occupations significantly decreased as mobilizations demanding agrarian reform increased.

Furthermore, in contrast to the situation in the 1990s, when massacres of rural activists triggered widespread public sympathy for the movement (Ondetti, 2006), there was not a single event to galvanize public support for large-scale land redistribution under either Lula or Dilma. In fact, the coverage of the MST's occupation in 2009 of the large orange operation owned by the Cutrale Corporation, especially a video of activists running over trees, represented the movement as a criminal actors bent on destroying property. In 2009, a survey by the Confederação da Agricultura e Pecuária do Brasil (Brazilian Confederation of Agriculture and Cattle Raising) and the Instituto Brasileiro de Opinião Pública e Estatística (Brazilian Institute of Public Opinion and Statistics) found that over 92 percent of the public considered occupations illegal, 75 percent thought that the MST should find other means to acquire property, and 57 percent held that the MST had strayed from its original purpose (Froufe, 2009). Without public sympathy and with state and economic conditions not in favor of the movement, the Landless Movement's ability to expand throughout Brazil via land occupations declined.

PROPITIOUS GOVERNMENTAL CONDITIONS

Despite certain unfavorable factors, Lula's election in 2002 improved governmental conditions for the movement in important ways. First, shortly after assuming power the government stopped applying the Cardoso decree that prohibited expropriation of occupied properties. This signaled to the Landless Movement that the government was supportive of agrarian reform in some form. Another change involved financing. INCRA's budget for various agrarian reform policies, including funds for officials' salaries, expropriating land, education, and credit, grew exponentially.

INCRA's mission also adapted. In developing a plan for rural development, the emphasis was now placed on building adequate infrastructure and production capacity as opposed to creating individualized, private landholdings (see Cardoso, 1997; Martins, 2000). Focusing on infrastructure and development meant that priorities included building roads, making economic production viable, and establishing working sanitation systems (Oliveira, 2010). Both the land and the credits distributed were considered *fondos perdidos* (lost funds), meaning that families who received resources were not expected to repay them (interview, INCRA official, Brasília, January 31, 2011). INCRA during the Rousseff administration continued these practices, changing, in 2014, Law 8629/1993 to remove explicit time frames from when families are supposed to receive definitive ownership of particular parcels of land. The National Audit Court took issue with these policies, pressuring INCRA to force families to purchase land and repay loans (CPMI da Terra, 2005; TCU, 2010).

Public policies that favored small farmers received additional resources from the PT. The monetary resources given to Brazil's school lunch program, which guaranteed that a certain percentage of the food served at schools came from family farms, increased from R$1 million to R$4 million (US$450,000 to US$1,800,000) between 2002 and 2014, affecting more than 43 million children (FNDE, 2014). In 2003, Law 10.696 created the Food Acquisition Program, which targeted small-scale producers, especially indigenous people, agrarian reform beneficiaries, fishers, Afro-descendants, and others. Through this program, small farmers sold their produce to the government in the event of poor market prices and institutions were used to direct food to marginalized communities. In 2009 and 2010 the percentage of financing that went to movement members rose from 8 percent to 12 percent while participating families in settlements increased from 7 percent to 11 percent (from 7,444 of 98,340 families to 10,440 of 94,398).

Increases in resources and programs did not, however, lead to harmonious relations between the Landless Movement and the government in general. At the federal level, right-wing legislators managed over PT opposition to organize congressional inquiries in 2002, 2005, and 2010 that targeted the MST and cut resources that were destined for financing movement educational and economic initiatives. Movement opponents cited alleged criminal behavior, specifically the misuse of public resources to promote violence and spread an antidemocratic ideology.[4] At the center of these claims was that the MST used public resources to engage in illegal land invasions by forming criminal organizations. Given that invasion (not occupation) was an illegal act, opponents of the MST's political project claimed that it broke the law, particularly the clauses of the constitution that enshrined productive property and the sections of the penal code that prohibited trespassing and stealing. Although none of the allegations was proven, the investigations were effective in periodically suspending the flow of public resources to programs that benefited movement members.

ACCUMULATION OF FORCES AND THE
MOVE TOWARD CONSOLIDATION

Economic, governmental, and state conditions changed considerably under PT rule. To craft a course of action amid such alterations, MST leaders issued two notebooks for debate. In the first, *Challenges Facing the Struggle for Agrarian Reform and the MST*, it was argued that "the struggle for agrarian reform today is a process of accumulating forces" (MST, 2009a), in particular acknowledging that opposition from large landowners and the Brazilian government had changed since Lula's election. "The agents of repression ha[d] begun to use other spaces and other facets of the state." The institutions identified included the National Audit Court, and the congressional inquiries were considered the primary means to halt movement efforts. The movement's second notebook, *Debating the MST's Internal Challenges*, raised a series of internal problems, among them overcentralization, lack of creativity among the rank and file, excessive attention to economic matters, and an absence of learning, debating, and reflection (MST, 2009b).

A critical change was the effort to create a new kind of leader, the militant-technician. Creating the movement's leaders from its own ranks rather than relying on outsiders had been a staple of the MST's mobilizational model (Veltmeyer and Petras, 2002), but the emphasis on producing the militant-technician differed in requiring official, usually formal training in addition to commitment to the movement. In a description of the pedagogical project of the Instituto de Nutrição Josué de Castro (Josué de Castro Educational Institute) issued in 2001, the school's goals were reported to include offering professional and high school education and the training of militants and technicians for work within the movement (ITERRA, 2004). Another description of the MST's professional training courses indicated that they would "help form militant technicians capable of influencing and organizing practical issues in settlements and providing political and technical assistance" (ITERRA, 2008). At the MST's Escola Milton Santos de Agroecología (Milton Santos School of Agroecology) in Paraná, I was told by one student that, in addition to receiving instruction about agroecology, they were "learning how to work and live collectively, with the idea of taking this back to where we live" (interview, Londrina, Paraná, July 6, 2011). MST schools teach practical skills while also promoting and consolidating the movement's collective form of organization.

Education, particularly, has gained more attention over the past 10–15 years during the MST's accumulation phase, but the movement's focus on education is not new. The first school administered by MST leaders emerged in the early 1980s in Rio Grande do Sul (MST, 1990). Demands for access to education increased throughout the 1990s, culminating in a national march in 1997. At this time, a coalition featuring the Confederação Nacional dos Trabalhadores na Agricultura (National Confederation of Agricultural Workers), the Confêrencia Nacional dos Bispos de Brasil (National Conference of Brazilian Bishops), and the MST held the first National Conference for Educators on Agrarian Reform in Brasília and demanded educational policies oriented around rural life. One result was the National Program for Education on Agrarian Reform. Since then, the program has grown to finance more than 25 courses at the secondary and postsecondary level in areas such as history, medicine, and cooperative management. In 2010 alone, over 10,000 students who were Landless Movement members participated in these courses, and participation has increased with the addition of the Movimento dos Pequenos Agricultores (Small Farmers' Movement), the Movimento dos Atingidos por Barragens (Movement of People Affected by Dams), and newer movements such as the Movimento dos Trabalhadores Desempregados (Movement of Unemployed Workers) (see Tarlau, 2015).

From the perspective of the MST and its allies, the accumulation of forces meant a coordinated attempt to consolidate its membership and organization. Consolidation and not expansion became the order of the day under PT rule because economic, governmental, and state conditions had changed. Consolidation fostered the development of members' capacity for critique and self-assessment while using public policies as needed.

CONSOLIDATION IN ACTION, THE POLITICIZATION OF AGROECOLOGY, AND MOVEMENT DIVISIONS

Under PT rule, movement leaders devised concrete ways to address the movement's economic crisis within its general strategic vision. A period of extended debate ensued in the early 2000s during the movement's transitional period (interview, MST regional director, Porto Alegre, Rio Grande do Sul, March 23, 2011). One result was the embrace of agroecological production. In addition to favoring labor-intensive forms of production, this mode of agricultural production attempts to mirror natural processes instead of dominating them, replacing purchased inputs with what is found locally (Altieri, 1987). Occupying land to secure it for families and developing production have been movement objectives for decades. Adopting an agroecological mode of production, in a sense, is a continuation of these earlier movement practices. One difference from the past, however, is the MST's explicit rejection of capital and chemical-intensive farming. Throughout the 2000s, leaders focused on and planned to confront the problems in economic production by coordinating individual and group transitions to labor-intensive technologies such as permaculture and away from mechanization.

In championing agroecology, the movement challenges corporations that promote the use of chemicals in production, the adoption of genetically modified organisms, and industrialized agriculture in general. The embrace of agroecology has prompted activists to lead occupations of territories owned by multinational corporations, among them in 2006 a site owned by the multinational seed corporation Syngenta in Paraná and one belonging to the Brazilian company Aracruz in Rio Grande do Sul. Technically, these occupations were of land in productive use if this term is understood as the use of 80 percent of it, but the MST considers this interpretation of the constitution's social-function clause too narrow. Its reasoning is that the promotion by multinational firms of industrialized agriculture, their extensive use of chemical inputs, and in some cases the alleged use of space in the public domain[5] violate the social-function clause's environmental section and what constitutes "rational use." One MST leader justified the movement's occupations of sites owned and used by agribusiness firms as follows (Chamber of Deputies, 2006):

> The action that took place, for example, in Aracruz, was precisely for the purpose to highlight for society the issue of land productivity. Right there in the constitution, it is written that land has a social function to produce and produce also food. Large multinational companies in Brazilian agriculture today are, in addition to establishing more large landowners (*latifundios*), abusing the environment, not respecting water, and not addressing social problems that exist in Brazil, such as hunger.

As this statement indicates, the MST has expanded its criteria for deciding which properties should be expropriated. The land occupation tactic, despite its diminished use during both the Lula and Dilma regimes, has remained important but in a different way.

The politicization of agroecology has led the MST to refashion its economic vision. In encampments, leaders teach families that "mechanization and the use of chemical inputs [are] capitalist practices and not appropriate for our nature. . . . Agroecology has to orient our practices. We have to find ways to teach members to become proficient in such practices for the development of a new form of economic production and a new social subject" (MST, 2001). Along these lines, in 2003 participants marched to a local area where 10 acres of transgenic soy were planted and burned to conclude the movement's annual agroecology conference (*Jornal Sem Terra*, 2003).[6] In 2005 the Venezuelan government, the Universidade Federal de Paraná, and the MST dedicated space in the Contestado settlement for the Escola Latino

Americana de Agroecologia (Latin American School for Agroecology), which is intended to "work with peasants and construct a new technological matrix that oppose[s] the conservative, transnational alternative provided by agribusiness" (*Jornal Sem Terra*, 2005). In short, agroecology became a major consideration under PT governments.

Other actors in the Landless Movement followed the MST's lead. The Movimento dos Atingidos por Barragens continued its opposition to privatization and adopted slogans such as "Water and Energy Are Not Commodities!" Similarly to the MST's incorporation of agroecology into its consolidation efforts, this movement encourages its members to conceive of private businesses and foreign companies as its principal opponents. The Movimento dos Pequenos Agricultores adopted agroecological production and the challenges to multinational agribusiness and issued training manuals for its members. Two notebooks, issued in 2014 for the movement's national congress, featured lengthy discussions of agroecology, critiques of the developmental policies promoted by the government, the role of women in the movement, and the importance of agroecology.[7] These three movements, along with allied student and religious organizations such as the Pastoral da Juventude Rural (Rural Youth Ministry) and the Movimento de Pescadores e Pescadoras Artesanais do Brasil (Artisanal Fishers' Movement) make up Brazil's branch of the transnational Via Campesina (Peasant's Way [Welch, 2005]).

The Via Campesina's banner of food sovereignty has become a regular demand made by the MST and its allies. The MST's first explicit reference to the concept in its publications was in the mid-1990s, when it commented on the way other Via Campesina groups were organizing protests at a United Nations meeting on food security (*Jornal Sem Terra*, 1995). Although there are only six other references to "food sovereignty" in MST publications from 1995 to 2000, the period from 2000 to 2012 saw 123 references to the term. Food sovereignty includes promoting decentralized, decommodified forms of using resources in food production and regular organized protests against the influence of agribusiness corporations in international summits organized by the United Nations (*Jornal Sem Terra*, 2009; 2012). A news item from a 2014 issue of *Jornal Sem Terra* documenting the thirteenth annual agroecology workshop hosted by the Landless Movement directly connects the MST's own history with the concept. In the story, one MST activist who had obtained land and adopted agroecological methods is quoted as saying, "It's important to keep and exchange seeds. It's even better to know that the seeds were produced on areas that people fought for in order to have food sovereignty" (*Jornal Sem Terra*, 2014).

The promotion of agroecology has led MST cooperatives to scale down and professionalize. In some cases, such as the Tapes agricultural cooperative, members decided to transition to agroecological production and sell the heavier equipment purchased with agrarian-reform credit. Others, such as the Novo Sarandi cooperative, declared bankruptcy and stopped operating (interview, director of Tapes agricultural production cooperative, Porto Alegre, Rio Grande do Sul, June 12, 2011). The movement also focused on "regional reference points"—special cooperatives that concentrated on training in production and finance (MST, 2008a). The movement recruited technicians from the Mondragón cooperatives of the Basque Country to teach members to manage finances and organize production in Sergipe and Paraná, an exchange that is intended to last at least 10 years (interview, director of Mundokide, near Rio Bonito, Paraná, July 25, 2011). This professionalization and scaling-back are aimed at collectivization. The difference between these efforts and past ones is that the current ones are more focused.

The director of the MST's confederation of cooperatives told me that the plan is to foment agroecological production practices among debt-burdened and in some cases insolvent or bankrupt producers (interview, Brasília, September 1, 2011). Producers who are insolvent have no legal access to production support, and this poses a problem for the movement because creating an alternative mode of economic production is critical to its revolutionary vision and success. As a way of addressing insolvency, leaders recruit bankrupt members into cooperatives where they can indirectly receive credit and access to markets (interview, director of milk producers' cooperative, near Pontão, Rio Grande do Sul, April 1, 2011).

Some in the Landless Movement saw the increase in resources as an opportunity. The government programs offered guaranteed markets for cooperatives and individual producers in settlements. While I was attending an MST-run high school, one day was devoted to instruction by a technician on how to register for the family farming program. Although neither the students nor the technician showed much enthusiasm for the subject, the technician noted that understanding public policies was important. At the annual conference of Bionatur, a seed cooperative created by the MST, movement members emphasized that the Food Acquisition Program was one of the main reasons the cooperative had survived a recent drought. Movement training manuals and newsletters praised public policies under PT governments and their support for small-scale production (*Jornal Sem Terra*, 2007; 2008; MST, 2008b).

Divisions have also emerged. I was told that efforts to standardize agroecological techniques outside of Paraná in movement training centers, while initially embraced, ended after leaders decided to prioritize other movement activities. More significant, 50 leaders from the MST, the Movimento dos Atingidos por Barragens, and the Movimento dos Trabalhadores Desempregados resigned from the Landless Movement in 2011 in the belief that such efforts distracted from radical forms of engagement (Passa Palavra, 2011).

Some describe the promotion of agroecological production as indicative of the Landless Movement's "peasant" nature. One danger in this characterization is reducing its economic activities to subsistence farming. Vergara-Camus (2014: 160–170), for instance, believes that subsistence farming is central to the MST's economic project and an anticapitalist alternative to neoliberalism. It is a mistake, however, to overemphasize the nonmarket nature of the MST's production practices. In fact, many of the MST's successful cooperatives and agroecological production practices embrace state-supported markets created through public policies. Some have claimed that the MST is radically "autonomous," existing adjacent to state structures of authority (Zibechi, 2012). Nevertheless, the Landless Movement's many complex, regular interactions with state authorities (e.g., accessing the public policies of local and federal governments) make such oversimplifications of autonomy problematic. Instead, the movement's turn to agroecological production is better considered part of its strategic shift in response to changing conditions.

The rapid increase in members and settlements that took place during the Cardoso years revealed the MST's limited capacity to train and incorporate new recruits. An activist who had been active principally at the national level during the 1990s but more recently retired from the movement told me that the MST's growth had resulted in the movement's "losing control of the settlements. . . . People, businesses, whatever, now come and go as they please. Agrobusiness sells seeds to people, and they are becoming small agribusiness" (interview, former MST state and national director, near Miguel do Iguaçu, July 12, 2011). The increase of resources through various public policies enabled the movement to engage with favorable governmental conditions.

WHAT'S NEXT?

Changing external conditions presented the Landless Movement with some opportunities and foreclosed others during the Lula and Dilma governments. The movement's actions toward consolidation during this period helped to build capacity for future resistance by creating new leaders, revising movement practices, and gaining resources while remaining in opposition to dominant political and economic elites. After Dilma Rousseff was removed from power in 2016, Michel Temer of the center-right Movimento Democrático Brasileiro (Brazilian Democratic Movement Party) rose to power. From the series of raids on Landless Movement schools in November of 2016 (Operation Castra) to the planned privatization of Brazil's remaining public utilities, Temer's administration showed that the time of "friendly" government was over. Bolsonaro since then has taken an even more austere approach to the movement. During and after President Rousseff's removal, mass protests, both against and in support of the PT government and its policies, periodically paralyzed Brazilian society. Central to the mobilizations on the political left was the Brazilian Frente Popular (Popular Front), bringing together more than 60 rural and urban movements, unions, and organizations including the Landless Movement. Former President Lula, in galvanizing movements across the left in opposition to Bolsonaro's authoritarianism and botched response to the COVID-19 pandemic, counts the MST as one group among many that intend to see the right-wing leader ousted either through impeachment or the ballot box. Since Bolsonaro became president the MST, in coalition with other leftist actors, has been acting as part of a vocal opposition. That the movement has managed to maintain this position, as well as continue to mobilize coalitions, show how the consolidation period under the PT governments has equipped it to weather difficult times.

With a new generation of leaders, it is safe to say that the Landless Movement has created the means to persist. External conditions—especially governmental ones, with the potential for Lula to return as president in the near future—is promising for the movement, especially in comparison with the first few years of Bolsonaro's administration. Yet the question remains, in the event of Lula's becoming president again, whether the movement will repeat the strategic mode of consolidating its organization of Lula's first term or find new modes of confrontation with a "friendly" government What is certain is that, with decades of experience behind the movement, there is plenty for leaders and members to draw upon to extend the struggle for agrarian reform into the foreseeable future.

EXTERNAL CONDITIONS AND THE
PT MOVING FORWARD

This chapter, in emphasizing the critical role of external conditions on the dynamics of social movement resistance, proposes a more nuanced way of conceiving of nonmovement factors than the political opportunity structure concept. Scholars have brought other terms, such as network, into debates in the literature on collective action without exploring adequately the different ways in which economics, the state, and government affect mobilization. Through a case study of the MST, this chapter highlights and differentiates such factors, illustrating how each, in turn, impacted the movement's efforts.

On this point of differentiating state, economic, and governmental conditions from one another, the place of the PT emerges as critical. First, the Lula and Dilma administrations managed to speak to territorial concerns— particularly over land tenure—in ways that went contrary to the MST's preferential mode of engaging in direct action land occupations to demand agrarian reform. This, in combination with declining economic inequality and improved export performance, allowed Brazil to reduce its external debt obligations, creating generally positive economic conditions when compared to the 1980s and 1990s. While the PT oversaw these changes, they also spoke to concerns of landless activists in the areas of education and production. Here, through targeted programs, as well as facilitating the growth of schools and the development of agroecology, government conditions—with the PT as the central player—directly helped the movement to consolidate. Changes in the economy and the state did not lead to this outcome. The PT's influence also triggered internal rifts, specifically over strategy.

Still, as the movement and its allies weather the Bolsonaro administration, they place their hopes firmly behind a return to Lula. The question moving forward is which Lula we will see—the center-left figure who tried to work with everyone, on the right and the left, or the more combative leftist of the 1970s and 1980s who unapologetically backed worker and peasant struggles.

NOTES

1. This chapter is a revised version of an article that appeared in *Latin American Perspectives* 47 (4): 206–222 (2020).

2. Among them the Conferência Nacional dos Bispos de Brasil (National Conference of Brazilian Bishops) and the Confederação Nacional dos Trabalhadores na Agricultura (National Confederation of Agricultural Workers) and small-farmer organizations such as the Movimento dos Atingidos por Barragens (Movement of People Affected by Dams) and the Movimento dos Pequenos Agricultores (Small Farmers' Movement).

3. In 2004 the movement organized 286 land occupations. In 2015 the Comissão Pastoral da Terra (Pastoral Land Commission—CPT) documented 86 (CPT, 2005; 2016).

4. The congressional inquiries began with alleged misuse of funds by MST-created nongovernmental organizations such as the Asociación Nacional de Cooperación Agrícola (National Association for Agricultural Cooperation), which held contracts with governmental entities.

5. Details on the occupation of land owned by Petrobras can be found at http: //g1.globo.com/espirito-santo/noticia/2015/05/familias-do-mst-ocupam-terreno-no-es-reservado-para-polo-da-petrobras.html. For more on Cutrale, see http://politica .estadao.com.br/noticias/geral,mst-acusa-cutrale-de-usar-terra-griladas,446913.

6. All issues of the *Jornal Sem Terra* can be found at http://www.docvirt.com/ docreader.net /docreader.aspx?bib=HEMEROLT&PagFis=2985.

7. Both notebooks can be found at https://issuu.com/comunicacaompa/docs/ caderno_de _estudo_congresso_i.

REFERENCES

Agamben, Giorgio
1998 *Homo sacer: Sovereign Power and Bare Life*. Stanford, CA: Stanford University Press.
Almeida, Paul
2019 *Social Movements: The Structure of Collective Mobilization*. Los Angeles: University of California Press.
Altieri, Miguel
1987 *Agroecology: The Scientific Basis of Alternative Agriculture*. Boulder: Westview Press.
ANDA (Associação Nacional para Difusão de Adubos e Corretivos Agrícolas)
2011 *Anuário estatistico do setor de fertilizantes, 1987–2006*. São Paulo: ANDA.
Arruda, Roldão
2014 "Esvaziado por ações do governo, MST chega aos 30 anos." *O Estado de São Paulo*, January 20.
Banford, Sue and Jan Rocha
2002 *Cutting the Wire: The Story of the Landless Movement in Brazil*. London: Latin America Bureau.
Brasil Econômico
2021 "Bolsonaro corte verba do MST e defende que a propiedad privada é sagrada." May 10. https://economia.ig.com.br/2021-05-10/bolsonaro-verba-mst.html.
Buechler, Steven M.
2016 *Understanding Social Movements: Theories from the Classical Era to the Present*. London: Routledge.
Cardoso, Fernando Henrique
1997 *Reforma agrária: Compromisso de todos*. Vol. 28. Brasília: Presidência da República, Secretaria de Comunicação Social.
Carter, Miguel (ed.).
2015 *Challenging Social Inequality: The Landless Rural Workers' Movement and Agrarian Reform in Brazil*. Durham, NC: Duke University Press.
Chamber of Deputies
2006 "Especial luta pela terra: Movimento Sem Terra (06'44")." April 17. http://www2.camara.leg.br/camaranoticias/radio/materias/REPORTAGEM-ESPECIAL/335615-ESPECIALLUTA-PELA-TERRA:-MOVIMENTO-SEM-TERRA-(06'-44%22).html.
CPMI da Terra (Comissão Parlamentar Mista de Inquérito da Terra)
2005 "Brasília: Republica Federativa do Brasil, Congresso Nacional."
CPT (Comissão Pastoral da Terra)
2002–2016 "Conflitos no campo Brasil." https://www.cptnacional.org.br/index.php/publicacoes-2/conflitos-no-campo-brasil.
Diani, Mario
2013 "Organizational fields and social movement dynamics," pp. 145–168 in Conny Roggeband, Jacquelien van Stekelenburg, and Bert Klandermans (eds.), *The*

Future of Social Movement Research: Dynamics, Mechanisms, and Processes. Minneapolis: University of Minnesota Press.

Diniz, Aldiva Sales and Bruce Gilbert

2013 "Socialist values and cooperation in Brazil's Landless Rural Workers' Movement." *Latin American Perspectives* 40 (4): 19–34.

Fernandes, Bernardo

2000 *A formação do MST no Brasil.* Petrópolis: Editora Vozes.

2008 "O MST e as reformas agrárias do Brasil." *Revista OSAL* 9: 73–85.

FNDE (Fundo Nacional de Desenvolbimento da Educação)

2014 "Datos estatísticos." http://www.fnde.gov.br/programas/alimentacao-escolar/alimentacao-escolar-consultas/alimentacao-escolar-dados-estatisticos.

Foucault, Michel

2007 *Security, Territory, Population: Lectures at the Collège de France, 1977–78.* New York: Springer.

Froufe, Celia

2009 "Ibope/CAN 92% condenam ocupações do MST." Estadão, December 9. https://politica.estadao.com.br/noticias/geral,ibopecna-92-condenam-ocupacoes-do-mst,485449.

Giovanaz, Daniel

2021 "Dos 1.133 assentamentos no balanço do Incra de 2020, só dois são da gestão Bolsonaro." March 15. https://www.brasildefato.com.br/2021/03/15/dos-1-133-assentamentos-no-balanco-do-incra-de-2020-so-dois-sao-da-gestao-bolsonaro.

Goodwin, Jeff

2013 "Social movements and revolutions," pp. 474–505 in Jeff Manza, Richard Arums, and Lynne Haney (eds.), *The Sociology Project: Introducing the Sociological Imagination.* Boston: Pearson.

Goodwin, Jeff and James M. Jasper

2004 *Rethinking Social Movements: Structure, Culture, and Emotion.* Lanham, MD: Rowman and Littlefield.

Hespanhol, Rosângela Aparecida de Medeiros

2013 "Programa de Aquisição de Alimentos: limites e potencialidades de políticas de segurança alimentar para a agricultura familiar." *Sociedade & Natureza* 25: 469–483.

ITERRA (Instituto Técnico de Capacitação e Pesquisa da Reforma Agrária)

2004 "Instituto de Educação Josué de Castro: método pedagogico." Cadernos de ITERRA 4.

2008 "O IEJC e a educação profissional." Cadernos de ITERRA 8.

Lázaro, Natália

2019 "Bolsonaro pretende classificar como 'terrorista' invasões do MST." https://www.metropoles.com/brasil/bolsonaro-pretende-classificar-como-terrorismo-invasoes-do-mst.

Lenin, Vladimir

1917 *The Dual Power.* http://www.marxists.org.

Loman, Herwin

2014 "Brazil's social challenges." *Economic Report*, January 9. https://economics .rabobank.com/publications/2014/january/brazils-social-challenges/.

Maisonnave, Fabiano and Lalo de Almeida

2020 "Amazonia sob Bolsonaro." *Folha de São Paulo*, October 24. https://temas.folha .uol.com.br/amazonia-sob-bolsonaro/sem-terra-de-direita/aumento-de-invasoes-de -areas-protegidas-revela-a-ascensao-dos-sem-terra-de-direita.shtml.

Martins, Mónica Dias

2000 "The MST challenge to neoliberalism." *Latin American Perspectives* 27 (5): 33–45.

McAdam, Doug

2010 (1982) *Political Process and the Development of Black Insurgency, 1930–1970.* Chicago: University of Chicago Press.

McAdam, Doug and Hilary Schaffer Boudet

2012 *Putting Social Movements in Their Place: Explaining Opposition to Energy Projects in the United States, 2000–2005.* Cambridge: Cambridge University Press.

McAdam, Doug, John D. McCarthy, and Mayer N. Zald (eds.).

1996 *Comparative Perspectives on Social Movements: Political Opportunities, Mobilizing Structures, and Cultural Framings.* Cambridge: Cambridge University Press.

McAdam, Doug, Sydney Tarrow, and Charles Tilly

2001 *Dynamics of Contention.* Cambridge: Cambridge University Press.

Migdal, Joel S.

2015 (1975) *Peasants, Politics, and Revolution: Pressures toward Political and Social Change in the Third World.* Princeton: Princeton University Press.

Mitchell, Timothy

1999 "Society, economy, and the state effect," pp. 76–97 in George Steinmetz (ed.), *State/Culture: State Formation after the Cultural Turn.* Ithaca, NY: Cornell University Press.

Morton, Gregory Duff

2015 "Managing transience: Bolsa Família and its subjects in an MST landless settlement." *Journal of Peasant Studies* 42: 1283–1305.

MST (Movimento Sem Terra)

1990 *Nossa luta é nossa escola: A educação das crianças nos acampamentos e assentamentos.* São Paulo: Brasil.

1995 *Caderno de Cooperação 5: O sistema cooperativista dos assentados.* São Paulo.

2001 *Caderno de Cooperação Agricola 10: O que levar em conta no acampamento.* São Paulo.

2006 *Balanço político da cooperação no MST.* São Paulo.

2008a *Cartilha de Cooperação 1.* São Paulo.

2008b *Cartilha de Apoio 2: Programa de formação para a cooperação e organização dos assentamentos.* São Paulo.

2009a *Cadernos de Debates 1: Desafios da luta pela reforma agraria popular e do MST.* São Paulo.

2009b *Caderno de Debates 2: Para debater os desafios internos do MST.* São Paulo.

Nascimento, Luciano

2015 "CPT considera reforma agrarian do governo Dilma a pior dos ultimos 20 anos." Agencia Brasil, January 7. https://agenciabrasil.ebc.com.br/geral/noticia/2015-01/cpt-considerareforma-agraria-do-governo-dilma-pior-dos-ultimos-20-anos.

Oliveira, Ariovaldo Umbelino

2011 "Não reforma agrária e contra reforma agrária no Brasil no governo Lula." Paper presented at the Thirteenth Conference of Latin American Geographers, San José, Costa Rica, July 25–29.

Oliveira, Augusto de Andrade

2010 "Critérios de avaliação de qualidade e a consolidação de assentamentos de reforma agrária no Brasil: a experiência do 'Programa de Consolidação e Emancipação (auto-suficiência) de assentamentos resultantes de reforma agrária–PAC.'" Ph.D. diss., Universidade Federal de Rio de Janeiro.

Ondetti, Gabriel

2006 "Repression, opportunity, and protest: explaining the takeoff of Brazil's Landless Movement." *Latin American Politics and Society* 48 (2): 61–94.

2008 *Land, Protest, and Politics: The Landless Movement and the Struggle for Agrarian Reform in Brazil.* University Park: Pennsylvania State University Press.

Pahnke, Anthony, Rebecca Tarlau, and Wendy Wolford

2015 "Understanding rural resistance: contemporary mobilization in the Brazilian countryside." *Journal of Peasant Studies* 42: 1069–1085.

Passa Palavra

2011 "Carta da saida de nossas organizações." http://www.passapalavra.info/2011/11/48866.

Peixinho, Albaneide Maria

2013 "A trajetória do Programa Nacional de Alimentação Escolar no período de 2003–2010: relato do gestor nacional." *Ciência & Saúde Coletiva* 18: 9009–9016.

Pereira, Anthony W.

2015 "Bolsa Família and democracy in Brazil." *Third World Quarterly* 36: 1682–1699.

Schmitt, Carl

2004 (1922) *Political Theology: Four Chapters on the Concept of Sovereignty.* Chicago: University of Chicago Press.

Scott, James C.

1977 *The Moral Economy of the Peasant: Rebellion and Subsistence in Southeast Asia.* New Haven: Yale University Press.

Silva, Luis Inácio Lula da

1999 "Interview." Roda Viva, January 10. http://www.rodaviva.fapesp.br/materia/67/entrevistados/luiz_inacio_lula_da_silva_1999.htm.

Skocpol, Theda

1979 *States and Social Revolutions: A Comparative Analysis of France, Russia and China.* Cambridge: Cambridge University Press.

Snow, David A.

2004 "Framing processes, ideology, and discursive fields," pp. 380–412 in David A. Snow, Sarah Soule, and Hanspeter Kriesi (eds.), *The Blackwell Companion to Social Movements.* London: Blackwell.

Souza, José Gilberto and José Jorge Gebara

2010 *PROCERA: Os resultados de assentamentos rurais frente à inepta política de crédito para a reforma agrária no Brasil*. São Paulo: FUNEP.

Tarlau, Rebecca
2015 "Education of the countryside at a crossroads: rural social movements and national policy reform in Brazil." *Journal of Peasant Studies* 42: 1157–1177.

Tarrow, Sidney G.
1998 *Power in Movement: Social Movements and Contentious Politics*. Cambridge: Cambridge University Press.

TCU (Tribunal das Contas da União)
2010 *Relatório e parecer prévio sobre as contas do Governo da República exercício de 2009*. Acórdão 557/2004. Brasília.

Tilly, Charles
1977 *From Mobilization to Revolution*. Boston: Addison-Wesley.

Todorov, João Claudio and Benicio Viero Schmidt
1997 *Primeiro censo da reforma agraria do Brasil*. Brasília: INCRA/University of Brasília.

Veltmeyer, Henry and James Petras
2002 "The social dynamics of Brazil's rural Landless Workers' Movement: ten hypotheses on successful leadership." *Canadian Review of Sociology/Revue Canadienne de Sociologie* 39 (1): 79–96.

Vergara-Camus, Leandro
2014 *Land and Freedom: The MST, the Zapatistas and Peasant Alternatives to Neoliberalism*. London: Zed Books.

Welch, Clifford
2005 "Estratégias de resistência do movimento camponês brasileiro em frente das novas táticas de controle do agronegócio transnacional." *NERA* 8 (6): 35–45.

Wolf, Eric R.
1969 *Peasant Wars of the Twentieth Century*. Oklahoma City: University of Oklahoma Press.

Wolford, Wendy
2010 *This Land Is Ours Now: Social Mobilization and the Meanings of Land in Brazil*. Durham, NC: Duke University Press.

Wright, Angus Lindsay and Wendy Wolford
2003 *To Inherit the Earth: The Landless Movement and the Struggle for a New Brazil*. Oakland, CA: Food First Books.

Zibechi, Raúl
2012 *Territories in Resistance: A Cartography of Latin American Social Movements*. Oakland, CA: Food First Books.

Chapter 3

Relations between Progressive Parties and Union Movements in the Southern Cone

A History of Encounters and Missed Connections

Fabricio Carneiro, Guillermo Fuentes,
and Carmen Midaglia
Translated by Victoria J. Furio

Most scholarly literature groups twenty-first-century progressive or Pink Tide governments in Latin America into two categories: the moderates, which generally retained the market reforms of the previous decades, and the radical or populist left, which sought to dismantle neoliberal policies and grant a greater role to the state.[1] The moderate left includes the parties that came to power in countries such as Brazil, Chile, and Uruguay, while the more radical left includes the governments of countries such as Bolivia, Ecuador, Venezuela, and, to a lesser extent, Argentina. However, a careful analysis of their histories makes evident important differences within these two analytical categories both at the economic and social levels and in their relations with their traditional electoral base, the unions. The relationship of union actors with progressive parties has been absent from the most influential studies on the left turn in the region. This chapter sheds light on these differences.

In Latin America the relationship between popular actors and the state has always been strained, largely because of the latter's strategy of co-optation as part of the incorporation of excluded sectors (Dangl, 2010: 5; Filgueira, 2013: 24). This type of linkage, built historically through contradictory political modalities, has become evident as leftist governments have attempted to preserve both the backing of broad sectors of the population in the context of coalitions that represented diverse ideological positions and the support of social movements, among them unions (Riethof, 2018: 7).

Prioritizing the topic of organized labor does not mean theoretically and empirically ignoring other forms of collective action that have been significant in the region (the landless, indigenous, feminist, and student movements and the *piqueteros*, among others). Some of these popular expressions are relatively new, while others are based on the ongoing demands for social justice that have confronted neocolonialism and the resistance to regional elites that opposed the modernization of the region in the previous century (Prevost, Oliva Campos, and Vanden, 2012). This renewed package of social demands tended to manifest itself in circumstances in which political opportunities presented themselves for processing claims, re-creating the public agenda, and promoting alternative modes of public protest (Tarrow, 1997: 147–148). The proposals of the labor movement reinforced and complicated the repertoire of popular demands in that its blueprint for action was focused on the conflict between capital and labor.

The links between progressive parties and unions have varied, especially in the Southern Cone countries. In this work we analyze the diverse paths of these interactions and argue that the relations between the two sets of actors during the so-called progressive era can be explained by the electoral strategies associated with putting together governing coalitions and the fragmentation of the union movement when those parties took office. The combination of these two factors established different formats for brokering labor interests that had a specific political impact in each of the cases analyzed. Contrary to the analysis that minimizes differences between Pink Tide governments´ links with social actors and those of the pro-neoliberal parties that predominated in the region before the left turn, we emphasize the convergence between some union movements and Pink Tide governments in the region. A closer analysis of these areas of convergence demonstrates that they are rooted in the historical links developed during the period of neoliberalism beginning in the 1980s.

Some union organizations viewed progressive governments as "friendly" allies, emphasized their "openness" to worker organization, and declared their expectation that Pink Tide governments would carry out policies to the benefit of organized workers. Needless to say, not all governments fulfilled that expectation to the same degree, and while some strengthened their links to workers' organizations others distanced themselves from union movements. Our argument is that closer links were created in cases in which progressive parties avoided electoral alliances with right-wing parties in order to reach power and retain it and in which workers' organizations were relatively united.

In some cases, the neoliberal policies of the 1980s and 1990s weakened the labor movement to such an extent that when progressive parties subsequently reached power, they were unable to strengthen the unions. The most prominent case is that of the Chilean Partido Socialista (Socialist Party—PS). In Uruguay, in contrast, the alliance between the governing Frente Amplio (Broad Front—FA) and the nation's main labor confederation allowed for a strong opposition during the neoliberal period. At the time of the FA's coming to power, not only was this relationship bolstered but it strengthened the workers' confederation. A third type of relationship can be identified in the case of Argentina, where the union movement was fragmented but Kirchnerism in power sparked a new reconfiguration of the ties between unions and party, with a clear revitalization of the labor movement. Lastly, in the case of Brazil, the close link of the country's largest union confederation during the 1990s with the Partido dos Trabalhadores (Workers' Party—PT) was unsustainable after Lula da Silva rose to the presidency.

This article examines the different types of relationships among actors that support economic distribution (progressive parties and unions) and whether they were strengthened during the Pink Tide period. The work is organized as follows: In the next section we analyze the differences in the ties established among progressive parties and union federations before and during the Pink Tide period. Then we will attempt to explain the variation in this relationship, focusing on union fragmentation and the types of political strategy employed by the progressive parties in order to reach power. In the last sections we analyze four country cases and then present our conclusions.

LINKAGES BETWEEN PROGRESSIVE PARTIES AND LABOR UNIONS IN THE SOUTHERN CONE

Relations between left parties and unions in the Southern Cone have displayed important variations since the transitions to democracy in the 1980s. While some left parties once in power sought to adapt to the new neoliberal "consensus" by implementing structural reforms contrary to their historical programmatic foundations, others, in alliance with organized labor, moderated or opposed reforms they had inherited from the neoliberal period.

The first group of countries manifests what has appropriately been called "neoliberalism by surprise" (Stokes, 2001). Some political parties that had been close to the workers' movement in the import-substitution industrialization period made a radical turn by adopting economic liberalization packages, labor flexibilization, and privatization that ended up blurring ideological divides (Roberts, 2014). Another adaptive strategy was the formation of electoral alliances with centrist parties that led to the weakening of the ties between progressive parties and the labor movement. This group included the Partido Justicialista (Justicialist Party—PJ) in Argentina under the government of Carlos Menem (1989–1999) and to a lesser degree the Partido Socialista (Socialist Party—PS) in Chile. In the late 1980s, the PJ began a process of far-reaching organizational and ideological change in order to appeal to a new electorate different from its traditional core, which was centered on urban industrial workers, and in response to an international environment that imposed limitations on its traditional program (Levitsky, 2003: 94). This transformation led to a distancing from its union base and a loss of labor's influence both within PJ structures and in Congress. The deunionization of the PJ signified a change in the party's political strategy, transforming it from a union-based party to one focused more on clientelist networks. In Chile, the PS began to move away from the labor movement in the waning days of the Pinochet dictatorship. The party, which represented the most radical wing of the governing Unión Popular (Popular) coalition under Salvador Allende's administration in the early 1970s, diametrically changed its program during the democratic transition. The traumatic experience of the Unión Popular led the PS to a critical reevaluation of liberal democracy and the risks of a radical redistribution program without a policy of alliances among classes and parties. The PS's ideological moderation and its alliance with the conservative Demócrata Cristiano (Christian Democrat—DC) party distanced the PS from the unions and transformed it into an electoral-professional party dominated by the political elite and their technical cadres. This transformation weakened the unions, marginalizing and fragmenting them while subordinating their demands to the dictates of the neoliberal model (Barrett, 2001).

In a second group of countries, left parties such as the PT in Brazil and the FA in Uruguay challenged the neoliberal model that predominated in the region, although they began moderating their programs as they grew stronger electorally and approached the seat of power. The PT from its inception maintained close ties to the union movement and specifically the powerful Central Única dos Trabalhadores (United Workers' Federation—CUT). Although the PT did not modify its program to the extent that the PJ did under Menem, it did go through a process of ideological "modernization" to adapt to the pressures of international markets (Hunter, 2010). As in the case of the PT, the FA before reaching power resisted neoliberal reforms, including the privatization promoted by the traditional parties, which allowed it to maintain its historical alliance with the union movement. Furthermore, it coordinated its actions with the labor movement in a manner that put into practice forms of direct democracy.

Pink Tide governments introduced significant changes that enhanced relations between the left and the labor movement. In Argentina, with Néstor Kirchner's victory in 2003 the PJ reshaped its links to worker organizations. The government, for instance, granted benefits to the *piquetero* movement (an organization of informal workers and the unemployed) with the expectation of rebuilding the PJ's historical alliance with organized social actors. The Kirchner government reactivated the system of collective bargaining, with a priority on negotiation by branches of industry, dismantled labor flexibilization laws, substantially increased the minimum wage, engaged in ongoing dialogues to resolve social and union conflicts, facilitated the consolidation of union control over social welfare programs, and promoted employment and reindustrialization in some sectors (Etchemendy, 2011). These measures helped transform the PJ in the context of the political delegitimization of the party system.

In Chile, in 2000 a socialist presidential candidate came to power for the first time since Allende but without changing in a significant way the relations between the labor movement and the party. Although the PS made overtures to labor by supporting labor reform, the moderate nature of its content divided the party at the same time that it left the unions weak. In Brazil the link between the labor movement and the PT weakened as the latter came closer to power. Once in government, the PT reached out to the unions with a policy of minimum wage increments, the creation of institutionalized mechanisms of consultation with the workers' federations, and the appointment of union leaders to government posts (Cardoso and Gíndin, 2009). Nevertheless, the party was unable to pass a labor reform bill, continued the previous government's macroeconomic policies, and became involved in numerous corruption scandals that undermined its support among the popular sectors.

In Uruguay, the FA pursued a path of ideological moderation like that of Brazil's PT, but once in power sustained its alliance with the union movement. The FA government's passage of numerous labor laws that expanded labor rights, along with some neocorporatist measures, ensured the continuation of an aligned union movement.

In summary, the links between unions and progressive parties before and after the latter came to power reveal a pattern of continuity in their positions in the case of Brazil and Uruguay and change in Chile and Argentina

Under Pink Tide governments in Chile, the PS remained distant from the union movement (as it had been prior to Ricardo Lagos's election in 2000). In Uruguay, the FA preserved its close relationship, promoting a package of public policies that benefited organized labor, especially with the reactivation of collective bargaining at the sectoral level. The PT, for its part, after coming to power, reformed such pillars of labor policy as retirement and social security and in the process weakened the party's historical alliance with the union movement. The PJ, which in the previous phase had moved away from the labor movement, reconfigured the alliance once in office under Néstor Kirchner.

The relations between parties and the labor movement impacted the power of unions. The liberalization of the 1990s weakened unions in Chile and Uruguay. The PS's advent to power in Chile only minimally strengthened them, while in Uruguay the power of unions of pre-liberalization years was largely restored during the period of FA rule. In Argentina and Brazil the unions retained a relative degree of strength during the economic liberalization of the 1990s, but in the 2000s they took different paths: resurgence in Argentina and weakening in Brazil (Table 3.1).

ELECTORAL STRATEGY AND
UNION FRAGMENTATION

As we have pointed out, the electoral victory of the progressive parties in southern Latin America did not involve uniform linkages with labor union movements. Differences were evident both in the area of labor policy and labor rights (Carneiro, 2017) and in the area of bipartite or tripartite negotiations. These differences can be explained by two political variables: the party's coalitional strategy and the degree of union fragmentation.

Regarding the first variable, the left parties that adopted a strategy of electoral coalitions with center and center-right political organizations moved the farthest away from the labor movement. This distancing occurred because of the left's difficulty in passing prolabor reforms because of obstruction by coalition partners. The union fragmentation suffered during the neoliberal period also impeded resurgence. A united labor movement facilitates coordinated protests and gives the government incentives to negotiate with labor as a unified actor capable of disciplining the unions when necessary (Murillo, 2001: 17). The scholarly literature points to the electoral strategies of governing parties in Europe as a key variable determining the links between

Table 3.1: Union Density (percent) in Selected Countries (1985–2010).

	Union Density			
Countries	1985–1990	1995–2000	2005–2010	*Difference*
Argentina	48.7	25.4	40.3	+14.9
Brazil	21.9	20.6	20.3	–0.3
Chile	13.4	11.4	11.6	+0.2
Uruguay	22.9	14.7	21.7	+7.0

Sources: For Argentina, figures for 1986, 1995, and 2008 from ILO (1998); for Brazil, Cardoso (2014); for Chile, Dirección de Trabajo, 2013; for Uruguay, figures for 1985–1997 from Cassoni, Labadie, and Fachola (2005) and for 2008 from Mazzuchi (2009).

the political left and unions and the distance between the two. Insofar as the left prioritizes capturing the "middle vote," it can be expected that these parties will choose to "liberate" themselves from strong commitments to organized labor.

The decline in industrial jobs and the increase in white-collar and professional occupations have presented new challenges for political representation and the brokering of labor interests. In the case of Latin America, this process had been under way for decades once the import-substitution industrialization model reached its limit. According to Weller (1998), the proportion of the economically active population employed in the secondary sector (mostly industry) fell from 25 percent to 23.7 percent between 1980 and 1990. As an offset, employment in the tertiary sector (services) rose from 46.7 percent to 53.9 percent. In Europe, neoliberal restructuring by social democratic parties in power has placed them on a collision course with the unions and created tensions that right-wing nationalist parties have capitalized on (Hyman and Gumbrell-McCormick, 2010).

An array of left parties in Latin America felt the same pressure as the European social democratic parties when they prioritized electoral objectives. In the four cases analyzed in this chapter, the parties developed electoral and government coalitions to increase their chances of winning the elections and then ensuring governability. The coalition strategies took different paths: while the FA in Uruguay partnered with Nuevo Espacio (New Space, a small center-left party that ended up joining the FA), the Frente para la Victoria (Front for Victory—FPV) in Argentina, and the PT in Brazil had to form coalitions with various parties (mostly left or center-left and center) to preserve congressional majorities. Lastly, from the end of the dictatorship on, the Chilean PS was part of the Concertación coalition, with a clear centrist orientation, made up of the DC, the Partido por la Democracia (Party for Democracy—PPD), and the Partido Radical Socialdemócrata (Radical Social Democratic Party—PRSD). These different coalition strategies determined the options for implementing reforms that benefited the traditional popular bases of these parties.

The late industrialization in Latin America never produced an industrial sector as extensive and significant as those of the industrialized democracies, and this led to highly fragmented labor markets. In addition, capital mobility and pressure from international markets in the region limited the autonomy that social democratic projects were able to develop in Europe (Roberts, 2008). In spite of these impediments, alliances between organized workers and political parties have been forged throughout Latin American history, as the cases of Uruguay and Argentina demonstrate. Throughout the twentieth century, while import-substitution industrialization fostered a favorable environment for the growth and empowerment of union activity and the unification of the labor movement, the adoption of a model geared toward the market and the institutional failures of democracy led to direct attacks on the organizational and mobilization capacity of the unions.

The transition to democracy that began in the cases studied from the mid-1980s coexisted with the change in the pattern of growth and accumulation geared toward international markets. These processes affected the labor movement in both its ability to influence decision making and its unity. For example, in the four cases analyzed, labor informality (measured by the number of workers who are not registered for social security) grew between 1990 and 2000, rising to 45.6 percent of workers in Argentina (Acuña, Kessler, and Repetto, 2002) and 52.5 percent in Brazil (Alejo and Parada, 2017). During the same period, unemployment increased from 5.9 percent to 14.8 percent in Argentina, from 4.5 percent to 11.4 percent in Brazil, from 8.7 percent to 10.8 percent in Chile, and from 8.9 percent to 13.5 percent in Uruguay (CEPALSTAT, n.d.). The distributive effects of the new economic model intensified the organizational weakness of the working classes by increasing income inequality and hindering collective action (Traversa, 2015). Promarket reforms, contrary to the assumptions that supported them, revealed that economic growth by itself did not reverse poverty, much less inequality. Indeed, the relation between growth and equity became a major topic of political debate (Patroni and Poitras, 2002: 211).

UNION-PARTY LINKAGE IN THE SOUTHERN CONE

Argentina

In Carlos Menem's Argentina, serious restructurings of the formal job market (erosion of labor contracts, outsourcing, etc.) had a severe impact on the unity of the labor movement (Etchemendy and Collier, 2008; Murillo, 2013). The historical Central General de Trabajadores (General Confederation of Workers—CGT) was subject to internal divisions. Its progovernment faction benefited from promarket policies that granted organized labor control over labor protection programs and participation in business operations stemming from privatization. The opposing current within the confederation considered itself the "opposition CGT" and called for state intervention in the economy. A third position was represented by the so-called blue-and-white CGT, which attempted to maintain some distance from the next Kirchnerist administration. Further fragmentation occurred in 1992 with the emergence of a new confederation, the Central de los Trabajadores Argentinos (Federation of Argentine Workers—CTA), which claimed to be independent of political parties and was mostly made up of state workers. The institutional power at the disposal of the CGR and CTA was unequal: the CGT had legal standing and therefore state authorization to handle union financing, while the CTA relied solely on union registration, which limited its capacity for action.

The coming to power of the Kirchners' FPV initiated a new relationship between the PJ and the labor movement. Among the political gestures undertaken by Néstor Kirchner's administration was the repeal of the Banelco Act, a law enacted during the government of Fernando de la Rúa that undermined labor relations by increasing the probationary hire period and providing companies with the upper hand in negotiations with labor. The repeal represented the debut of the FPV's congressional majority in 2004 and was approved 215 to 23. It counted on the support of the Unión Cívica Radical (Radical Civic Union—UCR) and the piquetero movement as well as the CTA, the progovernment CGT, and the "rebel" CGT (*La Nación*, December 15, 2003).

The system of collective bargaining was strengthened by the creation in 2003 of the National Plan for the Regularization of Work and the negotiation of a minimum wage increase through a tripartite mechanism. These developments tended to recentralize the negotiation processes that under neoliberalism had been decentralized at the company level (Trajtemberg, 2016). As a result, the collective bargaining coverage of total salaried employment increased from 43 percent to 55 percent between 2003 and 2012. Nevertheless, the policy of reconciliation between government and labor failed to reduce union fragmentation (Abal Medina, 2016).

Brazil

In the case of Brazil, the protracted process of economic liberalization coincided with the rise of the new unionism of the 1980s. This period set in place a fragmented pattern of union action, in which new federations not only held different views of capital-labor relations but also established distinct political formats for processing worker interests and establishing linkages with political parties. During the push for neoliberal policies under the presidencies of Fernando Collor de Mello and Fernando Henrique Cardoso, the labor movement assumed a defensive stance in order to preserve existing labor protections. The four major confederations, the CUT, the Força Sindical (Union Strength—FS), the Nova Central Sindical dos Trabalhadores (New Union Federation of Workers—NCST), and the União Geral dos Trabalhadores (General Union of Workers—UGT), displayed distinctive strategies for political action. The CUT, which obtained broad national representation and incorporated rural workers into its ranks, maintained close ties to the PT. The FS, which was second in importance, favored pragmatic unionism independent of political parties with the goal of facilitating exchanges with the business sector and the government. The NCST and UGT were created in the twenty-first century as reconfigurations of existing confederations (Radermacher and Melleiro, 2007).

The PT governments greatly improved union and worker benefits including substantial increases in the minimum wage, which registered a 54 percent increase by the end of Lula's second term in office (Cook and Bazler, 2013). However, the main government initiatives on labor barely attained partial approvals, and some capsized along the way (Radermacher and Melleiro, 2007). The two major reforms, which required a broad political consensus because they involved a major revision of the system of labor relations in areas such as union organization, collective bargaining, and the legal recognition of worker federations, generated divisions in the labor movement and political realignments in Congress.

A tripartite space for dialogue was instituted in the form of the Foro Nacional del Trabajo (National Labor Forum), but the agreements reached were subject to revisions by congressional committees in which business leaders managed to block some proposals, suggesting alternatives that were a far cry from the government's original program. In addition, the law on labor federations approved in 2008 intensified union fragmentation, fostering competition in a framework of scant regulation for the formation of new unions (Cook and Bazler, 2013). The limited results obtained in matters of labor reform can be explained by the PT's alliance with centrist parties such as the Partido do Movimiento Democrático Brasileiro (Brazilian Democratic Movement Party—PMDB) and by the fragmentation of the labor movement reflected in the existence of several confederations.

Chile

Augusto Pinochet's Labor Plan deregulated labor relations and promoted a market unionism. The new legal framework linked capital and labor, granted unions legal status but authorized actions only at the company level and limited strikes and collective bargaining, while granting freedom of action to employers to hire and fire workers (González and Zapata, 2015). The Central Unitaria de Trabajadores (United Workers' Federation—CUT) was reinstituted in 1988 as an interlocutor with government and industry, but its activity was framed within the labor code adopted in the authoritarian period. The new CUT renounced mobilization of the popular sectors at the same time that it moderated its demands (Gutiérrez, 2016).

The CUT's position coincided with the coalition strategy of the DC and the PS, which moderated social demands for economic distribution on the pretext of ensuring democratic stability (Drake, 2003). The predominance of the DC in the government coalition and the influence of its more conservative wing largely blocked more ambitious labor reforms that would have overturned the commodification of labor relations established in the Labor Plan. In this setting of political moderation without substantive change in the established rules for labor, a process of confrontation of different currents of opinion within the CUT broke out that eventually led to the breakup of traditional labor unity.

When the PS reached power with the presidential election of Ricardo Lagos (2000–2006), labor reform entered the public agenda, but only partial reformulations were reached (Frank, 2002; Gutiérrez, 2016). The diminished labor results exacerbated internal conflict and resulted in the breakdown of Chile's long tradition of labor unity, generating two new confederations: the Central Autónoma de Trabajadores (Autonomous Federation of Workers—CAT) and the Unión Nacional de Trabajadores (National Union of Workers—UNT). In addition, the political power of the CUT suffered another loss as a result of the distancing of the shop-floor unions, only a minority of which were federation members (Frías, 2008).

Uruguay

With the restoration of democracy in the 1980s, the Uruguayan labor movement maintained its traditional unity and ties with the left in the form of the FA. Indeed, the two forces carried out joint actions in opposition to neoliberal economic policies. The classic Convención Nacional de Trabajadores (National Workers' Convention—CNT) regained the traditional identity suppressed during the dictatorship and eventually took on the name Plenario Intersindical de Trabajadores–Convención Nacional de Trabajadores (PIT-CNT).

The absence of a labor code in the postdictatorship period facilitated the opening of spaces for collective bargaining but then their removal in the neoliberal years of the 1990s (Carneiro, 2017; Senatore, 2009). The joint actions of the PIT-CNT and the FA helped counter promarket reforms including the privatization of public services and tariff reductions (Notaro, 2012). Subsequently, the three FA presidencies (2004–2019) saw a strengthening of the PIT-CNT (González and Zapata, 2015). The FA governments enacted separate labor laws for the private and public sectors that favored workers by institutionalizing tripartite negotiations.

LABOR POLICIES IN THE POST–PINK TIDE YEARS

As we have stated above, the links between political parties and unions varied greatly under the Pink Tide governments of the Southern Cone. The types of coalitions formed by Pink Tide parties and the degree of fragmentation of labor federations were key factors in explaining worker inroads during the economic expansion of early twenty-first century. Beginning in 2015, a cycle of conservative and right-wing governments in the Southern Cone implemented promarket policies including cuts in social benefits, thus generating uncertainties regarding the future of social protections (Mauricio Macri in Argentina [2015–2019], Michel Temer [2016–2018], and Jair Bolsonaro [2019–present] in Brazil, Sebastián Piñera [2018–present] in Chile, and Luis Lacalle Pou [2020–present] in Uruguay). The right-wing resurgence coincided with the economic stagnation and crisis produced in part by the decline in international commodity prices. These governments have carried out markedly proemployer labor policies, particularly those associated with collective bargaining.

In Brazil, the Temer government passed a labor reform that dismantled part of the labor law and is considered the most restrictive measure of its kind since the Consolidation of Labor Laws of 1943. The reform promoted the flexibilization of the labor market particularly with regard to labor agreements, individual bargaining for certain types of workers such as those with higher education or higher wages, elimination of the union dues checkoff, and restrictions on financial resources for collective action. It also restricted workers' benefits. The Bolsonaro administration further deepened Temer's proemployer initiatives.

Similarly, the Macri government in Argentina modified the system of collective bargaining as the state began to play a less prominent role in the negotiation process and arbitration. During his presidency, the number of agreements and workers covered by them decrease (Pastrana and Trajtemberg, 2020). This decline was partly due to the increase in self-employment and nontraditional forms of contracting and to the government's opposition to agreements that exceeded its inflationary objectives. The Macri government attempted to carry out a labor reform consisting of important adjustments, but opposition from the FPV and other political organizations kept it from achieving the necessary majority. The project would have reduced the cost of employer compensation for layoffs, facilitated outsourcing, and introduced flexibility clauses regarding the workday and the revision of working condition requirements embodied in current collective agreements.

In Uruguay, the right-center parties that came to power in 2019 promoted fiscal austerity and adopted a hostile stance toward unions by limiting collective decision making in areas such as education policy as well as the right to strike. Taking advantage of its majority in the General Assembly, the government passed an all-encompassing law with 476 articles including emergency measures that limit public debate. As a reaction, social movements led by unions collected signatures to activate a referendum. The unions and the FA united in this endeavor, thus reinforcing the historical links between them.

Finally, Piñera's government in Chile attempted to pass a labor reform that it labeled "labor modernization." The initiative was halted by social protests in late 2019 that put forward the demand for a new constitution. The ensuing political crisis was intensified the following year by the COVID pandemic.

In short, this chapter has shown that Pink Tide governments developed distinct links with unions. Their relations were sometimes strengthened and sometimes led to confrontation, but the links were never broken. For this reason, once Pink Tide parties left office, they quickly converged with unions in their resistance to the austerity and dismantling policies of the neoliberal governments. Those who minimize the differences between Pink Tide governments and conservative or right-wing ones overlook these areas of convergence between progressive parties in power and social movements.

NOTE

1. This chapter is a revised version of an article that appeared in *Latin American Perspectives* 47 (5): 111–130 (2020). The Pink Tide category has been labeled "modern" (Castañeda, 2006), "social democrat" (Lanzaro, 2008), "social-liberal" (Levitsky and Roberts, 2011), and "moderate" (Weyland, 2011).

REFERENCES

Abal Medina, Paula
2016 "Los trabajadores y sus organizaciones durante los gobiernos kirchneristas." *Nueva Sociedad*, no.264, 72–86.
Acuña, Carlos, Gabriel Kessler, and Fabián Repetto
2002 "Evolución de la política social argentina en la década de los noventa: cambios en su lógica, intencionalidad y en el proceso de hacer la política social." *Proyecto Self-Sustaining Community Development in Comparative Perspective.* http://www1.lanic.utexas.edu/project/etext/llilas/claspo/overviews/argsocpol90s.pdf.
Alejo, Javier and Cecilia Parada
2017 "Desigualdad e informalidad en América Latina: el caso de Brasil." *Desarrollo y Sociedad* 78: 143–199.
Barrett, Patrick S.
2001 "Labour policy, labour–business relations and the transition to democracy in Chile." *Journal of Latin American Studies* 33: 561–597.
Cardoso, Adalberto
2014 "Os sindicatos no Brasil." *Boletin Mercado de Trabalho* 56 (February): 21–27.
Cardoso, Adalberto and Julián Gíndin
2009 *Industrial Relations and Collective Bargaining: Argentina, Brazil and Mexico Compared.* Geneva: ILO.

Carneiro, Fabricio
2017 "Desagregando reformas: comparando la regulación laboral en las izquierdas moderadas." MS, Universidad Torcuato Di Tella, Buenos Aires.
Cassoni, Adriana, Gastón J. Labadie, and Gabriela Fachola
2005 "The economic effects of unions in Latin America: their impact on wages and economic performance of firms in Uruguay," pp. 104–141 in Peter Kuhn and Gustavo Márquez (eds.), *What Difference Do Unions Make? Their Impact on Productivity and Wages in Latin America.* Washington, DC: Inter-American Development Bank
Castañeda, Jorge G.
2006 "Latin America's left turn." *Foreign Affairs* 85 (May/June): 28–43.
CEPALSTAT
n.d. "Tasa de desempleo." https://estadisticas.cepal.org/.
Cook, Maria Lorena and Joseph C. Bazler
2013 "Bringing unions back in: labour and left governments in Latin America." Cornell University School of Industrial and Labor Relations. http://digitalcommons .ilr.cornell.edu/workingpapers/166/.
Dangl, Benjamin
2010 *Dancing with Dynamite: States and Social Movements in Latin America.* Baltimore: AK Press.
Dirección del Trabajo de Chile.
2013 *Compendio de Series Estadísticas 1990–2013: Informe técnico.* Santiago: Departamento de Estudios de la Dirección del Trabajo.
Drake, Paul W.
2003 "El movimiento obrero en Chile de la Unidad Popular a la Concertación." *Revista de Ciencia Política 23 (2): 148–158.*
Etchemendy, Sebastián
2011 "El sindicalismo argentino en la era pos-liberal (2003–2011)," pp. 155–166 in Andrés Malamud and Miguel de Luca (eds.), *La política en tiempos de los Kirchner.* Buenos Aires: Eudeba.
Etchemendy, Sebastián and Ruth Berins Collier
2008 "Golpeados pero de pie: resurgimiento sindical y neocorporativismo segmentado en Argentina (2003–2007)." *Postdata* 13: 145–192.
Filgueira, Fernando
2013 "Los regímenes de bienestar en el ocaso de la modernización monservadora: posibilidades y límites de la ciudadanía social en América Latina." *Revista Uruguaya de Ciencia Política* 22 (2): 17–46.
Frank, Volker
2002 "The elusive goal in democratic Chile: reforming the Pinochet labor legislation." *Latin American Politics and Society* 44 (1): 35–68.
Frías, Fernández Patricio
2008 *Los desafíos del sindicalismo en los inicios del siglo XXI.* Buenos Aires: CLACSO.
González, Julio César and Francisco Zapata

2015 "Reformas estructurales y su impacto en las bases de poder del sindicalismo chileno y uruguayo." *Trabajo y Sociedad* 24 (Summer): 5–32.

Gutiérrez, Crocco Francisca
2016 "¿Sindicatos sin socios, pero representativos? Ideologías de la representatividad sindical en Chile." *POLIS Revista Latinoamericana* 15 (43): 533–555.

Hunter, Wendy
2010 *The Transformation of the Workers' Party in Brazil, 1989–2009*. New York: Cambridge University Press.

Hyman, Richard and Rebecca Gumbrell-McCormick
2010 "Trade unions, politics and parties: is a new configuration possible?" *Transfer: European Review of Labour and Research* 16: 315–331.

ILO (International Labor Organization)
1998 *World Labour Report, 1997–1998: Industrial Relations, Democracy and Social Stability*. Geneva: ILO.

Lanzaro, Jorge
2008 "La socialdemocracia criolla." *Nueva Sociedad*, no. 217, 40–58.

Levitsky, Steven
2003 *Transforming Labor-based Parties in Latin America: Argentine Peronism in Comparative Perspective*. Cambridge: Cambridge University Press.

Levitsky, Steven and Kenneth M. Roberts
2011 *The Resurgence of the Latin American Left*. Baltimore: Johns Hopkins University Press.

Mazzuchi, Graciela
2009 *Las relaciones laborales en el Uruguay: De 2005 a 2008*. Geneva: ILO.

Murillo, María Victoria
2001 *Labor Unions, Partisan Coalitions, and Market Reforms in Latin America*. Cambridge: Cambridge University Press.
2013 "Cambio y continuidad del sindicalismo en democracia." *Revista SAAP* 7: 339–348.

Neto, Octavio Amorim
2014 *De Dutra a Lula: La conducción y los determinantes de la política exterior brasileña*. Buenos Aires: Eudeba.

Notaro, Jorge
2012 "Sindicalismo, reformas estructurales y organización del trabajo: el caso uruguayo, 1985–2012." *Revista Gestión de las Personas y Tecnología* 5 (4): 64–71.

Pastrana, Federico and David Trajtemberg
2020 *La negociación colectiva en tensión: Nuevos y viejos condicionantes al régimen salarial argentino*. Bonn: Friedrich Ebert Stiftung.

Patroni, Viviana and Manuel Poitras
2002 "Labour in neoliberal Latin America: an introduction." *Labour, Capital and Society* 35 (2): 207–220.

Prevost, Gary, Carlos Oliva Campos, and Harry E. Vanden
2012 *Social Movements and Leftist Governments in Latin America*. London: Zed Books.

Radermacher, Reiner and Waldeli Melleiro.

2007 "El sindicalismo bajo el gobierno de Lula." *Nueva Sociedad*, no. 211, 5–18.

Riethof, Marieke

2018 *Labour Mobilization, Politics and Globalization in Brazil: Between Militancy and Moderation*. New York: Palgrave Macmillan.

Roberts, Kenneth M.

2008 "Is social democracy possible in Latin America?" *Nueva Sociedad*, no. 217, 70–86.

2014 *Changing Course in Latin America*. Cambridge: Cambridge University Press.

Senatore, Luís

2009 "Uruguay: 1992–2009: las políticas laborales y el sujeto sindical." *Revista Latinoamericana de Estudios del Trabajo* 22 (2): 53–76.

Stokes, Susan C.

2001 *Mandates and Democracy: Neoliberalism by Surprise in Latin America*. Cambridge: Cambridge University Press.

Tarrow, Sydney

1997 *El poder en movimiento: Los movimientos sociales, la acción colectiva y la política*. Madrid: Alianza Editorial.

Trajtemberg, David

2016 "Políticas públicas laborales tras doce años de gobierno de Néstor Kirchner y Cristina Fernández." FESUR, Análisis no. 17.

Traversa, Federico

2015 "Inequality, collective action and redistribution: a new indicator for assessing a complex relationship." *Revista Española de Investigaciones Sociológicas* 151: 167–182.

Weller, Jürgen

1998 "Los mercados laborales en América Latina: su evolución en el largo plazo y sus tendencias recientes." CEPAL Serie Reformas Económicas. http://archivo.cepal .org/pdfs/1998/ S9800094.pdf.

Weyland, Kurt

2011 "The left: destroyer or savior of the market model?," pp. 71–92 in Steven Levitsky and Kenneth Roberts (eds.), *The Resurgence of the Latin American Left*. Baltimore: Johns Hopkins University Press.

Chapter 4

Routines of Interaction between Latin American Feminists and the State

Progressive Government Legacies and the Conservative and Right-Wing Turn

Eduardo Moreira da Silva and
Clarisse Goulart Paradis
Translated by Luis Fierro

The literature of social movements has sought to theorize the relationship between these actors and the state.[1] While many studies have focused on contention and produced a rather homogeneous view of these actors, some studies on Latin America have considered this relationship more deeply, examining areas of political participation, social movement networks, and the political projects in dispute (Abers and von Bülow, 2011; Dagnino, Olvera, and Panfichi, 2006). Abers and von Bülow have identified forms of interaction between social movements and the state that justify new approaches to social movement theory, among them efforts to influence public policy through participation and inclusion in the state apparatus, making the connections between civil society and political society more complex than the previous literature had envisioned.

Studying the Lula government in Brazil, Abers, Serafim, and Tatagiba (2014) have sought to understand the interactions between society and the state in the areas of urban policy, agrarian development, and public security. They argue that new forms of interaction have emerged as a result of the inclusion of militants in the state apparatus and the heterogeneity of the

Brazilian state. With the aim of broadening the focus beyond contentious action, they modify McAdam, Tarrow, and Tilly's (2004) concept of the repertoire—the culturally codified ways in which people interact in the politics of conflict—to develop the idea of "interaction repertoires" that include collaborative relations between society and the state. This new notion allows them to "incorporate the diversity of strategies used by Brazilian social movements and examine how they have been used, combined, and transformed" (Abers, Serafim, and Tatagiba, 2014: 332).

They identify four interaction routines in the Brazilian case: (1) protest and direct action (even when there is collaboration with the state, which is viewed as an ally); (2) institutionalized participation (participatory budgets, public policy councils and conferences); (3) personal contacts with state actors facilitated by the expansion of links between the executive and these movements typical of leftist governments; and (4) occupation of positions in the bureaucracy. The last of these deserves particular attention because of the strong presence of social movement activists in governments of the left (Vaz, 2014). Although some writers view this phenomenon as leading to the co-optation of social leaders (Doimo, 1996), others have called it "institutional activism"—a strategy for promoting change through the institutional path but anchored in the previous trajectory of the actors and in the networks of which they are part (Abers and Keck, 2017; Abers and Tatagiba, 2016).

Recent protests can be characterized as a "new type of viral, rhizomatic, and diffuse political action" made up of "more mediatic and performative repertoires" (Bringel, 2013: 19). Similar approaches are adopted by analysts seeking to understand the mechanisms underlying the emergence of a "geopolitics of global indignation" expressed in protests in contexts as varied as North America, Europe, and Latin America (Bringel, 2013; Mayol and Azócar, 2011; Mella Polanco and Berrios Silva, 2013; Valerian, 2013). This chapter aims to examine the interaction repertoires in the policy sector for women on the basis of a comparison of Argentina, Bolivia, Brazil, and Chile. It focuses on the peak period of the Pink Tide, between 2009 and 2012, and also examines the emergence of the Blue Tide (the subsequent conservative wave) and its interactions within the feminist field. To this end, we analyze the feminist agenda of the state, especially the role of institutional mechanisms for the advancement of women,[2] and the participatory institutions and contours of feminist protests in these two periods.

The hypotheses of our research on repertoires during the Pink Tide period were as follows: (1) Women in the presidency and/or left-wing governments positively influence the institutional mechanisms for women's agenda. (2) The institutional and budgetary capacity of institutional mechanisms for women and participatory institutions facilitate the establishment of interactions between the executive branch of government and feminist and women's movements. (3) The presence of women in the legislature contributes to the establishment of interaction repertoires. (4) Protest functions as a component in the cycle of negotiations with the state. In turn, right-wing conservative coalitions are expected to undermine support for the feminist agenda and women's institutional mechanisms, disaggregate participatory policies, and thus incite more confrontational protests from feminist activists.

The thesis defended here is anchored in an analytical model with three interconnected dimensions. Its *normative* dimension supports a possible improvement in governance resulting from the presence of institutional channels for the participation of society in the formulation of public policy. Its *policy* dimension assumes that policies aimed at women can be enhanced if they have been shaped by the participation of women. Its *theoretical* dimension suggests combining studies of public policy and bureaucracy with studies of social movements and their interaction repertoires (Bebbington, Delamaza, and Villar, 2008).

REPERTOIRES OF INTERACTION BETWEEN FEMINISM AND THE STATE

The relationship between feminism and the state is part of an exhaustive but not exhausted debate with contributions from the North (Htun and Weldon, 2010; Kantola, 2006; Lovenduski, 2005; Mazur, 2002) and the Global South (Guzmán, 2001; Sardenberg and Costa, 2010) and from different currents of feminism (Paradis, 2013). More collaborative and confrontational approaches have permeated assessments of the strategies of feminist movements vis-à-vis the state, and in Latin America these approaches have been in constant dispute (Matos and Paradis, 2013). Abandoning a binary and Manichaean view, Matos and Paradis (2014) have suggested a new feminist synthesis of the state that takes into account the complexity of the relations between society and the state, monitors the state's political translations of the demands of feminist movements, considers how different groups of women are affected by state actions, and assesses the efforts of institutional mechanisms for women seeking to depatriarchalize the state. There is an important debate about the role of women presidents in this regard. It is obvious that women as a group do not all have the same interests, perspectives, and aspirations. As a result, there are examples of female presidents who have failed to pursue a feminist or gender agenda. At the same time, the election of a female president has undeniable symbolic content that can contribute to greater pressure from society and from the movements organized around feminist and women's demands.

In Latin America, all countries have institutional mechanisms for the advancement of women in their executive branch of government. Among the main characteristics of these institutions are dialogue with women's movements and organizations, efforts to sensitize and train public officials on gender issues, gender mainstreaming as a strategy for exercising power and achieving objectives, and a constant struggle to survive and increase their technical, budgetary, and political capacities (Paradis, 2013). Byrne et al. (1996) consider the relationship between institutional mechanisms for women and civil society strategy for influencing policy. There is also a relationship between the technical and budgetary capacities of these institutions and formal participatory structures along with higher levels of participation (Paradis, 2013).

The study of protest in Latin America has identified the existence of "cycles of confrontation" (Bringel, 2013; Tarrow, 1998; Tatagiba, 2014). The singularities of the most recent protests and, more important, the specificities of these countries' current social, political, and economic contexts may lead to the mistake of isolating certain historical contexts or establishing hasty parallels. Although it is important to avoid the "seduction of novelty" (Bringel, 2013: 24), in some countries it is possible to identify similar cycles of collective action in the struggle for democratization in recent decades (Tilly, 2006).

CASE STUDIES

Chile

The Servicio Nacional de la Mujer (National Women's Service—SERNAM) was established in Chile in 1992, the first time that an institutional mechanism for the advancement of women appeared in the top tier of the executive branch of government in Latin America (Paradis, 2013). The SERNAM was the strongest institutional mechanism for women among the countries analyzed here and one of the strongest in Latin America in terms of its bureaucratic structure and its budget. In 2011 it had 15 regional offices and just over 500 employees (including temporary ones) (Paradis, 2013). Its budget represented approximately 0.07 percent of the general budget, or US$4.60 per woman (Paradis, 2013). Despite not establishing a direct relationship with civil society, the SERNAM relied on a consultative council composed of government bodies and civil society movements and organizations that evaluated its policies and proposed action. In addition, it conducted public consultations, meetings with nongovernmental actors, and research (Chile, 2010). In March 2015, during Bachelet's second term, the first-tier Ministry of Women and Gender Equality was created and charged with formulating policies for women (Chile, 2016). This new ministry represented an important step in strengthening the state's capacity to provide policies for women.

In 2017, its budget increased considerably compared with the SERNAM's and the appointed minister had a recognized feminist trajectory (Paradis and Dos Santos; 2021).

The election of President Michelle Bachelet was considered a milestone for the incorporation of the gender equality agenda into the governments of the region (see Tobar, 2009: 21), although some challenges and weaknesses were present in her first term. In an excerpt from her inaugural speech, Bachelet recognized that her election was an expression of new times, in part because she was a woman (Chile, 2006). Early in her term she announced a parity cabinet (with 10 female ministers), including women in strategic sectors of the government such as the General Secretariat of the Presidency and the Ministries of the Economy, Planning and Cooperation, and Defense. In Planning, Health, and the General Secretariat, the female ministers had a recognized history of commitment to gender equality (Waylen, 2016). The number of women in the cabinet varied in the first term. After the initial parity, Bachelet was under pressure from her base and charged with having nominated people who were inexperienced or in some way "outsiders" from the perspective of the political elite to whom she owed allegiance. After female representation fell to 30 percent in October 2008, the government ended up with near-parity in 2010 (Waylen, 2016).

With regard to political support for the SERNAM, Fernández and Oliva (2012) point out that during Bachelet's term the institutional bodies for women obtained a significant increase in their budgets. According to Waylen (2016), the agency's prestige and influence increased in this period, since it was considered vital to advancing the interests of women and feminists, especially because there were few women in the legislature (15 percent in the Chamber of Deputies and around 5 percent in the Senate) (IPU, 2006). In general, however, the achievements of the first Bachelet government were considered limited. Escobar (2014: 5) described it as marked by an "economicist and technocratic conservatism, with some redistributive touches." Furthermore, the proposals for change that required congressional support were unsuccessful (Waylen, 2016). While in the 1990s the contradictions between feminists working in political institutions and those belonging to autonomous groups were latent, in the twenty-first century polarization opened the way for diversification and fragmentation that undermined the political support and further advances of the Bachelet government in favor of gender equality (Tobar, 2009). A significant part of the movement remained averse to collaboration with the state.

The protests that have taken place in Chile during the Pink Tide have been seen as a reaction to the inability of the political system to process the society's demands. Also observed is a pluralization of mobilization, with a predominance of action by young people mobilized through new networks and an increase in the support for student protest on the part of broad sectors of the population. In addition, other actors (including conservatives) took over the country's public space as part of the "social overflow" observed by Bringel (2013) in the Brazilian case regarding the presence in the public sphere of a wide range of actors that traditionally did not participate in protests.

The Chilean feminist movement today is marked by the pluralization represented by Mapuche feminism and the post-/de-/anti-colonial discourse of indigenous and Afro-descendant feminists, among others. Although Gajardo (2014) indicates a cooling of direct action and protest, Tobar (2009) points to the emergence of "young feminists," also identified in Brazil (Alvarez, 2014), with substantial participation in the national conference of feminists of 2005.

The return of the conservative-liberal coalition in Chile with Sebastián Piñera's election in 2018 was marked by significant instability, including a wave of protests of unprecedented magnitude, that permanently buried the fragile consensus in favor of postdictatorship stability (Titelman, 2019; Tanscheit, 2021). A fundamental component of this wave was the emergence of an organized mass feminist movement. From the university demonstrations in 2018 to the protests that brought together millions of women across the country on March 8, 2020, feminism shook the political scene in a process that has converged with the drafting of the new constitution.

Piñera's support for the feminist agenda has been selective and controversial. Amidst the feminist protests of 2018, the government presented an "agenda for gender equality," promoted as an initiative of the president after having "listened to the voice of women" (Chile, 2018). It included generic actions to combat violence, harassment, and discrimination against women and specific measures related to women's health and child care. Clearly, such actions present a gender agenda with technocratic content, far from the transformative claims of feminist protests. Its inaugural ministerial cabinet contained nearly 30 percent women, some of whom openly opposed feminist agendas such as the legalization of abortion. The Ministry of Women and Gender Equity, despite having maintained its administrative and budgetary structure, was marked by a considerable turnover of ministers, whose conservative and antifeminist profiles were largely rejected by organized women (Paradis and Dos Santos, 2020). In the midst of this process, Piñera responded to the "social outburst" with brutal repression and was denounced for abuse, torture, and murder (Tanscheit, 2021).

Argentina

After the redemocratization in Argentina, two new agencies focused on social assistance were created under the Ministry of Health and Social Action. The Consejo Nacional de la Mujer (National Women's Council—CNM), established in the presidency in 1992, was by 2011 only a third-tier agency with very limited technical capacity and budget (among the most deficient structures of this kind in Latin America). That year it had 28 employees, and its budget represented 0.002 percent of the general budget, or US$0.11 per woman. As a federal institution it brought together agencies responsible for policies for women at lower levels of government (Argentina, 2010). Matos and Paradis (2013) report that the council did not provide meaningful dialogue with the movements and gradually lost power, prestige, and resources. President Cristina Fernández de Kirchner was the first woman ever to be reelected in Latin America, with the highest presidential vote in 28 years of Argentine democracy (de Dios, 2011). In her inaugural speech in 2007 she recalled Eva Perón and recognized the role of the Madres y Abuelas de Plaza de Mayo in the construction of Argentine democracy (Argentina, 2007). Her initial cabinet had only three women, in social development, defense, and health. In 2008 she appointed a woman to head the Ministry of Industry (Salinas, 2015). According to Fernández and Oliva (2012: 128), gender policy during her term was marked by "discontinuity, lack of funding and ambiguity in the definition of equity."

Under the Mauricio Macri government, the policy agenda for women faced a series of setbacks. The reduction in number of female cabinet ministers included social security, from 50 percent in 2011 to 15 percent in 2015 (when Macri took office), labor, from 42 percent to 23 percent, and science, technology, and innovation from 43 percent to 0 (Canelo, 2021). Additional reversals included budget reductions, less budgetary transparency, and the replacement of the CNM by the Instituto Nacional de las Mujeres (National Women's Institute—INAM), thus replacing a collegiate body with a more executive one (Gherardi, 2017). Budget reduction especially held back the creation of a plan to fight violence (Canelo, 2021; Archenti and Tula, 2019; Sutton and Borland, 2019). Despite creating a plan to combat violence against women, Macri reduced the agency's budget, which led civil society organizations to sue to overturn the measure (Gherardi, 2017). Finally, Macri, in effect, masculinized the ministerial cabinet.

The women's and feminist movements in Argentina were characterized by three general tendencies: their presence in the human rights movements, collective action by the popular sectors, especially in periods characterized by fiscal adjustment and economic crisis, and the participation of middle-class women (Di Marco, 2011; Gajardo, 2014; Mayol and Azócar, 2011). The protests in 2001 in the context of the economic and political crisis were decisive in the incorporation of agendas from different sectors of the feminist field. The annual national women's conferences organized by various feminist movements and organizations since 1986 and the struggle for the legalization of abortion and for reproductive rights created what Di Marco (2011) has called "feminist people." The embracing of a feminist discourse by women of other social movements made it possible to construct a heterogeneous "women" in relation to a common adversary, the traditional and patriarchal forces, generating a political identity captured by Di Marco's term. The women's conferences became an ideal space for shaping common agendas and demonstrating women's activism (Di Marco, 2011) at the same time that they radicalized demands and contributed to the formation of a more autonomous field but one that was not totally averse to the state.

In addition, the significant presence of women in the legislature fostered by the quota law meant that interaction routines were centered more on the legislative than on the executive branch. More recently, Argentine feminists have produced new waves of protest. The broad feminist response, using primarily social networks and employing the hashtag #niunamenos, to the cruel murder of a pregnant 14-year-old by her boyfriend in April 2015 catalyzed mobilizations (Rovetto, 2015: 18). The incident brought 200,000 people onto the streets and attracted the attention of many public figures (Cué, 2015). The protest was replicated in 120 other cities and towns and in countries such as Uruguay and Chile and became a permanent campaign with a public agenda. Its demands included public policies, access to justice, and actions aimed at cultural transformation.

Recently, the struggle for the legalization of abortion carried out by women's and feminist movements stands out. Sutton and Borland (2019) reveal how the rights of activists to legalize abortion in Argentina included an expansion of the "frames" present in the discursive repertoire of actors. One of the main elements of this expansion is related to the human rights argument, which was central to the national campaign for the right to legal, safe, and free abortion that was approved in 2020 (Sutton and Borland, 2019). Part of the power of the human rights frame derives from its ability to provide legitimacy to political demands, given its political acceptance and the instruments it makes available to carry them out, such as national and international law. Furthermore, as had happened during the organization for the Beijing conference actions, the category of human rights was appropriated locally and led to a degree of unity among the groups involved in the struggle. This was what happened with the national campaign for the right to legal, safe, and free abortion in 2005. On its tenth anniversary, in 2015, more than 300 organizations and countless individuals joined the walks for women's lives. The coalition included political parties, labor organizations, academic institutions, human rights groups and others. The movement highlighted five central strategies: connecting national and international law, constructing coalitions, widening and narrowing the focus in the fight for abortion, connecting with local discourse, and disputing the legitimacy of the antiabortion discourse (Sutton and Borland, 2019: 28).

Brazil

In Brazil, the Conselho Nacional dos Direitos da Mulher (National Council for Women's Rights—CNDM) was created in 1985 and, linked to the Ministry of Justice, served as the country's first institutional mechanism for the advancement of women's rights. It functioned as a political space for articulation of representatives of government and civil society in relation to the demand for democratization and the expansion and deepening of women's public agenda. Its deliberative character and its financial and administrative autonomy were ensured only until 1989, when it became a consultative body (Bohn, 2010; Montaño, 2003).

In 2003 the Partido dos Trabalhadores (Workers' Party—PT) government created the Special Secretariat for the Promotion of Women's Policies, with ministry status under the Presidency, but by 2011 it was receiving only a very small portion of the general budget (0.005 percent), or US$0.52 per woman. Despite not having a local structure, it provided considerable institutional and budgetary support for the establishment and maintenance of institutional mechanisms for women at state and local levels.

The election of Dilma Rousseff had important repercussions. In her inaugural speech, she affirmed her commitment to women: "I come to open doors so that many other women can also, in the future, become president, and so that—today—all Brazilian women will feel the pride and the joy of being a woman" (Brazil, 2011). Despite not having gender parity in her cabinet during her first term, she appointed women for social areas, culture, the environment, and planning, budget, and management. In 2011 the Chief of Staff of the Presidency and the Minister of Institutional Relations were replaced by women. Luiza de Bairros of the Ministry of Racial Equality and Eleonora Menicucci of the Special Secretariat for Women's Policies had strong connections with the women's movement and recognized feminist trajectories. Like Rousseff, Menicucci had been arrested and tortured during the military dictatorship. While there was a significant increase in the ministry's budget between 2012 and 2015, only 30 percent of it was spent (Carvalho, 2018). Under strong political pressure and experiencing an economic crisis and a drastic reduction of public resources, in September 2015 Rousseff created the Ministry of Women, Racial Equality, and Human Rights and reduced the status of the Special Secretariat.

With the creation of the Special Secretariat in 2003, the role of the CNDM had changed from being responsible for formulating policies to monitoring equality policies for women (Brazil, 2008). It is one of a few deliberative women's councils in Latin America. Another mechanism of participation was the Conference of Women's Policies, the first three of which (in 2004, 2007, and 2011) involved around 200,000 women in municipal, state, and national events in all the country's federative units. These conferences were instrumental in the development of a national women's policies plan. Considerable evidence shows that the relationship between the movements and the Special Secretariat was close and as a result at least two-thirds of the Secretariat's budget financed projects presented by civil society and local state actors (Matos and Paradis, 2013; Bohn, 2010). In this context, Sardenberg and Costa (2010) have identified the emergence of a participatory state feminism facilitated by the growth of activism and the articulation of feminist and women's movements, the rise of the PT, with its commitment to participatory forms of government, and awareness that the patriarchal political system limited women's representation in the executive, legislative, and judiciary branches of government.

The pluralization of the feminist field in Brazil encompassed relationships established with increasingly broad sectors of society, in particular the less institutionalized sectors (Alvarez, 2014: 34). In addition to the popularization of feminism among students, there was a shared desire for feminist action in the streets and for a multiplication of popular feminisms in the city and countryside. One of the important protests of popular feminism was the 2000 March of the Margaridas (named for a union leader), which brought together about 20,000 women from throughout the country. In 2003 the number of women marching doubled, in 2007 about 50,000 rural workers participated, and in 2011 more than 100,000 women gathered in Brasília (IPEA, 2013). These and other mobilizations combined training, denunciation, and pressure with political dialogue and negotiation with the state, especially during the PT governments, that resulted in some achievements (CONTAG, 2015). The March of the Margaridas and the participation of its leaders in councils, conferences, and policy monitoring committees produced documentation policies for rural women, credit for production, property titles for women, and policies to combat violence against women.

Rousseff's impeachment in 2016 was widely denounced as a parliamentary coup. The academic feminist field also framed the coup as a backlash permeated by political violence against the president (Biroli, 2016; Araújo, 2018). For Biroli (2016), such violence was applied not only to remove Rousseff and the PT from power but also to attack feminist activism, especially state activism, in a context of the increasing influence of feminism on the state and Brazilian society. The murder of the councilwoman Marielle Franco in March 2018 marked the cruelty of the political shift to the right and specifically the frontal attack on organized black women, who were at the forefront of resistance and struggles for democracy.

Vice President Temer's government was marked by significant instability, massive protests, and substantial changes in labor legislation in favor of structural adjustment. Furthermore, the dismantling of the feminist agenda was accentuated. The cabinet did not contain any women, and its discourse reinforced traditional gender roles. Four different ministers, one of them openly antifeminist, were appointed to the Secretariat for Women's Policy during this short period of government. In addition, the government reduced allocations for programs to combat violence. Jair Bolsonaro's election represented a shift toward the extreme right. His government attempted to combat the legacy of the PT and the feminist agenda at the state level. It also made moves to eliminate the term "gender" from official written statements, which began to underscore the defense of family values. Part of this shift involved the creation of the Ministry of Women, Family, and Human Rights, whose minister was an ultraconservative Christian missionary. Furthermore, the president himself has committed numerous acts of symbolic violence against women.

Bolsonaro's rise in 2018 sparked significant feminist protests including actions in the streets and a social media campaign based on the hashtag "Ele não" (Not him). Over a two-month period, there were 50 million posts, as well as 294 street demonstrations throughout the country (Mussi and Zanini, 2021).

Bolivia

The presidential election of Evo Morales of the Movimiento al Socialismo (Movement toward Socialism—MAS) in Bolivia in 2005 gave rise to a sharp rupture in the country's social imaginary that involved the protagonism of the indigenous population and the state's construction of a new societal framework. In 2009, the government created the Vice Ministry for Equal Opportunities, linked to the Ministry of Justice. Only a second-tier institution, the vice ministry had a precarious budget—in 2012, 0.001 percent of the general budget, around US$0.3 per woman. The vice ministry was responsible for implementing policies for women, children, youth, the elderly, and people with special needs (Bolivia, 2012). It had no formal channels for the participation of civil society and at times was led by a man, thus reinforcing the idea that it was not designed to be feminist. In Morales's second term a cabinet with gender parity was created with the appointment of female heads of the Ministries of Justice, Planning, Transparency, Development, Employment and Welfare, the Environment, Cultures, Health, and Rural Development (Uriona, 2010). Many of them were indigenous and came from social and labor organizations close to the MAS base (Díaz Carrasco, 2013).

After the approval of the new constitution in 2009, which included the goal of "decolonizing the state," the women's organizations framed a demand agenda around the "depatriarchalization" of the Bolivian state and society (Chávez et al., 2011; Paredes, 2012). One of the results was the creation in

2010 of the Depatriarchalization Unit within the Ministry of Cultures. On the one hand, the unit represented a milestone in recognizing that patriarchy was a political problem and had to be the object of state action (Cárdenas et al., 2013; Ybarnegaray Ortiz, 2012; Uriona, 2010). Nowhere else in Latin America has the state dedicated itself to the deconstruction of structurally entrenched powers such as colonialism and patriarchy. On the other hand, the unit was created as a fourth-tier subordinate agency and was soon rife with internal contradictions (Bolivia, 2014). The Ministry of Cultures itself recognized a struggle within the state to expand its institutionality and understood that the term "depatriarchalization," although it had captured the collective imagination of Bolivian society, was only beginning to be theoretically developed (Cárdenas et al., 2013).

Some writers have pointed to contradictions between the indigenous and the feminist agendas (Htun and Ossa, 2013; Ybarnegaray Ortiz, 2012) that permeated both the Depatriarchalization Unit and the Vice Ministry of Equal Opportunities. The prevailing view in the government, associated with the notion of gender complementarity, did not recognize the importance of specific instances of gender disparity in the public sphere (Htun and Ossa, 2013). In addition, in the Ministry of Cultures the term "depatriarchalization" appears to have acquired a meaning at odds with "different variants of feminism," seen as external and in contradiction to the indigenous worldview.

The protests of feminist and women's movements in Bolivia sought to include the demand for gender equality in national legislation and in the state. Although the constituent process incorporated a wide range of demands from feminist and women's movements, it was not successful "in recognizing the principle of depatriarchalization as a pillar of the process of transformation, inclusion, and disruption of power relations that exclude and oppress women," which was incorporated only later (Uriona, 2010: 34). The elections of 2010 did, however, culminate in the presence of 47 percent women in the Senate and 25 percent in the Chamber of Deputies (Uriona, 2010). Today parity is a reality in both chambers.

In summary, protests under the Morales government assumed the character of negotiation and reinforcement of the state's commitment to decolonization and depatriarchalization. At the same time, feminist agendas retained their most contentious demands, especially those of radical feminists in favor of sexual and reproductive rights and those of the rural and indigenous sectors in opposition to the government's extractive policies. Also noteworthy was the significant increase in female representation in the legislature as a result of the electoral law. Furthermore, a broad participatory institutionality was created, especially at the local level, that enabled yet another channel of frequent communication between the state and the social movements. The success in creating a national agenda for feminist and women's movements was expressed in the creation of new laws and the establishment of the Depatriarchization Unit. The interaction between the feminist movement and the state manifested itself the most at the legislative level as opposed to the rather weak Vice Ministry of Equal Opportunities.

The government of Jeanine Añez, which came to power through a civil/military coup in 2019, was guided by religious conservatism and a radically changed orientation, since the president associated indigenous people with Satan. The composition of the cabinet reflected the strategy of gaining support from the military with the appointment of members of the upper classes and whites. Protests with a significant presence of indigenous women broke out and were repressed with strong police violence. The government broke relations with the progressive governments of Venezuela, Mexico, and Argentina, resumed relations with the United States, which had been interrupted for 11 years, and changed some 80 percent of the diplomatic corps. It did not have time, however, to dismantle the structure of participation, since Law 341 on participation and social control remained in force (Zilla and Andrade, 2020). As is shown by Paradis and Dos Santos (2011), the interim government sought to replace the state's decolonization and depatriarchalization agenda with one based on a conservative technocracy, expressed in the nomination of women managers who were far from aligned with the organized women's movement.

REPERTOIRES OF INTERACTION OF THE FEMINIST MOVEMENT IN COMPARATIVE PERSPECTIVE

The interaction repertoires of the four countries are shown in Table 4.1.

The analysis undertaken in this article has sought to reinforce the thesis presented in social movement literature that interactions between feminists and the state are not simply contentious but also collaborative. The occurrence of the two types of interaction is influenced by the dominant political project of the state, the profile of the institutional mechanisms of advancement for women, the formal channels of participation, support for the feminist and gender agenda by presidents, and female presence in the legislature.

The interactions of feminist movements during the Pink Tide governments both in participatory spaces and through protest actions contributed to the advancing of the feminist agenda. In Chile, interactions occurred more with the executive branch than with the legislative power, as well as through the consultative council, which included representatives of civil society. Protests were somewhat fragmented and more contentious than collaborative. In the Piñera governments, gender technocracy distanced itself further from the

Table 4.1: Interaction Repertoires of Latin American Feminists during the Pink Tide.

Country	Institutional Mechanisms for Women	Women in Parliament	Women in Executive Branch	Formal Participatory Spaces	Nature of Protests
Chile	Strong: first-tier, considerable budget, considerable personnel and administrative structure	Low: 14 percent (IPU, 2011)	Female president supporting gender equality; parity in the cabinet during most of the government, some ministers with feminist trajectories	Civil Society Council	Fragmented movement, increase of autonomist sectors, therefore more contentious than collaborative
Brazil	Relatively strong: first-tier, medium-sized budget, with difficulties in execution, reduced structure, but strong support for subnational mechanisms	Low: approximately 8 percent (IPU, 2011)	Small number of female ministers; minister of women's policies and minister of racial equality both feminists.	National Council for Women's Policies and national conferences, among others	More collaborative, with growth of contentious actions and sectors since 2013
Bolivia	Weak: fourth-tier, divided between Ministry of Justice and Ministry of Cultures, very limited budget	High, especially after the approval of constitution and parity law	Parity in the cabinet	Constituent process	More collaborative; mostly women's movements in the base of MAS

Argen- tina	Weak: fourth-tier, large bud- get deficit	High because of quota laws: approxi- mately 37 percent (IPU, 2011)	President has ties with the Madres de Plaza de Mayo; few women appointed to ministries	n.a.	Contentious and occa- sionally collab- orative (feminist confer- ences)

feminist agenda, and protests became massive in favor of a refoundation of the state.

In Brazil, interactions were more centered on the executive and formal spaces for participation, which periodically brought together a significant number of women's organizations. Protests were part of a continuum of interaction that combined participation in councils with mobilization at conferences. The shift to the right after 2016 limited spaces for participation, reduced the number of women in the cabinet, and cut the budget for women's policies. This resulted in the intensification of contentious protests. In contrast to the absence of women in Temer's government, the Bolsonaro government has opened institutional spaces, but they are based on a conservative discourse of defending the family, which is central to the mobilization of the government's base of support.

In Bolivia, interactions with the executive branch's institutions were less beneficial for the women's movement. In contrast, the constituent process created a meaningful space for interaction between government, parties, and women's movements and organizations that was instrumental in creating the parity law. The 2019 coup brought neoliberalism, racism, authoritarianism, and a cabinet composed of the upper classes and whites. Militant protests were violently repressed.

Finally, in Argentina, given the weakness of the institutional mechanisms for women, interaction took place primarily in the legislative sphere where deputies had considerable impact. The national women's conferences provided opportunities for alliances among women's movements and the formulation of political proposals. The Ni Una Menos protests provided a platform for demands. When Macri replaced the CNM with the INAM, which had a reduced budget, civil society organizations went to court. The human rights argument was central to what became a successful national campaign in support of legal, safe, and free abortion.

The interactions between women's movements and Pink Tide governments were not free of controversy, and in all four countries under study there were contentious actions and organized sectors that mobilized outside the collaborative frameworks with the state. Contradictions in the projects of these progressive governments have reinforced the emergence and strengthening of more autonomous sectors. However, collaborative interaction became so prevalent in the region that Matos (2010) has suggested that it is now one of the main characteristics of a new feminist wave. This process was marked by a significant reinforcement of state feminism, which under progressive governments was characterized by strong collaboration with women's movements and feminists of recognized trajectory. As Paradis and Dos Santos (2021) point out, under Pink Tide governments qualitative changes in state feminism favoring a more transformative agenda displaced the technocratic agendas that until the end of the twentieth century dominated the debate on public policies for women. The subsequent rise of conservative and rightist governments has resulted in the isolation of state institutions, which were previously more open to feminist proposals, at the same time that convergences between progressive parties and social movements have emerged around contentious actions.

NOTES

1. This chapter is a revised version of an article that appeared in *Latin American Perspectives* 47 (5): 40–57 (2020).
2. By "institutional mechanisms for the advancement of women" we mean the agencies of the executive branch of the state that are responsible for the implementation of gender equality policies (see Paradis, 2013).

REFERENCES

Abers, Rebeca and Margaret E. Keck
2017 *Autoridade prática: Ação criativa e mudança institucional na política das águas do Brasil*. Rio de Janeiro: Fiocruz Editora.
Abers, Rebeca, Lizandra Serafim, and Luciana Tatagiba
2014 "Repertórios de interação estado-sociedade em um estado heterogêneo: a experiência na Era Lula." *Dados* 57: 325–357.
Abers, Rebecca and Luciana Tatagiba
2016 "Institutional activism: mobilizing for women's health from inside the Brazilian bureaucracy," pp. 73–101 in Federico M. Rossi and Marisa von Bülow (eds.), *Social Movement Dynamics: New Perspectives on Theory and Research from Latin America*. New York: Routledge.
Abers, Rebeca and Marisa von Bülow
2011 "Movimentos sociais na teoria e na prática: como estudar o ativismo através da frontera entre Estado e sociedade?" *Sociologias* 13 (28): 52–84.
Alvarez, Sonia

2014 "Para além da sociedade civil: reflexões sobre o campo feminista." *Cadernos Pagu*, no. 43, 13–56.

Araújo, Clara
2018 "Incongruências e dubiedades, deslegitimação e legitimação: o golpe contra Dilma Rousseff,"pp. 33–50 in Linda Rubim and Fernanda Argolo (eds.), *O golpe na perspectiva de gênero*. San Salvador: Edufba.

Archenti, Nélida and María Inés Tula
2019 "Teoría y política en clave de género." *Colección* 30 (1): 13–43.

Argentina
2007 "Discurso de la Presidenta Cristina Fernández de Kirchner en la Asamblea Legislativa." https://www.casarosada.gob.ar/informacion/archivo/16462-blank -35472369.
2010 "Informe ante la Undécima Conferencia Regional Sobre la Mujer de América Latina y El Caribe." https://www.cepal.org/sites/default/files/events/files/argentina .pdf.

Bebbington, Anthony, Gonzalo Delamaza, and Rodrigo Villar
2008 "El desarrollo de base y los espacios públicos de concertación local en América," pp. 28–79 in Cristina Almeida Cunha Filgueiras and Carlos Aurélio Pimenta de Faria (eds.), *Governo local, política pública e participação na América do Sul*. Belo Horizonte: Editora PUC Minas.

Biroli, Flávia
2016 "Political violence against women in Brazil: expressions and definitions." *Revista Direito e Práxis* 7: 557–589.

Bohn, Simone
2010 "Feminismo estatal sobre a presidência Lula: o caso da Secretaria de Política para as Mulheres." *Revista Debates*, no. 4, 81–106.

Bolivia
2012 "Estructura orgánica del Ministerio de Justicia." http://www.justicia.gob.bo/ images/stories/pdf/organigrama%20=2012.pdf.
2014 *Resolución ministerial n.1008/2014*. Bogotá: Ministerio de Culturas y Turismo.

Brazil
2008 *Decreto no. 6.412*. March 26. Brasilia.
2011 "Dilma Rousseff, Presidenta da República: discurso durante Compromisso Constitucional perante o Congresso Nacional." Brasília: Sistema Integrado de Planejamento e Orçamento do Governo Federal, Painel do Orçamento Federal. https://www1.siop.planejamento.gov.br/QvAJAXZfc/opendoc.htm?document =IAS%2FExecucao_Orcamentaria.qvw&host=QVS%40pqlk04&anonymous=true &sheet=SH06.

Bringel, Breno
2013 "Sentidos e tendências do levante brasileiro de 2013." https://www.academia. edu/10068329/_2013_As_Jornadas_de_Junho_em_perspectiva_global.

Byrne, Bridget, Julie Koch Laier, Sally Baden, and Rachel Marcus
1996 "National machineries for women in development: experiences, lessons and strategies for institutionalising gender in development policy and planning."

BRIDGE 36. http://www.bridge.ids.ac.uk/sites/bridge.ids.ac.uk/files/reports/re36c.pdf.

Canelo, Paula Vera

2021 "Género y poder en Argentina: las elite ejecutivas de Fernández de Kirchner, Macri y Fernández." 87: 127–150.

Cárdenas, Felix, Idon Chivi, Sandro Canqui, and Francisca Alvarado

2013 *Despatriarcalización y chachawarmi: Avances y articulaciones posibles*. La Paz: Ministerio de Culturas y Turismo/Viceministerio de Descolonización.

Carvalho, Layla Pedreira

2018 "A SPM e as políticas para as mulheres no Brasil: saltos e sobressaltos em uma institucionalização das demandas das agendas feministas," pp. 81–107 in Marlise Matos and Sonia E. Alvarez (eds.), *Quem são as mulheres das políticas para as mulheres no Brasil? O feminismo estatal participativo brasileiro*. Porto Alegre: Editora Zouk.

Chávez, Patricia, Toonia Quiroz, Dunia Mokranis, and María Lugones

2011 *Despatriarcalizar para descolonizar la gestión pública*. La Paz: Vicepresidencia del Estado Plurinacional de Bolivia, Dirección de Participación Ciudadana.

Chile

2006 "Discurso presidenta Michelle Bachelet." http://www.archivochile.com/Chile_actual/Elecciones_2005/Bachelet/11_03_2006.pdf.

2010 "Informe ante la Undécima Conferencia Regional Sobre la Mujer de América Latina y El Caribe." https://www.cepal.org/sites/default/files/events/files/chile.pdf.

2016 "Comienza el nuevo Ministerio de la Mujer y la Equidad de Género." http://www.gob.cl/comienza-nuevo-ministerio-la-mujer-la-equidad-genero/.

2018 "#TodosPorTodas: Presidente Piñera anuncia agenda de equidad de género." Ministerio Secretaría General de Gobierno. https://msgg.gob.cl/wp/2018/05/23/todosportodas-presidente-pinera-anuncia-agenda-de-equidad-de-genero/.

CONTAG (Confederação dos Trabalhadores da Agricultura)

2015 "Marcha das Margaridas 2015: caderno de textos." http://www.contag.org.br/index.php?modulo=portal&acao=interna&codpag=402&dc=1&nw=1.

Cué, Carlos E.

2015 "Argentina se mobiliza pela primeira vez contra assassinatos machistas: manifestação sem precedentes é ponto alto em processo que une políticos e celebridades." *El País Internacional*, June 13. http://brasil.elpais.com/brasil/2015/06/03/internacional/1433356172_949785.html.

Dagnino, Evelina, Alberto Olvera, and Aldo Panfichi

2006 *A disputa pela construção democrática na América Latina*. São Paulo: Paz e Terra.

de Dios, Fernando

2011 "Cristina Kirchner comemora reeleição na Argentina." IG, October 24. https://ultimosegundo.ig.com.br/mundo/cristina-kirchner-comemora-reeleicao-na-argentina/n1597314636800.html.

Díaz Carrasco, Marianela Agar

2013 "¡De empleada a ministra!: despatriarcalización en Bolívia." *Íconos* 45: 75–89.

Di Marco, Graciela

2011 *El pueblo feminista: Movimientos sociales y lucha de las mujeres en torno de la ciudadania*. Buenos Aires: Editora Biblos.

Doimo, Ana Maria

1996 *A vez e a voz do popular nos movimentos sociais e participação política no Brasil pós-70*. São Paulo: Cortez Editora.

Escobar, Luis Eduardo

2014 "Michelle Bachelet en busca de la transformación de Chile." *Nueva Sociedad*, no. 252, 4–14.

Fernández Ramil, María de los Ángeles and Daniela Oliva Espinosa

2012 "Presidentas latinoamericanas e igualdad de género: un camino sinuoso." *Nueva Sociedad*, no. 240, 119–133.

Gajardo, Antonieta Vera

2014 "Moral, representación y 'feminismo mapuche': elementos para formular una pregunta." *Polis* 13 (38): 301–323.

Gherardi, Natalia.

2017 "La violencia de género: desafíos de políticas públicas" in E. Faur (comp.), *Mujeres y varones en la Argentina de hoy: Géneros en movimiento*. Buenos Aires: Siglo XXI Editores, 2017.

Guzmán, Virginia

2001 "La institucionalidad de género en el estado: nuevas perspectivas de análisis." *Serie Mujer y Desarollo CEPAL*, no. 32, 5–40.

Htun, Mala and Juan Pablo Ossa

2013 "Political inclusion of marginalized groups: indigenous reservations and gender parity in Bolivia." *Politics, Groups, and Identities*, no. 1, 4–25.

Htun, Mala and Laurel Weldon

2010 "When do governments promote women's rights? A framework for the comparative analysis of sex equality policy." *Perspectives on Politics* 8 (1): 207–214.

IPEA (Instituto de Pesquisa Econômica Aplicada)

2013 "Marcha das Margaridas: perfil socioeconômico e condições de vida das mulheres trabalhadoras do campo e da floresta." http://transformatoriomargaridas.org.br/sistema/wp-content/uploads/2015/02/pesquisa-ipea-marcha-das-margaridas.pdf.

IPU (Inter-Parliamentary Union)

2006 "Women in national parliaments: situation on 31 December 2006." http://archive.ipu.org/wmn-e/arc/classif311206.htm.

2011 "Women in national parliaments: situation on 31 December 2011." http://archive.ipu.org/wmn-e/arc/classif311211.htm.

Kantola, Johanna

2006 *Feminists Theorize the State*. New York: Palgrave Macmillan.

Lovenduski, Joni (ed.).

2005 *State Feminism and Political Representation*. New York: Cambridge University Press.

Matos, Marlise

2010 "Movimento e teoria feminista: é possível reconstruir a teoria feminista a partir do Sul global?" *Revista de Sociologia e Política* 18 (36): 67–92.

Matos, Marlise and Clarisse Paradis

2013 "Los feminismos latinoamericanos y su compleja relación con el Estado: debates actuales." *Íconos* 45: 91–107.

2014 "Desafios à despatriarcalização do Estado brasileiro." *Cadernos Pagu,* no. 43, 57–118.

Mayol Miranda, Alberto and Carla Azócar Rosenkranz

2011 "Politización del malestar, movilización social y transformación ideológica: el caso 'Chile 2011.'" *Polis* 10 (30): 163–184.

Mazur, Amy

2002 *Theorizing Feminist Policy.* New York: Oxford University Press.

McAdam, Doug, Sidney Tarrow, and Charles Tilly

2004 *Dynamics of Contention.* Cambridge: Cambridge University Press.

Mella Polanco, Marcelo and Camila Berrios Silva

2013 "Gobernabilidad, democratización y conflictividad social en Chile: escenarios posibles para un nuevo equilibrio." *Polis* 12 (35): 429–458.

Montaño, Sonia

2003 "As políticas públicas de gênero, um modelo para armar: o caso do Brasil," pp. 7–22 in Sonia Montaño, Jacqueline Pitanguy, and Thereza Lobo (eds.), *As políticas públicas de gênero, um modelo para armar: O caso do Brasil.* Serie Mujer y Desarollo CEPAL, no. 45. Santiago: CEPAL.

Mussi, Daniela and Débora Zanini

2020 "#Eles não! O confronto eleitoral feminino contra Trump e Bolsonaro," pp. 143–166 in Flávia Biroli, Luciana Tatagiba, Carla Almeida, Cristina Buarque de Hollanda, and Vanessa Elias de Oliveira (eds.), *Mulheres, poder e ciência política: Debates e trajetórias.* Campinas: Editora Unicamp.

Paradis, Clarisse Goulart

2013 "Entre o Estado patriarcal e o feminismo estatal: o caso dos mecanismos institucionais de mulheres na América Latina." Master's thesis, Universidade Federal de Minas Gerais.

Paradis, Clarisse Goulart and Carla Beatriz Rosário Dos Santos

2021 "Contrastes en el campo feminista y la crisis del ciclo progresista en América Latina: una comparación entre Bolivia, Brasil y Chile." *Revista Tejedoras* 2 (2): 135–151.

Paredes, Julieta

2012 "La opresión que se recicla," pp. 196–210 in Coordinadora de la Mujer (ed.), *Mujeres en diálogo: Avanzando hacia la despatriarcalización en Bolivia.* La Paz: Coordinadora de la Mujer.

Rovetto, Florencia Laura

2015 "Violencia contra las mujeres: comunicación visual y acción política en 'Ni Una Menos' y 'Vivas Nos Queremos.'" *Contratexto,* no. 24, 14–34.

Salinas, Lucia

2015 "Transición democrática: como fueron los primeros gabinetes, de Néstor Kirchner a Macri." https://www.clarin.com/politica/primeros-Gabinetes-Nestor -Kirchner-Macri_0BJ7lX6yYDQg.html.

Sardenberg, Cecilia and Ana Alice Alcântara Costa

2010 "Contemporary feminisms in Brazil: achievements, shortcomings, and challenges," pp. 255–284 in Amrita Basu (ed.), *Women's Movements in a Global Era: The Power of Local Feminisms*. Boulder: Westview Press.

Silva, Eduardo Moreira da
2013 "As ressignificações da representação e da legitimidade política." Ph.D. diss., Universidade Federal de Minas Gerais.

Sutton, Barbara and Elizabeth Borland
2019 "Abortion and human rights for women in Argentina." *Frontiers: A Journal of Women Studies* 40 (2): 27–61.

Tarrow, Sidney
1998 *Power in Movement: Social Movements and Contentious Politics*. New York: Cambridge University Press.

Tanscheit, Talita São Thiago
2021 "Das ruas à Constituinte: a reinvenção da ação coletiva no Chile." Jacobin Brasil, June 18. https://jacobin.com.br/2021/06/das-ruas-a-constituinte-a-reinvencao-da-acao-coletiva-no-chile/.

Tatagiba, Luciana
2014 "1984, 1992 e 2013: sobre ciclos de protestos e democracia no Brasil." *Política & Sociedade* 13 (28): 35–62.

Tilly, Charles
2006 *Regimes and Repertoires*. Chicago: University of Chicago Press.

Titelman, Noam
2020 "La derecha chilena en su laberinto: Nueva Sociedad." *Nueva Sociedad,* no. 289. https://nuso.org/articulo/derecha-chilena-en-su-laberinto/.

Tobar, Marcela
2009 "Feminist politics in contemporary Chile: from democratic transition to Bachelet," pp. 21–44 in Jane Jaquette (ed.), *Feminist Agendas and Democracy in Latin America*. Durham, NC, and London: Duke University Press.

Uriona, Katia
2010 "Desafíos de la despatriarcalización en el proceso político boliviano." *Tinkazos,* no. 28, 33–49.

Valerian, Devrim
2013 "Street protests and class power: reflection on current events in Turkey, Egypt, and Brazil and aftermath of the Arab Spring." https://libcom.org/library/street-protests-class-power.

Vaz, Alexander Cambraia Nascimento
2014 "Capacidades estatais para o desenvolvimento: entre a burocratização e a política como elementos de ação do Estado." Ph.D. diss., Universidade Federal de Minas Gerais.

Waylen, Georgina
2016 "Gendering politics, institutions, and the executive: Bachelet in context," pp. 13–38 in Georgina Waylen (ed.), *Gender, Institutions, and Change in Bachelet's Chile*. New York: Palgrave Macmillan.

Ybarnegaray Ortiz, Jenny

2012 "Feminismo y descolonización: notas para el debate." *Nueva Sociedad*, no. 234, 159–171.

Zilla, Claudia and Madeleyne Aguilar Andrade

2020 "Bolivia after the 2020 general elections: despite the return to power of the MAS, a new political era could be about to begin." *SWP Comment* no. 55, November. https://www.swp-berlin.org/10.18449/2020C55/

Chapter 5

Critical Collaboration, Self-Management, and Cooperative Economics

Convergence and Divergence in Feminist Movement Pathways in El Salvador and Nicaragua

Daniel P. Burridge

As the Latin American Pink Tide ebbs and the region's lefts continue to be reinvented (Motta, 2013), many scholars are debating how, why, and to what extent leftist governments in Latin America have converged with social movements in the pursuit of emancipatory objectives and how movements and governments have diverged in these efforts. In this chapter I address this debate through the lens of the understudied cases of El Salvador and Nicaragua. I draw on my extensive ethnographic research in the two countries to show that feminist movements have taken a variety of interactional pathways in relation to their allegedly allied governments both across countries and even within the same country. Additionally, I highlight practical and theoretical insights specific to the Salvadoran and Nicaraguan cases that contribute to our knowledge of the wave of experiments in democratic innovation and redistributive justice that has characterized the Latin American region in the past 20 years.

Scholars have frequently interrogated the radical and social democratic leftist governments of the Pink Tide (Ellner, 2014) and the social movements that brought these governments to state power and constituted their social bases (Silva, 2009; Stahler-Sholk, Vanden, and Kuecker, 2008). Fewer studies have foregrounded the *interactions* between leftist social movements and left-controlled state institutions. Some studies frame these interactions in terms of dichotomies such as confrontation vs. co-optation (Prevost, Oliva Campos, and Vanden, 2012). While such a binary may superficially apply in some countries—such as Nicaragua and Ecuador—where governments have provided movements with little space to maneuver (Becker, 2013; Zaremberg, 2012), most movement-state dynamics in the region play out in the broad "gray zones" (Auyero, 2007) between these heuristic poles.

As George Ciccarriello-Maher (2013) demonstrates in the case of Venezuela, for instance, popular movements harnessed their explosive constituent power from below to force the Chávez government to radicalize an initially reformist project and reconstitute state power. In similar fashion, Evo Morales's Movimiento al Socialismo (Movement toward Socialism—MAS) in Bolivia grew out of the popular rebellions that toppled neoliberal governments in the 2000s to then collaborate with diverse movements in implementing new forms of plurinational citizenship and communal democracy (Cameron, Hershberg, and Sharpe, 2012). However, in both Venezuela and Bolivia, state attempts to institutionalize the vehicles of popular power led to setbacks in revolutionary goals and reductions in movements' strategic power vis-à-vis state institutions (Fernandes, 2010; Oikonomakis and Espinoza, 2014).

Given the difficulties of transcending such verticalist political logics and the perceived failures of revolutionary processes in the twentieth century, many movements now pursue greater independence from established political actors, though this need not always mean disengagement from formal political institutions. Rather, some movements increasingly work "within and against the state" to transform the bureaucratic and authoritarian tendencies of the state itself (Ciccariello-Maher, 2013). Other movements maintain their own agendas and autonomous spaces while engaging with the state tactically and strategically through "cautious negotiations" that further movement demands while avoiding co-optation (Conway, 2013; Stahler-Sholk, Vanden, and Becker, 2014).

Feminist movements in Latin America have been particularly adept at negotiating their objectives with Pink Tide governments and have thus contributed to "deepening democracy" through the reshaping of state institutions and societal norms regarding gender and sexuality (Horton, 2015). Though uneven, this progress increasingly occurs as a result of feminist movements' combining "autonomous" and "institutional" strategies to retain their collective self-determination in relations with parties and state institutions while simultaneously building women's individual and collective autonomy in society (Horton, 2015). Even when such negotiations have proved impossible, feminist movements have creatively pursued their goals in whatever ways were available to them, including through contentious street protests or through more subtle initiatives to create cultural change around gender relations from the bottom up. In this paper, I explore three cases—one in El Salvador and two in Nicaragua—of interactions between feminist movements and leftist governments that have deepened democracy in different ways by either empowering citizens in relation to government, restructuring public administrative apparatuses, or both (Goldfrank, 2011).

   In the first half of the chapter, I analyze an instance of what I call feminist cogovernance in El Salvador, in which feminist movements from the semi-urban territory of Suchitoto have collaborated with state institutions administered by the leftist Frente Farabundo Martí para la Liberación Nacional (Farabundo Martí Front for National Liberation—FMLN) in order to cogovern or share sociopolitical power in gender politics. Referred to as "critical collaboration" by the feminists themselves, this strategy entails movement organizations' working alongside government bodies in the formulation, implementation, and oversight of public policies addressing violence against women, the defense of women's rights, and gender equality in community development. When combined with intensive grassroots organizing among women, feminist organizations' critical collaboration with state and partisan institutions remakes certain state institutions into more flexible, responsive systems of social management.

   In the second half of the chapter, I analyze two cases of territorialized feminist movements in Nicaragua, both of which diverge sharply from the Salvadoran case study. First, I analyze Mujeral en Acción in the town of León, a case of feminist self-management of cases of sexual violence and defense of women's rights, given the Sandinista government's hostility toward feminist frames of reproductive justice. I then examine Nuevo Amanecer, a women's cooperative in the rural mountainous Miraflor region of Estelí, where women have abandoned public work on sexual and reproductive rights altogether in order to privilege interactions with Sandinista state institutions that provide them technical and financial resources to pursue their cooperative economic initiatives.

THE TRAJECTORY, STRATEGIES, AND DILEMMAS
OF SUCHITOTO'S FEMINIST MOVEMENT

During the country's civil war of 1980–1992, all five of the guerrilla factions that made up the FMLN laid claim to military strongholds in the mountains surrounding Suchitoto, thus making it an ideal site for understanding localized expressions—historically and contemporarily—of leftist struggles to transform Salvadoran society. Importantly, in contrast to other revolutionary movements in Latin America, a vanguardist FMLN emerged not as a preestab-lished structure that sought to recruit adherents but in response to the strategic goals of diverse popular movements and guerrilla groups that sought to maxi-mize their attempts to overthrow a repressive regime (Montgomery, 1995).

The FMLN's internal diversity and grassroots power sharing in the Suchitoto area during the war led to a strong capacity for negotiation and a tolerance for ideological pluralism afterward. In the postwar period, four feminist organizations became consolidated. These organizations operate in the context of a social movement community (Staggenborg, 1998) in which they often work in coalition and are sustained by the overlapping networks, relationships, and loyalties that make up the local feminist movement. The feminist social movement community of Suchitoto is one of the most pow-erful civil society sectors in the municipality. According to various actors within and outside it, its organizations even assume functions of governance, particularly in the areas of violence against women and local development. Activists from other local social movement organizations (such as peasant and environmental groups) allege that it is feminist organizations' financial support for the municipal government that enables their disproportionate influence over both formal and informal governance processes, while many of the women participants attribute their power to their movement's capac-ity for both electoral and contentious mobilization. Critical collaboration as feminist cogovernance in Suchitoto, both as a social movement strategy and as a movement-state relation, derives from three conditions: (1) the local state's relative weakness and the movement's concomitant ability to leverage funding (through international aid chains) to buttress the state's capacities, (2) the grassroots strength and personal/economic autonomy of women in the area, and (3) the organizational and ideological autonomy of feminist orga-nizations, which mediates grassroots power and financial/technical leverage.

THE EMERGENCE AND CONTOURS OF A POPULAR FEMINIST SOCIAL MOVEMENT COMMUNITY

Despite its basis in diverse popular movements and organizations, the FMLN consistently relegated women's issues to the realm of "special interests" dur-ing the war years, citing the need to unify around the more urgent socioeco-nomic goals of their cause and to the political-military demands of their daily struggle against the Salvadoran military regime (Viterna, 2013). Thus, when the Peace Accords were signed in 1992 and the FMLN became a formal polit-ical party, pent-up feminist demand that had simmered within the FMLN's political-military organizations for a decade—nourished by the transnational feminist discourses of that moment (Horton, 2015)—burst forth. Numerous women commanders broke away from the party's androcentric and internally authoritarian political culture to form their own organizations for foregrounding women's rights, needs, and interests (Viterna, 2013; Navas, 2012).

In Suchitoto, the first women's organization to be founded, the Concertación de Mujeres (Coalition of Women—La Concerta), initiated organization and awareness raising that led to the emergence of additional organizations, among them the Asociación para el Desarrollo de las Mujeres (Women's Development Association—APDM) and the Asociación de Parteras Rosa Andrades (Rosa Andrades Midwives' Association—Las Parteras), which provided services in midwifery and sexual and reproductive health. These organizations were committed to working for the collective empowerment of women, and in Suchitoto this meant forging critical collaboration—an explicit focus on autonomous interactions between their organizations and government institutions (Herrera et al., 2008). Indeed, the struggles of women and their incipient organizations were no longer "subordinated to the military-political struggle of the FMLN," according to Morena Herrera, a former upper-level commander in the FMLN, a native and resident of Suchitoto, and a founder of the Colectiva Feminista para el Desarrollo Local (Feminist Collective for Local Development—La Colectiva), which has operated out of Suchitoto since the mid-2000s. Morena describes this historical moment as one in which women's and feminist organizations "had their own agendas and didn't ask permission of anyone."

Outside Suchitoto, many feminist and women's organizations remained within the FMLN's formal orbit (Navas, 2012), as did most movements in other social sectors (campesino, unionist, student, and environmentalist). In this sense, the FMLN can be considered a "movement-party" in which only semantic or strategic distinctions differentiate movement and party organizations and many individuals practice *doble militancia* (active membership) in both the party and allied social movement organizations. Paul Almeida (2014) has called this dynamic "social movement partyism" in the Central American context to suggest a parity in power between movement and party, though he acknowledges that the FMLN began focusing on electoral concerns at the expense of grassroots movement building as it became consolidated as a political party. This consolidation exacerbated the already stark disparities in political power and socioeconomic status between the commanders-turned-party-leaders of the FMLN and its popular base (Sprenkels, 2018). Thus, while the FMLN retained a discursive focus on popular empowerment, collaborated with aligned movements in resistance to neoliberal economic policies, and made significant electoral gains through the 1990s and 2000s (Almeida, 2014), internal hierarchies persisted, and popular movements were increasingly subordinated to the party.

Nevertheless, for El Salvador's first free and fair elections in 1994, the FMLN was the clear choice for all sectors of the left—"old" and "new" currents alike—including feminists in Suchitoto who had diverged organizationally from the FMLN political structure but were still undergirded by socialist ideologies of collective liberation nurtured within the FMLN. From the FMLN's initial municipal victory in Suchitoto, women of the feminist social movement community endeavored to "support the good" that the local FMLN government did and "critique what was bad" in order to prioritize their own movement objectives. Morena and the women of the Concerta were at the very first negotiating tables in the Suchitoto municipal council with the specific goal of ensuring adequate representation for women in that space.

By the late 1990s, critical collaboration as a strategy of the local feminist movement had yielded significant fruits. A fifty-fifty quota for men and women on the council was municipal code, and informally the women's organizations began naming one specific representative to the council. The year 2000 saw the approval of a municipal gender equity policy in Suchitoto, the first of its kind in the country. This policy mandated strict protocols for cases of violence against women and gender-equitable hiring practices internal to the municipality (Herrera et al., 2008).

The establishment of the Colectiva further consolidated the feminist social movement community. At a discursive level, it provided it with an explicit— if controversial—feminist frame for much of its work, the three original organizations having operated with the objectives of "holistic" care for women and "defense of women's rights." Also, while the other three organizations were exclusively embedded in the *local* grassroots communities of Suchitoto, the Colectiva began extending the model of critical-collaboration-based local development to municipalities across the country. It also led the formation of national platforms such as the Agrupación Ciudadana por la Despenalización del Aborto (Citizens' Group for the Decriminalization of Abortion—La Agrupación), a broad coalition of organizations that seeks to legalize abortion under four minimal conditions—when the pregnancy endangers the mother's life, when the fetus has no chance of survival outside the uterus, and in cases of sexual violence or trafficking.

In broad strokes, the coordination across the four organizations in the Suchitoto social movement community and the grassroots organizing and cooperative economic activity of ordinary women are best understood as undergirded by an ethos of popular feminism, a commitment by women of the popular sectors to activism to combat gendered hierarchies and violence regardless of ideological differences (given that not all women consider themselves "feminists") (Lebon, 2014). Within Suchitoto, the feminist social movement community works to promote the individual and collective autonomy of women in both sexual-reproductive and economic terms. A leading member of the Concerta, Eva Martínez, describes her organization's territorial work as focused on "empowering women, so that they discover the leader that they have within them, and a vision for a future in which society is more just." The Concerta's provision of direct services and opportunities for economic empowerment—such as micro-credit banks and cooperatives—is accompanied by informal or popular education (*formación*) that enables women to "understand their rights so that they can defend them . . . and *exercise* them" (interview, Suchitoto, July 20, 2016). Other activist women agreed that the Concerta and other organizations have had a transformative effect on culture and socialization in the territory, empowering women to denounce abuse and be more economically autonomous both individually vis-à-vis male partners and collectively with other women. Improvements in gender equity in the social fabric of the communities of Suchitoto are palpable even among women such as Ofelia, who have never attended an activity sponsored by a women's or feminist organization and "dislike the term 'feminism'" but still recognize that the women's and feminist organizations' work in the communities has contributed to the reduction of violence against women and "improvements in sharing household work between men and women" (interview, El Barrillo, March 13, 2018).

THE "SCALING UP" OF CRITICAL COLLABORATION

Localized critical collaboration preceded FMLN presidential administrations, but feminist movement leaders "took it national" in 2009 when the FMLN won presidential elections through its alliance with the journalist Mauricio Funes. The FMLN's basis in popular organizing and its commitment to social transformations combined with Funes's novelty as a critical political outsider to present social movements on the left with unprecedented openings to push their agendas. Women's and feminist movements were among the most aggressive in harnessing these opportunities, forming a coalition—with prominent participation from Suchitoto leaders—to negotiate their previously existing feminist agendas with officials in national-level state institutions. These negotiations led to concrete feminist gains, in institutional terms, in two areas.

The first area—most directly the result of critical collaboration—entailed the formulation, approval, and implementation of multiple national-level policies to promote gender equity: the Special Law for a Life Free from Violence for Women, which drew on elements of Suchitoto's municipal laws regarding gender equity and violence against women, and the Law of Equality, Equity, and Eradication of Discrimination against Women, which prohibits sex- and gender-based discrimination in all public and private institutions. Finally, a new article of the Law of Political Parties was passed in 2013 to stipulate that women make up 30 percent of the candidates for popular election. Second, and somewhat controversially, both the Funes government (2009–2014) and the subsequent, entirely FMLN government, led by the former guerrilla commander Salvador Sánchez Cerén (2014–2019), incorporated numerous feminist activists into leadership and decision-making positions in state institutions. The FMLN also transformed the Instituto Salvadoreño para el Desarrollo de la Mujer (Salvadoran Institute for Women's Development— ISDEMU) from a marginalized, defunded shell to a dynamic state institution staffed by feminists from movement organizations who implemented new policies regarding gender equity—including *within* state agencies—and established substantive programs to empower women in economic, legal, reproductive, and psychological terms.

While critical collaboration by feminists brought important policy advances on some issues, it was unable to sway the FMLN leadership with regard to more controversial feminist demands such as the abortion rights campaign led by the Agrupación and the Colectiva. Still, in contrast to those feminist groups whose leaders were absorbed into government ranks as movement "contributions" in support of the FMLN's state-based project, the feminist organizations committed to critical collaboration retained their historical leaders. These leaders led the process of "scaling up" (Tarrow, 2011) of critical collaboration in interactions with national-level state institutions to further their emancipatory agendas regardless of government directives. To do so, they drew on practices institutionalized in municipalities like Suchitoto.

CRITICAL COLLABORATION WITH STATE INSTITUTIONS AS LOCAL MOVEMENT STRATEGY

One of the main ways in which feminist organizations transform the state is through legislation with regard to violence against women (Ferree, 2012), but ensuring its implementation, enforcement, and oversight remains an obstacle (Horton, 2015). The feminist social movement community in Suchitoto has focused on and excelled in these areas, demonstrating its ability to cogovern gender politics with state institutions. Feminist activists themselves provide training to state officials (at both municipal and national levels) in non-revictimizing methods of attention to victims of violence against women. This training ensures that police officers, judges, health care personnel, and teachers comply with the new requirements pursuant to gender equity. Activists of Suchitoto's feminist social movement community have also worked with local state officials to create and maintain a municipal Roundtable on the Prevention of Violence against Women in which the four women's organizations, the municipality, the police, the public health agencies, the courts, and the schools cooperate to ensure compliance with the Special Law on Violence against Women. Observations of these meetings and interviews with women who participate reveal that feminist organizations exercise leadership in cogovernance relationship around violence against women in terms of both moral-political authority and access to financial and organizational resources.

Some local government representatives see feminist organizations' leadership in these issues as undercutting state mandates or simply as "unsustainable" because of its alleged overreliance on international cooperation. Feminist activists such as Eva counter that they have every intention of "training state officials to do their jobs properly and forming professionals to assume these strategic positions in the state once they are ready" (interview, Suchitoto, July 20, 2016). Though this has largely not yet occurred, feminist movement leadership in cogovernance around violence against women has resulted in safer, more empowered women and a state-society matrix that is more attuned to gender equity given collaborative relationships with leftists in political power.

Feminists in Suchitoto have extended critical collaboration to other state institutions to ensure that community development occurs in ways that are equitable for women. For instance, a project called Community Water Systems with Gender Equity (with funding obtained by the Colectiva from the Basque Country) was executed according to a critical-collaboration framework through shared work by the Concerta, the Colectiva, and the municipality. It improved the physical infrastructure and the social administration of 15 community-based water systems in the Suchitoto area while ensuring that the administration and distribution of water was managed in gender-equitable ways—another clear example of feminist movements and state institutions' cogoverning vital spheres of social life (Burridge, 2021).

There are two valid ways to explain the ability of the women's social movement community to accumulate and maintain power and influence with both local and national state institutions. The first follows its public discourse in claiming that its local success—in terms of women's formal political representation, gender-sensitive policies, and cultural change on gender issues—derives from its embeddedness in women's organizations. These ties enable it to mobilize large numbers of people for contentious or electoral purposes, determining the fortunes of parties and maintaining independence in interactions with parties and state institutions.

The second explanation is simply that the feminist social movement community's ability to engage in critical collaboration with state institutions derives from its ability to provide financial support to state institutions in the context of critical collaboration. This claim was made most fervently by members of historical peasant organizations in the Suchitoto territory, who attributed the influence of the feminist social movement community on the municipality to the Colectiva's sharing of project funds with the government as a partner and joint executor. For activists outside the feminist social movement community such as Javier, a longtime militant of the Asociación de Desarrollo Municipal PROGRESO (PROGRESO Municipal Development Association), a grassroots peasant organization, such financial arrangements constitute a tool for bending the municipal government to the movement community's will in ways that marginalize other organizations and movement sectors (interview, Suchitoto, March 14, 2018). It makes perfect sense that these economic incentives would guide the municipal government's close relationship with the feminist social movement community. By providing financial and legitimation opportunities to state institutions, feminist organizations ensure the success of their critical-collaboration strategy across various issues.

NICARAGUAN CASES: FEMINIST SELF-MANAGEMENT VS. STATE SUPPORT FOR WOMEN'S COOPERATIVES

One case of women's or feminist activism in Nicaragua is an instance of feminist self-management, in which a relatively small collective of feminist activists in the historic colonial city of León attempt to protect women's sexual and reproductive rights through direct community-based support for women victims of violence in their communities. Another is a women's cooperative in the remote rural community of Sontule, Estelí, which has focused on women's economic empowerment by seeking out financial and technical support from Sandinista state institutions. These two cases reveal the difficulties and the opportunities of operating in the Nicaragua of Daniel Ortega and Rosario Murillo.

Empirical Feminism and Self-Management: Mujeral en Acción

The triumph of the Sandinista Revolution on July 19, 1979, showed that spontaneous urban insurrection could combine with organized guerrilla warfare not simply to bring down a corrupt and unpopular authoritarian regime but also to usher in a revolutionary government that could prioritize popular education, free health care, the formation of rural cooperatives, democratic governance, and a mixed economy in the face of a systematic and violent U.S. campaign for social and economic destabilization. The commitment of the Sandinista government led by Daniel Ortega to democracy and popular participation through the 1980s eventually led to its relinquishing of power in 1990 to the Liberal Violeta Chamorro, who led a coalition of opposition forces to begin implementation of a neoliberal restructuring of Nicaraguan society and economy (Robinson, 2003). In retrospect it appears that, as a result of this defeat, Ortega began prioritizing the pursuit of power over democratic-socialist ideals. By the end of the 1990s he had brokered a power-sharing deal with Arnoldo Alemán, the main Liberal strongman and former president, to put independent state institutions under partisan control in order to shield the two of them from prosecution (Aleman on corruption charges connected with embezzlement of international donations after Hurricane Mitch in 2001 and Ortega on charges of sexual abuse of his step-daughter) (Close, 2016; Walker and Wade, 2016). Upon winning the elections of 2006, the Ortega-led Sandinistas returned to state power and began bringing various state institutions and societal actors under partisan control (Close, 2016). This process led to a tumultuous relationship with independent social movements (Zaremberg, 2012), particularly the environmental movement (which crystallized around resistance to the Interoceanic Canal) and the feminist movement. The issue of sexual abuse and violence served as the original detonator and continuing wedge between the Nicaraguan feminist movement and the Sandinista government.

In the wake of the Sandinistas' electoral defeat in 1990, many women leaders had left the official Sandinista party ranks to found their own women's organizations in order to work on issues such as reproductive justice, but it was not until 1998, when Daniel Ortega's stepdaughter, Zoilamérica Narváez Murillo, accused him of sexual abuse and rape, that this rift became irreconcilable. This national scandal saw women's and feminist organizations taking Zoilamérica's side while loyal Sandinistas, including the victim's mother, Vice President Rosario Murillo, accused her of being a mentally unstable seductress. To this day, women's leaders criticize the government for covering up instances of violence against women and furthering a vacuous "traditional-religious" sense of gender equality based on women's role in the family, legislative quotas for women, and the growing influence of Murillo herself in the government and country. For its part, the Sandinista government alleges that feminism is a foreign ideology that disrupts families and that feminist organizations "prey on the people's poverty" in an effort to unseat a revolutionary government.

Within these "mainstream" feminist movements in Nicaragua, then, there are two variants: organizations that are interested in national-level work centered in Managua and organizations and activists engaged in more local and territorialized work in their respective municipalities. The Mujeral en Acción collective in León is an organization of this latter type. In many ways León is similar to Suchitoto; both were strongholds of revolutionary forces during the

1980s, and both are vibrant cultural and tourism hubs in contemporary times. But while Suchitoto has four strong feminist and women's organizations with considerable international financing and local grassroots bases, León has only Mujeral, which is not a traditional or legal social movement organization at all. Rather, it is an informal collective, a flexible and horizontal group whose actions are self-financed by its members (some of whom run businesses in the city). It accompanies women who have been victims in cases of sexual violence (perpetrated by both domestic partners and formal health care providers), and it privileges interventions in the sociocultural fabric of León through workshops and presentations in the city and territory and on social media. Relations between Mujeral and the municipal government of León also parallel national dynamics; a ruinous falling-out between the Sandinista municipal government of León and Mujeral was precipitated by impunity around a case of sexual violence perpetrated by a high-level administrator at the León headquarters of the Universidad Nacional Autónoma de Nicaragua against a female student.

It would be simplistic, however, to transpose global and national-level flows of ideas around feminism and women's rights to the local scene. For instance, when I questioned, Mujeral activist Silvia about government declarations that women like herself were deluded by foreign conceptions of gender, she responded that she considered herself to have come to feminism "empirically" as a result of the gendered abuses she had experienced and observed in her own life. She explained that the fact that she has borrowed some of the theories she uses to understand those abuses from other countries does not change the content of the gendered violence and injustice in Nicaragua or the need to struggle for women's rights and gender equality (interview, León, November 12, 2017).

At a philosophical level, Mujeral is explicitly based on ideas of self-management (or autonomy) with regard to its work on violence against women, in which it draws on local networks of neighbors, friends, and progressive entrepreneurs—as opposed to local or state agencies—to shelter survivors of sexual violence and to finance its work to raise awareness among youth and adults. While such a strategy may pertain to a "new social movement" as described in this volume, Mujeral's autonomy in relation to state institutions is not so much a strategic choice influenced by outside thinkers or funders as a necessity for operation, given the government's rejection of feminist claims and persecution of feminist activists and organizations. Feminists working with Mujeral acknowledge how difficult it is to work for feminist change without the support of the government but seem to view their independence as a badge of honor. One of the founders, Janet, said, "We don't want judicial personhood. .. . . . We don't want to become an NGO [nongovernmental organization]. With self-management and volunteerism and with what people want to contribute, we will do as much as we can" (interview, León, October 29, 2017).

Women's Cooperative Economics: Nuevo Amanecer

The Nicaraguan department of Estelí is characterized by rugged mountainous terrain, sparsely populated rural communities, much agricultural activity (primarily coffee, potatoes, and cabbage because of its high altitudes and cooler temperatures), and strong affiliation with the FSLN. It was a Sandinista bastion during the Revolution of the 1980s and was consolidated as such through the creation of a dense network of agricultural cooperatives and cooperative-style social structures that would be the bedrock of a new socialist society. As a result, this area was also a primary target of Contra attacks, which routinely burned cooperative buildings and kidnapped, raped, and killed cooperative leaders and their family members (Walker, 1987).

Despite this adverse history, cooperativism survived through the neoliberalization of the Nicaraguan economy and society during the 1990s, faring particularly well in rural areas far from centers of capitalist development. Sontule is one of the best-organized communities in the Miraflor, a "protected area" in northeastern Estelí. During three month-long visits in 2015–2017, I researched its three cooperatives: one male-dominated and coffee-focused, created by Sandinista operatives sent from Managua in the early 1980s, another, also male-dominated, that had split from the first in a dispute over leadership and decision making, and a third entirely made up of women who had seen the benefits of cooperativism and wanted to form a cooperative of their own. Beginning in the early 1990s these women formed Nuevo Amanecer (New Dawn), but because (in contrast to the men) they had no land they focused on the affective and associative aspects of their cooperative (leadership training, awareness raising around women's economic and social rights, and opposition to sexual violence). In the 2000s they began economic initiatives around ecotourism and an incipient organic fertilizer project.

Cooperatives in Estelí had very little interaction with state institutions in the postrevolutionary period. Relationships with state institutions have begun only recently, primarily through a newly formed state institution, the Ministerio de Economía Familiar, Comunitaria, Cooperativa y Asociativa (Ministry of the Family, Communitarian, Cooperative and Associative Economy—MEFCCA), which was inaugurated in 2012 to support and channel (or, in more cynical terms, co-opt) the economic capacities of cooperatives it considers part of the popular economy.

In 2016 Nuevo Amanecer began navigating the acquisition of a lucrative (US$10,000) MEFCCA project that they hoped would enhance their incipient attempts to produce and market organic fertilizer to be sold in neighboring communities. While the women had already decided that they wanted to produce organic fertilizer, their "business plan" had been largely provided to them by city-based MEFCCA technicians through a series of visits to Sontule and workshops that the women attended in Estelí (a couple of which I was able to observe). These workshops were characterized by a palpable disparity in power between the women of Sontule and the well-educated and well-dressed technicians of the MEFCCA who were sent there to teach them about budgeting, finances, and market analysis. The women tried to say whatever was appropriate to secure the funding for their project. They knew that they could not let the opportunity pass them by.

In subsequent conversations, the women expressed considerable hesitancy and pessimism regarding their chances of executing their project but assumed that they would receive assistance throughout the process from the MEFCCA technicians. Indeed, through my conversations with the technicians, I learned that this was also their aim. They planned to "promote" cooperatives such as Nuevo Amanecer: to fund them, train their members in budgeting and financial administration, ensure that they got their legal papers in order, connect them to services in local municipalities, and eventually integrate them into regional and (trans-)national economic networks. The support of the MEFCCA was significant because in the past Nuevo Amanecer had been forced to seek outside funding from "international cooperation." With this aim, they had joined the second-tier cooperative UCA Miraflor—essentially a nonprofit that connected small-scale producers to international actors—in 1995 in order to be able to conduct projects with foreign donors. While the Sandinista government did not disband or persecute these cooperatives involved in international commerce (as it had done with various other international nongovernmental organizations), with the founding of the MEFCCA state institutions would seek to be the primary funders, administrators, and patrons of local-level popular economic activity in places like Sontule. Supporting community-based cooperatives would become the terrain of the Sandinista state.

This account depicts the Sandinista government's attempt to break many popular groups' dependence on international players and highlights its co-optation of civil society through political logics that subordinated independent social movements and, in this case, economic initiatives to the party-state (Prevost, Oliva Campos, and Vanden, 2012). At the same time, many of the women themselves and particularly the cooperative's leaders expressed deep gratitude to the Sandinista government for its generous financial support and felt that this was the appropriate way for state institutions to relate to community organizations—stressing that "no other government had ever been worried about supporting women's cooperatives in the countryside."

This cooperative-state relationship could be understood as co-optation or as a redistribution of wealth and power from the state toward society consistent with a process of dual power construction. It is also, however, an example of how a group of women—only a minority of whom identified as feminists at all—gained access to crucial state financial and technical resources from a leftist state to pursue their own objectives. Though the larger Nicaraguan context of state repression and persecution of independent social movement leaders should be condemned, the sorts of economic redistribution described here should not be lightly dismissed, especially in a region and community that had scarcely ever been able to access such significant financial support for a locally led project. That this project was led by women is all the more significant given the government's conservative stance on women's rights. To be sure, the fact that this particular project was able to receive government support indicates that it did not challenge government interests but rather bolstered them and attests to the women's creativity, hard work, and capacity for self-management.

These two Nicaraguan cases show that women in the country are by and large not publicly permitted to advocate for their sexual rights but encouraged to pursue their collective economic rights—a crucial distinction for analysts of the Nicaraguan government's relations with social movements under Sandinista rule. While we see a stark bifurcation of categories of women's rights in Nicaragua under a decidedly closed leftist government, we see how explicitly feminist activism in El Salvador vis-à-vis a more open and less powerful leftist government resulted in women's empowerment in both sexual and economic terms.

COGOVERNANCE AND SELF-MANAGEMENT AS HORIZONS OF STATE-SOCIETY TRANSFORMATION

The three cases in this chapter highlight a number of practical and theoretical insights for the region's scholars and activists as leftist forces learn and reinvent themselves in response to experiences of state power. First, local and national government institutions must be open to the possibility of restructuring public administrative apparatuses along emancipatory lines based on substantial, critical input from social movements. Leftist control of the state is a necessary but not sufficient condition for this, since various leftist governments in the region have proven to be quite opposed to negotiations with independent movements. Second, movements must accrue a high level of power or leverage with regard to the state to achieve their objectives. The feminist social movement community of Suchitoto had merged autonomist and institutionalist currents of activism with its grassroots social bases and diverse forms of leverage to critically collaborate with government officials to slowly transform the "male" state (MacKinnon, 1982) to a more nongendered apparatus, while empowering organized women and feminists to share in practicing more equitable forms of governing gender (Brush, 2003). In other words, movement leverage with ostensibly allied state and partisan actors—whether electoral, contentious, financial, or all three—is crucial to furthering movement agendas.

Third, social movement organizations have the potential for effectively and democratically managing particular social goods/fields on the basis of their local knowledge and sectorial expertise (Bamyeh, 2009) in a variety of situations. Movements' relations with state institutions as they pursue this social management are a crucial variable. Critical collaboration has led to nominally successful cogovernance of gender politics in Suchitoto and suggests a more viable model for promoting gender equity than exclusively state-led initiatives. In León, the state was absent and hostile in the terrain of gender politics, and therefore the local feminist collective practiced total self-management of its own more "autonomous" strategy. In Sontule, cooperatively organized women were able to obtain valuable financial support from the state for their economic projects in part because they avoided contentious issues around reproductive justice altogether. In all cases, women's and feminist movements navigated complicated relationships with leftist governments to pursue their objectives on their own terms, contributing to the incremental but radical remaking of certain elements of the state and society in the long run.

Whether in terms of political independence (see Munck in this volume) or the "autonomy of the organizations of the popular masses" (Poulantzas, 1980), what is clear from the cases presented in this chapter is that social movements from below must be able to self-organize, self-manage, and leverage resources to construct strategic relations with state institutions (themselves a series of social relations), even ostensibly allied ones. Looking ahead to new rounds of struggle, as movements strengthen themselves to construct cogovernance with the leftist state institutions of the present and future, it is more likely that social and political change will be put at the service of truly emancipatory ends.

NOTES

1. This chapter is a revised version of an article that appeared in *Latin American Perspectives* 47 (4): 150–169 (2020).

2. In numerous visits over four years, I did 23 interviews with activists and others in Suchitoto, residents of both the urban center and various rural communities. I have accumulated thousands of hours of lived experience in the area and numerous

observations of women's organizations' activities such as assemblies on women's economic initiatives and meetings of the municipal Roundtable on Violence Against Women.

3. The women's and feminist organizations have also undertaken extensive educational and awareness-raising processes with primary and high school students on themes of self-esteem, respect, and cooperation and sexual and reproductive rights, including issues around adolescent pregnancy.

4. When participants wished that their identifying information be concealed, I provided them with a single-name pseudonyms.

5. Some feminist activists in Suchitoto—and in other more autonomist circles—saw this "departure" of "comrades" from movement organizations as a form of movement-weakening co-optation or even movement "decapitation" by FMLN governments.

6. Feminist leaders were disappointed by the FMLN's withdrawal of support for the abortion rights issues at the end of the 2018 legislative session. They speculate that the FMLN feared further electoral loss if they supported abortions rights too strongly (see http://www.contrapunto.com.sv/sociedad/genero/defensoras-de-derechos-de-la-mujer-no-debimos-confiar-en-el-fmln-/6655).

7. See https://colectivafeminista.org.sv/wp-content/uploads/2020/07/MEMORIA-DE-LABORES-2018-2019.pdf for quantitative and qualitative descriptions of activities aimed at making women safer and more empowered in the Suchitoto area in 2018–2019.

8. The creation of the MEFCCA and its relations with cooperatives was the brainchild of Orlando Núñez, a sociologist who was the architect of various agrarian reforms during the 1980s and produced a study for the Sandinista government in the 2000s demonstrating that 75 percent of the country's employment and 43 percent of its gross domestic product came from economic networks associated with the popular social economy (families, communities, cooperatives, and other sorts of associative economics) and suggesting that the government needed to attempt to harness and expand these activities.

REFERENCES

Almeida, Paul D.
2014 *Mobilizing Democracy: Globalization and Citizen Protest*. Baltimore: Johns Hopkins University Press.
Auyero, Javier
2007 *Routine Politics and Violence in Argentina: The Gray Zone of State Power*. New York: Cambridge University Press.
Bamyeh, Mohammed
2009 *Anarchy as Order: The History and Future of Civic Humanity*. Lanham, MD: Rowman and Littlefield.
Becker, Marc

2013 "The stormy relations between Rafael Correa and social movements in Ecuador." *Latin American Perspectives* 40 (3): 43–62.

Brush, Lisa
2003 *Gender and Governance.* Walnut, CA: Altamira Press.

Cameron, Maxwell A., Eric Hershberg, and Kenneth E. Sharpe
2012 *New Institutions for Participatory Democracy in Latin America: Voice and Consequence.* New York: Palgrave Macmillan.

Ciccariello-Maher, George
2013 *We Created Chavez: A People's History of the Venezuelan Revolution.* Durham, NC: Duke University Press.

Close, David
2016 *Nicaragua: Navigating the Politics of Democracy.* London: Lynne Rienner Publishers.

Conway, Janet
2013 *Edges of Global Justice: The World Social Forum and Its "Others."* New York: Routledge.

Ellner, Steve
2014 *Latin America's Radical Left: Challenges and Complexities of Political Power in the 21st Century.* Lanham, MD: Rowman and Littlefield.

Fernandes, Sujatha
2010 *Who Can Stop the Drums? Urban Social Movements in Chavez's Venezuela.* Durham, NC: Duke University Press.

Ferree, Myra Marx
2012 *Varieties of Feminism: German Gender Politics in Global Perspective.* Stanford, CA: Stanford University Press.

Goldfrank, Benjamin
2011 *Deepening Local Democracy in Latin America: Participation, Decentralization, and the Left.* University Park: Pennsylvania State University Press.

Herrera, Morena Soledad, Blanca Mirna Benavides, Christine Hopkins Damon, and Flora Blandon de Grajeda
2008 *Movimiento de mujeres en El Salvador 1995–2006: Estrategias y miradas desde el feminismo.* San Salvador: Fundación Nacional para el Desarrollo.

Horton, Lynn
2015 "Women's movements in Latin America," pp. 79–87 in Paul Almeida and Allen Cordero Ulate (eds.), *Handbook of Social Movements across Latin America.* New York: Springer.

Lebon, Nathalie
2014 "Brazil: popular feminism and its roots and alliances," pp. 147–165 in Richard Stahler-Sholk, Harry E. Vanden, and Marc Becker (eds.), *Rethinking Latin American Social Movements: Radical Action from Below.* Lanham, MD: Rowman and Littlefield.

MacKinnon, Catherine A.
1982 "Feminism, Marxism, method, and the state: an agenda for theory." *Signs: Journal of Women in Culture and Society* 7 (3): 515–544.

Montgomery, Tommie Sue

1995 *Revolution in El Salvador: From Civil Strife to Civil Peace.* 2d edition. New York: Routledge.

Motta, Sara C.

2013 "Reinventing the lefts in Latin America: critical perspectives from below." *Latin American Perspectives* 40 (4): 5–18.

Navas, María Candelaria

2012 *Feminismo y sufragismo: Visibilizando a las mujeres.* San Salvador: Centro de Estudios de Género, Universidad de El Salvador.

Oikonamakis, Leonidas and Fran Espinoza

2014 "Bolivia: MAS and the movements that brought it to state power," pp. 285–305 in Richard Stahler-Sholk, Harry E. Vanden, and Marc Becker (eds.), *Rethinking Latin American Social Movements: Radical Action from Below.* Lanham, MD: Rowman and Littlefield.

Poulantzas, Nicos.

1980 *State, Power, Socialism.* London: Verso.

Prevost, Gary, Carlos Oliva Campos, and Harry E. Vanden (eds.)

2012 *Social Movements and Leftist Governments in Latin America: Confrontation or Co-optation?* New York: Zed Books.

Robinson, William I.

2003 *Transnational Conflicts: Central America, Social Change, and Globalization.* London: Verso.

Silva, Eduardo

2009 *Challenging Neoliberalism in Latin America.* New York: Cambridge University Press.

Sprenkels, Ralph

2018 *After Insurgency: Revolution and Electoral Politics in El Salvador.* South Bend, IN: Notre Dame University Press.

Staggenborg, Suzanne

1998 "Social movement communities and cycles of protest: the emergence and main-tenance of a local women's movement." *Social Problems* 45 (2): 180–204.

Stahler-Sholk, Richard, Harry E. Vanden, and Glen David Kuecker (eds.)

2008 *Latin American Social Movements in the Twenty-first Century: Resistance, Power, and Democracy.* Lanham, MD: Rowman and Littlefield.

Stahler-Sholk, Richard, Harry E. Vanden, and Marc Becker (eds.)

2014 *Rethinking Latin American Social Movements: Radical Action from Below.* Lanham, MD: Rowman and Littlefield

Tarrow, Sydney G.

2011 *Power in Movement: Social Movements and Contentious Politics.* Cambridge: Cambridge University Press.

Viterna, Jocelyn

2013 *Women in War: The Micro-Processes of Mobilization in El Salvador.* New York: Oxford University Press.

Walker, Thomas W. (ed.)

1987 *Reagan versus the Sandinistas: The Undeclared War on Nicaragua.* Boulder: Westview Press.

Walker, Thomas W. and Christine Wade
2016 *Nicaragua: Emerging from the Shadow of the Eagle*. Boulder: Westview Press.
Zaremberg, Gisela
2012 "'We're either burned or frozen out': society and party systems in Latin American municipal councils (Nicaragua, Venezuela, Mexico, and Brazil)," pp. 21–52 in Maxwell A. Cameron, Eric Hershberg, and Kenneth E. Sharpe (eds.), *New Institutions for Participatory Democracy in Latin America: Voice and Consequence.* New York: Palgrave Macmillan.

PART 2

Social Movements and Progressive Governments in Brazil and Argentina

The governing progressive parties in Brazil and Argentina contrasted sharply with those of Bolivia, Venezuela, and Ecuador in having a strong electoral presence during the two decades prior to reaching power. The Peronist party was by far historically the strongest in Argentina. In Brazil the Partido dos Trabalhadores (Workers' Party—PT) was the most disciplined party, judging from voting patterns in Congress. The Movimento dos Trabalhadores Sem Terra (Landless Workers' Movement—MST) in Brazil and the *piqueteros* in Argentina—the largest social movements in their respective countries—maintained mixed relationships, both contentious and supportive, with their progressive governments. Both countries saw a convergence of social movements and progressive parties (the Peronist party and the PT) in their opposition to neoliberal reforms following the right-wing pushback beginning in 2015.

Gabriel Funari explores the transformation of Brazil's PT from an "agglomeration of social movements" to a ruling party by focusing on its relation to two constituent assemblies, the one in 1987–1988 and President Dilma Rousseff's proposed plebiscite on a new one in response to mass protests in 2013. With its participation in the first, he reports, the party "began to occupy positions within both constituted and constituent power," while Rousseff's abortive initiative marked the point when it could no longer maintain the uneasy consensus that had made it the nation's leading political party. In addition, he points to two dimensions of Brazilian democracy as they relate to the PT: "the consolidation of democratic institutions through popular mobilization" and "the distribution of graft and patronage to ensure governability." The resultant tensions within the PT consisted of confrontations between the party's militant base, partly tied to social movements, and party members who were mostly interested in winning elections by channeling energy through the electoral process.

Leandro Gamallo points to the emergence in the 1990s of diverse social movements that "involved autonomous and novel processes of organization such as citizen neighborhood assemblies" and the unemployed workers known as *piqueteros*. He points out that the 12-year rule of presidents Néstor Kirchner and Cristina Fernández de Kirchner was closely connected to the social movements that had challenged the neoliberal order in previous years. Kirchnerism "fragmented them with regard to their support or opposition to the government" and "altered their tactics and modes of organization." Referring to the movements that were supportive of the Kirchner government, Gamallo argues that "not all participation in the state implies weakness, subordination . . . or co-optation" as some social movement theorists assert. He also points to a "bifurcation" in which "regressive social movements" beginning in 2012 filled in for the weak and divided opposition parties by beginning "to erode support for the government and produce effective oppositional articulations," thus paving the way for the triumph of the conservative presidential candidate Mauricio Macri in 2015. Gamallo suggests that the challenge facing the Pink Tide President Alberto Fernández, who replaced Macri in 2019, and the social movements, some of which hold state positions, is "again how to build a constructive relationship between the two."

Chapter 6

Social Movement Mobilization or Governability

Tracing the PT's Constitutionalist Junctures

Gabriel Funari

Understanding contemporary Brazil inevitably involves contending with the Partido dos Trabalhadores (Workers' Party—PT).[1] Since the party's establishment in 1980, no other political actor has immersed itself so profoundly in both institutionalized rule and social movements in Brazil. Established during the waning days of the military dictatorship, the PT grew in tandem with Brazil's democratization process by becoming the principal node through which the politics of alterity was expressed in the country (Baiocchi, 2004). Its historical progression is intertwined with the formation, consolidation, and ongoing disputes surrounding Brazil's democratic regime.

In order to understand the PT's transformation from an agglomeration of social movements to a national ruling party, it is imperative to grasp the party's fluctuating policies regarding the 1988 constitution. Social scientists have neglected these programmatic disputes in favor of studying the PT's electoral performances (Avritzer, 2016; Hunter, 2010; Keck, 2010), a historical narrative that aptly identifies the ideological sacrifices the PT made to attain power. However, any study of the PT's impact on the Brazilian political system must contend with the different ways that the party has interpreted and sought to influence constitutional arrangements.

With that in mind, this study examines two cases in which the PT directly grappled with the constitution—the party's participation in the 1987–1988 constituent assembly and President Dilma Rousseff's proposal to hold a plebiscite on a new constituent assembly following the mass protests of June 2013. The theoretical framework of constituent and constituted power helps delineate the party's mediation of the demands of its militant base and social movements, on the one hand, and the logic of institutional governability, on the other. Examining the PT in the framework of constituent and constituted power also exposes the party's role in reinforcing the two defining dynamics of Brazilian democracy: the consolidation of democratic institutions through popular mobilization and the distribution of graft and patronage to ensure governability.

The PT's constitutionalist shifts illustrate the ceaseless confrontations between the radical impetus of the party's militant base in part tied to social movements and its insistence on winning political power by abiding by established norms. It is precisely through these programmatic tensions—those of a radically transformative political project continuously molded by ordered imperatives—that the PT's political power became bound to Brazil's constitutional regime.

This tussle between the PT's militant backbone and the party's programmatic imperative to attain institutional power reflects the creative tension between social movements and Pink Tide governments explored throughout this book. A significant portion of the PT's foundational leaders were leaders of social movements. Indeed, the party became a national political force by becoming the partisan hub for labor unions, landless peasants tied to the Movimento dos Trabalhadores Sem Terra (Landless Workers' Movement—MST), and adherents of liberation theology (Keck, 2010). While these disparate social movements allied themselves with the PT, they retained autonomy and critical distance to hold the party accountable to its progressive agenda (Baiocchi, 2004).

As the PT began to win mayoral, gubernatorial, and eventually presidential elections, the party and its allied social movements maintained a dynamic of targeted approximation in specific policy areas. The PT appointed leaders of social movements to influential positions in the state bureaucracy, particularly in agencies tasked with implementing hunger alleviation, land reform, and labor policies (Abers, Serafim, and Tatagiba, 2014). During Lula's first term (2003–2007), 26 percent of senior government positions were filled by union activists tied to the Central Única dos Trabalhadores (Unified Workers' Central—CUT) labor union and other labor organizations, a figure that decreased to 16 percent during Lula's second term (2007–2011) (Abers, Serafim, and Tatagiba, 2014). Frei Betto, a Dominican friar and one of the most prominent exponents of liberation theology in Brazil, led Lula's successful hunger alleviation program. Meanwhile, on the rhetorical front, successive PT governments publicly praised social movements in advancing the party's egalitarian ideals throughout Brazil (Singer, 2016).

At the same time, social movements were unable to influence critical aspects of the PT's governance agenda. Allied social movements failed to restrain the free-market imperatives of the PT federal administrations, with particular criticism of the government's austere fiscal measures during 2003 and 2004 and its subsidies to Brazilian corporations (Singer, 2016). As a result, social movements accused the PT of betraying its democratic socialist ideals throughout the party's 13 years at the helm of the federal government. For the PT, its free-market policies and increasingly close ties to traditionalist and crony-based right-wing parties were seen as pragmatic and necessary concessions to stay in power (Singer, 2016).

The study utilizes an array of primary and secondary sources to outline the PT's policies regarding the 1988 Constitution. Resolutions from party conferences and speeches given by PT delegates during the 1987–1988 constituent assembly were obtained from the Fundação Perseu Abramo, the think tank founded and operated by the PT. The June 2013 protests are examined through news articles that trace the escalation of the street demonstrations and the plebiscite proposal as well as through transcripts obtained from the website of the Presidency of the Republic of Rousseff's speeches in response to the protests.

The constituent assembly in 1987–1988 marked the point at which the PT began to operate within formal institutions at the national level. Despite holding only 3 percent of the assembly's seats, the PT successfully advocated for the inclusion of participatory governance mechanisms in the constitutional text (Keck, 2010). The PT deputies voted against the final constitutional text but agreed to sign the *magna carta* (Ribeiro, 2003). By doing so they acknowledged the party's participation in the deliberative process and signaled their willingness to collaborate with the newly formed democratic institutions. Luiz Inácio Lula da Silva's presidential election in 2002 vindicated the PT's decision to immerse itself in the mechanisms of government. Nonetheless, in taking power within the constitutional arrangement set in place in 1988, the PT increasingly distanced itself from its radical origins. It distributed bribes to pass legislation, allied itself with conservative parties, and committed to a market-oriented economic platform (Avritzer, 2017).

The conflict between constituent and constituted power in Brazil erupted with the massive street protests that broke out throughout the country in June 2013, initiated mainly by the Movimento Passe Livre (Free Fare Movement), which advocated free public transportation (Nobre, 2013). A central critical point could be derived from the diverse complaints formulated by protesters: a complete aversion to the established distribution of political power (Nogueira, 2013). Specifically, protesters voiced their displeasure at the transactional nature of policymaking, in which a fragmented multiparty Congress bargains with the executive branch to attain (often by corrupt means) benefits in exchange for votes. Heeding the protesters, on June 24, 2013, President Rousseff proposed a plebiscite on whether to hold a constituent assembly. Vice President Michel Temer led a coalition to block the proposal (Taylor, 2016). In the face of stringent opposition from its congressional base, the government was forced to backtrack on its constituent proposal by the following day (Nogueira, 2013).

From June 2013 on, the dynamic of critical autonomy and occasional approximation that social movements maintained with the PT government faced decisive setbacks. Rousseff's plebiscite proposal originated in a petition by the CUT labor union and the student organization União Nacional dos Estudantes (UNE) (Silva Júnior and Souza Júnior, 2017). The plebiscite proposal represented a fleeting moment of convergence between the PT and its progressive social movement allies. However, in accepting the advice of her congressional coalition and rejecting the plebiscite proposal, Rousseff prioritized the PT's partisan allies in Congress over its critical support base in social movements. Her plebiscite proposal is therefore crucial to understanding the escalating dispute between constituted power and constituent power, largely underpinned by social movements, that has assailed the Brazilian political system since 2013. Her fleeting proposal to alter the institutional balance of power in Brazil made explicit what had remained under the surface since Lula's election—that the PT continued to be a political actor formed and defined by insurgent constituents intent on exposing the inequalities and injustices of the political system.

The decisive victories won by the far right in Brazil since 2013, the foremost of which was Jair Bolsonaro's election in 2018, were all fueled by elitist, patriarchal, and traditionalist anger at the PT's representative potential (Nicolau, 2020). With the ascendancy of the far right, Brazilian social movements have lost all forms of productive dialogue with the federal government. Instead of following in the PT's footsteps in seeing social movements as important stakeholders and potential partners in policymaking, Bolsonaro and his allies are increasingly concerned with the armed repression and criminalization of social movements as part of their efforts to dismantle the remaining strands of the democratic consensus inaugurated in 1988 (Funari, 2021). In turn, Bolsonaro's criminalization efforts have led the social movements to reactivate their close alliance with the PT, thereby strengthening bonds between the party and its militant base that had withered during the PT's rule.

The consolidation of democratic rule and the PT's political prominence developed in the interplay between reconstituted state power and incipient constituent power. By operating within institutions while maintaining its popular roots, the PT mirrored Brazil's democratization trajectory. The events of 1988 and 2013 exemplify formative moments and critical junctures in Brazil's recent political history—the first for the consolidation of a new mode of governance and the second for the manifestation of the eroded legitimacy of that system of rule.

This study is divided into four sections. The first section details the theoretical framework of constituent and constituted power and its applicability to the PT's historical trajectory. The second and third sections present the two case studies and are followed by concluding remarks.

DELINEATING CONSTITUENT AND CONSTITUTED POWER

The theoretical framework of constituent and constituted power is deployed because the PT's distinctive origin as an agglomeration of marginalized political subjects and disparate social movements offers invaluable glimpses into the determination of all political discourse by the dissonance between rulers and the ruled. In a country marked by a violently imposed and strictly ordered social hierarchy, Brazilian political discourse has always been characterized by a deficit in popular representation (Singer, 2013). Since its inception, the PT has sought to overcome this deficit by propelling factory workers, leaders of peasant movements, and black activists into elected office (Keck, 2010). The party's experience can therefore elucidate how the theoretical concepts of constituent and constituted power manifest themselves in political society.

Lefort (1986) identifies constituent power as a concept emanating from the secularization of European society in the eighteenth century. He argues that modern political regimes are derived from the body politic of monarchism, under which the compact between constituted and constituent power was divinely sanctioned. As democratic revolts abolished divine monarchy, the locus of modern power became an empty place that could never be fully reoccupied. Previously united in the body of the monarch, constituent and constituted power became the two poles that define modern political discourse (Lefort, 1986; Schmitt, 2008). Agamben (1998) notes that under modern forms of political power, constituent and constituted power are intertwined in an unresolved dialectic in which the potentiality of a transformative populace ceaselessly opposes the actuality of established authority.

Constituent power including social movement mobilization is inevitably compelled to grapple with formalized rule. Dussel (2008) acknowledges that it is only through institutions that the mechanisms of governance can take on an organized form. He goes on to claim that constituted power is a "necessary imperfection" because it is both a constricting institutional space and the central reference point for the resolution of political disputes (Dussel, 2008: 45). Schmitt (2008) perceives the constitution as the binding mechanism between constituent and constituted power that makes up the modern state.

Without a divine executive, the modern state is an ephemeral entity that relies on the codified legality of the constitution in order to ground itself in society. Constitutions are therefore living texts that seek to give form to disembodied power (Schmitt, 2008).

Formed by historically marginalized political subjects, the PT has been able to expose the way the Brazilian state perpetuates unequal and violent living conditions through both direct government policy and extrainstitutional privilege. The exclusionary functions of constituted power—the lack of civil liberties and free-market imperatives of dictatorial rule and the extralegal violence perpetrated by agents of the state—helped shape the political subjectivity of the constituents who created the PT. In order to transform the unequal power paradigms of the Brazilian state, diverse constituents that included prominent social movements came together to form the PT. The PT therefore sought to ensure that the new democratic regime would be influenced by the voices of political subjects that had previously been excluded from the political process.

THE PT AND THE 1987–1988 CONSTITUENT ASSEMBLY

During its first seven years of existence, the PT was mainly active outside of political institutions (Branford, 2015). As a radical party that rejected corporate financing and avoided alliances with mainstream political operatives, it struggled to achieve electoral relevance during the democratic transition (Keck, 2010). During the first open elections in 1982 and 1985 that initiated the democratic transition, the PT emphasized class struggle and never disguised its objective of achieving democratic socialism (Keck, 2010). The party performed poorly in both elections, electing eight members of Congress and two mayors in 1982 and only one mayor in 1985 (Branford, 2015).

The PT's distance from formal political power in the 1980s identified its ethos as a radical, novel political experiment (Brandão, 2003). The party assumed an antagonistic position with regard to the controlled democratic transition led by the military, its allied political party Aliança Renovadora Nacional (National Renewal Alliance—ARENA), and the formal opposition Partido do Movimento da Democracia Brasileira (Brazilian Democracy Movement—PMDB) (Brandão, 2003). The ARENA, the PMDB, and the military had been the only legal channels of political expression during the dictatorship and agreed to transfer power to civilian government without any transitional justice for the dictatorship's crimes (Nobre, 2008).

After José Sarney became president in 1985, the PT made persistent demands to make the democratic transition more inclusive. In a resolution published after the PT's national assembly in January 1985, the party demanded the annulment of the National Security Law and all other emergency decrees set up by the dictatorship (PT, 1985). Additionally, it called for the establishment of a constituent assembly to consolidate the democratic transition (PT, 1985). The Sarney government passed a law in November 1985 making the Congress responsible for writing the new constitution (Power, 2000). Critically, it was to be written not by an independent body possibly influenced by the social movements but by the agents of constituted power, which included many of the congresspeople selected during the military dictatorship (Avritzer, 2016). Additionally, the structure of Brazil's electoral regime ensured that the Congress that wrote the constitution would be dominated by conservative representatives from rural areas while the electorate located in urban centers would go underrepresented (Avritzer, 2016).

In June 1986, PT delegates at the party's fourth national assembly debated whether it should field candidates for the legislature that was going to be tasked with writing a new constitution. PT delegates were hostile to the way the PMDB had constricted the democratic transition (PT, 1986). With considerable experience as a union negotiator, Lula persuaded a majority of the delegates to participate in the constituent assembly. At the same time, however, the party issued a resolution affirming its commitment to democratic socialism and continued resistance to Sarney's market-oriented economic policies (PT, 1986).

With its electoral support concentrated in urban centers, the PT elected 16 candidates to Congress, 3 percent of the chamber (Keck, 2010). Despite the difficulties that it faced with an unfair electoral system, the nature of the PT's appeal was evident when Lula was elected to the constituent assembly with the most votes nationwide (Keck, 2010). Voters also elected other prominent PT delegates, including the union leader Djalma Bom, the sociologist Florestan Fernandes, and the former guerrilla fighter José Genoino (Keck, 2010). The constitutive process was fundamentally determined by the PMDB. The party controlled the presidency and all the state governments except Sergipe's (Avritzer, 2016). More important, 303 PMDB delegates were elected to the assembly, making up 54 percent of its members and thereby ensuring the party's absolute majority (Power, 2000). The PMDB's status as the only legal opposition during the dictatorship had enabled the party to build unrivaled electoral alliances on a national scale. It appointed its delegates and partisan allies to head all of the assembly's commissions and ultimately held veto power over all constitutional proposals (Power, 2000).

The assembly's first session took place on February 1, 1987. Under pressure from the PT, the regimental commission that was responsible for determining how the assembly was going to function approved various motions for popular participatory mechanisms. Commission sessions were open to the public, and citizens were able to submit their own amendments if they contained more than 30,000 signatures (Avritzer, 2017). Citizens submitted 122 amendments backed by more than 12 million signatures (Keck, 2010). In an effort to resist the PMDB's supremacy over the deliberative process, the PT became the only party in the assembly to write a full constitutional text. The PT's version of the constitution was written by the prominent jurist Fabio Konder Comparato (Lima, 2013). It sought to limit property rights, granted the state a full monopoly in important areas related to national security, prohibited presidential reelection, maintained the presidentialist form of government, and abolished the Senate (Garcia, 1987).

The PT's constitution was submitted on May 6, 1987, and was immediately rejected (Lima, 2013).

The political culture of Brazil's new democracy was influenced by the confrontation in the assembly between the dominant conservative faction of the PMDB and the left-leaning delegates. Nobre (2013) argues that the constituent assembly gave rise to a new political culture that he termed *peemedebismo*. The term arose from the alliance that the Sarney government and Ulysses Guimarães, the president of the constituent assembly and PMBD leader, had formed with smaller conservative parties. *Peemedebismo* is an explicitly transactional form of legislating that provides the opportunity for political parties to increase their electoral funds by exchanging congressional votes for payouts from the executive branch or appointments to key government ministries and state-owned companies (Nobre, 2013). Following the 1987–1988 constituent assembly, *peemedebismo* became firmly ingrained in the policy-making process and governance predicated on acquiescing to the conservative congressional contingent (Nobre, 2013).

The conservative alliance, which became known as the Centrão, clashed with the progressive wing of the PMDB and the leftist parties in the assembly, including the PT. The progressives in the assembly tried and failed to pass constitutional provisions related to substantial land reform, parliamentarianism, and term limits (Nobre, 2013). Land reform was one of the PT's top demands throughout the assembly, but the party's attempt to authorize the expropriation of unproductive plots was easily defeated by the conservative coalition (PT, 1988b).

With the Centrão's victory over the progressive contingent in the assembly, the final constitutional text was approved on October 5, 1988 (Avritzer, 2016). Despite conservative dominance, there was still consensus among the delegates on deepening democratic frameworks. The constitution made states responsible for the military police, gave municipalities greater authority over tax collection, created a national health service, enhanced the independence of the judiciary and of the Federal Prosecutor's Office, and established participatory councils in the areas of health, urban reform, and social security (Avritzer, 2016; Gargarella, 2013; Nobre, 2008). PT delegates unsuccessfully proposed constitutional provisions to reduce working hours, reform the education system, abolish obligatory military service, and curb the over-representation of rural communities in the electoral system (PT, 1988b). The drawing up of ordinances for participatory councils was the only significant policy platform advocated by the PT to make it into the final text (PT, 1988b). Crucially, the 1988 Constitution reinforced the presidential supremacy put in place by the military dictatorship (Gargarella, 2013; Limongi, 2008). The leading delegates of the constituent assembly were obsessed with the question of governability (Avritzer, 2017). With the hyperinflation crisis assailing the country at the time, they were intent on maintaining a powerful executive branch that could respond quickly to crises (Abranches, 1988).

The combination of an executive empowered with legislative initiative and a multiparty Congress gave rise to coalitional presidentialism (Abranches, 1988). It is only in such a system that a political culture like *peemedebismo* can arise (Nobre, 2013). Coalitional presidentialism incentivizes a patronage-based system in which reaching the presidency becomes a means of distributing the spoils of government among partisan allies (Abranches, 1988). Consequently, the parties in Congress are constantly vying to ally themselves with the executive for self-serving purposes (Nobre, 2013). Governance becomes explicitly transactional as legislative actors demand material goods in exchange for support for the executive's initiatives (Mello and Spektor, 2018). The constant transactions required to maintain coalitions in the Brazilian political system facilitate rampant corruption at the hands of political operatives (Mello and Spektor, 2018). Thus the centralization of authority in the presidency and the enhanced social rights codified in the constitution produced a paradoxical political environment in which egalitarian policies aiming to improve the lives of marginalized political subjects are enacted through patronage and graft.

The PT's initial resistance to the operational logic produced by the 1988 Constitution exposed the contradictions of the new democratic regime. In July 1987, PT delegates voted in favor of the draft constitutional text in order to ensure that the new democratic framework could continue to be developed during a second round of assembly deliberations (PT, 1988a). Nonetheless, its delegates warned in a press release that the preliminary version of the constitution would maintain a system heavily centralized in the executive, which would in turn perpetuate injustice, impunity, and socioeconomic inequalities (PT, 1988a).

Since the final text failed to change the presidentialist system, the PT decided to vote against the constitution. Even as it did so, however, it signed the final document as proof of the party's participation in the constituent assembly (Keck, 2010). This decision lent credibility to the new democratic regime. The party's critical posture toward dominant political actors did not stop it from recognizing the legitimacy of that regime. The PT and its constituents as well as its social movement allies were fundamentally opposed to the conservative vision of centralized constituted power, but the party never relinquished its willingness to work alongside its adversaries in the new democratic order. Indeed, the 1988 Constitution served to shore up the land demands of the MST in subsequent years.

Social scientists emphasize Lula's second-place finish in the 1989 presidential election as the definitive moment at which the PT became a national political force (Brandão, 2003; Keck, 2010). Despite having achieved poor electoral results in executive-level elections, defending a radical political platform, and lacking any financial support to run a national campaign, Lula almost reached the presidency (Keck, 2010). Nonetheless, prior to the 1989 election the PT's actions in the constituent assembly were integral to making the party an influential political actor on the national level. It was during the constitutive process that the party had its foundational experience in national politics. Lula and his supporters learned how to build interparty coalitions and to engage with their conservative adversaries (Keck, 2010). Additionally, it was during the assembly that the PT was able to bring its massive constituent strength underpinned by social movements into the formal political process.

Thus, the constituent assembly marked the moment at which the PT began to occupy positions within both constituted and constituent power. The party's refusal to compromise on its radical positions further legitimized it in the eyes of its militant base and social movement activists. Simultaneously, its willingness to participate in the constituent assembly and abide by its procedures convinced its adversaries that the party was not a hostile extrainstitutional actor. Rather than an inscrutable adversary, the PT became a potential partner in the institutions of government. After its actions during the assembly, the PT was conclusively positioned within the formal paradigm of political power in Brazil.

JUNE 2013 AND CONSTITUENT REVOLT

Throughout the 1990s, the PT became the leading opposition party by emphasizing transparency and ethics in government (Ribeiro and Floriano, 2003). The party shifted from voting against the constitution in 1988 to defending it ardently during successive center-right Partido da Social Democracia Brasileira (Social Democratic Party—PSDB) administrations (Nobre, 2008). At the time, President Fernando Henrique Cardoso issued 35 executive orders to alter constitutional amendments aimed at facilitating privatization (Gargarella, 2013). The PT unsuccessfully fought against the executive orders in Congress, but its willingness to protect the constitutional text from

Cardoso's privatization initiatives signaled that the party and many of its members had embraced the new democratic order (Nobre, 2008).

Since any significant political change under the 1988 Constitution is made by the president, the PT's foundational imperative to combat Brazil's socioeconomic inequality could only be fulfilled by gaining control of the executive branch (Limongi, 2008). This was accomplished with Lula's election as president in 2002, his reelection in 2006, and Dilma Rousseff's election in 2010 and 2014. The first 10 years of PT federal administrations saw an increase in the independence of the judiciary, greater utilization of participatory councils and public policy conferences, and the elevation of social reforms in the federal policy-making process (Power, 2014). It was during that period that approximately 25 million people propelled themselves out of poverty with the help of the PT's conditional cash transfer programs such as Bolsa Família (de Castro, Koonings, and Wiesebron, 2014). The PT also created Fome Zero, a hunger alleviation program that eradicated starvation nationwide for the first time in Brazilian history (Abers, Serafim, and Tatagiba, 2014). These unprecedented social welfare programs were crucial in ensuring that social movements with national-level scope like the MST and the CUT backed the PT in elections despite increasing militant unease over the party's political alliances and market-oriented economic policies.

Nonetheless, dissecting the way these social welfare programs were passed into law sheds light on the PT's problematic position within both constituent and constituted power. During Lula's first two years as president, the PT governed through a minority coalition in Congress. Despite holding only 18 percent of congressional seats, the PT controlled 60 percent of Lula's cabinet seats (Avritzer, 2016). Its control of such a large proportion of key government positions went against the rules of *peemedebismo*, wherein the executive is expected to reward its congressional allies with prominent ministries (Nobre, 2013). Instead, the PT orchestrated a vote-buying scheme known as the Mensalão in which the party would issue monthly bribes to members of Congress in order to pass its landmark proposals (Avritzer, 2016). When the Mensalão scandal broke in 2005, the PT was forced to reassess the composition of its government. Lula brought the PMDB into his coalition in order to avoid the risk of impeachment and to boost his reelection chances in 2006 (Nobre, 2013). Thereafter, the PMDB became increasingly prominent within the PT government, eventually being granted the vice presidency on the joint ticket with Rousseff in 2010 (Avritzer, 2016).

The PT's implementation of social welfare policies increased its legitimacy within constituent power. Furthermore, its massive expansion of federal participatory councils continued its earlier efforts in municipal government to give members of social movements firsthand exposure to the policy-making process (Abers, Serafim, and Tatagiba, 2014). Simultaneously, the party perpetuated the transactional imperatives of coalitional presidentialism for the sake of governability. It is therefore impossible to assess the PT's advancement of historic social welfare programs without acknowledging the political logic that made it possible. The party improved the material conditions of Brazil's poorest and opened direct access to popular participation in government while bolstering the transactional political culture of *peemedebismo*. Predictably, during the first decade of PT governments, the transactional nature of Brazilian political culture increasingly came into conflict with popular demands for greater transparency and an end to the impunity of public officials. The implementation of innovative egalitarian policies by the PT failed to curb the political system's dependence on graft and patronage (Mello and Spektor, 2018). As a consequence, the constituted regime became increasingly unable to fulfill constituent expectations.

Rousseff was inaugurated in January 2011 with no prior experience in elected office (Power, 2014). She also lacked internal support within the PT, having joined the party only in 2000. She inherited the PMDB coalition from Lula and came to rely on it to make up for her lack of negotiating ability (Power, 2014). Lula's modus operandi since his union days was centered on mediating opposing forces (Keck, 2010). In contrast, Rousseff did not negotiate; she either won or lost (Avritzer, 2016). While she depended on the PMDB to ensure governability, she positioned herself as an anti-*peemedebismo* figure seeking alternative pathways to efficient governance that did not involve rampant corruption (Nobre, 2013). During the first two years of Rousseff's government, her public approval ratings remained high and Congress was willing to comply with her agenda (Nobre, 2013). In 2013, however, her government failed to appease public discontent over deficient public services (Santos, 2014). Simultaneously, social movements that had previously provided nearly unconditional support to the PT were increasingly disillusioned by the party's inability to enact radical reforms in the area of land reform, urban housing, curbs to extractive industries in protected environmental areas, and wealth taxation (Alonso, 2017). The PT's insistence on providing subsidies for Brazilian companies doing business abroad, the so-called National Champions, even as they increasingly sought to undermine labor regulations at home also contributed to disillusionment amongst the social movements. Furthermore, the end of a long commodities boom caused the economy to contract and unemployment to increase. Entrenched in constituted power, the PT became increasingly isolated, unable to tap into its constituency and social movement allies to deal with the challenges it was facing as the ruling party. Meanwhile, the rampant corruption perpetuated by *peemedebismo* became an increasing source of public discontent (Nobre, 2013).

The first public expressions of discontent with the political order occurred in São Paulo in June 2013 with the Movimento Passe Livre (Free Transport

Movement—MPL), a nonpartisan social movement mobilizing against a 20-cent increase in public transport fares (Saad-Filho, 2013). The military police responded violently to the peaceful rally, which provoked thousands to join MPL rallies over the course of the following week. Protests broke out throughout the country amid intensified media coverage of the MPL rallies and continued police repression. Over the following days, constituent demands were no longer centered on the increase in transportation fares. While the protests quickly incorporated a wide array of political agendas, the central demand was political reform, which involved greater accountability measures to combat government corruption and a more effective system of voting distribution that would make Congress more representative. Constituents from both the left and the right of the political spectrum decried a crisis of representation (Alonso, 2017; Taylor, 2016).

In contrast to previous popular mobilizations that had either been led or supported by the PT and its allied social movements (including the Diretas Já prodemocracy protests in 1984 and the protests in favor of President Fernando Collor's impeachment in 1992), the June 2013 protests were dominated by members of the middle class who had never voted for the PT and were ready to turn the party into the principal target of public disgust (Singer, 2013). The fact that a party that had been dedicated to transparent, participatory governance had embraced the patronage-based political system helped to galvanize the millions who marched in June 2013. The protests reached their peak on June 20, when 1.4 million people marched in 130 cities, forcing Rousseff to cancel a trip to Japan (G1.com, 2013). Speaking to the nation on live TV on June 21 (Portal do Planalto, 2013), the president attempted to sympathize with the public dissatisfaction and insisted that her government was going to maintain public order. After her public address failed to put a halt to the demonstrations, Rousseff called a meeting of her cabinet, all 27 state governors, and the mayors of the country's largest cities on June 24. With the media filming the meeting, the first point put forward by the president was a proposal to hold a constituent assembly (Nogueira, 2013). The initiative consisted of a plebiscite to be held in September 2013 in which voters would choose whether to establish a sovereign body to write a new constitution (Singer, 2013). This proposal came in response to a petition submitted by social movements allied with the PT during the June protests that gathered 7.4 million signatures demanding a constituent assembly (Locatelli, 2014).

The constituent assembly proposed by Rousseff was aimed specifically at reforming laws relating to campaign finance, the electoral system, senatorial surrogates, interparty coalitions, and secret votes in Congress (Nobre, 2013). It therefore sought to dismantle the entire transactional structure of coalitional presidentialism. The proposal was instantly criticized by preeminent jurists, who claimed that a constituent assembly would have to rewrite the entire constitution and not just focus on particular policy areas (Oliveira, 2013). More important, members of the Rousseff government, including Vice President Michel Temer, immediately rejected the proposal and made it clear that the PMDB contingent in Congress would never approve a plebiscite on holding a constituent assembly (Avritzer, 2016). The party that had dominated the constitution-making process in 1988 had no intention of relinquishing its influence over the policy-making process.

On the following day, Rousseff sent her minister of justice, José Eduardo Cardozo, to declare that the administration was not advocating a constituent assembly but merely wanted to gauge public sentiment toward political reform (Locatelli, 2014). Unlike other new left parties throughout Latin America (in Venezuela, Bolivia, and Ecuador) that had effectively turned public disgust with the state into a transformational constitutional project, the PT was afraid of hinging its future electoral prospects on a project of substantial political reform. The government failed to recognize that the June revolt was an expression of the crisis of legitimacy of the political system that required a decisive response (Nogueira, 2013).

Rousseff's attempt to create a constituent assembly magnified the PT's conflicting positions within constituted and constituent power. The fact that her proposal was so quickly and so emphatically rejected by her coalition partners demonstrated that the PT's origins as a radical transformational party rooted in social movements remained an element to be feared. Despite having led the national government for over a decade, the PT was still seen as an anomaly within the partisan system (Nogueira, 2013; Singer, 2013). In order to prevent the PT from recovering its radical constitutive strength, the party's conservative allies refused to comply with Rousseff's plebiscite proposal.

Dismayed at the institutional failure to initiate political reform, members of over 400 social movements, including the most prominent ones such as the MST, the CUT, and the Movimento dos Trabalhadores Sem Teto (Homeless Workers' Movement—MTST), came together in September 2014 for an informal plebiscite on whether to hold a constituent assembly. These social movements still supported the PT in elections but were highly critical of the party's inability to lead a process of constitutional change (Silva Júnior and Sousa Júnior, 2017). By holding the informal plebiscite, the PT's constituents openly repudiated Rousseff's failure to formally explore institutional pathways toward writing a new constitution. Approximately 5 percent of the electorate (7.7 million people) voted in the informal plebiscite, with 97 percent voting in favor of a constituent assembly (Maretti, 2014).

Meanwhile, within formal constituted power, the impetus for political reform was quickly undermined by the Centrão. All attempts to promulgate significant reform, including a curb on the creation of political parties and attempts to make all congressional votes public, were shelved by Congress

(Silva Júnior and Souza Júnior, 2017). With her failure to institute political reform, Rousseff's approval ratings plummeted. At 80 percent at the beginning of 2013, following the June protests they collapsed to less than 30 percent (Saad-Filho, 2013). Rousseff was able to win reelection in an extremely close contest in 2014, but the PT's failure to act on the demands of its social movement base and Rousseff's repudiation of *peemedibismo* damaged her ability to govern (Taylor, 2016).

Thus, the June 2013 protests and the failed plebiscite proposal marked the point at which the PT could no longer maintain the uneasy consensus that had allowed it to become the nation's leading political party. The advancement of inclusive social welfare policies within a political system centered on distributing spoils was no longer a viable mode of governance. From 2013 on, the PT's relationship to the Centrão gradually deteriorated. Frustrated at the PMDB's rejection of her reform proposals, Rousseff sidelined Temer and his allies from all decision making in government, in a drawn-out escalation of tensions with her congressional base that would culminate in her impeachment in 2016 (Santos and Guarnieri, 2016).

While the June 2013 plebiscite proposal attempted to resurrect the PT's innovative initiatives in the 1987–1988 constituent assembly, the party lacked its previous programmatic vision. The PT had submitted a constitutional text of its own in 1987, which displayed an ambitious and comprehensive political agenda (Keck, 2010). When the June 2013 protests erupted, the Rousseff government proposed a constituent assembly without a viable strategy for constitutional change (Nogueira, 2013). Even with over 7 million people formally calling for constitutional change through significant mobilization of social movements throughout Brazil, the party could not reignite its mass appeal. Ensconced in constituted power, the PT was unable to replicate its transformative vision of 1987–1988.

Meanwhile, radical right-wing forces began to tap into popular discontent with the political system. Bolsonaro and his allies combined the rhetoric of anticorruption and disgust with pork-barrel politics with his long-held radical views on shoot-to-kill policing, gun rights, and the criminalization of social movements (Funari, 2021). A large proportion of the middle-class protesters who marched in June 2013 coalesced around this discourse, which fused long-held racist and traditionalist views with contemporary anger toward the ruling political actors. By effectively articulating these various popular demands, Bolsonaro was able to position himself as the spearhead of anti-PTism, the messianic alternative to the PT. Unable to offer constitutional alternatives while still in power (which was the essence of Rousseff's constituent assembly proposal), the PT helped to pave the way for antagonistic politicians like Bolsonaro with agendas centered around dismantling all of the progressive gains made by the party while it was in power.

Nevertheless, since Rousseff's impeachment in 2016, radicalism on the right has galvanized the unification of social movements and political parties on the left. Having been increasingly distant from constituted power through successive electoral defeats since 2016, the PT now has fewer qualms about realigning itself with its foundational allies in the social movements. As a result, the party is able to play a leading role in this resurging broad-based alliance of progressive political parties and social movements, all of which face existential threats under Bolsonaro's authoritarian agenda.

CONCLUSION

In examining the PT's actions during the 1987–1988 constitutional assembly and the June 2013 protests, I have sought to examine the dual movement of constituent and constituted power, the conflicting political forces that have determined the party's historical trajectory. The PT's advocacy of subaltern demands during the 1987–1988 constituent assembly and its gradual acceptance of the constitution helped consolidate the new democratic regime (Nobre, 2008). While in government, the PT's implementation of poverty alleviation programs, its support of allied social movements, and its establishment of participatory councils served to solidify the compact between constituents and the state. The PT initially navigated the institutional tensions of Brazilian constitutionalism to maintain political stability and provide material improvements to the lives of millions of citizens.

Nevertheless, constituent demands for institutional transparency and the elimination of entrenched constituted impunity manifested themselves on an unprecedented scale in June 2013 (Tatagiba, 2014). In proposing a plebiscite on a new constituent assembly, the Rousseff government unearthed the transformative potential of the PT. However, its failure to lead a process of constitutional change confirmed that the PT had become dependent on its congressional coalition and could no longer mobilize its radical constituent origins. In decisively distancing itself from its allied social movements, the PT became vulnerable to the intrigues of its unreliable crony allies in Congress. In failing to lead a process of political reform at the behest of social movements such as the CUT and the UNE, which had submitted the petition for constitutional reform, the PT distanced itself from its voter base and helped to exacerbate the crisis of legitimacy of the political system.

Since June 2013, the political system to which the constitution gave birth has become the central battleground of the conflict between constituent and constituted power. From intensified public discontent with political representatives and ongoing disputes between the three branches of government to elected officials' openly repudiating democratic norms (which has accelerated at an unprecedented rate during the Bolsonaro administration), all the contemporary political struggles in Brazil are influenced by the distribution of power enshrined in 1988.

In 2021, massive street protests took place throughout Brazil. Organized by an array of social movements and left-wing parties including the PT, they called for Bolsonaro's removal as a result of his catastrophic handling of the pandemic and his efforts to dismantle the constitutional regime. After Rousseff's contentious impeachment in 2016, the party had consistently pointed to the vulnerability of the political system to cronyism and authoritarianism (Nicolau, 2020). Nevertheless, in once again defending the existing system despite its paradoxes and vulnerabilities, the PT is renewing its foundational commitment to established institutional rules while heeding popular demands. At the same time, the united efforts of the PT and social movements to combat the ascendancy of the authoritarian far right can reenergize the transformative potential of the various strands of constituent power that originally helped make the PT a bulwark of democratic constitutionalism.

NOTE

1. This chapter is a revised version of an article that appeared in *Latin American Perspectives* 47 (5): 163–178 (2020).

REFERENCES

Abers, Rebecca, Lizandra Serafim, and Luciana Tatagiba
2014 "Changing repertoires of state-society interaction under Lula," pp. 36–62 in Fábio de Castro, Kees Koonings, and Marianne Wiesebron (eds.), *Brazil under the Workers' Party: Continuity and Change from Lula to Dilma*. Basingstoke, UK: Palgrave Macmillan.
Abranches, Sergio
1988 "Presidencialismo de coalizão: o dilema institucional brasileiro." *Dados* 31: 5–9.
Agamben, Giorgio
1998 *Homo sacer: Sovereign Power and Bare Life*. Stanford, CA: Stanford University Press.
Alonso, Angela
2017 "A política das ruas: protestos em São Paulo de Dilma a Temer." *Novos Estudos*, June, 49–58.
Avritzer, Leonardo
2016 *Impasses da democracia no Brasil*. Rio de Janeiro: Civilização Brasileira.

2017 "Participation in democratic Brazil: from popular hegemony and innovation to middle-class protest." *Opinião Pública* 23 (1): 43–59.

Baiocchi, Gianpaolo

2004 "The party and the multitude: Brazil's Workers' Party (PT) and the challenges of building a just social order in a globalizing context." *Journal of World-Systems Research* 10 (1): 199–215.

Brandão, Marco Antonio

2003 *O socialismo democrático do Partido dos Trabalhadores: A história de uma utopia (1979–1994)*. São Paulo: Annablume.

Branford, Sue

2015 *Brazil under the Workers' Party: From Euphoria to Despair*. Rugby: Practical Action Publishing.

de Castro, Fábio, Kees Koonings, and Marianne Wiesebron

2014 "Introduction," pp. 1–10 in Fábio de Castro, Kees Koonings, and Marianne Wiesebron (eds.), *Brazil under the Workers' Party: Continuity and Change from Lula to Dilma*. Basingstoke, UK: Palgrave Macmillan.

Dussel, Enrique

2008 *Twenty Theses on Politics*. Durham, NC: Duke University Press.

Funari, Gabriel

2021 "'Family, God, Brazil, guns . . . ': the state of criminal governance in contemporary Brazil." *Bulletin of Latin American Research*, Online Version. https://doi .org/10.1111/blar.13240

G1.com

2013 "Especial: resultados das manifestações." http://g1.globo.com/brasil/linha -tempo-manifestacoes-2013/platb/.

Garcia, Marco Aurelio

1987 "Boletim Nacional n. 27: Nosso Projeto de Constituição, Fundação Perseu Abramo, O PT e a Constituente 1985–1988." https://fpabramo.org.br/csbh/wp -content/uploads/sites/3/2017/04/08–4.perseu6.documentos.pdf.

Gargarella, Roberto

2013 *Latin American Constitutionalism, 1810–2010: The Engine Room of the Constitution*. Oxford: Oxford University Press.

Hunter, Wendy

2010 *The Transformation of the Workers' Party in Brazil, 1989–2009*. Cambridge: Cambridge University Press.

Keck, Margaret

2010 *PT—A lógica da diferença: O Partido dos Trabalhadores na construção da democracia brasileira*. Rio de Janeiro: Centro Edelstein.

Lefort, Claude

1986 *Democracy and Political Theory*. Cambridge: Polity Press.

Lima, Wilson

2013 "Constituição do PT vetava reeleição e previa monopólio estatal no País." August 25. http://ultimosegundo.ig.com.br/politica/2013-10-05/constituicao-do-pt -vetava-reeleicao-eprevia-monopolio-estatal-no-pais.html.

Limongi, Fernando

2008 "O poder executivo na Constituição de 1988," pp. 23–56 in Ruben George Oliven, Marcelo Ridenti, and Gilda Marçal Brandão (eds.), *A Constituição de 1988 na vida brasileira*. São Paulo: Editora Hucitec.

Locatelli, Piero

2014 "Entenda a reforma política." October 31. http://www.cartacapital.com.br/ politica/entenda-a-reforma-politica-6840.html.

Maretti, Eduardo

2014 "Plebiscito por constituinte tem quase 8 milhões de votos; resultado será levado a Brasília." September 24. http://www.redebrasilatual.com.br/politica/2014/09 /plebiscitopor-reforma-politica-tem-adesao-de-quase-8-milhoes-e-resultado-sera-levado-a-brasilia-9996.html.

Mello, Eduardo and Matias Spektor

2018 "Brazil: the costs of multiparty presidentialism." *Journal of Democracy* 29 (2): 113–127.

Nicolau, Jairo

2020 *O Brasil dobrou à direita: Uma radiografia da eleição de Bolsonaro em 2018*. Rio de Janeiro: Zahar.

Nobre, Marco

2008 "Indeterminação e estabilidade: os 20 anos da Constituição Federal e as tarefas da pesquisa em direito." *Novos Estudos CEBRAP* 82: 97–106.

2013 *Imobilismo em movimento: Da abertura democrática ao governo Dilma*. São Paulo: Companhia das Letras.

Nogueira, Marco Aurelio

2013 *As ruas e a democracia: Ensaios sobre o Brasil contemporâneo*. Brasília: Fundação Astrojildo Pereira.

Oliveira, Mariana

2013 "Juristas questionam proposta de Constituinte para reforma política." June 24. http://g1.globo.com/politica/noticia/2013/06/juristas-questionam-proposta-de-constituinte-parareforma-politica.html.

Portal do Planalto

2013 "Pronunciamento da Presidenta da República, Dilma Rousseff, em cadeia nacio-nal de rádio e TV." June 21. http://www2.planalto.gov.br/acompanhe-o-planalto /discursos/discursos-da-presidenta/pronunciamento-da-presidenta-da-republica-dilma-rousseff-em-cadeianacional-de-radio-e-tv.

Power, Timothy

2000 "Political institutions in democratic Brazil: politics as a permanent constitu-tional convention," pp. 17–36 in Peter R. Kingstone and Timothy J. Power (eds.), *Democratic Brazil: Actors, Institutions, and Processes*. Pittsburgh: University of Pittsburgh Press.

2014 "Continuity in a changing Brazil: the transition from Lula to Dilma," pp. 10–36 in Fábio de Castro, Kees Koonings, and Marianne Wiesebron (eds.), *Brazil under the Workers' Party: Continuity and Change from Lula to Dilma*. Basingstoke, UK: Palgrave Macmillan.

PT (Partido dos Trabalhadores)

1985 "Encontro Nacional Extraordinario 12–13 de Janeiro de 1985: Resolução." https://fpabramo.org.br/csbh/wp-content/uploads/sites/3/2017/04/08–4.perseu6. documentos.pdf.

1986 "4o Encontro Nacional do Partido dos Trabalhadores 30 de Maio–1o de Junho de 1986 Resoluções." https://fpabramo.org.br/csbh/wp-content/uploads/sites/3 /2017/04/08-4.perseu6.documentos.pdf.

1988a "Declaração de voto do PT." https://fpabramo.org.br/csbh/wp-content/uploads /sites/3/2017/04/08–4.perseu6.documentos.pdf.

1988b "Declaração na votação do texto final da Constituição."https://fpabramo.org.br /csbh/wp-content/uploads/sites/3/2017/04/08–4.perseu6.documentos.pdf.

Ribeiro, Pedro and Jose Floriano

2003 "O PT sob uma perspectiva sartoriana: de partido anti-sistema a legitimador do sistema." *Política & Sociedade* 2 (3): 45–70.

Saad-Filho, Alfredo

2013 "Mass protests under 'left neoliberalism': Brazil, June-July 2013." *Critical Sociology* 39: 657–669.

Santos, Eduardo Heleno

2014 "Crise de representação política no Brasil e os protestos de junho de 2013." *Liinc em Revista* 10 (1): 86–95.

Santos, Fabiano and Fernando Guarnieri

2016 "From protest to parliamentary group: an overview of Brazil's recent history." *Journal of Latin American Cultural Studies* 25: 485–494.

Schmitt, Carl

2008 *Constitutional Theory*. Translated and edited by Jeffrey Seitzer. Durham, NC: Duke University Press.

Silva Júnior, Gladstone Leonel da and José Geraldo de Sousa Júnior

2017 "A luta pela constituinte e a reforma política no Brasil: caminhos para um 'constitucionalismo achado na rua.'" *Revista Direito e Práxis* 8: 1008–1027.

Singer, Andre

2013 "Brasil, junho de 2013, classes e ideologias cruzadas." *Novos Estudos CEBRAP* 97: 23–40.

2016 *O Lulismo em crise: Um quebra cabeça do período Dilma (2011–2016)*. São Paulo: Companhia das Letras.

Tatagiba, Luciana

2014 "1984, 1992 e 2013: sobre ciclos de protestos e democracia no Brasil." *Política & Sociedade* 13 (28): 35–62.

Taylor, Matthew

2016 "Brazil in the crucible of crisis." *Current History* 115 (778): 68–74.

Chapter 7

Dynamics of Contention

Social Movements and Democracy in Argentina (1989–2019)

Leandro Gamallo
Translated by Mariana Ortega-Breña

The analysis of social conflicts that follows will address three fundamentals of collective action as they relate to Argentina in the twenty-first century: the actors in contention, their demands, and their modes of struggle.[1] These categories will be linked to the dynamics of political-institutional processes and, to a lesser extent, to different models of economic development. These three aspects will be viewed as independent but interrelated in such a way that drastic alterations in one lead to changes in the others. Transformations in institutional policy and macroeconomic models will be considered as part of the fundamental context for various historical struggles. More specifically, the chapter will contrast the relations between social movements and neoliberal governments with those of Pink Tide governments between 2003 and 2015 and then after 2019.

My theoretical framework is based on the so-called emerging synthesis developed by McAdam, McCarthy, and Zald (1999) and used by McAdam, Tarrow, and Tilly (2005) and will include both empirical and theoretical contributions with regard to resource mobilization and the structure of political opportunities under both neoliberal and anti-neoliberal governments. I will survey some of the research on transformations in the field of conflict using databases of contentious actions, in-depth interviews with social leaders, and ethnographies on social organizations.

STRUGGLES AGAINST NEOLIBERALISM
AND ITS BREAKDOWN (1989–2001)

The military dictatorship of 1976–1983 dealt a major blow to organized labor (Villarreal, 1985), a trend intensified under the administrations of Carlos Menem (1989–1999), which implemented even more radical neoliberal policies affecting smaller industrial branches and the purchasing power of workers. Policies including economic openings, financial liberalization, selective regulation of markets, and the furthering of a new kind of state based on a broad privatization of public goods and services (Cantamutto and Wainer, 2013) were introduced in response to an acute 1988–1990 economic crisis characterized by hyperinflation and a sharp increase of poverty and social marginality.[2] During 1989 Argentina experienced a wave of looting of unprecedented proportions in recent history that prefigured transformations in the collective action of the popular sectors. The looting not only represented new forms of confrontation that went beyond existing channels for participation and shed light on Argentina's "new social issue," the structural poverty of a significant portion of the population (Serulnikov, 2017).

Given the decline of the labor movement due to defeats and the disarticulation of its social base (as a result of unemployment, informality, outsourcing, etc.), the social conflict of the time was characteristically diverse, including a multiplication of contentious actors, the appearance of heterogeneous demands and claims, and new forms of struggle. A new labor confederation, the Central de Trabajadores de Argentina (Argentine Workers' Central—CTA), emerged in opposition to the traditional Peronist Confederación General del Trabajo (General Confederation of Labor—CGT). However, many of the decade's most important conflicts involved actors playing unprecedented major roles, including the families and friends of victims of police repression and/or abuse of power, retirees, the unemployed, human rights organizations, workers in recovered factories, and neighborhood assemblies (Schuster et al., 2006). Many of these groups remained outside the traditional institutions in charge of processing social demands. Many of them also proclaimed their autonomy from the state and political parties and unions, but others subscribed to political traditions such as Peronism or variants of Marxism. Their demands were heterogeneous, some of them corporate (such as pension increases and social assistance plans for the unemployed) and others political (changes in the economic model, replacement of certain governmental representatives) and identity-based. These new actors resorted to unusual modes of performance to satisfy unmet demands or to solve their problems in the face of state inaction. Direct action, understood as "forms of contentious action that are not mediated by the dominant institutionality" (Pérez and Rebón, 2012: 21), expanded. Popular protests surpassed traditional channels of participation and were expressed through disruptive modalities such as street and highway blockages, building takeovers, encampments and blockades, *escraches*,[3] looting, and even uprisings (Antón et al., 2010; Auyero, 2002; Merklen, 2010).

These novel types of protest formed part of the popular resistance to neoliberalism, which turned into what was termed a new repertoire of action of Argentine social movements (Auyero, 2002; Merklen, 2010; Svampa and Pereyra, 2003). Many of these new dimensions persisted even when the political and economic conditions changed. Strictly speaking, the new forms of organization and struggle did not replace but complemented the old ones. Both the provincial uprisings and *puebladas* (popular revolts) and the expansion of the *piquetero* movement, made up of factions of the unemployed, were based on experiences of union resistance that found new channels of action via new modes of organization (Auyero, 2002). This change in the repertoire of collective action should be understood not as a simple empirical inventory of relatively new and more powerful modes of action but as a set of new forms of socialization and political participation. Underpinning the development was the transformation of "workers" into "the poor" (Merklen, 2010)—in other words, the shift from the factory to the neighborhood (Svampa, 2005). Territorialization became the most important factor in the "reaffiliation" of the popular universe once all references to the world of formal work had been lost.

This social fabric, woven around cooperation (which often effectively replaced the state), was based on political and social organizations, such as those of the piqueteros, with strong territorial anchoring. Transformations of popular struggle were related to the urgent need for more and better tools for obtaining resources in a context of accelerated impoverishment and the creation of new networks that would provide an identity and collective anchor for these modes of popular participation.

All these transformations in social conflict increased toward the end of the decade, when Argentina experienced widespread rejection of the neoliberal model as it went through its worst economic, social, and political crisis as a nation. In 1999 Fernando de la Rúa of the Unión Cívica Radical (Radical Civic Union) became president and increased fiscal adjustment and economically orthodox measures. Between 1999 and 2002, economic activity dropped by almost 20 percent, social indicators such as poverty and unemployment worsened dramatically, and the system of democratic representation underwent a deep political crisis.[4] Intense and belligerent social conflict took over the streets of the country.

Resistance on the part of the various sectors affected by neoliberal policies (largely the piquetero movement) grew as the model's collapse became increasingly evident. By late December 2001, in response to a series of government measures meant to deal with the fiscal deficit and the abysmal default on the foreign debt, protesters began demanding the resignation of the minister of the economy and, finally, the president himself. December 19 and 20, 2001, represented the apex of the cycle of protests begun years before, in which the popular and middle sectors demonstrated en masse, issuing different demands but using a common slogan: "They Must All Go!" The mobilizations, looting, street and highway blockages, and clashes with security forces throughout the country not only put an end to the de la Rúa administration but inaugurated a new national political-economic stage. Despite the collapse of the economic model itself (which gave rise to disputes among the ruling class regarding how to proceed),[5] the political change in early-twenty-first-century Argentina cannot be understood without accounting for the popular struggles that finally put an end to the pattern of accumulation that had governed the country for 25 years.

The social movements called attention to the injustice produced by the neoliberal model and broke up its consensuses, but they failed to overcome their own fragmentation or form strategic alliances with other actors to initiate a new hegemony (Muñoz, 2010; Retamozo, 2011). Lacking alternatives from the world of popular organizations, political reconstruction had to be carried out by "traditional" actors, albeit using other political-symbolic references and employing different power relations between the ruling class and the subaltern sectors. After de la Rúa's resignation on December 20, 2001 (and an interim of five different presidents within a week), the Peronist Eduardo Duhalde (a former candidate defeated by de la Rúa in the 1999 elections) managed to obtain majority support from his party and was proclaimed president until the end of the period. Duhalde had to acknowledge the protests and recognize the damage produced by neoliberalism, thus accepting the legitimacy of the demands. Among other measures, he implemented a massive income program called Unemployed Heads of Households that issued 150 pesos per month (US$50) to almost 2 million families. In a society faced with unprecedented levels of unemployment and poverty,[6] state intervention was meant to guarantee a minimum subsistence level for the most disadvantaged social groups and neutralize potential social outbreaks (Perelmiter, 2012). Thus, despite not having led the way out of the crisis through direct participation, the social movements served as a force behind the formulation of public policies and even the dynamics of representative democracy. After the murder of two piquetero militants by police on June 26, 2002, during a protest for an increase in unemployment benefits, Duhalde had to call for early elections. In April 2003, his candidate of choice, Néstor Kirchner, became president with only 22 percent of the vote after Carlos Menem (who had received 25 percent of the votes during the first round) resigned.

KIRCHNERISM AND THE SOCIAL
MOVEMENTS (2002–2007)

The Kirchner government consolidated a new model of accumulation initiated by Duhalde. Neodevelopmentism (Costantino and Cantamutto, 2017) took advantage of an upward economic cycle based on favorable international conditions for commodity exports to promote the expansion of the domestic market, the recovery of purchasing power across important portions of the working population, and an improvement in various social indicators such as unemployment, poverty, and social inequality. That said, several indicators only reached precrisis levels. Conscious of its low percentage of votes, the government began to channel multiple civilian demands and form innovative political alliances. In spite of having belonged to the party that carried out the neoliberal reforms of the 1990s, Kirchner developed a progressive rhetoric that portrayed the state as the space for social problem resolution and social integration (Muñoz and Retamozo, 2008). He also identified previous leading actors—financial speculation, multilateral credit organizations such as the International Monetary Fund, the last civil-military dictatorship and even Menemism—as enemies.

Changes in social conflict became evident. During the first years, the piquetero movement remained the most dynamic actor with the greatest veto power. The new official discourse appealed to a sector of this movement: those who saw themselves as belonging to the national-popular tradition of combative Peronism of the 1960s and 1970s. Both because of the ideological affinity with this sector and the government's explicit tactic of building alliances with social movements, a broad set of organizations (the most numerous in number of militants and adherents) became progovernment and were given political posts across various state levels. This not only further fragmented the piquetero movement but produced changes in the goals, tactics, and modes of organization of the now progovernment groupings, which conceived their social militancy as linked to their work within the state (Perelmiter, 2012). Additionally, a type of collective action that had been infrequent until then was introduced: mobilizations in support of the government or against government adversaries. The Kirchner administrations built a contentious social base using these sectors, often to confront economically powerful actors (Perelmiter, 2012; Pérez and Natalucci, 2010).

However, not all piqueteros were moved by the administration's discourse. A heterogeneous sector that included fractions of left-wing Peronism, traditional Marxism, and autonomism maintained its opposition to the state while retaining its previous tactics, mainly street blockage and encampments. Although the government deactivated repression as a way to confront these conflicts, it managed to isolate this sector with relative success not only by fragmenting old alliances but by delegitimizing the piquetero movement and picketing (street blockage) itself as an anachronistic mode of struggle. As some of the specialized literature maintains (McAdam, McCarthy, and Zald, 1999: 38), the presence of a "radical wing" benefited the progovernment sector in its "dialogist" role as a conflict mediator. Furthermore, the overall movement was not greatly harmed by the containment of both sectors; the goals attained included an increase in the number of productive enterprises, cooperatives, and social subsidies financed by the state (Perelmiter, 2012).

At the same time, the sustained expansion of the domestic market led to a growing reincorporation of large numbers of the unemployed into the labor market, although many of them were in precarious conditions. The gradual recovery in employment levels weakened the social base of the organizations of the unemployed and strengthened union power as promoted by the government during collective negotiations (through institutions in charge of the wages and working conditions assigned to unions, the state, and the business sector). Thus the government made explicit its desire to reinstitutionalize social conflict, incorporating some demands and actors into the formal political system and rechanneling the most disruptive street protests. The conflict map slowly changed in terms of actors, demands, and forms of struggle. Until 2002 the struggles were mainly carried out by the unemployed; during the following years, it was unionized workers who were responsible for most of the protests, usually in the form of strikes (Antón et al., 2010; Etchemendy and Collier, 2007). Although a significant portion of the popular sectors (particularly the unemployed and workers in the informal sector) continued protesting outside institutional margins, by the middle of the first decade of the century conflict in Argentina had moved from the streets and openly disruptive actions to mostly institutionalized and regulated forms of protest (Antón et al., 2010).

This process of "union revitalization" (Senén González, 2011) did not entail a return to the typical union model of import-substitution industrialization of the postwar years. The process only reached formal unionized workers, while a third of the economically active population remained structurally outside the registered labor market. Indeed, the tripartite negotiation involving the state was termed "segmented neocorporativism" because the new basis for union power and negotiation resided mainly in the registered sector of the economy, leaving out the greater mass of workers who remained in precarious conditions in the informal sector (Etchemendy and Collier, 2007: 149). Although unions retained a pragmatic autonomy with regard to the government, several union leaders held ministerial and congressional posts during those years (Etchemendy and Collier, 2007).

Despite the renewed prominence of labor conflict, Argentine struggles retained the complex and heterogeneous character of the 1990s. Two types of demands, driven by different actors, came to occupy center stage. One was the demand for justice in the fight against insecurity. The government of Néstor Kirchner took swift action in favor of the historical claims of human rights organizations and, during its first two months, repealed impunity laws that protected political and military personnel from being charged with crimes against humanity during the last de facto government. However, by the mid-1990s the fight against impunity had taken on new meaning, with insecurity with regard to crime becoming one of Argentine society's greatest concerns (Kessler, 2011; Pereyra, 2011). This reached a tipping point with the kidnapping and murder of Axel Blumberg, the son of the businessman Juan Carlos Blumberg, in March 2004. Over 200,000 people participated in the ensuing protest, one of the largest of the period. Although the movement led by Blumberg quickly decreased in size, the government acknowledged some of the demands and bolstered the penal code with more punitive legislation. The demand for security would become the source of numerous collective actions (some of them violent) during this period, even though the proportion of violent crimes decreased (Gamallo, 2017; Kessler, 2011).

The twenty-first century also saw the emergence of socio-environmental struggles. The very rationale of the development model (based, in part, on the processing of natural resources) led to tensions in the form of social conflict. Resistance to a prospective gold mine in Esquel in 2002 (a turning point in the history of environmental resistance) and protests in the city of Gualeguaychú, Entre Ríos, against the installation of pulp mills on the Uruguayan side of the Uruguay River became emblematic struggles. There were also numerous local conflicts involving indigenous communities' claims of landownership, protests by peasant organizations against compulsory fumigation, resistance to the clearing of virgin land in response to the expansion of the agricultural frontier, and urban struggles over the contamination of rivers and the relocation of landfills (Merlinsky, 2013).

Many of these struggles involved autonomous and novel processes of organization such as citizen neighborhood assemblies (Bottaro and Sola Álvarez, 2012). The calling of assemblies was a direct inheritance from the critical December 2001 days and represented a form of direct democracy and autonomy vis-à-vis the state. Not surprisingly, the organizations behind these assemblies were less permeable and remained the most oppositional and intransigent. Although some demands have led to institutional changes,[7] environmental demands in general were not processed at the institutional level and, in some cases, were actually repressed (Costantino and Gamallo, 2015).

GOVERNMENT VERSUS AGRICULTURAL BOURGEOISIE: THE CRISTINA FERNÁNDEZ ADMINISTRATIONS (2008–2015)

The Néstor Kirchner government that ended in December 2007 managed to overcome the political-institutional crisis that gave birth to it and build its own legitimacy around an economic recovery[8] and the creation of new social consensuses underpinned by social movements (Muñoz, 2010). All of this contributed to the election of Cristina Fernández de Kirchner (Néstor's wife) as president for the 2007–2011 term. Although social conflict seemed to continue along the same lines, an unusual event would disrupt not only the political situation but the very universe of social protest. At the beginning of 2008, during record increases in international commodity prices, a government project that tried to increase the fees on grain exports met unexpected resistance among the upper echelons of the entrepreneurial class. Entrepreneurial protests began with lockouts and then the use of a tactic used by the unemployed—the blocking of strategic routes across the nation. The unexpected consequences of this cycle of protests[9] were due not only to the ironclad defense of corporate interests, even though leading economic sectors historically had little direct influence on the state, but also to the capacity of a belligerent rural-based elite to link up with a heterogeneous group that included other economic sectors and political factions opposed to the government. The conflict became a political opportunity for scattered opposition groups to unite around a common political identity: anti-Kirchnerism (Gamallo, 2012). An indicator of the effectiveness of this articulation was the massive mobilizations in opposition to the government in the nation's large cities. This brought back the *cacerolazos* (banging on pots and pans) now repeatedly used by the middle and upper classes in protest against the government.

This conflict led to the most important political crisis since December 2001 and forced the government to temporarily suspend implementation of the measure, which then went to Congress for consideration. During the months of congressional deliberations, hundreds of thousands of citizens mobilized throughout the country to support either the agricultural front or the governing alliance. As a reaction against the opposition, dozens of social organizations, piqueteros, and unions played a central role when they took to the streets in support of the government, disputing public space with their antagonists. The opposition, however, demonstrated greater street presence, and this was reflected in Congress. The Chamber of Deputies approved the project, but the Senate then rejected it: the vice president broke the tie by voting against the project promoted by his own government. Nevertheless, the incident demonstrated the mobilization capacity of popular social movements and their essential role in the survival of the Cristina Fernández government, particularly in the case of CGT-affiliated unions and piquetero groups close to the government.

This conflict led to major transformations in political and social arenas. It began a process of polarization that would increase over time with confrontations centering on Kirchnerism. After its defeat, the government lost allies both from a sector of Peronism (including cabinet members) and from allied parties. In addition, alliances with some economically powerful actors began to crack at the same time that mass media conglomerates became fiercely oppositional. These factors, coupled with economic stagnation due largely to the international crisis that began in 2008, were responsible for the electoral defeat of the ruling party in the midterm elections of 2009.

From then on, the government radicalized certain measures as well as its discourse. It nationalized the pension funds that had been privatized in the 1990s, issued a universal subsidy to children, promoted antitrust legislation to regulate media conglomerates, and approved the law of equal marriage, acknowledging sexual-minority civil rights. These measures and the confrontation with sectors of the economic elite gained the support of center-left groups enthusiastic over the idea of a sovereign and popular government. Two milestones marked this new stage: the multitudinous celebrations for the national bicentennial (which assembled more than 2 million people between May 21 and 25, 2010) and the death of Néstor Kirchner on October 27, 2010.

These events were accompanied by the emergence of a new Kirchnerism, reconfigured by unprecedented confrontations and strengthened by a new relationship with social movements. The government began to promote the creation of social organizations and pro-government factions within existing ones (such as unions and student groups), at the same time that there was an escalation of progovernment mobilizations. After Kirchner's death, thousands of young people across the country joined pro-government social organizations such as La Cámpora, a group with organic ties to the national government, in national mourning (Vázquez and Vommaro, 2012). While Kirchnerism had from the beginning engaged in a dispute for the "streets," this feature was now accentuated, as La Cámpora, closely associated with Cristina Fernández, sought to lead not only the Partido Justicialista (Justicialist Party) but also the social organizations identified with the ruling party. This eagerness to direct and subordinate the social movements would end up breaking up the official coalition years later, as many organizations left the progovernment camp. The Kirchnerist groups—heterogeneous and often in competition among themselves—supported the government by convening hundreds of thousands of people and participating in official events, celebrations, commemorations, and festivals.

Thus the universe of mobilization in Argentina began to split into two opposing camps. Official collective actions celebrating the government's triumphs by local groups, parties, unions, and numerous unaffiliated citizens sought to take over streets and squares. Though some maintained a conflictive relationship with the government over the administration of resources or political differences (Natalucci, 2012), the general approach of the groups that identified themselves as Kirchnerist was to support the government in its confrontations with adversaries. At the same time, other social movements and opposition groups took to the streets to combat the government and make concrete demands. There were two political blocs in this latter group: a leftist one with an anticapitalist discourse and an antileftist one with a completely different symbology and forms of participation, which took to the streets with heterogeneous slogans but the explicit goal of discrediting the Kirchner experiment (Antón et al., 2010).

In this polarized scenario, popular organizations unrelated to the government and unaligned with the right-wing opposition found it difficult to find legitimate space for their claims. In spite of the obstacles, the struggle of some opposing piquetero organizations and pro-leftist grassroots unions continued. One of these mobilizations was the occupation of the Parque Indoamericano, an undeveloped area in southern Buenos Aires. During the early days of December 2010, some 15,000 people from informal settlements took over the property to protest their overcrowded living conditions and the absence of a state housing policy. Their main goal was to begin construction while negotiating a series of governmental measures aimed at solving the housing problem (Zapata, 2013). The national and local governmental response, however, took the form of violent eviction (ordered by a local judge) using federal and local forces. The conflict at the Parque Indoamericano demonstrated that urban planning had continued along the lines of the neoliberal model to the extent that urban inequalities (transport, access to housing, etc.) had in fact intensified in spite of the development model promoted by the Kirchners (Ciccolella, 2009; Guevara, 2014).

The economic recovery of 2010–2011 and the political initiatives implemented by the government during these years facilitated Fernández de Kirchner's reelection with 54 percent of the votes in late 2011. However, in mid-2012 protests against her, publicized mainly through social networks, were staged in upper-middle-class neighborhoods of major cities, complemented by cacerolazos across the nation (Gamallo, 2012). Though the first spontaneous gatherings of that year took place exclusively in Buenos Aires's most affluent neighborhoods, the subsequent ones were massive and occurred with increasing levels of organization in practically all of the country's important urban centers. Some of the protests were held outside of public buildings. The trigger was the implementation of new restrictions on the purchase of foreign currency, but in fact the demands were quite diverse (Pereyra, 2016). The main drive was opposition to the government. The protests of 2012 displayed on the streets the regrouping of the conservative opposition as would be repeated electorally several years later. Additionally, they demonstrated the continued capacity of the middle to high sectors to contest the space of social protest that had come to the fore in 2008.

Another major source of conflict of Cristina Fernández's second administration involved the unions. The rupture of the alliance with the CGT shifted a group of unions toward the camp of the opposition. Beyond the sector's specific demands, the conflicts can be partially explained by the government's attempt to subordinate the unions and the determination of some leaders to occupy positions within the state and on electoral slates (Gamallo, 2012). During Cristina Fernández's second term, the CGT called five general strikes with a great impact. Meanwhile, social organizations and opposition piqueteros continued to demand increases in state subsidies for the poor (Natalucci, 2012).

Toward the end of the period, new mobilizations of social movements took place including those of the women's movement against patriarchy and the informal workers organized by the recently created Confederación de Trabajadores de la Economía Popular (Confederation of Popular Economy Workers—CTEP), which merged several existing organizations. The women's movement led a mobilization of over 300,000 on June 3, 2015, to protest femicide and gender violence (expressed by the slogan *¡Ni una menos!* [Not One Woman Less!]). This resulted in the creation of an official registry of femicides by the judicial branch. Although the government strengthened some measures such as the partial nationalization of the YPF oil company in 2012 and the creation and increase of subsidies to various sectors of the population, the economic model began to show signs of exhaustion, and social indicators were not at all favorable (Kulfas, 2017). In this context, Cristina Fernández slowly lost the political capital she had achieved with her overwhelming victory in 2011. The government met defeat in the 2013 legislative elections after the massive mobilizations of 2012. Its 2015 presidential candidate, Daniel Scioli, lost to the right-wing Mauricio Macri, inaugurating a new stage for the country and for Argentine social movements.

SOCIAL MOVEMENTS IN A NEW NEOLIBERAL CYCLE

Despite the fact that during the campaign Macri had promised to continue many of the more progressive measures of the previous government, once in power he quickly demonstrated that his real objective was to roll out conservative reforms. In the first months of government, he oversaw a marked transfer of income from workers to wealthier sectors (Scaletta, 2017). In the long run the aim was to transform the balance of power between the ruling classes and subordinate sectors in a regressive direction. In this sense, the 2015 elections not only represented a democratic shift but also marked a change in the previous development model (Scaletta, 2017). What is unique about this situation is that the changes occurred in the absence of any economic, social, or political crisis that would have justified the reorientation. For this reason, the reform plan for fiscal adjustment and economic orthodoxy did not arouse the popular support that, for example, it had in the 1990s in response to the hyperinflationary crisis. From the outset of his government, social movement resistance to the measures escalated.

This new scenario saw the reconfiguration of old alliances and fractures. The state policy toward collective action also changed, since Macri promoted a smear campaign accompanied by a selective but growing repression of social protest. This is why the protests against repression and in favor of human rights gained prominence in the period. This included the enormous mobilizations of human rights organizations in response to the disappearance of Santiago Maldonado in August 2017[10] and the massive outcry of May 2017 promoted by the Madres de Plaza de Mayo and various human rights organizations against a Supreme Court ruling that benefited those convicted of crimes against humanity committed during the last dictatorship. As a result of these protests, the Supreme Court backed off.

In this context, the CGT staged several general strikes. Various sectors, such as teachers and state workers, carried out massive mobilizations and strikes that in some cases were successful. The CTEP, which brings together informal and unemployed workers, played a leading role forcing the implementation of the Social Emergency Law, which created a registry of informal workers and granted them public health insurance. Women's organizations also led demonstrations and pushed for a congressional debate of the Voluntary Interruption of Pregnancy bill in 2018.[11]

A turning point in the political conjuncture was the protests against the reduction in pensions implemented in December 2017. Despite the fact that the bill was approved in Congress, the unity and articulation between sectors shown in those marches, as well as the radicalization of the protests (which included episodes of collective violence), forced the government to back down. The impact of the protests, along with the negative perception of the repressive response by the government, undermined the image of the president, who had emerged victorious in the legislative elections in October of that year. The protests led into the formation of the Frente de Todos (Everyone's Front)—the electoral instrument unifying the different sectors of Peronism and the center-left opposition that defeated Macri in October 2019 after two years of economic crisis, decline in real wages, and foreign indebtedness. Social movements have been an active part of the formation of the Frente de Todos: piqueteros, unionists, and social leaders have been incorporated into electoral slates. They have also been part of the local and provincial governments as a result of the electoral triumphs of Peronism.

CONCLUSIONS

Following the cycle of protests that put an end to the neoliberal model at the beginning of the twenty-first century, collective action increasingly became part of Argentine political-institutional life. In the past two decades, collective action has expanded to include multiple actors and forms of protest. Just as Kirchnerism cannot be explained without addressing the social movements that challenged the neoliberal order, the experience of 12 years of Peronist government radically transformed those movements. It not only fragmented them with regard to their support or opposition to the government and altered their tactics and modes of organization but also constructed a new field of political confrontation that revolved around the state and, specifically, the ruling coalition. This partly explains the emergence of numerous pro-government social organizations as well as antigovernment social movements that were conservative both in the class background of those they mobilized and in their slogans and types of protest. This social movement bifurcation is peculiar to this period and calls into question some of the postulates that were first raised by new social movement theorists: not all participation in the state implies weakness, subordination, treason, or co-optation (as suggested by Svampa, 2008, among others), nor does the action of social movements necessarily imply democratization or expansion of rights. In fact, Macri's candidacy and subsequent victory in 2015 can be partly explained by the emergence of the "regressive social movements" that in 2012 staged massive protests in the face of a fragmented political opposition and began to erode support for the government and produce effective oppositional articulations.

The victory of a right-wing government in 2015 opened a new field of confrontation in which old divisions and alliances have been reconfigured. Once more, social movements were a step ahead of the political leadership, promoting unity of resistance to the initiatives of the Macri government and collaborating in the Peronist bid to return to power. The progressive government of Alberto Fernández elected in 2019 again opened space and "political opportunities" for progressive social movements. The challenge facing both Fernández and the social movements (the pro-Peronist piqueteros, unionists, and cooperative members, some of whom play an active role in the government and hold leading posts) is again how to build a constructive relationship between the two. For that to happen, the Fernández government needs to channel the demands that sustain the electoral contract between the Peronist leadership and its base without demobilizing the latter.

NOTES

1. This chapter is a revised version of an article that appeared in *Latin American Perspectives* 47 (4): 96–111 (2020).

2. According to the World Bank (2018a), the inflation rate in 1989 reached 3,080 percent, while in 1990 it was 2,313 percent.

3. *Escraches* were collective performances enacted during the 1990s by human rights organizations in which they "scribbled" or pointed to the homes or workplaces of those accused of participating in crimes against humanity during the last military dictatorship in Argentina but were nevertheless free.

4. In the legislative elections of 2001, 20 percent of voters cast blank votes or invalid ones, referred to as "votes of anger" against the political system.

5. Leading groups of the Argentine bourgeoisie clashed when faced with the exhaustion of the economic model; some wanted to dollarize the economy while others wanted to devalue the currency. Duhalde's administration opted for the latter.

6. The national poverty rate amounted to 42.3 percent of the population in October 2002, and 16.9 percent were destitute, one of the highest rates in recent Argentine history (Arakaki, 2011).

7. The better-known cases are the appointment of the environmentalist lawyer of Gualeguaychú, Romina Picoloti, as secretary of the environment under the Néstor Kirchner administration. Later, in 2010, the government of Cristina Fernández, spurred on by social movements, approved the Glacier Law.

8. According to World Bank (2018b) data, between 2003 and 2007 the gross domestic product grew by an average of 8.68 percent per year.

9. In 2008 the contentious actions of these organizations outnumbered those of workers and the unemployed (Antón et al., 2010).

10. Maldonado disappeared in the course of the violent repression of a Mapuche protest in Argentina's Patagonia. Several days later his cadaver was found 400 meters from where he had last been seen.

11. That year the Chamber of Deputies approved the proposed law, which was then rejected in the Senate. The law was finally passed in December 2020 and signed by the progressive president Alberto Fernández.

REFERENCES

Antón, Gustavo, Jorge Cresto, Julián Rebón, and Rodrigo Salgado
2010 "Una década en disputa: apuntes sobre las luchas sociales en la Argentina."
    OSAL 28: 95–116.
Arakaki, Agustín

2011 *La pobreza en Argentina 1974–2006: Construcción y análisis de la información.* Buenos Aires: Universidad de Buenos Aires.

Auyero, Javier

2002 "Los cambios en el repertorio de la protesta social argentina." *Desarrollo Económico* 42 (166): 187–220.

Bottaro, Lorena and Maria Sola Álvarez

2012 "Conflictividad socioambiental en América Latina: el escenario post-crisis de 2001 en Argentina." *Política y Cultura* 37: 159–184.

Cantamutto, Francisco and Andrés Wainer

2013 *Economía política de la convertibilidad.* Buenos Aires: Capital Intelectual.

Ciccolella, Pablo

2009 "Buenos Aires: una metrópolis postsocial en el contexto de la economía global," pp. 35–62 in Pedro Pírez (ed.), *Buenos Aires, la formación del presente.* Quito: OLACHI.

Costantino, María Agostina and Francisco Cantamutto

2017 "Neodesarrollismo, el programa de la industria ante la crisis neoliberal." *Márgenes* 3 (3): 9–26.

Costantino, María Agostina and Leandro Gamallo

2015 "Los conflictos socioambientales durante los gobiernos kirchneristas en Argentina," pp. 277–308 in Luis Daniel Vázquez (ed.), *De la democracia liberal a la soberanía popular: Articulación y crisis en América Latina.* Mexico City: FLACSO.

Etchemendy, Sebastián and Ruth Collier

2007 "Golpeados, pero de pie: resurgimiento sindical y neocorporativismo en Argentina (2003–2007)." *Politics and Society* 35 (3): 145–192.

Gamallo, Leandro

2012 "Entre paros y cacerolazos: apuntes sobre la conflictividad social en la Argentina reciente." *Anuario del Conflicto Social* 2012: 877–908.

2017 "Linchamientos, ataques y estallidos: las acciones colectivas de violencia punitiva en Argentina (2009–2015)." Ph.D. diss., Universidad de Buenos Aires.

Guevara, Tomás

2014 "Transformaciones territoriales en la Región Metropolitana de Buenos Aires y reconfiguración del régimen de acumulación en la década neo-desarrollista." *QUID* 16 (4): 115–136.

Kessler, Gabriel

2011 *El sentimiento de inseguridad: Sociología del temor al delito.* Buenos Aires: Siglo XXI.

Kulfas, Matías

2017 *Los tres kirchnerismos: Una historia de la economía argentina 2003–2005.* Buenos Aires: Siglo XXI.

McAdam, Doug, John D. McCarthy, and Mayer N. Zald

1999 "Oportunidades políticas, estructuras demovilización y marcos interpretativos culturales," pp. 21–46 in Doug McAdam, John D. McCarthy, and Mayer N. Zald (eds.), Madrid: Istmo.

McAdam, Doug, Sidney Tarrow, and Charles Tilly

2005 *Dinámica de la contienda política*. Barcelona: Hacer.

Merklen, Denis

2010 *Pobres ciudadanos: Las clases populares en la era democrática (Argentina, 1983–2003)*. Buenos Aires: Gorla.

Merlinsky, Gabriela

2013 "Introducción: la cuestión ambiental en la agenda pública," pp. 19–60 in Gabriela Merlinsky (ed.), *Cartografías del conflicto ambiental en Argentina*. Buenos Aires: Fundación CICCUS.

Muñoz, María Antonia

2010 *Sísifo en Argentina: Orden conflicto y sujetos políticos*. Villa María and Mexico City: EDUVIM/Plaza y Valdés.

Muñoz, María Antonia and Martín Retamozo

2008 "Hegemonía y discurso en la Argentina contemporánea: efectos políticos de los usos de 'pueblo' en la retórica de Néstor Kirchner." *Perfiles Latinoamericanos*, no. 31, 121–150.

Natalucci, Ana

2012 "Políticas sociales y disputas territoriales: el caso del Programa Argentina Trabaja." *Revista Perspectivas de Políticas Públicas* 3: 126–147.

Perelmiter, Luisina

2012 "Fronteras inestables y eficaces: el ingreso de organizaciones de desocupados a la burocracia asistencial del Estado. Argentina (2003–2008)." *Estudios Sociológicos* 30: 431–458.

Pereyra, Sebastián

2011 *¿La lucha es una sola? La movilización social entre la democratización y el neoliberalismo*. Los Polvorines and Buenos Aires: Universidad Nacional Gral. Sarmiento/Biblioteca Nacional.

2016 "La estructura social y la movilización: conflictos políticos y demandas sociales," pp. 233–255 in Gabriel Kessler (ed.), *La sociedad argentina hoy: Radiografía de una nueva estructura*. Buenos Aires: Siglo XXI.

Pérez, Germán and Ana Natalucci

2010 "La matriz movimentista de acción colectiva en Argentina: la experiencia del espacio militante kirchnerista." *América Latina Hoy* 54: 97–112.

Pérez, Verónica and Julián Rebón

2012 *Las vías de la acción directa*. Buenos Aires: Aurelia Rivera.

Retamozo, Martín

2011 "Movimientos sociales, política y hegemonía en Argentina." *Polis: Revista de la Universidad Bolivariana* 10 (28): 243–279.

Scaletta, Claudio

2017 *La recaída neoliberal: La insustentabilidad de la economía macrista*. Buenos Aires: Capital Intelectual.

Schuster, Federico, Germán Pérez, Sebastián Pereyra, Melchor Armesto, Martín Argelino, Analía García, Ana Natalucci, Melina Vázquez, and Patricia Zipcioglu

2006 *Transformaciones de la protesta social en Argentina 1989–2003*. Instituto de Investigaciones Gino Germani Documentos de Trabajo 48.

Senén González, Cecilia

2011 "La revitalización sindical en Argentina durante los Kirchner." *Trabajo y Sindicatos durante los Gobiernos de Izquierda en América Latina* 5 (8): 39–64.

Serulnikov, Sergio

2017 "Como si estuvieran comprando: los saqueos de 1989 y la irrupción de la nueva cuestión social," pp. 137–176 in G. Di Meglio and S. Serulnikov (eds.), *La larga historia de los saqueos en la Argentina: De la independencia a nuestros días.* Buenos Aires: Siglo XXI.

Svampa, Maristella

2005 *La sociedad excluyente: La Argentina bajo el signo del neoliberalismo.* Buenos Aires: Taurus.

2008 *Cambio de época: Movimientos sociales y poder político.* Buenos Aires: Siglo XXI.

Svampa, Maristella and Sebastián Pereyra

2003 *Entre la ruta y el barrio: La experiencia de las organizaciones piqueteras.* Buenos Aires: Biblos.

Vázquez, Melina and Pablo Vommaro

2012 "Con la fuerza de la juventud: aproximaciones a la militancia kirchnerista desde La Cámpora," pp. 149–174 in Germán Pérez and Ana Natalucci (eds.), *Vamos las bandas: Organizaciones y militancia kirchnerista.* Buenos Aires: Nueva Trilce.

World Bank

2018a "Datos del Banco Mundial." https://datos.bancomundial.org/indicador/FP.CPI .TOTL.ZG?end=2018&locations=AR&start=2018&view=bar.

2018b "Datos del Banco Mundial." https://datos.bancomundial.org/indicador/NY .GDP.MKTP.KD.ZG?locations=AR.

Zapata, María Cecilia

2013 "Toma de tierras en la ciudad de Buenos Aires: un análisis de las causas estructurales que anunciaron el conflicto del Indoamericano." *Pampa* 9: 45–71.

PART 3

Social Movements and Progressive Governments in Venezuela, Bolivia, and Ecuador

Of all the Pink Tide governments, those of the Andean nations Venezuela, Bolivia, and Ecuador are considered the farthest to the left. They all declared socialism as a goal, belonged to the proleftist Alianza Bolivariana para los Pueblos de Nuestra América (Bolivarian Alliance for the Peoples of Our America—ALBA), founded by Fidel Castro and Hugo Chávez, and had tense relations with the United States. The Ecuadorian President Rafael Correa ordered the withdrawal of U.S. troops from the Manta military base, while Evo Morales of Bolivia and Chávez expelled U.S. ambassadors in response to Washington's alleged attempts at destabilization and regime change. In addition, in all three countries the leftist governing party was institutionally weak. In Venezuela and Bolivia these parties initially considered themselves "movements," and in Ecuador the governing party consisted of a makeshift alliance founded just prior to Correa's election in 2006.

Bolivia and Ecuador have strong indigenous movements that have confronted the government over environmentally precarious projects involving the exploitation of oil in Ecuador's Yasuní National Park and the construction of a highway in Bolivia's Isiboro Sécure National Park and Indigenous Territory. The relations between the government and social movements in Bolivia contrasted, however, with those in Ecuador. While social movements were instrumental in the Pink Tide's return to power in Bolivia in 2020, the Ecuadorian indigenous movement largely refused to take sides in the 2021 presidential elections that pitted the Pink Tide candidate Andrés Arauz against the neoliberal Guillermo Lasso.

Lucas Koerner explores the potentials and shortcomings of the Bolivarian process in Venezuela with a close examination of the campesino movement and its relations with the Partido Socialista Unido de Venezuela (United Socialist Party—PSUV). He argues that much of the scholarship on the relations between Pink Tide governments and social movements has over-emphasized the role of endogenous causes, neglecting the "unremitting aggression on the part of the world's most powerful imperialist state," the United States. His analysis shows that the tensions and dialogue between the peasant movement and the government were overshadowed by aggression from Washington, which prevented the process from moving forward. Koerner points out that the government of Nicolás Maduro received critical support from vocal campesino organizations, which in 2018 organized the "most ambitious mobilization" in over a decade. Their "far-reaching agrarian reform agenda" was designed to "transform the relationship of the state to the *campesinado* and thus advance the revolutionary process" and included establishing "local campesino-run 'peace courtrooms' and placing state agencies . . . under decentralized grassroots control."

In his chapter on Bolivia, John Brown points to different stages in the relations between the Pink Tide party Movimiento al Socialismo (Movement toward Socialism—MAS) and the nation's vibrant social movements. In the heat of the struggle against neoliberal presidents, the social movements forged a strategic alliance with the MAS that continued after Morales's election "in a common struggle to push forward with constitutional reform in the face of elite resistance" that became "a virtual undeclared civil war in the Eastern lowlands." At the same time social movement leaders "received funding for local projects . . . from the central government while positions in government were opened to local actors." Nevertheless, creative tension stemmed from the social movement adherence to radical demands dating back to the anti-neoliberal struggles of previous years, which included the nationalization and industrialization of natural gas.

The discontent intensified after Morales's reelection in 2009, when the far-right opposition was apparently subdued and "for many grassroots members of popular organizations in El Alto [on which Brown bases his study] the process was moving too slowly." Nevertheless, Brown quotes one social movement official as saying, "We must remain by the government's side. The workers of El Alto cannot align with parties of the right." The tensions, however, intensified to the point that the nation's right took advantage of social movement protests in the lead-up to the coup that ousted Morales in 2019. Under the succeeding government of Jeanine Áñez, "the reemergence of the racist right provided a common enemy that witnessed a re-convergence between divided wings of El Alto's popular organization." Brown concludes, "While movements must walk a tightrope in challenging a left party from the left without strengthening a common enemy on the right . . . the use of excessive party-base linkages to curb contestatory mobilization may ultimately act as the greatest support to the forces of capital."

The case of the "creative tensions" in Ecuador contrasts with that of Bolivia. Alejandra Santillana and Sebastián Terán point out that some of the policies of the Rafael Correa government met the demands of the Ecuadorian social movements but others, particularly those in support of extractive projects, resulted in head-on clashes and imprisonments. Thus the "strong government role in the economy and progressive policies on the social front . . . sharply contrasted with neoliberalism" and significantly reduced poverty. At the same time, however, the strengthening and modernization of the state "entailed the systematic weakening of the social movements and the replacement of the 'popular camp.'" In addition, they note that "the Correa period also saw an attempt to meet the indigenous movement's long-standing demand for Ecuador to become a plurinational state . . . even though the social movements were not as central as they were in Bolivia during the Evo Morales period."

The negative aspects of the Correa presidency were exacerbated under the neoliberal governments that succeeded it. As an example, Santillana and Terán point to the significant reduction in the budget dealing with gender-based violence "in a country where a woman is murdered every three days." They end their chapter with reflections on the electoral triumph of the neoliberal presidential candidate Guillermo Lasso in 2021 "largely because a divided left was unable, even for pragmatic reasons, to work together," a scenario that contrasted with the return of progressive rule in 2020 in Bolivia. The failure of the indigenous movements to become a "counterhegemonic force" was at least partly due to their "inability or unwillingness to engage with the Marxist and Correist left." Nevertheless, they express some hope that convergence based on self-criticism, particularly on the part of Correa and his followers, will prevail: "The popular camp will, no doubt, build its strength on its control of the National Assembly and the ongoing discussions within and across the various sectors of the left."

Chapter 8

In the Empire's Crosshairs

Toward a World-Systemic History of Venezuela's Campesino Movement

Lucas Koerner

One hundred and sixty-two years ago, a liberal rebel army of indigenous and Afro-descendant peasants under the command of "General of the Sovereign People" Ezequiel Zamora rose up against Venezuela's conservative landed oligarchy in what would be known as the Federal War.[1] Despite his being assassinated and his campesino followers' being betrayed by the liberal elites, Zamora's battle cry "Oligarchs tremble!" would long haunt the country's propertied classes, animating future national-popular struggles up to the present. In 1999, Venezuelan peasants once again took up Zamora's banner in their fight for land and liberty, this time after having elected one of their own to the presidency and rewritten the national constitution. The entirely novel historical scenario opened by Hugo Chávez and the Bolivarian Revolution coincided with the beginnings of a concerted U.S. counterinsurgency campaign aimed at defeating the Pink Tide spearheaded by Venezuelan peasants alongside urban semiproletarians and subsequently carried forward by popular forces across the continent. In this article, I endeavor to reframe the history of the past two decades from the neglected vantage point of Venezuela's campesino movement, whose relitigation of the land question clarifies the potentialities and impasses of the Bolivarian process. I argue that we cannot properly account for the successes and shortcomings of the peasant movement and the Bolivarian project writ large without placing them in the context of unremitting aggression on the part of the world's most powerful imperialist state.[1] Scholars have by and large ignored this question of imperialism, tending to present the Bolivarian Revolution and the Pink Tide it initiated as a failure whose causes are mostly endogenous. This represents a serious obstacle to the study of the social movements and the progressive experiments they bring into being.

THE VENEZUELAN CASE IN BROAD CONTEXT

In recent years, a significant body of literature has emerged to evaluate the "end of the progressive cycle" in Latin America and the role of states and social movements in its purported failure. On the right end of the political spectrum, the Pink Tide is the "chronicle of a death foretold": social movements cede the analytical stage to a pan-ideological "populism" that inevitably corroded the foundations of liberal democracy, as it did in the United States by paving the way for the election of Donald Trump (Weyland and Madrid, 2019; Levitsky and Ziblatt, 2018). At the same time, many left-identified writers inquire why Latin American social movements were unable to achieve structural change, blaming progressive governments' anti-democratic "co-optation" of grassroots organizations and/or intensification of resource extraction (Machado and Zibechi, 2017; Webber, 2017; Lander and Arconada, 2019; González, 2019; Svampa, 2019; Riofrancos, 2020) in what Ellner (2021) terms the "neo-extractivism thesis." This left critique is regularly leveled at Venezuela's Bolivarian Revolution, notwithstanding its well-deserved reputation as the most radical of Pink Tide experiments. According to these scholars, Venezuela's current crisis is the result of the failure of the Chavista administrations to fundamentally restructure the inherited petro-state and rentier accumulation regime. Most point to a combination of "subjective" factors, including what they identify as the Bolivarian government's authoritarian verticalism, systemic corruption, and "extractivist" economic policies (López Maya, 2018; Lander and Arconada, 2019; González, 2019), while others emphasize "objective" constraints such as Chavismo's limited reach beyond its urban poor social base and opposition disruption, among other elements (Rojas, 2018; Buxton, 2020).

However, the vast majority of this literature on Venezuela fails to grapple with the agency of the United States as a central analytical variable. The same goes for the precrisis scholarship on Venezuelan social movements, which is largely focused on "internal" state-society relations (Fernandes, 2010; Ciccariello-Maher, 2013; 2016; Valencia, 2015; Azzellini, 2018). There is indeed a disconnect between these two bodies of literature and that examining U.S. foreign policy vis-à-vis Venezuela (Golinger, 2006; Corrales and Romero, 2013; Gill, 2019; Gill and Marshall, 2020). Following Ellner (2020a), I argue that the Bolivarian process and the social movements that constitute its motive force can only be evaluated in the context of virtually unceasing U.S. aggression. But in order to examine Washington's role in molding the terrain on which Venezuelan social movements maneuver, we must overcome "methodological nationalism," which cordons off the "internal" sphere of state/society relations from the "external" one, in this case U.S. "foreign" policy (Wimmer and Schiller, 2003). In other words, we need a holistic approach mapping the dialectical relationship between the U.S. Empire and Venezuela's state and social formation.

IMPERIALISM IN VENEZUELA: A "RELATIONAL" APPROACH

My point of departure in sketching the contours of U.S. imperialism in Venezuela is the state theory of Nicos Poulantzas. A number of scholars have made contributions in applying Poulantzas's "relational" approach to the Venezuelan context (Nelson, 2013; 2020; Enríquez and Newman, 2016; Ellner, 2017; Lubbock, 2020). What is lacking, however, is a theory of how the U.S. imperial state—itself the "material condensation" of a relationship of metropolitan class forces hegemonized by U.S. monopoly capital—participates in shaping the "strategic field" of peripheral states like Venezuela's (Poulantzas, 1978: 128, 136). Beginning under the early-twentieth-century Gómez dictatorship, Washington and Western oil companies in alliance with a new comprador bourgeoisie established a neocolonial development model predicated on U.S. hegemony over oil production, internal security, mass media, consumer culture, and foreign policy (Quintero, 2007; Tinker Salas, 2009). The distinction here between the U.S. state and U.S. multinational firms must be viewed "not as the boundary between two discrete entities but as a line drawn internally, within the network of institutional mechanisms through which a social and political order is maintained" (Mitchell, 2006: 170).[2] What we have, then, is the "internalization . . . of the foreign capital within the power blocs of these social formations . . . affect[ing] their state, a state that intervenes in the reproduction of the dominant imperialist relations at the heart of its own social formation" (Poulantzas, 2008: 315).

The Venezuelan state petroleum company PDVSA played precisely such a role during the 2002–2003 oil lockout: bourgeois state power was displaced from the Chavista-controlled executive and legislature to the opposition-aligned company management (Poulantzas, 1978: 138; Nelson, 2013: 178), which launched an economic coup d'état aimed at ousting Chávez and preserving imperialist relations based on the extraction of oil rent by U.S. and European capital via the local bourgeoisie (Sánchez Otero, 2012). However, even after the Chavista seizure of PDVSA, the Washington-backed opposition retained powerful enclaves within the "expanded state," including the judiciary, the public prosecution, the private media, the traditional universities, and nongovernmental organizations (NGOs), which would prove instrumental in subsequent coup attempts. U.S. federal agencies provided funding and technical assistance to anti-Chavista NGOs (Gill, 2019), the rabidly *golpista* private media remained in the hands of oligarchs closely tied to the United States and Europe (Golinger, 2006), and the Euro-descendant upper middle class born of Western oil companies' neocolonial "social engineering" project continued to supply most of the country's judges, prosecutors, and university professors (Tinker Salas, 2009: 5, 185–186; Emersberger and Podur, 2021: 164–166). Moreover, the traditional bourgeoisie maintained a stranglehold on the economy, especially in the import and retail sectors, which it leveraged to drain hundreds of billions of state-supplied petrodollars from the country through import fraud and other mechanisms (Sutherland, 2016). And while the Bolivarian government made efforts to expand the state and communal sectors as well as secure tactical alliances with "patriotic businesspeople," these emerging fractions engaged in illicit accumulation much as did their traditional counterparts (Ellner, 2020b). Reformist elements likewise remained entrenched within the bureaucracy and the ruling party, undermining the government's socialist agenda and later consolidating their hegemony as the imperialist offensive intensified under the Nicolás Maduro administration.

Imperialism is a hierarchical structure of sustained value transfer from the countries of the African, Asian, Caribbean, and Latin American "periphery" to the U.S., Western European, and Japanese "core" (Dussel, 2013; Cope, 2019). This structure is not merely "external" but "internalized . . . inserted in and modify[ing] the relations of force between classes of these countries . . . articulat[ing] the specific contradictions . . . that appear, in certain of their aspects, as the induced reproduction of contradictions in the imperialist chain" (Poulantzas, 2008: 316). Modified by the implantation of neocolonial relations, Bolivarian Venezuela's state and social formation came to constitute a decisive battleground in the international class war: the national-popular movement raising anew the banner of socialism in its fight for substantive democratization of the country (Pascual Marquina and Gilbert, 2020: 16) and the creation of a regional anti-imperialist bloc (Aponte García and Amézquita Puntiel, 2015; Cusack, 2018) posed an "extraordinary threat" to U.S. hegemony in its own "backyard." Washington and its local allies responded with no fewer than six coup attempts (Emersberger and Podur, 2021), in addition to economic warfare first during the 2002 oil lockout and then, after 2017, international sanctions that remain in force (Weisbrot and Sachs, 2019; Rodríguez, 2021). As in the case of other Global South countries devastated by Western hybrid warfare (Moyo and Yeros, 2007; Kadri, 2019; Capasso, 2020), the economic destruction of Venezuela is not a mere side effect of the

U.S. regime-change strategy but an indispensable modality of accumulation. Yet Venezuela has been targeted not only because it sits on the world's largest proven oil reserves but because of its representing a *"socialist example* that once inspired the world" (Pascual Marquina and Gilbert, 2020: 15–16). The two-decade-long imperial counterinsurgency has aimed to terminate the most ambitious revolutionary experiment of the present century and in so doing strike a blow to labor regionally, if not globally. It is no coincidence, then, that the escalating assault on Venezuela in the wake of Hugo Chávez's 2013 death was followed by the lawfare operation in Brazil that ousted Dilma Rousseff and jailed Lula da Silva, the 2019 overthrow of Evo Morales in Bolivia, and the failed 2018 "soft coup" in Nicaragua, in each case spearheaded by U.S.-backed opposition forces attempting to roll back the left-in-power's impressive social achievements and reimpose Washington's diktat.

To buttress my argument for bringing an analysis of imperialism "back in" to the study of Latin American social movements, I will now turn to Venezuela's campesino movement. The case study offers a sorely neglected vantage point for examining the Bolivarian process in a world-systemic context.

WAR ON THE LATIFUNDIO

In recent years, a rich body of literature has emerged evaluating agrarian development policies under the Bolivarian Revolution (Enríquez, 2013; Purcell, 2017), especially the government's contradictory efforts to promote food sovereignty and agro-ecology (Enríquez and Newman, 2016; Felicien, Schiavoni, and Romero, 2018; Lubbock, 2019). However, outside of rural communes (Ciccariello-Maher, 2016), Venezuela's campesino movement has been understudied compared with its regional counterparts (Vergara-Camus and Kay, 2013). The South American country has a long history of peasant militancy, from the nineteenth-century War of Independence and Federal War through the early-twentieth-century underground organizations known as *cajas rurales* and later the *ligas campesinas* (peasant leagues) to the present (Ciccariello-Maher, 2013: 204–205). And while campesino struggles continued under the adverse conditions of the pacted Puntofijista regime that preceded Chávez (Lavelle, 2014: 145), it was the latter's election and 2001 promulgation of the Land Law that "changed things 100 percent" (Virigay, 2010: 56). For the first time ever, Venezuela's indigenous and Afro-descendant peasants had elected one of their own who was committed to the transformation of production relations in the savagely unequal countryside. On the eve of Chávez's election, Venezuela had one of the most unequal landholding distributions in the world, with 75 percent of arable land in the hands of just 5 percent of landowners (Wilpert, 2006: 252). The enactment of the Land Law was thus a watershed moment, sanctioning the occupation and expropriation of idle land with the aim of eliminating the large estates known as latifundios and thereby democratizing land tenure.

But the revolutionary offensive beginning with the Land Law and 48 other decrees issued by Chávez in 2001 did not go unopposed. In a televised press conference, the president of the ranchers' lobby, José Luis Betancourt, ripped up a copy of the law in what was unambiguously a declaration of war against campesinos and the Chávez government. Indeed, the Land Law was "one of the main motivations for the April 2002 coup attempt and the 2003 shutdown of the oil industry" (Wilpert, 2006: 253–254). Though both coup attempts ultimately failed, the landed oligarchy unleashed a low-intensity war in the countryside, their hit men (*sicariato*) assassinating 75 campesinos in a seven-month period between 2001 and 2002 alone (Virigay, 2010: 57). While the Chávez government's simultaneous efforts to expand state regulation of the oil and fishing industries as part of the 49 decrees undoubtedly threatened the interests of key fractions of the country's comprador bourgeoisie, it was the land question that, in the words of the 47-hour-dictator Pedro Carmona (2005), was especially "delicate." Chávez (2006a) himself emphasized the centrality of the countryside in Venezuela's class struggle, quoting the Peruvian socialist revolutionary José Carlos Mariátegui: "The regime of landed property determines the political and administrative regime of every nation." Revolutionizing agrarian production relations under campesino hegemony—the sine qua non for food sovereignty—menaced not only the laatifundista elite but also transnational agro-industrial capital like Polar, whose oligopolistic control of the agrifood system is premised on continued import dependence (Sánchez, 2019a; Felicien, Schiavoni, and Romero, 2018: 6–7). Both class fractions are deeply interlinked with imperialist capital, on which they depend for technology and productive inputs purchased with petrodollars historically provided at preferential rates by the Venezuelan state (Purcell, 2017). Drawing on the historical legacy of the Federal War, Chávez and the campesino movement's "war on the latifundio" threatened to uproot this neocolonial social metabolism based on the comprador bourgeoisie's usurpation of the land and petroleum rents of the subsoil, which maintains the country permanently vulnerable to U.S.-led aggression (Coronil, 1997).

The first years following the Land Law's enactment were, in the words of Plataforma de Lucha Campesina (Campesino Struggle Platform) leader Andrés Alayo (2020: 240), "characterized by an enormous popular momentum. Hundreds of campesino cooperatives were formed, and the Venezuelan people witnessed thousands of cases of vacant land's being occupied." During this period, the immense bottom-up mobilization that defeated the U.S.-backed opposition efforts to oust Chávez in the coup, oil strike, and recall referendum pushed the Venezuelan president to deepen the revolutionary process. After distributing 2.3 million hectares of state land in 2003–2004, the government finally set its sights on private estates in 2005 (Wilpert, 2006: 257). An emblematic case is the 13,000-hectare El Charcote cattle ranch, owned by the Vestey Group, a meat products conglomerate belonging to one of England's wealthiest aristocratic families. The estate was initially occupied by 26 campesinos in 2000, only to be later joined by hundreds of families who proceeded to form cooperatives with assistance from state institutions (Lemoine, 2003). The peasants' direct action pushed the government first to intervene and later to expropriate the ranch alongside several other large estates (Venezuelanalysis, 2006). Yet despite the popular impetus of these early years, the pace of expropriations remained exceedingly slow, with a total of just 2.5 million hectares of privately held land redistributed during the entire 2005–2011 period (Wilpert, 2013: 6). Contrary to Lord Vestey's fears, Venezuela had not "done a Zimbabwe," namely massively transferred land to the racialized peasantry (Venezuelanalysis, 2006; Moyo and Yeros, 2007).

APPARATUSES OF REACTION

The biggest challenge faced by the campesino movement came, paradoxically, from within the state itself. The judicial apparatus continued to be staffed by "lawyers and judges [who] share the same cultural background and class origins as the landowners and latifundistas" (Edward Ellis, quoted in Emersberger and Podur, 2021: 165). Still under opposition control, the Supreme Court struck down two vital provisions of the Land Law in 2002. Article 89 allowed campesinos to preemptively occupy estates that met the criteria for expropriation pending litigation, while Article 90 exonerated the government from compensating landowners for investments made on the land (Wilpert, 2006: 256). Though the Chávez government attempted to legalize the occupations by issuing temporary land-use charters (*cartas agrarias*) and in 2005 effectively reinstating Article 90, the judicial obstructionism nevertheless "represented a severe blow to the land-reform process because it made it far more expensive and far slower than it would otherwise have been" (Wilpert, 2013: 6). The ruling came around the same time that the president of the court enjoyed close relations with Washington, which "sought to steer the . . . [court] in a particular direction on a range of issues," including supporting a recall referendum against Chávez, refraining from prosecuting the U.S.-funded opposition NGO Súmate, and blocking unfavorable legislation such as tougher telecommunications regulations (Gill, 2019: 302–303). This context illustrates the tilted nature of the institutional playing field, where imperialist-aligned forces clearly retained the upper hand. At the local and state levels, courts frequently ruled in favor of large landowners challenging the legality of the land-use charters (Wilpert, 2006: 256). This put peasants at risk of eviction by state police and the National Guard, whose role remained "ambiguous at best" (Lavelle, 2013: 144–145). Even newly created agrarian reform bodies like the Instituto Nacional de Tierra (National Land Institute—INTI) at times opposed land occupations (Lavelle, 2013: 145–146), in addition to being hobbled by a lack of institutional capacity and of interagency coordination (Enríquez, 2013; Enríquez and Newman, 2016).

But the most serious barrier to land reform was systematic impunity with regard to the landlord violence that was responsible for 130 deaths by 2005 alone (Wilpert, 2006: 259). As Alayo (2020: 240) and many other campesino leaders have repeatedly pointed out, "The truth is that the state's institutions—the Prosecutor's Office, the Office of the Ombudsman, the courthouses, the judges, and the justice system as a whole—never showed much willingness to bring to justice those responsible for murdering *campesinos*." The alignment of the judicial apparatus with the latifundistas and the comprador bourgeoisie as a whole is not simply a function of judges' and prosecutors' elite class extraction (Miliband, 1969) but reflects the "antipopular" logic of key state institutions, which can reproduce itself even after the "democratization of personnel recruitment" (Poulantzas, 1978: 157; Koerner, 2020).[3] At different conjunctures, the Chávez administration attempted to reform the police, the public prosecution, the courts, and the prisons and/or bypass them by creating parallel structures (Ellner, 2014: 194), but it did not significantly modify the legal system's "relation . . . to the popular masses" (Poulantzas, 1978: 157). In an effort to shift the balance of forces within the state, thousands of peasants marched on Caracas in 2005 and 2006 to demand that the government take decisive action to advance land reform and end impunity, including designating local agrarian officials in consultation with grassroots organizations, dispatching prosecutors to investigate assassinations, and cracking down on corrupt police and military personnel (FNCEZ, 2006). But the government failed to meet the movement's core demands, mostly because doing so would have required the radical transformation of the judicial apparatus and other state structures still totally or partially in opposition hands, which it was not prepared to carry out. Indeed the project of land reform was always limited by the bourgeois legality of the ancien régime: rather than simply declaring all landholdings exceeding a certain size illegal and seizing them without compensation, the government opted for compensated expropriation only of latifundios that failed to provide legal documentation, even though land titles in Venezuela were generally issued by corrupt authorities beholden to the landed oligarchy (Wilpert, 2006: 252–253, 257–258; Ciccariello-Maher, 2013: 209). The institutional rupture that thoroughgoing land reform demanded was at odds with the electoral road to revolutionary political and socioeconomic change embodied in the Bolivarian process (Enríquez and Newman, 2016: 595). Leftist critics such as the former vice minister of planning Roland Denis (2015) have accused the Chávez government of failing to seize on the defeat of the 2002 coup to overhaul the inherited bourgeois state as dissident sectors of the armed forces led by Chávez (2006b) had planned to do in the wake of the thwarted February 4, 1992, civic-military uprising.

However, rarely are the world-systemic constraints on radicalization factored into the analysis, among them the potential U.S. response, which might have taken the form of crushing economic sanctions and other modalities of hybrid warfare currently being employed against Venezuela and other Global South countries that have likewise carried out social revolutions or national liberation struggles. This constant menace in part deterred the government from combating impunity not just for landlords and their sicarios but for U.S.-sponsored perpetrators of coups and counterrevolutionary destabilization across the board. We should recall that in 2004 a U.S. congressional representative met with the Venezuelan prosecutor Danilo Anderson and threatened to block a US$45 million World Bank loan for judicial modernization if the latter pursued his case against Súmate (Gill, 2019: 303). Anderson, who also led the investigation into the 2002 coup, was killed by a car bomb several weeks later. The murder came just six months after a foiled assassination attempt on Chávez, who blamed both attacks on the Washington-and Bogotá-backed opposition (Emersberger and Podur, 2021: 106, 229–230). In the face of such low-intensity warfare, and with the United States bogged down in Iraq, the Bolivarian process might have been more successful had it confronted Washington and the local oligarchy head-on through a bottom-up strategy relying on the momentum of the popular masses to force a revolutionary breakthrough.

REFORM FROM ABOVE

The campesinos' historic 2006 march marked the end of the popular offensive that began with the enactment of the Land Law (Alayo, 2020: 240). Rather than double down on the strategy of bottom-up land reform as enshrined in Article 89 (Wilpert, 2013: 6), the Chávez government shifted to a top-down policy of taking over vacant estates and placing them under the direct control of the Land and Agriculture Ministry, which administered large state enterprises employing peasants as wage laborers (Alayo, 2020: 241). The change in policy was not the will of any single individual or class fraction but instead emerged from the "collision" of contradictory social forces, comprador and national-popular, old and new (Poulantzas, 1978: 135–136). It was during this period that Chávez became increasingly disconnected from the popular masses both in the countryside and in the urban barrios, which began to demobilize (López, 2015: 139–140; Gilbert, 2021) as reformist bureaucratic fractions cemented their leadership within the revolutionary process via the Partido Socialista Unido (United Socialist Party—PSUV), freshly forged from the proverbial rib of the bourgeois state (Ellner, 2014: 174; Hetland, 2016). According to Enríquez and Newman (2016: 607), the emerging agrarian model "entailed a change in the state's emphasis, from promoting small farms and cooperative agricultural initiatives through land redistribution . . . to consolidating state farms and a rapprochement with large farmers (with increased food imports to supplement domestic production)." The new policy direction stabilized the position of the imperialist-linked class fractions—agro-industrial monopoly capital and large landowners—which continued their low-intensity war against the Bolivarian process through capital flight and targeted killings of campesino and other popular leaders. By 2011, more than 260 peasants had been assassinated without a single landlord's being brought to justice (Wilpert, 2013: 9). The antipopular logic undergirding key state institutions' relations to the peasantry thus remained unchanged, as exemplified not only in the systematic impunity sustained by the judicial apparatus but also in state enterprises like Agropatria (Prado, 2020: 52). Created from the 2010 nationalization of transnational agricultural inputs supplier AgroIsleña, Agropatria was intended to provide small- and medium-sized producers with seeds, agrochemicals, and fertilizers at regulated prices. And while it did significantly expand access to inputs in the early years, the nationalized firm did not fundamentally break with the imperialist social metabolism embodied in AgroIsleña, which had sold its technological packages from Monsanto and other Northern conglomerates, imported with Venezuelan state-issued preferential dollars, at monopoly prices, driving many small farmers into bottomless debt (Purcell, 2017: 305; Reardon, 2010). Agropatria never broke from the mold of AgroIsleña as a local distributor of largely transnational-sourced seeds, fertilizers, and other essentials (Sánchez, 2019b) that its administrators would resell on the black market at inflated prices, inciting popular protest (Purcell, 2017: 306–307; ALBA TV, 2011). These structural continuities in Agropatria, together with growing dependence on food imports paid for with subsidized dollars provided to the comprador bourgeoisie, evidence the persistent embeddedness of imperialist relations.

While the post-2006 period was characterized by overall popular demobilization and bureaucratic retrenchment, there were also countervailing tendencies at work, especially during Chávez's final years. It was paradoxically after 2009—when the structural vulnerabilities of the hybrid post-neoliberal economic model became more apparent (Schincariol, 2020: 111–114)—that Chávez and the popular movement embarked upon the

Bolivarian Revolution's most innovative political experiment: the commune as the foundation of socialist democracy (Gilbert, 2017). Across the country, grassroots militants answered Chávez's call to form communes based on direct democracy and socialized control of the means of production, building on prior organizing experiences both during and preceding the Bolivarian process (Kozarek, 2019–2021). It is no coincidence, then, that many of the most successful communes were founded in rural areas by campesinos continuing the centuries-long struggle for land, which would put them at odds with key sectors of the bureaucracy. For instance, the El Maizal communards in Lara fought a protracted battle to take control of lands that Chávez had ordered expropriated and turned over to them in 2009 but the Venezuelan Food Corporation, allegedly colluding with private landlords, had refused to place in communal hands (Ciccariello-Maher, 2016). Such conflicts would only sharpen amid the escalating imperialist assault of the years following Chávez's death as reformist elites gained hegemony within the government at the expense of campesinos and other organized popular sectors.

IMPERIALIST OFFENSIVE, SHARPENING STRUGGLE

Hugo Chávez died on March 5, 2013, after a lengthy battle with cancer, which some speculate may have been induced by Washington (Golinger, 2016). His successor, Nicolás Maduro, secured a narrow win in a snap election. The U.S.-backed opposition baselessly cried fraud and took to the streets in insurrectionary violence that caused the deaths of nine people (Venezuelanalysis, 2013), egged on by the Obama administration's refusal to recognize Maduro's victory for months after the rest of the international community had done so. The opposition would unleash similar rounds of violent street mobilizations (*guarimbas*) aimed at ousting the Maduro government in 2014 and 2017, with firm U.S. support. Meanwhile, the Venezuelan economy was hard hit by the post-2014 collapse of global oil prices and the imposition of a de facto financial blockade under Obama's sanctions (Vivanco, 2016), later formalized by Trump in 2017 with the explicit aim of toppling the Maduro government (Weisbrot and Sachs, 2019). It is in this context of mounting destabilization that the top-down model of state-directed, large-scale agricultural production fell into crisis and began to be dismembered by comprador fractions within the bureaucracy (Alayo, 2020: 242). As we have seen in the case of Agropatria, the state firm became "'a pioneer of *bachaqueo*,' profiteering from reselling or manipulating access to subsidized agrarian inputs often en masse over the border in Colombia" (Purcell, 2017: 306). The dismantling of the state agricultural sector dovetailed with a rise in violent evictions of campesinos occupying idle land carried out by state security forces on the orders of regional INTI officials (Boothroyd-Rojas, 2017). What was emerging in the post-Chávez era was a new landlord class fraction closely linked to sectors of the bureaucracy and the PSUV, which the land and agriculture minister Wilmar Castro Soteldo (2018) would later christen the "revolutionary bourgeoisie."

The new direction in state agrarian policy was not so much a response to any single top-down decision as a reflection of the shifting terrain of class struggle, in which campesinos were no less an actor than landlords and bureaucrats. One early example of campesino resistance to the nascent "revolutionary bourgeoisie" was the January 2017 occupation of an unproductive ranch in Yaracuy that reportedly belonged to the wife of an air force captain and former PSUV mayor. Members of the local Negro Miguel Commune seized the abandoned estate and held it for 12 days amid efforts by the state police and the National Guard to dislodge them (Kozarek, 2017). That same year, El Maizal communards similarly occupied the Venezuelan Food Corporation–managed Porcinos del ALBA pig farm together with its employees. The public enterprise had been established as part of an agreement with Cuba but left in a state of ruin by company managers allegedly intending to privatize it (Comuna El Maizal, 2019). The campesinos carried out the occupation in late June 2017 amid the third and bloodiest round of U.S.-backed *guarimbas*, which paralyzed the country for months and left scores dead. While the timing may have been fortuitous, it is nevertheless quite likely that the context of right-wing violence targeting state institutions, especially in the agrifood area (Felicien, Schiavoni, and Romero, 2018), made it harder for hostile bureaucratic sectors to repress an occupation so clearly Chavista-identified as this one.

The rural class struggle only intensified in 2018. In the face of ongoing evictions, continuing impunity for over 300 peasant assassinations, and bureaucratic lethargy in granting land titles and agrarian charters, the campesino movement sought to leverage the conjuncture of presidential elections to push the government to the left on agrarian policy (Pascual Marquina, 2018). Peasants launched what was perhaps the most ambitious mobilization since the 2005–2006 occupations of Caracas, the Admirable Campesino March. Following a similar route as Simón Bolívar's 1813 Admirable Campaign, campesino representatives from 10 states marched 435 kilometers to demand a far-reaching agrarian reform agenda that would transform the relationship of the state to the peasantry and thus advance the revolutionary process. Their demands included not just the long-standing calls for prosecution of violence by landlords and state functionaries as well as land and productive inputs for small farmers but also deep structural reforms such as establishing local campesino-run "peace courtrooms" and placing state agencies like Agropatria under decentralized grassroots control

(Sieveres and Ortega, 2020: 225–228). After some initial tensions, Maduro and senior state officials held a two-hour public meeting with peasant leaders, who in one of the most remarkable political episodes of the post-Chávez era powerfully berated government institutions on live television and demanded that the president take decisive action (VTV, 2018). The moment of popular ferment was violently cut short two days later when a pair of explosive-laden drones was shot down at a military ceremony, detonating just meters away from Maduro. While no evidence surfaced directly tying Washington to the incident, it is undeniable that relentless hostility—which included the unprecedented sanctioning of the sitting president and refusal to recognize his reelection victory—created the conditions for the assassination attempt (Ellner, 2018). The grassroots momentum dissipated as the peasant struggle disappeared from the national spotlight and with it the possibility, however limited, of shifting the correlation of class forces in the wake of Maduro's reelection (Escalona, 2018). Though campesinos continued to mobilize over the following months, their demands were corralled within bureaucratic channels as the government pursued a liberalizing economic agenda in alliance with landed elites, old and new.

(NEO)LIBERALIZATION AND THE GUAIDÓ ERA

On January 23, 2019, a previously little-known opposition legislator recently chosen to head the National Assembly, Juan Guaidó, swore himself in as "interim president" and was immediately recognized by Washington, which broadened existing financial sanctions into a full-fledged oil embargo aimed at starving the country into submission. Thus began the sixth U.S.-backed coup effort (Emersberger and Podur, 2021), which was almost immediately countered by nationwide Chavista demonstrations (Venezuelanalysis, 2019), with campesinos taking the lead in mobilizing against the coming right-wing offensive as early as January 10 (Tatuy TV/Venezuelanalysis, 2019). Yet the peasantry also continued producing the fruits and vegetables feeding the millions of people left hungry by spiraling inflation and dwindling food imports severely exacerbated by years of tightening sanctions, thereby "hamper[ing] the possibility of a social explosion, which is one of the U.S. State Department's aims" (Alayo, 2020: 243). Notwithstanding campesinos' anti-imperialist protagonism, the unprecedented imperialist escalation would only strengthen the hand of the domestic class forces arrayed against them.

Assassinations continued at an alarming rate, with 19 peasants killed just in the eight months following the meeting with Maduro (ALBA TV, 2019). Impunity was virtually absolute for their killers, as it remained for Guaidó and the other U.S. clients behind the latest coup and its prior iterations. The government likewise mostly failed to fulfill its promises to grant titles for idle lands seized by peasants and halt evictions ordered by local INTI functionaries. In response to government inaction——itself a function of the "contradictory structure of the state" (Poulantzas, 1978: 134)—campesinos mounted a two-month-long vigil inside the INTI's Caracas headquarters to increase pressure on the Maduro administration while simultaneously standing with it against the accelerating U.S. onslaught (Vaz, 2019).

However, despite repeated protests, campesinos and other social movements were unable to halt the progressive dismantling of the Bolivarian national-popular project, in part because of the political demobilization of the late Chávez years and the atomizing effects of an economic downturn intensified by U.S. sanctions that further weakened grassroots organizations increasingly dependent on institutional support. The chief beneficiaries of this new balance of forces were comprador state fractions tied to agro-industry and the import sector, which seized the opportunity to push through a liberalizing agenda of dollarization, abrogation of price controls and labor protections, and sweeping privatization of state companies starved of funds by U.S. sanctions and deliberate disinvestment (Salas and Pascual Marquina, 2021). While privatization had begun in piecemeal fashion as early as 2015, it did not formally become state policy until 2019, when the government began a massive transfer of state lands and enterprises to the "revolutionary bourgeoisie" under the banner of "strategic alliances" with private capital (Pérez, 2021). For instance, in the leading agrarian state of Portuguesa, the installations and agricultural machinery belonging to the state-run Pedro Carmejo company were turned over to "an entrepreneur close to the [state] governor," and numerous other state firms met a similar fate (Tatuy TV, 2020). Emblematic of this policy shift was the 2020 Anti-Blockade Law, which under the pretext of skirting sanctions opened the way for even more aggressive privatizations such as that of Agropatria (Fuentes, 2020; Dobson, 2020). Yet the emerging bourgeois fraction was never as "revolutionary" as Castro Soteldo (2018) claimed, frequently siding with the traditional bourgeoisie in its U.S.-sponsored war on the Bolivarian process. The dramatic expansion of the agro-industrial firm El Tunal in recent years offers an instructive example: the firm's owner, Alejo "El Tornillo" Hernández, received 5,000 hectares of state land in Portuguesa despite having openly agitated for Maduro's overthrow and allegedly contracted sicarios to assassinate workers years before (Alayo, 2020: 244; ALBA TV, 2013). Ellner (2020b) is therefore correct that this "new" sector is basically undifferentiated in its antagonism toward the Bolivarian Revolution from "older" bourgeois fractions, likewise eager to topple the remaining national-popular institutional pillars. What has changed is that the Bolivarian government's pragmatic policy of forging "tactical" alliances with the former in response to U.S.-led destabilization has evolved into a "strategic" embrace of private capital as the engine of economic recovery and development. Paradoxically, the Maduro administration's gradual implementation of structural adjustment policies has in no way mollified Washington, which has only intensified its offensive, actively targeting rising agrifood import magnates like Alex Saab, who was illegally detained in Cape Verde and extradited to the United States in October 2021 for his role in supplying the government's food distribution program. This is because economic (neo)liberalization is secondary to the objective of annihilating the Bolivarian process as a precursor to complete recolonization.[4] As long as the Bolivarian government stays in power, the door remains open to popular struggle capable of possibly reversing the reformist tide and reactivating the revolutionary potentialities of Chavismo, without succumbing to the catastrophe of neocolonial restoration.[5]

The 2021 regional and municipal elections evidence the promise and peril of the present moment. The ruling socialist party's crushing defeat in Chávez's home state of Barinas and other former rural strongholds might be read as an index of the deep discontent with the broader rightist turn, in which the agrarian question has played no small part. Yet the mayoral victory of El Maizal Commune spokesperson Ángel Prado in Simón Planas, in the context of Chavismo's overall electoral triumph, suggests that the Bolivarian flame is far from extinguished.

CONCLUSION

I have proposed a reframing of the history of Bolivarian Venezuela from the largely overlooked standpoint of the campesino movement. Peasants' struggle for land and justice in the countryside lays bare the lingering possibilities and deepening contradictions within the Bolivarian process, which I argue cannot be understood outside the world-systemic context of imperialist relations fundamentally shaping the national terrain of class war. It is therefore imperative to bring the study of imperialism back into the analysis of social movements, especially now that the left is tentatively returning to power across the region.

NOTES

1. I thank Steve Ellner, Ronaldo Munck, Matteo Capasso, Ricardo Vaz, Cira Pascual Marquina, Chris Gilbert, Max Ajl, and an anonymous reviewer for their thoughtful comments and revisions.

2. As the U.S. National Security Council itself admitted, "oil operations, are for all practical purposes, instruments of our foreign policy towards these countries" (Tinker Salas, 2009: 205–206).

3. "It is thus not merely that many state institutions remained staffed by holdovers from the pre-Chávez ancien régime now "dress[ed] in red" (Virigay, 2010: 54) but that functionaries who had come up through the ranks of the Chavista movement have perpetuated an antipopular logic and have occasionally defected to the opposition.

4. I am indebted to Max Ajl for this insight.

5. Reradicalization is not unprecedented, as is seen, for example, in the case of the Mexican Revolution under the government of Lázaro Cárdenas in the 1930s.

REFERENCES

Alayo, Andrés
2020 "*Campesinos* defending Chávez's project: a conversation with Andrés Alayo," pp. 238–248 in Cira Pascual Marquina and Chris Gilbert (eds.), *Venezuela: The Present as Struggle—Voices from the Bolivarian Revolution*. New York: Monthly Review Press.
ALBA TV
2011 "Campesinos toman sede de Agropatria en El Vigía." April 7. https://www .albatv.org/Campesinos-toman-sede-de.html.
2013 "Sicarios patronales y Policía Militar atacan a trabajadores en Lara." February 27. https://www.albatv.org/Sicarios-patronales-y-Policia.html.
2019 "Eight months later, the campesino march walks on but solutions are yet to arrive." Venezuelanalysis, April 29. https://venezuelanalysis.com/analysis/14449.
Aponte García, Maribel and Gloria Amézquita Puntiel (eds.)
2015 *El ALBA-TCP: Origen y fruto del nuevo regionalismo latinoamericano y cari-beño*. Buenos Aires: CLACSO.
Azzellini, Dario
2018 *Communes and Workers' Control in Venezuela: Building 21st-Century Socialism from Below*. Leiden and Boston: Brill.
Boothroyd-Rojas, Rachael
2017 "Investigation launched into violent eviction of rural families in Venezuela." Venezuelanalysis, March 14. https://venezuelanalysis.com/news/12975.
Buxton, Julia
2020 "Continuity and change in Venezuela's Bolivarian Revolution." *Third World Quarterly* 41: 1371–1387.
Capasso, Matteo
2020 "The war and the economy: the gradual destruction of Libya." *Review of African Political Economy* 47 (166): 545–567.
Carmona Estranga, Pedro
2004 "Mi testimonio ante la historia." https://dokumen.tips/documents/mi-testimonio -ante-la-historia.html.
Castro Soteldo, Wilmar

2018 "Cultivando patria no. 99." https://www.youtube.com/watch?v=7DYCTRePl6g.

Chávez, Hugo

2006a "Aló Presidente no. 249." June 8. http://todochavez.gob.ve/todochavez/4032
-alo-presidente-n-259.

2006b "Intervención del Comandante Presidente Hugo Chávez, en la inauguración de
la Unidad Oncológica 'Kléber Ramírez Rojas' del Hospital Luis Razetti." October
5. http://www.todochavez.gob.ve/todochavez/3438-intervencion-del-comandante
-presidente-hugo-chavez-en-la-inauguracion-de-la-unidad-oncologica-kleber
-ramirez-rojas-del-hospital-luis-razetti.

Ciccariello-Maher, George

2013 *We Created Chávez: A People's History of the Venezuelan Revolution.* Durham,
NC: Duke University Press.

2016 *Building the Commune: Radical Democracy in Venezuela.* London: Verso.

Comuna El Maizal

2019 "UP Porcinos El Maizal." https://comunaelmaizal.wordpress.com/up-porcinos
-el-maizal/.

Cope, Zak

2019 *The Wealth of (Some) Nations: Imperialism and the Mechanics of Value
Transfer.* London: Pluto Press.

Coronil, Fernando

1997 *The Magical State: Nature, Money, and Modernity in Venezuela.* Chicago:
University of Chicago Press.

Corrales, Javier and Carlos A. Romero

2012 *U. S.-Venezuela Relations since the 1990s.* London: Taylor & Francis Group.

Cusack, Asa K.

2018 *Venezuela, ALBA, and the Limits of Postneoliberal Regionalism in Latin
America and the Caribbean.* New York: Palgrave Macmillan.

Denis, Roland

2015 "Roland Denis: 'Chávez didn't dare to do what he had to between 2002 and
2003.'" Venezuelanalysis, June 12. https://venezuelanalysis.com/analysis/11414.

Dobson, Paul

2020 "Venezuelan government privatises state-run Agropatria." Venezuelanalysis,
November 30. https://venezuelanalysis.com/news/15064.

Dussel, Enrique

2013 *16 tesis de economía política: Una filosofía de la economía.* Buenos Aires:
Editorial Docencia.

Ellner, Steve

2014 *El fenómeno Chávez: Sus orígenes e impacto hasta 2013.* Caracas: Fundación
Celarg.

2017 "Implications of Marxist state theory and how they play out in Venezuela."
Historical Materialism 25 (2): 29–62.

2018 "What will result from Venezuela's drone explosions." *Latin American Advisor,*
August 16. https://www.thedialogue.org/analysis/what-will-result-from-venezuelas
-drone-explosions/.

2020a "Introduction: Latin America's Pink Tide governments: challenges, break-throughs, and setbacks," pp. 1–19 in Steve Ellner (ed.), *Latin America's Pink Tide: Breakthroughs and Shortcomings*. Lanham, MD: Rowman and Littlefield.

2020b "Class strategies in Chavista Venezuela: pragmatic and populist policies in a broader context," pp. 163–191 in Steve Ellner (ed.), *Latin America's Pink Tide: Breakthroughs and Shortcomings*. Lanham, MD: Rowman and Littlefield.

2021 "Introduction: Rethinking Latin American extractivism," pp. 1–28 in Steve Ellner (ed.), *Latin American Extractivism: Dependency, Resource Nationalism, and Resistance in Broad Perspective*. Lanham, MD: Rowman and Littlefield.

Emersberger, Joe and Justin Podur
2021 *Extraordinary Threat: The U.S. Empire, the Media, and Twenty Years of Coup Attempts in Venezuela*. New York: Monthly Review Press.

Enríquez, Laura J.
2013 "The paradoxes of Latin America's 'Pink Tide': Venezuela and the project of agrarian reform." *Journal of Peasant Studies* 40: 611–638.

Enríquez, Laura J. and Simeon J. Newman
2016 "The conflicted state and agrarian transformation in Pink Tide Venezuela." *Journal of Agrarian Change* 16: 594–626.

Escalona, Julio
2018 "The rumble of the campesinos: will it break the silence?" Venezuelanalysis, August 1. https://venezuelanalysis.com/analysis/13972.

Felicien, Ana, Christina M Schiavoni, and Liccia Romero
2018 "The politics of food in Venezuela." *Monthly Review* 70 (2): 1–19.

Fernandes, Sujatha
2010 *Who Can Stop the Drums? Urban Social Movements in Chávez's Venezuela*. Durham, NC: Duke University Press.

FNCEZ (Frente Nacional Campesino Ezequiel Zamora)
2006 "Zamora retoma Caracas." *Aporrea,* March 27. https://www.aporrea.org/actualidad/n75217.html.

Fuentes, Federico
2020 "Venezuela: Maduro's anti-blockade law deepens debate over revolution's future." *Green Left Weekly,* October 30. https://www.greenleft.org.au/content/venezuela-maduro-anti-blockade-law-deepens-debate-over-revolution-future.

Gilbert, Chris
2017 "The Chávez hypothesis: vicissitudes of a strategic project." *Counterpunch,* May 19. https://www.counterpunch.org/2017/05/19/the-chavez-hypothesis-vicissitudes-of-a-strategic-project/.

2021 "How the left got where it is in Venezuela (and what to do about it)." Venezuelanalysis, February 4. https://venezuelanalysis.com/analysis/15110.

Gill, Timothy M.
2019 "Shifting imperial strategies in contemporary Latin America: the U.S. Empire and Venezuela under Hugo Chávez." *Journal of Historical Sociology* 32 (3): 294–310.

Gill, Timothy M. and Joseph Marshall

2020 "Two decades of imperial failure: theorizing U.S. regime change efforts in Venezuela from Bush II to Trump." Class, Race and Corporate Power 8 (2).

Golinger, Eva

2006 *The Chavez Code: Cracking U.S. Intervention in Venezuela*. Northampton, MA: Olive Branch Press.

Golinger, Eva and Mike Whitney

2016 "The strange death of Hugo Chavez: an interview with Eva Golinger." *Counterpunch*, April 22. https://www.counterpunch.org/2016/04/22/the-strange -death-of-hugo-chavez-an-interview-with-eva-golinger/.

González, Mike

2019 *The Ebb of the Pink Tide: The Decline of the Left in Latin America*. London: Pluto Press.

Hetland, Gabriel

2017 "From system collapse to Chavista hegemony: the party question in Bolivarian Venezuela." *Latin American Perspectives* 44 (1): 17–36.

Kadri, Ali

2019 *Imperialism with Reference to Syria*. Singapore: Springer.

Koerner, Lucas

2020 "Antonimias institucionales: militancia y burocratización en el Ministerio de Comunas de Venezuela." *Estudios Sociales del Estado* 6 (11): 145–183.

Kozarek, Katrina

2017 "Land occupation! Venezuelan Commune Negro Miguel occupies unproductive ranch." Venezuelanalysis, January 19. https://venezuelanalysis.com/video/12892.

2019–2021 "In Commune documentary series." Venezuelanalysis. https:// venezuelanalysis.com/tag/commune.

Lander, Edgardo and Santiago Arconada

2019 *Crisis civilizatoria: Experiencias de los gobiernos progresistas y debates en la izquierda latinoamericana*. Bielefeld: Bielefeld University Press.

Lavelle, Daniel

2014 "A twenty-first-century socialist agriculture? Land reform, food sovereignty and peasant–state dynamics in Venezuela." *International Journal of Sociology of Agriculture and Food* 21 (1): 133–154.

Lemoine, Maurice

2003 "Venezuela: the promise of land for the people." *Le Monde Diplomatique*, October. https://mondediplo.com/2003/10/07venezuela.

Levitsky, Steven and Daniel Ziblatt

2018 *How Democracies Die*. New York: Crown.

López, Ociel

2015 *¡Dale más gasolina! Chavismo, sifrinismo, y burocracia*. Caracas: Casa Nacional de las Letras Andrés Bello.

López Maya, Margarita

2018 "Populism, 21st-century socialism and corruption in Venezuela." *Thesis Eleven* 149 (1): 67–83.

Lubbock, Rowan

2020 "The hidden edifice of (food) sovereignty: rights, territory, and the struggle for agrarian reform in Venezuela." *Journal of Agrarian Change* 20 (2): 289–310.

Machado, Decio and Raúl Zibechi

2017 *Cambiar el mundo desde arriba: Los límites del progresismo.* Quito: Huaponi Ediciones.

Miliband, Ralph

1969 *The State in Capitalist Society.* New York: Basic Books.

Mitchell, Timothy

2006 "Society, economy, and the state effect," pp. 169–186 in Aradhana Sharma and Akhil Gupta (eds.), *The Anthropology of the State: A Reader.* Malden, MA, and Oxford: Blackwell.

Moyo, Sam and Paris Yeros

2007 "Intervention: the Zimbabwe question and the two lefts." *Historical Materialism: Research in Critical Marxist Theory* 15 (3): 171–204.

Nelson, Marcel

2013 "Institutional conflict and the Bolivarian Revolution: Venezuela's negotiation of the free trade area of the Americas." *Latin American Perspectives* 40 (3): 169–183.

2020 "Walking the 'tightrope' of socialist governance: a strategic relational analysis of twenty-first-century socialism," pp. 59–84 in Steve Ellner (ed.), *Latin America's Pink Tide: Breakthroughs and Shortcomings.* Lanham, MD: Rowman and Littlefield.

Pascual Marquina, Cira

2018 "Venezuela: Maduro sides with campesinos against big landowners." Venezuelanalysis, April 10. https://venezuelanalysis.com/news/13763.

Pascual Marquina, Cira and Chris Gilbert (eds.)

2020 *Venezuela: The Present as Struggle—Voices from the Bolivarian Revolution.* New York: Monthly Review Press.

Pérez, Leander

2021 "From nationalization to privatization." Venezuelanalysis, March 1. https://venezuelanalysis.com/analysis/15135.

Poulantzas, Nicos

1980 *State, Power, Socialism.* London: Verso.

2008 *The Poulantzas Reader: Marxism, Law, and the State.* London and New York: Verso.

Prado, Angel

2020 "Grapes of wrath in rural Venezuela: a conversation with Angel Prado," pp. 48–55 in Cira Pascual Marquina and Chris Gilbert (eds.), *Venezuela: The Present as Struggle—Voices from the Bolivarian Revolution.* New York: Monthly Review Press.

Purcell, Thomas F.

2017 "The political economy of rentier capitalism and the limits to agrarian transformation in Venezuela." *Journal of Agrarian Change* 17 (2): 296–312.

Quintero, Rodolfo

1976 *La cultura del petróleo.* Caracas: Universidad Central de Venezuela.

Reardon, Juan

2010 "From agribusiness to agroecology? An analysis of Venezuela's nationalization of AgroIsleña." Venezuelanalysis, October 19. https://venezuelanalysis.com/
analysis/5723.

Riofrancos, Thea

2020 *Resource Radicals from Petro-Nationalism to Post-Extractivism in Ecuador.*
Durham, NC: Duke University Press.

Rodríguez, Francisco

2021 "Sanctions and oil production: evidence from Venezuela's Orinoco Basin."
Franciscorodriguez.net. https://franciscorodriguez.net/2021/03/26/sanctions-and
-oil-production-evidence-from-venezuelas-orinoco-basin/.

Rojas, René

2018 "The Latin American left's shifting tides." *Catalyst* 2 (2).

Salas, Luis and Cira Pascual Marquina

2020 "Venezuela's economy under siege: a conversation with Luis Salas."
Venezuelanalysis, June 19. https://venezuelanalysis.com/interviews/14913.

Sánchez, Clara

2019a "Venezuela en la geopolítica de los alimentos." Alimentos y Poder, June
5. https://alimentosypoder.com/2019/06/05/venezuela-en-la-geopolitica-de-los
-alimentos/.

2019b "Venezuela en la geopolítica de los alimentos II (III Parte)."Alimentos y
Poder, December 22. https://alimentosypoder.com/2019/12/22/venezuela-en-la
-geopolitica-de-los-alimentos-ii-iii-parte/#_ftn6.

Sánchez Otero, Germán

2012 *La nube negra: Golpe petrolero en Venezuela.* Caracas: Vadell Hermanos
Editores.

Schincariol, Vitor Eduardo

2020 *Society and Economy in Venezuela.* Cham: Springer International Publishing
AG.

Sieveres, Gerardo and Arbonio Ortega

2020 "Struggling against the 'revolutionary bourgeoisie' in rural Venezuela: a conversation with Gerardo Sieveres and Arbonio Ortega," pp. 222–230 in Cira Pascual
Marquina and Chris Gilbert (eds.), *Venezuela: The Present as Struggle—Voices
from the Bolivarian Revolution.* New York: Monthly Review Press.

Sutherland, Manuel

2016 "Crítica a la política económica del 'socialismo del Siglo XXI': apropiación
privada de la renta petrolera, política de importaciones y fuga de capitales."
Estudios Latinoamericanos 38: 39–63.

Svampa, Maristella

2019 *Neo-extractivism in Latin America: Socio-environmental Conflicts, the
Territorial Turn, and New Political Narratives.* Cambridge: Cambridge University
Press.

Tatuy TV

2020 "Pedro Camejo: another victim of state-led privatisation in Venezuela."
Venezuelanalysis, April 3. https://venezuelanalysis.com/analysis/14833.

Tatuy TV/Venezuelanalysis

2019 "Platform for peasant struggle holds anti-imperialist march against international aggressions." January 14. https://venezuelanalysis.com/video/14220.

Tinker Salas, Miguel

2009 *The Enduring Legacy: Oil, Culture, and Society in Venezuela*. Durham, NC: Duke University Press.

Valencia, Cristobal

2015 *We Are the State! Barrio Activism in Venezuela's Bolivarian Revolution*. Tucson: University of Arizona Press.

Vaz, Ricardo

2019 "Free men and liberated land: defending Chávez's legacy in the Venezuelan countryside." Venezuelanalysis, June 24. https://venezuelanalysis.com/analysis/14598.

Venezuelanalysis

2006 "Land dispute between English company and Venezuelan government resolved." April 4. https://venezuelanalysis.com/news/1683.

2013 "Venezuelan Attorney General: Opposition violence after elections left 9 deaths and 78 injured." April 25. https://venezuelanalysis.com/news/8830.

2019 "What is going on in Venezuela? Testimonies of the ongoing coup." February 4. https://venezuelanalysis.com/analysis/14273.

Vergara-Camus, Leandro and Cristóbal Kay

2017 "Agribusiness, peasants, left-wing governments, and the state in Latin America: an overview and theoretical reflections." *Journal of Agrarian Change* 17: 239–257.

Virigay, Ramón

2010 "Ramón Virigay and Adriana Ribas, Jacoa Cooperative, Ezequiel Zamora National Campesino Front (Jacoa, Barinas)," pp. 46–62 in Carlos Martínez, Michael Fox, and Jojo Farrell (eds.), *Venezuela Speaks: Voices from the Grassroots*. Oakland, CA: PM Press.

Vivanco, Pablo

2016 "Despite profit motive, US banks and markets squeezing Venezuela's economy." teleSUR English, October 18. https://www.telesurenglish.net/opinion/US-Banks-and-Markets-Squeezing-Venezuelas-Economy-20161017-0009.html.

VTV

2018 "Completo: Maduro recibe la Marcha Campesina Admirable que recorrió 500 kms para verlo." https://www.youtube.com/watch?v=hHMdePV594I&t=1616s.

Webber, Jeffery R.

2017 *The Last Day of Oppression and the First Day of the Same: The Politics and Economics of the New Latin American Left*. Chicago: Haymarket Books.

Weisbrot, Mark and Jeffrey Sachs

2019 "Economic sanctions as collective punishment: the case of Venezuela." CEPR. https://cepr.net/images/stories/rzeports/venezuela-sanctions-2019-04.pdf.

Weyland, Kurt and Raúl L. Madrid (eds.)

2019 *When Democracy Trumps Populism: European and Latin American Lessons for the United States*. Cambridge: Cambridge University Press.

Wilpert, Gregory

2006 "Land for people not for profit in Venezuela," pp. 249–264 in Peter Rosset, Raj Patel, and Michael Courville (eds.), *Promised Land: Competing Visions of Agrarian Reform*. Oakland, CA: Food First Books.

2013 "Chávez's legacy of land reform for Venezuela." T.H.E. Journal 3: 1–13.

Wimmer, Andreas and Nina Glick Schiller

2003 "Methodological nationalism, the social sciences, and the study of migration: an essay in historical epistemology." *International Migration Review* 37: 576–610.

Chapter 9

Party-Base Linkages, Contestatory Mobilization, and "Creative Tensions" in Bolivia

John Brown

In the course of left-led processes in Latin America in the past two decades, relations between ruling left parties and constituent movements followed complex paths.[1] At times, popular organizations mobilized in defense of the party—electorally and on the streets—while at other moments there was friction. In the case of Bolivia, the left turn initially followed "a classic mode of incorporation from below via a mass mobilization party" (Silva, 2017: 93), and the government presented itself as a "government of the social movements." However, tensions emerged between sectors of the movement base and the ruling party, the Movimiento al Socialismo (Movement toward Socialism—MAS). Fontana (2013: 31) argues that "it is clear that the typical oppositional politics of Bolivian social movements have not changed even with a more progressive administration." The vice president during Morales's presidencies, Álvaro García Linera, described these as natural "creative tensions" that act as a motor for constructing socialism. Others (Veltmeyer, 2014; Webber, 2017) question García Linera's analysis, stating instead that popular demands for a more rapid transformation had been sidelined.

To understand the evolution of party-movement relations and to account for both convergence and divergence it is necessary to understand that the MAS-led process, and popular organization support for it, was underpinned by rejection of neoliberalism. Tensions emerged where the MAS diverged from an anti-neoliberal course. This raises several questions. Why did the MAS moderate the process? Did this moderation trigger party-base tensions? And if so, what form did they take, and how can we explain this?

To engage with these questions, it is necessary to locate analysis of party-base relations in a wider framework that accounts for the evolving power relations between the left-led government and a pro-neoliberal opposition bloc. To understand whether a left party governs from the left and retains popular movement support, we must understand the nature of opposition power. Moreover, movements and party may converge when confronting a universal enemy, allowing the forging of new party-base linkages, but we must address whether such linkages act as conduits for movements to shape the reform process from below or whether they are used by party officials to curb the contestatory mobilization capacity of movements. Responding to the above concerns, this chapter offers a framework for evaluating party-movement relations in conjunction with party-opposition relations before turning to an analysis of the Bolivian case via the lens of popular organizations in the city of El Alto.

THE LEFT-LED STATE, ORGANIZED
POPULAR SECTORS, AND ECONOMIC
ELITES: A RELATIONAL ANALYSIS

To explore why constituted forces enter into confrontation with their constituent bases calls for a framework accounting for the relative power of economic elites, the organized popular base, and the left government. Jessop's (2008) strategic-relational approach is useful in this regard. Jessop (2008: 1) starts from the proposition that the state is a social relation that reflects the changing balance of power between social forces. He continues (2008: 6): "Putting states in their place like this does not exclude (indeed, it presupposes) specifically state-engendered and state-mediated processes. It does require, however, that they be related both to their broader social context and to the strategic choices and conduct of actors in and beyond states." State managers' selection of strategies, projects, and policies will influence the opportunities for groups to achieve their goals, and at the same time the balance of forces in society will influence the range of policy options available to state managers. While elected leftist politicians are key exercisers of state power, they act in relation to and influence a wider balance of social forces (the organized popular sectors and capital). Therefore, to study the relation between the left-led state, the organized popular base, and economic elites, "we must consider how state powers are exercised and aligned (or not) with specific class interests in particular societies and conjunctures, and vice versa" (Jessop, 2016: 96). To do this we must identify both what increases the power of capital and the popular base to exert pressure on state managers and what increases state managers' capacity to influence the power of both groups.

Where the structural power of capital is robust, the range of policy options available to state managers who challenge the interests of capital is narrowed. Building on earlier debates among theorists such as Nicos Poulantzas, Ralph Miliband, and Fred Block, among others, Culpepper (2015: 396) says that structural power results from the fact that "capital holders control the investment decisions on which the economy depends for growth." Furthermore, as Robinson (2012: 353–358) notes, in a globalized setting the neoliberal drive toward a "single unified field for global capitalism" has significantly boosted the structural power of transnational capitalists, thereby limiting the autonomy of state managers, who face pressure to promote an environment friendly to transnational economic elite interests. However, state managers are not wholly constrained by the power of capital and may strategically select policies that, in certain conjunctures, favor popular-class interests over those of capital (Jessop, 1990: 248–272). Indeed, state-capital relations cannot be understood outside of a wider analysis that accounts for state–popular-base relations.

A key measure of the popular base's ability to influence state managers is its capacity to engage in what Silva (2017) labels "informal contestatory interest intermediation"—"routinized interactions where the government proposes a policy, affected popular sector organizations protest vigorously, negotiation ensues, and government abides by agreements" (Silva, 2017: 96). This intermediation involves "principles, norms, processes and routines that are not enshrined in law" (Silva, 2017: 103) but understood by base and party alike. It is influenced by the mobilizational capacity of the popular base, which in turn is dependent upon that base's organizational strength and unity and its degree of autonomy from the left party (Anria, 2016). The greater the disruptive scale, duration, and frequency of its mobilizations, the greater the capacity of the popular base to influence the decision making of state managers.

Whether informal contestatory interest intermediation is regularly used depends on the relationship between base and state, which in turn is influenced by state-capital relations. A common agenda or universal enemy facing the base and the party is more conducive to a base-party ally-type relationship, and therefore lower levels of contestatory mobilization may be expected. In ally relationships it is also more likely that there will be extensive and intensive linkages between base and party. Extensive linkages are "loose political ties based largely on an exchange of particularistic goods" including clientelist/selective side-payments and patronage payouts (Anria and Cyr, 2017: 1256, 1268). Intensive linkages include the integration of popular organizations into the formal bureaucratic party structure (Anria and Cyr, 2017). Where extreme intensive linkages are built, popular organizations

are more likely to become deeply invested in the party and to prove depend-
able allies.

Conversely, where the power of capital over state managers is strong and
the party adopts capital-friendly policies, an adversarial base-party relationship is more likely and contestatory intermediation more frequent. State
managers in turn may seek to limit the space for successful intermediation.
Furthermore, extensive and intensive linkages forged during ally-type relations may actively undermine the independent capacities of the popular base.
Extensive linkages may buy off movement leaders and reduce the likelihood
of contestatory mobilization, even where party decisions impinge on the
well-being of the social movements' grassroots base, while intensive linkages are likely to weaken movements' autonomy. Moreover, if state managers
are seen by ordinary members of social movements as favoring capital over
popular demands and the leadership of the movement fails to call for contestatory mobilization because of co-optation, tensions *within* the movement
are likely. These tensions may fracture the unity and organizational strength
of the base, thereby ensuring a smoother governance environment in which
left state managers seek to avoid radical challenges to the interests of capital.

ADVANCES AND SETBACKS IN
BOLIVIA'S PROCESS OF CHANGE

The initial support bloc of the MAS was a heterogeneous coalition of popular
actors with a strategic alliance with a more autonomous bloc of movement
organizations. The MAS emerged from a resistance movement of coca producers and relocated miners in the Chapare, and actors and organizations
based in this province make up its core constituency. The focus here, however,
is on strategic partners, because government-base tensions most frequently
developed with these groups. The analysis centers on the experiences of the
popular organizations in El Alto that were at the heart of the anti-neoliberal
protests that helped bring Morales to the presidency. Primary data collection
centered on groups that continuously supported Morales and the MAS and
groups that had initially supported the president but whose relationship shifted
from ally to adversary. Thirty-five interviews completed in 2017 focused on
the key local popular organizations, the Federación de Juntas Vecinales–El
Alto (El Alto Federation of Neighborhood Associations—FEJUVE) and the
Central Obrero Regional–El Alto (El Alto Regional Workers' Union—COR).
To increase the generalizability of the findings, interviewees were chosen
from both grassroots members and the executive committees.

2003–2005: ANTI-NEOLIBERAL MOBILIZATION
AND POPULAR DEMANDS IN EL ALTO

In October 2003, residents of El Alto "mounted massive demonstrations after the neoliberal president Gonzalo Sánchez de Lozada unveiled plans to give concessions to transnational corporations to pipe natural gas from the eastern lowlands to Chilean ports for export to the United States" (Postero, 2010: 61). The "terms of the concession to foreign capital, framed as a giveaway, turned the issue into a symbol of the popular sector's exclusion from market society" (Silva, 2009: 134–135). There was rising disenchantment with market-oriented policies, while across the country there was utter exhaustion with the traditional parties, whose technocratic decision making excluded popular sector voices. As Luis Flores, a central actor in the FEJUVE leadership during the 2003–2005 period, noted, "the organization leaderships and the grassroots base were united in the idea that the COR and the FEJUVE had to reclaim control over their organizations, which had been instrumentalized by political parties in the city" (interview, El Alto, August 23, 2017). Alfredo Cahuaya, a resident of District 4 and an active participant in the protests, said that "democracy had reached its limits in 2003, whereby the people, instead of being incorporated or included in the plans for the development of the city and the country, were excluded. The COR and FEJUVE leaderships simply followed the demands of the parties" (interview, La Paz, August 18, 2017). The parties in turn "adhered to the demands of foreign capital" (Carlos Arze of the Centro de Estudios para el Desarollo Laboral y Agrario, interview, La Paz, August 25, 2017). There was a sense among Alteños of both political and socioeconomic exclusion—that the city had been "forgotten" by successive governments that instead pandered to the demands of powerful national and foreign economic actors (Espósito and Arteaga, 2006: 79, 86).

In this context, the COR and the FEJUVE elected new leaders who were not beholden to any party and who outlined a set of demands calling for wholesale nationalization and the reclamation of control over the extraction and industrialization of Bolivia's natural gas. As Carlos Barrera, vice-president of the FEJUVE in 2003, told me, "Our ultimate objective was to advance a revolutionary political program, to advance profound structural changes in the country. The neoliberal system had to end" (interview, El Alto, June 27, 2017). The COR and FEJUVE demands, reflecting the concerns of the popular base, also centered on state provision of nonprecarious employment as well as basic services such as sewerage, drinking water, gas connections, and lighting. Known as the "October Agenda," this set of demands became a unifying program that drove further waves of mass mobilization in the city's gas wars between 2003 and 2005. These protest waves were driven not simply by demands for more control over national resources and state provision of services but by the demand that the entire political structure be cleansed of corrupt parties and actors beholden to the interests of capital. In December 2005, Evo Morales was elected, with support from El Alto's organized popular sectors, with a mandate "to restore a measure of national economic and political autonomy, to open political participation and power to heretofore marginalized leftist and other popular sector leaders, and to protect the overwhelmingly poor and indigent mestizo and indigenous popular sectors from the ravages of the market" (Silva, 2009: 143).

2005–2010: THE MAS IN EL ALTO AND STRATEGIC RELATIONS

In response to the October Agenda and a constituent assembly process convened during Morales's first term, the Eastern lowland elites began to struggle for regional autonomy in a bid to avoid the proposed changes in the status of private property rights, land reform, and redistribution of state revenue. By August 2008 there was a virtual undeclared civil war in the Eastern lowlands. A strategic alliance was forged between the MAS, the COR, and the FEJUVE, who were united in a common struggle to push forward with constitutional reform in the face of elite resistance. Having witnessed the mobilizational power of El Alto's organizations, Morales wanted to ensure the support of their leaderships not only electorally but also in defending against the conservatives' destabilization tactics (Anria, 2013). Meanwhile, FEJUVE and COR leaders saw in the MAS an opportunity to gain access to the state and push toward achieving both the October Agenda and El Alto's development via state provision of basic services and nonprecarious jobs (Franklin Troche, international press officer for the COR, interview, El Alto, July 13, 2017). Positions in government or direct access to decision making were exchanged for loyalty (Anria, 2013), which entailed mobilizing the base for elections, engaging in defensive protests against elite destabilization efforts, and ensuring that large-scale protests against MAS policies would not erupt (former vice president of the FEJUVE, interview, El Alto, June 27, 2017). The COR had "very good relations with the central government ever since. We supported the government in the Constituent Assembly; we supported them against the autonomists. The government and the COR, we were very close. We had to defend the process" (spokesperson for the COR, interview, El Alto, July 13, 2017). As Franklin Troche told me, "We are workers, we are leftists. We had to be beside Evo Morales and the government because it is a party of the left" (interview, El Alto, July 13, 2017). The FEJUVE also shared an ideological affinity with the anti-neoliberal stance of the MAS. The

"FEJUVE supported the process led by the MAS because it shared the same principles. This doesn't mean the FEJUVE was part of the MAS. But there was a shared philosophy" (Daniel Gutiérrez, international press officer for the FEJUVE, interview, El Alto, August 9, 2017).

Summarizing Morales's first term via the strategic-relational framework, we can see that he sought to fulfill popular demands for increased political and economic inclusion, thereby challenging the interests of the traditional Bolivian elites. With the lowland elites engaging in aggressive destabilization efforts, Morales was vulnerable to the mobilization or defection of popular organizations. Moreover, the elite's efforts to remove Morales from power and block constitutional reforms that would boost the inclusion of the popular sectors meant that the MAS, the COR, and the FEJUVE were united against a common pro-neoliberal enemy. Popular organizations in El Alto and across the country were at the height of their mobilizational capacity during this period and therefore capable of both defending the government from destabilization tactics and holding it to their demands (Silva, 2017). With the popular movements capable of bringing the country and government to a standstill and of surrounding and isolating autonomist forces in the East, Morales called for a referendum on whether to accept the draft constitution, which passed in 2009.

During this struggle against autonomist forces, intensive and extensive linkages were forged between the MAS and El Alto's popular organizations whereby COR and FEJUVE leaders received funding for local projects such as street repairs and water and gas installations directly from the central government while positions in government were opened to local actors. However, these linkages would become an issue once elite destabilization efforts had been quashed.

2010–2016: EMERGENT TENSIONS AND FRACTURING RELATIONSHIPS

Before Morales's reelection in 2009, "Bolivian politics was characterized by sharp polarization between the opposition on the right and the government and its allies on the left" (Ellner, 2013: 17). However, with the promulgation of the new constitution and the retreat of the erstwhile secessionists into institutional channels of opposition, the MAS was no longer able to rally the base against a common enemy (Fontana, 2013). In fact, after the secessionist drive was defeated tensions escalated between party and base. To explain why, it is necessary to outline the nature of government–transnational corporation relations after 2010.

To fulfill the promises to boost social citizenship in the new constitution, Morales depended on revenues from the country's natural-resource industries. However, he had inherited an extractive industry with path-dependencies that imbued transnational corporations with high levels of structural power (Kaup, 2010). Natural-gas extraction requires continued large-scale investment in exploration, but the state gas company, YPFB, and the hydrocarbon sector in general had received very little investment since the late 1990s. Furthermore, the gas industry was dominated by Petrobras and Repsol, which had long-term contracts giving them access to hydrocarbon reserves that bi- and multilateral trade agreements legally guaranteed (Kaup, 2013).

In this setting, while Morales was elected promising to eliminate the worst excesses of economic exclusion, the Bolivian economy was underdeveloped and reliant on commodity exports, the state extraction company was underfunded and outdated, and transnational extractive firms were contractually and infrastructurally embedded in the economy and had the extractive capacity and capital to invest in new explorations. Consequently, Morales could not realistically push for wholesale nationalization (Kaup, 2010: 135). As Bolivia's former minister for mining, César Navarro, told me, "productive models do not change just because of good intentions or decrees. They are the material outcome of decades. Extractivism characterized colonialism, liberalism, state capitalism, and neoliberalism" (electronic interview, September 2017). Nevertheless, taxes and royalties on transnational corporations were increased, boosting state income from gas exports from US\$673 million in 2005 to more than US\$5 billion in 2013. YPFB increased its role, both operationally and as an auditor, while it had a greater voice in determining the destination of investments. Moreover, service contracts of joint ventures between YPFB and transnational extractive firms allowed the state company "to participate in operations and develop its productive and technological capacities" (Paz and Ramírez-Cendero, 2021: 138, 144). Despite these advances, the state sought only to regain control of previously capitalized assets, and the firms holding these assets extracted a small percentage of Bolivia's gas (Kaup, 2010). Hence, most of the hydrocarbon value chain was not nationalized. The state's increased share of hydrocarbon revenues, and the plans to direct these funds to social spending programs, did, however, represent a significant policy shift from the previous neoliberal governments.

While Morales strategically calculated how far he could push given the embedded, structural power of transnational capital, transnational corporation elites also engaged in strategic decision making. Until 2009, transnational extractive firms had taken an aggressive stance toward Morales, supporting the lowland political elites in their pursuit of autonomy. However, after the 2009 presidential and congressional elections and the 2010 departmental elections, the MAS dominated the political sphere, and transnational corporation elites came to realize that relying solely on an alliance with right-wing political parties to protect their interests was futile (Wolff, 2016). In this scenario, in which Morales was reliant on the transnationals but they depended on his maintaining a healthy profit-making environment, their relations evolved from confrontation to dialogue and, ultimately, cooperation (Wolff, 2016). The outcome of such strategically calculated, structurally oriented action was a compromised nationalization that, while appeasing capital, brought the MAS into confrontation with sectors of its own support base.

For some Alteños who had taken to the streets between 2003 and 2005, the moderated nationalization represented a reneging on Morales's earlier promises to adhere to the October Agenda. As one executive committee member of the 2003 FEJUVE said, "The MAS gave a few little crumbs, a stadium and other trinkets, but this is not what we fought for in 2003" (interview, El Alto, August 8, 2017). According to the Alteños drinking tea at a stall in La Ceja, El Alto, "Nothing changed here. Evo forgot us once he became president. We still have no jobs, no security. We are still poor." As another member of the FEJUVE executive committee during the 2003 protests (interview, El Alto, August 24, 2017) put it,

> The October Agenda demanded complete nationalization, not a negotiation on the price TNCs [transnational corporations] pay. The government has not demanded that the TNCs leave. This is not nationalization. All the TNCs and businesses have actually been given even more help by the government. The elites, now more than ever, have grabbed hold of the government.

This analysis was echoed by Carlos Rojas, a central actor in El Alto's wave of anti-neoliberal struggles and long-time activist: "Not even a pencil belonging to the multinationals has been expropriated, and, as a result, the revolutionary program of 2003 has been destroyed" (interview, El Alto, June 28, 2017). State–transnational-corporation relations, perceptions that the government had failed to provide sufficient jobs and essential public services, and the belief that Morales had reneged on promises to guarantee spaces for popular participation in decision making led many Alteños I spoke with to describe Morales as "not much better than [former presidents] Mesa, Goni, and all the other neoliberals" (conversation with minibus driver, El Alto, August 4, 2017). Indeed, echoing Zibechi's (2010) analysis, a key factor leading to disaffection with Morales was the feeling that decision making remained hierarchical and exclusionary.

While there were tensions between the MAS and some sectors of the base regarding the scope of reforms and how decisions were made, it is important to stress that there was also convergence between the party and popular organization leaders who supported the project, even if they critiqued the speed of reforms. Franklin Troche of the COR captured this sentiment: "The government has to adhere to the October Agenda. This is the mandate from the city of El Alto. Some leftist organizations are reducing their support for Don Evo Morales because the industrialization of our natural resources has not yet been completed" (interview, El Alto, July 13, 2017). He went on to say that, despite the divergence between popular expectations and the realities delivered by the MAS government, "we must remain by the government's side. The workers of El Alto cannot align with parties of the right. We can have different lines of thinking toward the government, but our institution must always be of the left . . . and the MAS is leftist."

While some organization leaders accepted that the structural constraints on the MAS government limited its capacity to engage in more rapid nationalization, industrialization, and subsequent creation of nonprecarious employment as well as increased social spending, the fact remains that for many grassroots members of popular organizations in El Alto the process was moving too slowly. However, the central vehicles for contestatory interest intermediation, the COR and the FEJUVE, in general did not call for mass demonstrations against government policy (Carlos Arze, interview, La Paz, August 25, 2017). Arteaga (2015) states that from 2010 on, following the end of the standoff between the government and the Eastern elites, there were increasing efforts by the MAS to accommodate El Alto's popular organizations. According to a member of the FEJUVE leadership during the gas war, COR and FEJUVE leaders were offered political positions within the MAS, thereby using the popular organizations as "trampolines to become deputies, senators, city council members, to run for mayor" (interview, El Alto, August 9, 2017). However, Daniel Gutiérrez (interview, El Alto, August 9, 2017) of the FEJUVE told me that the organization

> supports the social programs of the government, and we participate in the public announcements that the MAS organizes, and this has led to confusion regarding our relationship. We are not simply an allied entity. The FEJUVE will always be on the side of defending our neighborhoods. For this reason, the FEJUVE has had an affinity with the MAS, but we are not part of the political party.

Although it is understandable that a popular organization with a socialist ideology would support the MAS, the nature of the linkages between some organization leaders and the party did cause frictions. Indeed, a MAS politician on the municipal council of El Alto admitted to me that the MAS "committed many errors by co-opting and controlling the COR" (anonymous interview, El Alto, July 13, 2017). The "problem with all this is that the COR has lost its capacity to hold the government to account" (Carlos Arze, interview, La Paz, August 25, 2017). Despite such critiques, the spokesperson for the COR said that the organization did engage in contestatory interest intermediation but only when it was prudent to do so: "What would happen if we were to push Evo and he were to fall? The right would return, the military governments would return. So we cannot push too quickly" (interview, El Alto, July 13, 2017).

These nuanced viewpoints from local actors who all reject neoliberalism highlight the difficult balancing act facing popular organization leaders when a leftist party is elected to office. The incorporation of popular organization leaders into state structures, sometimes as MAS candidates, and the provision of much-needed funding by the MAS government to local organizations represents a significant deepening of the quality of democratic participation for long-excluded sectors. These intensive and extensive linkages, however, are double-edged, since they can also dampen the willingness of popular organization leaders to engage in contestatory mobilization. For example, a member of the COR executive committee told me (anonymous interview, El Alto, August 7, 2017) that Eliseo Suxo, head of the COR, was deeply damaging the organization because "one minute he is openly supporting Evo Morales, the next he is not. The COR has been sullied and dirtied, and it must be purged. We should have kept our autonomy. Perhaps after supporting the government during the constituent assembly, we got too close to be critical."

Linkages between the MAS and the FEJUVE executive also raised issues for contestatory intermediation. For example, in 2010, at the sixteenth FEJUVE congress, Fanny Nina was elected president. The new leadership of the FEJUVE was extremely critical of the MAS's failure to adhere strictly to the October Agenda, stating that "the MAS simply maintains the same capitalist economic system and the neoliberal political system" (FEJUVE–El Alto, 2010: 11). Furthermore, it said that, while the MAS was elected with the support of the indigenous populations and the popular classes, these groups were increasingly being excluded from political decision making and were in fact being taken over by the MAS to "legitimize itself as a government of the social movements." It was therefore vital that "the executive power of the FEJUVE practice political independence from parties of both the left and the right at the national, departmental, and municipal level." The concern of portions of the FEJUVE executive and the grassroots base was that the offering of access to political positions within the MAS (intensive linkages) and promises of direct funding to loyal leaders (extensive linkages) were debilitating the organization's capacity to critique the central government's relations with transnational corporations (Fanny Nina, interview, El Alto, July 25, 2017).

Elected in 2010 because of her forceful calls for a FEJUVE leadership that was more open and more responsive to its base, Nina quickly encountered resistance from sectors of the FEJUVE executive. She was removed from her position by a bloc of the executive committee that accused her of working for personal interests and against the FEJUVE (Fanny Nina, interview, El Alto, July 25, 2017), and Rúben Paz took over as president (Paz would later become secretary general of governability for La Paz under the MAS mayor Zacarías Maquera). According to Javier Tarqui, El Alto council member for the Sol.Bo party, the new FEJUVE executive was "closely aligned with the MAS" and "the organization failed to offer any coherent challenge to the central government" (interview, El Alto, July 27, 2017). Sandro Ramírez, executive of the FEJUVE, however, rejected such assessments, repeating a phrase I often heard during interviewing that "just because we are with the government does not mean that we are the MAS" (interview, El Alto, July 26, 2017). Ramírez noted that the FEJUVE supports the MAS because the government responds to the needs of the city (El Alto). The problem, however, was that while close linkages between the MAS and some local organization leaders had indeed brought benefits to the city, the scope of these benefits and the speed at which changes occurred were facing popular scrutiny. Disappointment with the depth of change with regard to hydrocarbon nationalization and the perceived lack of funding for El Alto's development raised questions about the relationship between the MAS and popular organization leaders.

The popular organizations in Alto that coordinated anti-neoliberal mobilization before Morales's election had raised popular expectations regarding a radical anti-neoliberal transformation. However, the balance of forces shifted in Morales's second term. No longer facing immediate internal threats from autonomists, thereby lessening the government's reliance on the defensive mobilizations of the popular base, and facing imposing structural constraints set by the government's reliance on transnational exporters, Morales opted to moderate the reform process. This strategy irked sectors of the popular base, but booming gas prices facilitated increased social spending, as Morales retained the steadfast backing of the core popular organizations who played a foundational role in establishing the MAS and whose voices were incorporated into the policy-making process. Moreover, by making use of linkages forged during his first term he was able to limit contestatory interest intermediation from strategically allied popular organizations, thereby ensuring a relatively smooth governing environment and continued electoral success. The problem with this strategy, however, was that limiting the scope for strategically aligned organizations to engage in contestatory mobilization caused discontent with the reform process to build up inside the organizations themselves.

2016–2018: CRACKS IN THE BASE AND
PARALLEL ORGANIZATIONS

In a scenario in which sections of the FEJUVE and COR executives had forged tight linkages with the MAS but popular discontent was rising with regard to the nature of both government-capital relations and top-down government-base relations, ruptures emerged within the popular organizations. In conjunction with emerging rifts, Soledad Chapetón of the right-wing Unidad Nacional (National Unity), with ties to business interests, was elected mayor. Chapetón's election was the result of public frustration surrounding the performance of the MAS mayor (and former head of the COR) Edgar Patana, "who failed to provide employment . . . or projects for the base" (Daniel Ramos, regional coordinator for the MAS in El Alto, interview, El Alto, August 10, 2017) and was facing corruption allegations. With cracks emerging in the COR and the FEJUVE and with the MAS and Unidad Nacional now seeking to forge intensive and extensive linkages, the popular organizations split into two competing bodies.

Using existing channels, the MAS continued to offer funding and support to a "loyal" bloc of leaders while using its media influence to sideline the voices critical of the moderated nationalization process, the tightening of relations between the government and transnational corporations, and the lack of economic diversification (Arteaga, 2015). Meanwhile the bloc that sought to reclaim autonomy from the MAS because of its alleged reneging on the anti-neoliberal agenda was ultimately linked to the right-wing Unidad Nacional, which, once in control of municipal funds, offered financing to the "contestatory" branches of the COR and the FEJUVE.

Divisions within the FEJUVE leadership led to a scenario in 2016 in which two congresses were organized simultaneously to select a new leadership, one based in the original site of the FEJUVE on Avenida 6 de Marzo and recognized by the MAS and a second based in Villa Dolores and recognized by the rightist-backed mayor, Chapetón. Likewise, the result of the MAS linkages to "loyal" COR leaders fostered a schism in the organization that was encouraged by Unidad Nacional, which supported and financed the development of a parallel COR (Daniel Gutiérrez, interview, El Alto, August 9, 2017).

Carlos Rojas, formerly of the FEJUVE–6 de Marzo, became part of the leadership of the FEJUVE–Villa Dolores and called the FEJUVE–6 de Marzo a "puppet" of the MAS. For Rojas, the true FEJUVE, headed by Benigno Siñani, was in Villa Dolores and was "contestatory, combative, and organic" (interview, El Alto, June 28, 2017). Siñani said, "We leave politics in the house, and we enter the FEJUVE to work with no political allegiances. Unfortunately, the central government labels us as being right-wing. Any type of organization that is not supporting the government, they always label them right-wingers" (interview, El Alto, June 26, 2017). However, Daniel Gutiérrez of the FEJUVE–6 de Marzo questioned the contestatory nature of the FEJUVE–Villa Dolores, pointing out that at the initial congress establishing the new executive committee of FEJUVE–Villa Dolores, members of Chapetón's team were present, congratulating the new leaders and drinking beer with them (interview, El Alto, August 9, 2017): "We call it the yellow FEJUVE after the colors of Unidad Nacional . . . a FEJUVE created by Soledad Chapetón."

There were claims and counterclaims from leaders of the two FEJUVEs. When I discussed accusations that the FEJUVE–Villa Dolores was a "yellow FEJUVE" with a Unidad Nacional politician on the city council (interview, El Alto, July 20, 2017) they said,

> It is true that Soledad Chapetón asked me personally to take my role as council member for Unidad Nacional. While you are correct to ask about autonomy and my links to the FEJUVE leadership in Villa Dolores and the Unidad Nacional, you need to understand that political parties will come and go, and so they can be used to achieve the goals and demands of the base.

Meanwhile, the head of the FEJUVE–6 de Marzo, Sandro Ramírez (interview, El Alto, July 26, 2017), told me,

> We support the [MAS] government because it has opened doors to El Alto's benefit. Listen, if the mayor [Chapetón] invited me tomorrow to do something that would benefit the city and I had to work with her in return, I would do it, because it is for the benefit of the neighborhood base that we must work.

Although such sentiments may be a political reality in the city, the formation of extensive and intensive linkages with the parties (whether of the left or the right) meant that the popular organizations did not act as a funnel for contestatory mobilization as they did in the 2003–2005 period. According to Carlos Arze, organizations "must walk a tightrope, responding to popular needs and avoiding open confrontation with their benefactor parties" (interview, La Paz, August 25, 2017). One social movement activist stated, "The problem with the divisions and co-opting in FEJUVEs and CORs is that today in El Alto there is no popular force. What can the organizations do when they are in the service of the parties? Nothing! What are they going to demand? Nothing!" (FEJUVE executive committee member 2003, interview, El Alto, August 24, 2017). As Carlos Barrera (former vice president of the FEJUVE, interview, El Alto, June 27, 2017) summed up, the loss of autonomy and the divisions within the FEJUVE and the COR means that "El Alto's organizations are pawns between political parties . . . co-opted and useless, incapable of defending our radical 2003 agenda."

2019–2021: CONVERGENCE AGAINST A COMMON ENEMY BUT DIVERGENCE WITH THE MAS

In 2019, Morales won elections with the support of many popular organizations. Previously, he had lost a 2016 referendum in which he sought a change to the constitution to allow him to run for reelection. The Supreme Court ruled, however, that the constitution allowed for reelection without term limits, a move that unified the divided political opposition while delegitimizing Morales in the eyes of some critical former strategic allies. The 2019 election results were immediately disputed by the Organization of American States (OAS), whose "deep concern" about a "change in trend" in voting patterns created the impression that fraud had taken place. A report later released by researchers at MIT's Election Data and Science Lab would prove that the OAS analysis was deeply flawed, discrediting it and its secretary general, Luis Almagro (Williams and Curiel, 2019).

With the Electoral Court's announcement of the results in favor of Morales, and with the OAS casting doubts over their legitimacy, large-scale protests erupted in urban areas. While the initial protesters were middle-class voters angered by perceived fraud, they were subsequently joined by formerly strategically allied popular organizations that resented the failure to comply with the results of the 2016 referendum. The protests, however, were eventually co-opted by far-right elements embodied in Luis Camacho, head of the Civic Committee of Santa Cruz. Camacho bound together sectors of the opposition bloc that had remained somewhat muted post-2008 because of Morales's political power and popular support. Camacho and allied racist figures incited violent protests across the country and called on the police to "stand on the side of the people." With police mutinies in Cochabamba, Santa Cruz, and Sucre and police mingling with protesters in La Paz, General Williams Kaliman "suggested" that Morales step aside, and he did. While there is no doubt Morales was ousted, the issues of top-down interference in popular organizations and parallelism dealt him a double blow. On the one hand, a once powerful and unified base was fractured and made less capable of mass-defensive mobilization. On the other, precisely in response to efforts to curb popular organization autonomy, some popular organizations engaged in offensive mobilization against Morales.

With the ouster of Morales, Jeanine Añez was declared caretaker president. Añez, from the Unidad Democrática (Democratic Unity) party headed by the ultraconservative Rubén Costas, governor of Santa Cruz, immediately installed a new cabinet with deep ties to Bolivia's right-wing sectors. The Añez government persecuted MAS leaders, arbitrarily detained critics of the coup government, shut down critical media outlets, called members of the MAS "animals," and deployed the armed forces to repress anticoup protesters at Sacaba and Senkata in El Alto, killing at least 23 and injuring hundreds (Achtenberg, 2020; International Human Rights Clinic and University Network for Human Rights, 2020).

The reemergence of the racist right provided a common enemy that witnessed a re-convergence between divided wings of El Alto's popular organizations. In the course of 2018–2020, the FEJUVE had fractured into three blocs; the "contestatory" bloc aligned with the right-wing Unidad Nacional, which had lost relevance, and two blocs that contested control over the FEJUVE–6 de Marzo. One wing, headed by Fernando Condori, sought to reclaim organizational autonomy from the MAS, while the other, headed by Basilio Villasante, retained tight linkages with the MAS. These struggles were pushed aside temporarily as the leaders of both factions called for mass demonstrations demanding immediate presidential elections. The elections were finally held in October 2020, with the MAS ticket of Luis Arce and David Choquehuanca winning more than 55 percent of the vote.

In El Alto, Morales had lost some legitimacy because of his decision to run for reelection in 2019, while the perceived reneging on the October Agenda and the formation of extreme intensive and extensive linkages with some popular organization leaders had led to tensions between the government and sectors of the popular base. The convergence of the MAS and El Alto's popular organizations had from the outset been based on resistance to neoliberalism, and divergences between party and base emerged when the party was perceived to be moving away from its anti-neoliberal path. However, while the tensions, and MAS's response to them had damaged the legitimacy of the party and its leadership in the eyes of some former supporters, the MAS remained the only viable national party capable of acting as a bulwark against the neoliberal right's reclaiming state power. In the face of a universal common enemy, both wings of the FEJUVE–6 de Marzo backed the MAS ticket in the October 2020 elections. Moreover, El Alto voters dramatically increased their electoral support for the MAS candidates in comparison with the 2019 election, in which large sectors of the electorate had rejected Morales. This unification of El Alto's citizens and organizations to confront a common enemy is crucial to understanding the city and its capacity to influence national politics. As Franklin Troche of the COR told me (interview, El Alto, July 13, 2017),

> While we may have our own tensions in El Alto, when confronted with danger we offer our hands to each other and the people unite. This has happened many

times. When the autonomists were dividing our country (in 2008), we were divided here in the city too. However, in the face of danger, we forget our divisions and come out together; we know who the enemy is, those with a different political tendency.

Unification to confront a common enemy, however, does not mean that tensions between popular organizations and the MAS disappear once the critical confrontational moment with the neoliberal right has passed.

Following Arce's election, the two blocs of the FEJUVE–6 de Marzo called for the organization's unification. Condori stated, "I am not part of the MAS, but I am part of the process of change, and because of this, we have decided with Villasante to unify this emblematic institution." Meanwhile, Villasante, echoing earlier statements by FEJUVE leaders aligned with the MAS, highlighted that the only party willing to work with the FEJUVE for El Alto's development was the MAS and that the two organizations would work together. This achievement of unity, however, proved short-lived. The old issue of linkages and autonomy between the FEJUVE and the MAS reemerged, with Condori accusing Villasante of using the organization to gain political positions with the party (ElAltoDigital, 2020; ExitoNoticias, 2020). During the mayoral elections in March 2021. Eva Copa, a former MAS senator from El Alto, with the backing of the Condori-led wing of the FEJUVE, split from her party to run for El Alto's mayorship on the new Jallalla La Paz ticket. She claimed to be responding to demands from the grassroots of local popular organizations to reclaim organizational autonomy from the MAS. Morales verbally attacked Copa and predicted that the MAS's candidate, Zacarías Maquera, would easily win, but Copa triumphed with 68.7 percent of the vote.

KEEPING PARTY-BASE TENSIONS CREATIVE: LESSONS FROM BOLIVIA

Throughout the period of Morales's leadership, as in other Pink Tide countries, tensions between the governing left party and sectors of its constituent base emerged. To help frame the causes and consequences of such tensions, a strategic-relational approach (Jessop, 2008) that accounts for the balance of power between the left-led state, the organized popular base, and the economic elite is useful. Indeed, the Bolivian case highlights the risks facing popular organizations and movements in dealing with left-led states in an environment where "structural path-dependent economic constraints can impede fundamental transformations over the short and medium term" (Kohl and Farthing, 2012: 234).

While the MAS and El Alto's popular organizations were united in confronting a common enemy during Morales's first term, over time the linkages forged between the party and organization leaderships became a barrier to contestatory mobilization. To maintain his legitimacy and to conform to the 2009 Constitution, which sought to enhance the quality of social citizenship for excluded sectors, Morales required a rapid increase in state finances. In the context of an underdeveloped economy, he increased state income from hydrocarbon exports. Veltmeyer (2014) argues, however, that the superior negotiating position of the agents of global capital ultimately limited the capacity of the MAS government to respond to popular demands for a fundamental restructuring of the hydrocarbon sector. Understanding the state as a social relation that reflects the changing balance of power between capital and society helps us grasp this scenario. While Morales was ideologically committed to an anticapitalist model, his actions post-2009 appeared in many ways to have favored domestic and transnational economic elites, reflecting the power of the groups on which his development strategy depended. These strategic selectivities fostered tensions with sections of a popular base that had demanded (perhaps unrealistically, given the structural power of capital) wholesale nationalization and direct inclusion in the development of national policy.

García Linera (2011: 24) argues that friction between base and party should be understood as "creative tensions" within "the national-popular bloc"—"tensions between the very sectors that are leading the process of change." Such "creative tensions" may emerge between the centralized monopoly of power by the state and the decentralized nature of decision making by social movements (Fuentes, 2014). These unavoidable tensions, according to García Linera, "have the potential to help drive forward the course of the revolution itself" if they are resolved through constant struggle and conflict (Fuentes, 2014). As Fuentes (2014: 118) says, "Herein lies the real importance of struggle from below, which brings such tensions to the fore and allows for the creation of a correlation of forces that can best enable the process of change to advance." However, the case of El Alto's popular organizations raises key issues regarding implications of García Linera's concept that tensions from below can be used to drive the process forward.

As MAS-transnational relations tightened and the limits of moderated nationalization became more apparent to sectors of the base, the intensive and extensive linkages forged between the MAS and the COR and FEJUVE leaderships during Morales's first term became barriers to contestatory interest intermediation. Despite popular critique of the extent of reforms, the strategically allied COR and FEJUVE leaderships in general failed to call for mass mobilization to challenge the government. The El Alto case demonstrates that participatory spaces in Bolivia were open—but principally to those who did not challenge the MAS's relations with the transnationals. Popular discontent built up to the point where, once the unified and powerful organizations split, opportunities opened for right-wing parties to take advantage. While movement leaders in El Alto who accepted funding from the right-wing Unidad Nacional claimed that they were simply using the party to gain funding that the MAS denied them, they were in fact contributing to the legitimization of that party, adding to the confusion of the grassroots, and furthering the splits in the once unified popular organizations. Fracturing organizational unity weakened the very popular power on which Morales's electoral victories were built and, as García Linera points out, the future of the process depended.

While the reemergence of the far right in 2019–2020 led to a re-convergence to confront the common enemy between the divided popular organizations and the MAS, once the critical confrontational moment had passed the issues of organizational autonomy and the depth of the anti-neoliberal project under the MAS came to the fore again. Indeed, while the MAS emerged as a political vehicle for social movement demands to move beyond neoliberalism and remained the dominant party at the national level, MAS-base tensions opened space at the local and regional levels for new parties representing popular demands. Looking ahead, the direction of Bolivia's process of change will depend on how the MAS leadership responds to criticism from below and from its left, both in the electoral arena and on the streets. Failure to reopen spaces for critical internal debate may mean a further fracturing of the popular bloc, thereby reducing the possibilities of challenging pro-neoliberal opposition forces.

The tensions in the Bolivian case highlight issues regarding movement–left-party relations in general. The extrademocratic destabilization tactics of conservative forces and the pressures imposed by transnational capital to curb efforts to increase the quality of social citizenship tend to foster a centralization of power in the executive (Brown, 2018; Cannon and Brown, 2017). This issue chimes with the concerns of Zibechi (2010; 2012) and Holloway (2002) that the state not be the focus of emancipatory struggles because by its very nature it reproduces vertical power relations. These writers tend to reject parties and propose "changing the world without taking power" (Holloway, 2002). In contrast, Katz (2012: 48) argues that both movements and parties are essential: "No emancipatory project can evolve exclusively in the social realm, nor can it do without the specific platforms—the links between demands and power strategies—that party groupings provide." He therefore advocates that the state be the target of all social demands, since its transformation is the condition for any anticapitalist transition.

While Katz is correct, Holloway's and Zibechi's concerns regarding vertical power relations between party and base cannot be ignored. It is clear that when the power of capital over left state managers is most pronounced, the risks of tensions' emerging between a left party and its constituent base are increased. It is therefore essential that popular movements be strong in their own right, since only strong movements will ensure that a left-led state moves in a leftist direction (see Ciccariello-Maher, 2013; Poulantzas, 1978). A mobilized public requires that popular organizations remain internally democratic. In the Bolivian context, while Morales opened formal channels of participation for popular voices during confrontations with a common enemy, over time these party-base linkages ossified, leading to blockages in the flow of demands from below. As Jaime Solares, former leader of the Central Obrera Boliviana (Bolivian Workers' Center—COB) and a key figure in the 2003–2005 anti-neoliberal protests, told me, "We allowed our popular vehicles to be taken over by Morales. Our organization leaders became distanced from their base. This was an error" (interview, La Paz, June 12, 2017). As the El Alto case demonstrates, when the forces of capital pressure a left party to moderate its programs, without a vent for popular discontent regarding the direction of the process, internal organization tensions will increase and parallel organizations controlled by the right may emerge. This process reduces mobilizational power by fracturing the unity and organizational capacity of the base. Although this occurred at the national level as well, Morales hardly abandoned his anti-neoliberal commitments, thus explaining why social movement activists who were critical of his government rallied behind his party's return to power in 2019–2020. While movements must walk a tightrope in challenging a left party from the left without strengthening a common enemy on the right and while "unity, unity, unity" is necessary at national election time, the use of excessive party-base linkages to curb contestatory mobilization may ultimately act as the greatest support for the forces of capital.

NOTE

1. This chapter is a revised version of an article that appeared in *Latin American Perspectives* 47 (5): 40–57 (2020).

REFERENCES

Achtenberg, Emily
2020 "MAS party under threat as Bolivia moves towards new elections (without Evo)." *NACLA Rebel Currents*, January 10. https://nacla.org/blog/2020/01/10/mas -party-under-threat-bolivia-new-elections-without-evo.

Anria, Santiago
2013 "Social movements, party organization, and populism: insights from the Bolivian MAS." *Latin American Politics and Society* 55 (3): 19–46.
2016 "Democratizing democracy? Civil society and party organization in Bolivia." *Comparative Politics* 48: 459–478.

Anria, Santiago and Jennifer Cyr
2017 "Inside revolutionary parties: coalition-building and maintenance in reformist Bolivia." *Comparative Political Studies* 50: 1255–1287.

Arteaga, Walter
2015 "Building citizenship in the context of the debate on the post-2015 agenda in Bolivia." *Community Development Journal* 50: 571–588.

Brown, John
2018 "Escaping the confines of market democracy: lessons from Venezuela." *Socialism and Democracy* 32 (2): 14–31.

Cannon, Barry and John Brown
2017 "Venezuela 2016: el año de vivir peligrosamente." *Revista de Ciencia Política* (Santiago) 37: 613–634.

Ciccariello-Maher, George
2013 "Constituent moments, constitutional processes: social movements and the new Latin American left." *Latin American Perspectives* 40 (3): 126–145.

Culpepper, Pepper
2015 "Structural power and political science in the post-crisis era." *Business and Politics* 17: 391–409.

ElAltoDigital
2020 "La Fejuve de El Alto avanza rumbo a la unificación." October 21. https://www.elaltodigital.com/politica/la-fejuve-de-el-alto-avanza-rumbo-a-la-unificacion/.

Ellner, Steve
2013 "Latin America's radical left in power: complexities and challenges in the twenty-first century." *Latin American Perspectives* 40 (3): 5–25.

Espósito, Carla and Walter Arteaga
2006 *Movimientos sociales urbano-populares en Bolivia: Una lucha contra la exclusión social, económica y política.* La Paz: UNITAS.

ExitoNoticias
2020 "Se rompe el pacto de unidad entre Basilio Villasante y Fernando Condori." *ExitoNoticias* December 11. https://exitonoticias.com.bo/index.php/2020/12/11/se-rompe-el-pacto-de-unidad-entre-basilio-villasante-y-fernando-condori-se-toman-instalaciones-de-la-fejuve-de-el-alto/.

Fontana, Lorenza Belinda
2013 "On the perils and potentialities of revolution: conflict and collective action in contemporary Bolivia." *Latin American Perspectives* 40 (3): 26–42.

Fuentes, Federico
2014 "'Bad left government' versus 'good left social movements'?: Creative tensions within Bolivia's process of change," pp. 103–125 in Steve Ellner (ed.), *Latin America's Radical Left: Challenges and Complexities of Political Power in the Twenty-first Century.* Lanham, MD: Rowman and Littlefield.

García Linera, Álvaro
2011 *Las tensiones creativas de la Revolución: La quinta fase del proceso de cambio.* La Paz: Vicepresidencia del Estado Plurinacional.

Holloway, John
2002 *Change the World without Taking Power.* London: Pluto Press.

International Human Rights Clinic and University Network for Human Rights
2020 "They shot us like animals: Black November and Bolivia's interim government." https://www.humanrightsnetwork.org/bolivia.

Jessop, Bob
1990 *State Theory: Putting the Capitalist State in its Place.* Cambridge: Polity.
2008 *State Power: A Strategic-Relational Approach.* Cambridge: Polity.
2016 *The State: Past, Present, Future.* Cambridge: Polity.

Katz, Claudio
2012 "Socialist strategies in Latin America," pp. 31–48 in Jeffery Webber and Barry Carr (eds.), *The New Latin American Left: Cracks in the Empire.* Lanham, MD: Rowman and Littlefield.

Kaup, Brent
2010 "A neoliberal nationalization? The constraints on natural-gas-led development in Bolivia." *Latin American Perspectives* 37 (3): 123–138.
2013 "Transnational class formation and spatialities of power: the case of elite competition in Bolivia." *Global Networks* 13 (1): 101–119.

Kohl, Ben and Linda Farthing
2012 "Material constraints to popular imaginaries: the extractive economy and resource nationalism in Bolivia." *Political Geography* 31: 225–235.

Paz, María and Juan Ramírez-Cendrero
2021 "Extractivism and resource nationalism in Bolivia: foreign direct investment policy and development under Evo Morales," in Steve Ellner (ed.), *Latin American Extractivism: Dependency, Resource Nationalism, and Resistance in Broad Perspective.* Lanham, MD: Rowman and Littlefield.

Postero, Nancy
2010 "The struggle to create a radical democracy in Bolivia." *Latin American Research Review* 45 (4): 59–78.

Poulantzas, Nicos
1978 *State, Power, Socialism.* London: NLB.

Robinson, William
2012 "Global capitalism theory and the emergence of transnational elites." *Critical Sociology* 38: 349–363.

Silva, Eduardo
2009 *Challenging Neoliberalism in Latin America.* New York: Cambridge University Press.
2017 "Reorganizing popular sector incorporation: propositions from Bolivia, Ecuador, and Venezuela." *Politics and Society* 45 (1): 91–122.

Veltmeyer, Henry
2014 "Bolivia: between voluntarist developmentalism and pragmatic extractivism," pp. 80–113 in James Petras and Henry Veltmeyer (eds.), *The New Extractivism: A*

Post-Neoliberal Development Model or Imperialism of the Twenty-first Century?
London and New York: Zed Books.

Webber, Jeffery

2017 *The Last Day of Oppression and the First Day of the Same: The Politics and Economics of the New Latin American Left.* Chicago: Haymarket Books.

Williams, Jack and John Curiel

2019 "Analysis of the 2019 Bolivia election." *CEPR*, February 27. https://cepr.net/report/analysis-of-the-2019-bolivia-election/.

Wolff, Jonas

2016 "Business power and the politics of postneoliberalism: relations between governments and economic elites in Bolivia and Ecuador." *Latin American Politics and Society* 58 (2): 124–147.

Zibechi, Raúl

2010 *Dispersing Power: Social Movements and Anti-State Forces.* Oakland, CA: AK Press.

2012 *Territories in Resistance: A Cartography of Latin American Social Movements.* Oakland, CA: AK Press.

Chapter 10

Progressive Government, Neoliberalism, and the Popular Camp in Ecuador

A Crisis of Hegemony

Alejandra Santillana Ortiz and
Sebastián Terán Ávalos
Translated by Ronaldo Munck

Ecuador, as embodied in the government of Rafael Correa between 2007 and 2017, represents a limit case in the conflictual/cooperative relations between progressive governments (*progresismo*)[1] and social movements in Latin America. Compared, for example, with the Bolivian government of Evo Morales (2006–2019), which had a close, albeit sometimes fraught, relationship with social movements, Correism was largely distant from them, not least the relatively powerful and influential indigenous movement (see Becker, 2011). This distance, which went far beyond the "creative tensions" that were present in other countries, led to the emergence of a minority right-wing government in 2021 as the indigenous movement candidate called for abstention in the runoff between the Correist candidate and the right-wing one. By contrast, in Bolivia the progressive option prevailed in the 2021 elections over the supporters of the 2019 coup, partly because of strong backing from social movements. To understand this outcome, we need to explore the nature of the crisis of hegemony in Ecuador, the very particular relations between progressive politics and social movements, and the defining conjunctures of the 2019 semi-insurrectional strike and the 2021 elections.

MANAGING THE CRISIS

The complex crisis that Ecuador has lived through—which has an economic and a political aspect but is ultimately a crisis of hegemony—has posed a challenge for all governments but also for their opposition, constraining its ability to offer a viable and sustainable alternative to neoliberalism. It has influenced society's ability to contest the commodification of all aspects of human life. The nation-state is also in question, as Fernández-Savater (2020: 15) explains, "los[ing] autonomy with regard to the powers that define reality and becom[ing] subordinate to them." Thus the neoliberal project of subordinating all human life to the market and accumulation through dispossession becomes increasingly authoritarian in that alternatives are unsustainable. The crisis also, of course, has an impact on a state that, as Segato and Gutiérrez (2017) argue, cannot even guarantee life, as is seen in Ecuador most clearly in the anguish caused by the failure to display even a minimum of competence with the COVID crisis.

In this situation, politics becomes totally polarized, as María Galindo (2021) explains; debate is closed off, politics becomes a binary game, and we are unable even to consider new possibilities or forms of life. The people are defined as consumers and "maintained strictly on the margins of decision making with regard to all issues that impact them, leaving them able only to complain, vote, or express their opinions via social media" (Fernández-Savater, 2021: 16). The issue is to what extent the progressive option in Ecuador has been able to break this model and offer an alternative to hegemonic neoliberalism. Until such an alternative is forged, society in Ecuador, as in the rest of Latin America, is condemned to experience constant crisis, with destabilizing and volatile institutions and levels of security.

Neither society nor the state in Ecuador has been able, despite modernization and institutionalization, to create political and institutional stability or an economy not based on debt and rents that benefits more than a small minority. The dramatic failure in dealing with the COVID crisis continues to expose this deficit. What it also demonstrates in a broader sense is a failure of governmentality, defined by Foucault (2002: 56) as "the ensemble formed by the institutions, procedures, analyses and reflections, the calculations and tactics that allow the exercise of this very specific albeit complex form of power, which has as its target: population, as its principal form of knowledge: political economy, and as its essential technical means: apparatuses of security." What we have seen instead in Ecuador is a near-permanent state of exception, a constant threat of social exclusion, and living conditions marked by daily scarcity.

At most, the state seeks to manage the crisis. The neo-bureaucratic political tradition in Latin America holds that society can be contained and managed by the state. This has been the case with most populist, presidential, reformist, and *caudillista* regimes (Roth Deubel, 2015). This role was deepened by the pro-neoliberal neoinstitutionalist tradition that prevailed in the 1980s and 1990s, which held that "the logic of the market must correct the failings and dysfunctions of the state" (Roth Deubel, 2015: 46). The ideological supremacy of the capitalist market effectively weakened the national state and even sought to bring about the "end of politics."

However, in Ecuador as elsewhere, politics was not solely linked to the state. A vibrant nonstate public domain was constructed through the collective endeavor of social movements from the 1990s on. The clearly dominant indigenous movement developed a triple way of relating to the state—working with it and against it and seeking to go beyond it by creating its own institutions (see Santillana, 2019). Thus indigenous social structures, economic relations, and political expressions became major players in national politics. These social movements emerged and developed in the context of repeated failures in the management of the crisis, producing widespread popular discontent and massive mobilizations in a context of corruption, political instability, bank closures, unemployment, and migration. It was in this context that progressive governments emerged across Latin America, taking the particular form of Correism in Ecuador. But was the "long night" of the neoliberal era going to be replaced by "twenty-first-century socialism," as some proclaimed? Could Correism resolve the crisis of the state in Ecuador and construct a stable hegemonic system?

AFTER NEOLIBERALISM

In the context of failing legislative political legitimacy, a mood of *¡Que se vayan todos!* (Out with all of them!), referring to politicians, and rising fuel prices, Correism began a process of much-needed state reform. Essentially it was seeking to embed constitutionally the principles of an efficient market system that could be institutionalized and controlled. This involved both reliance on the traditional state bureaucracy and an embrace of the new public management discourse (see Munck, 2003), balancing what was needed to keep both the foreign investors and the poor satisfied. The Correa period also saw an attempt to meet the indigenous movement's long-standing demand for Ecuador to become a plurinational state, which was significant even though the social movements were not as central as they were in Bolivia during the Evo Morales period. This initiative was part of the broader commitment of

Correism to what has been called "neoconstitutionalism,"[2] which sought the constitutional institutionalization of state reforms.

Under Correa there was a marked reduction of poverty and considerable economic reactivation: between 2006 and 2016, poverty decreased from 36.7 percent to 22.5 percent and annual per capita growth of the gross domestic product was 1.5 percent (compared with 0.6 percent over the prior two decades). However, Correa also presided over a government in which the extractivist state was openly promoted, social protest was criminalized, and market mechanisms were given free rein (such as in the reform of higher education), all clothed in the mantle of the Citizens' Revolution. The so-called progressive decade under Correa basically put into practice the idea that the return of politics meant essentially the strengthening of the state. This was the mantra that was meant to overcome the dire heritage of neoliberalism and the cycles of political instability caused by the weakness of the political parties. The modernization of the state, however, entailed the systematic weakening of the social movements and the replacement of the "popular camp"[3] by the new liberal citizen at the heart of the Citizens' Revolution.

The management of the ongoing crisis of hegemony by Correa in his decade in office did lead to considerable social investment, but corruption was institutionalized and there was a marked increase in labor precarity. The greater institutionalization of business rules did lead to an increased flow of foreign investment, and Correa was able to stabilize the political order and secure a considerable personal following, including in the middle classes, that generated a degree of political legitimacy. However, this expansion of the middle class did not emerge from the historical process of capital accumulation; it did not get to own the means of production (Rodríguez López, 2018: 97). Rather, it was a response to the needs of a technocratic regime that required competent professionals to implement the rational technical management of natural resources and the efficient circulation of ideas, commodities, and people. It was this new middle class that acted as a social base for the progressive political order and helped attenuate historical conflict over inequality.

The stability under much of the Correa presidency contrasted with the unstable order of the 1980s and 1990s, and this created the material and subjective conditions for a more dynamic reformist capitalist order. The rational administration of affairs was once more seen as possible. The technocratic middle classes acted as a mechanism for governmentality and the synchronization of private, state, and foreign capital. It was the progressive state that played the key role in generating this new order and led to the creation of a new subjectivity—as Rodríguez López (2018: 98) puts it, "a people of the state (*pueblo del estado*), a fed and clothed people, that was at the same time left on the political sidelines."

The policies of the Correa presidency were characterized by both continuities and change with respect to the neoliberal governments that came before and after it (Lenin Moreno, his chosen successor [2017–2021], and Guillermo Lasso, beginning in 2021). On the one hand, the Correa model was based on a strong government role in the economy and progressive policies on the social front, which sharply contrasted with neoliberalism. However, not least by its failure or refusal to construct a counterhegemonic social movement, it was unable to overcome the crisis of hegemony (see Mazzolini, 2021), and the neoliberal framework remained operative, for example, in the continuation of the economy's dollarization.

In the period before Correa's unexpected victory in the 2006 elections, there were various permutations of the neoliberal economic and political model in terms of the class coalitions formed and their policies. In the first phase, during the 1990s, the dominant class bloc was led by the bankers and the agro-export sector. Its alignment with the hegemonic global order was symbolized by the dollarization of Ecuador's economy in 2000. Given the economic and political crisis that the country was experiencing, the adoption of the U.S. dollar as legal tender was designed to ensure financial stability and, of course, secure the support of the International Monetary Fund (IMF), which was to continue to review the macroeconomic program and eventually to disburse a US$500 million loan in 2019. After dollarization it was the import sector that achieved hegemony within the dominant class bloc.

When Correa and his Citizens' Revolution came into office in 2007, a more complex and contradictory ruling coalition emerged. The first component was a number of left intellectuals and activists affiliated with social movements, particularly the indigenous movement. They formed the inner circle of Alianza PAIS [Patria Altiva i Soberana] (PAIS Alliance), the political party formed by Correa, who had no party background. Emblematic of these cadres was Alberto Acosta, who occupied the strategic position of minister for mines and energy and was also elected president of the constituent assembly. However, he resigned in 2007 in a dispute over extractivism, and this group as a whole began to lose influence as the constituent assembly was sidelined. The second fraction of Correa's support was a group of mainly progressive technocrats that emphasized the role of the state and the public sector in a modernizing direction. A third fraction consisted of a group of business leaders that depended on the expansion of the internal market and had been relatively marginal during the neoliberal period. The economic policies of the Correa period well expressed the interests of this group in that they expanded consumption for the middle classes while marginalizing small-scale commerce and nonmodernized agriculture. The final and dominant fraction was composed of the business sector that depended on government contracts and acted as an intermediary with international capital in the pursuit of infrastructure projects and the modernization of the primary goods sector (see Ospina, 2017).

HIGHER EDUCATION

The reform of higher education in Ecuador reflects the continuities and discontinuities of the Correa era. In 2000 a new law, the Organic Law of Higher Education, asserted the need for a regulated system with standard quality control measures. However, it was only with the 2008 Constitution that the quality control mechanisms were actually institutionalized and broader access to higher education for the population was established. It was estimated that only half the population had access to higher education, and the Correa government emphasized the importance of democratizing access as part of the proclaimed Citizens' Revolution (*El Universo*, 2019). In addition to ensuring the quality of higher education, the emphasis was on higher education as a right, a public good, and not a commodity (Minteguiaga, 2010). In the pursuit of academic excellence, 14 universities were closed down by the Correa government, but 4 new ones were opened (CACES, 2019) although they were not immediately operational. The logic of this restructuring was not entirely clear. Under the Moreno government the higher education budget was cut, and it is acknowledged that only half of the student demand for a university education is currently being met.

This calls into question the success of the higher education reforms carried out in the progressive decade. There were also inconsistencies in that the principle of free access to the higher education system was subverted by the emergence of private providers set up to provide leveling-up services at a price (Ramírez, 2010). This partial privatization was carried out more consistently under the unambiguously neoliberal regime of Lasso that came into office in 2021.

Overall, the higher education reforms were successful in ensuring more open access and a standardization of mechanisms of quality control. However, there is no significant difference between *progresismo* and neoliberalism with regard to community engagement, which was unevenly implemented, as nearly all the emphasis was placed on enterprise engagement (see Acosta, 2021). Thus both regimes acted within a technocratic logic of "innovation," which was designed to facilitate market mechanisms, including those that provided skilled "human resources" for the transnational sector of the economy.

THE POST-CORREA YEARS

This complex dominant class bloc was an unstable and not particularly coherent formation. The progressive intent of Correa was blunted by the reality of the coalition of interests that kept him in office and allowed him to win three elections. The main beneficiaries of this period were the construction, real estate, and credit sectors, which thrived on the increased capital flows, the extractive rents accrued from the primary sector and, of course, the expansion of the middle classes and the internal consumer market. In 2017 Alianza PAIS put forward Vice President Lenín Moreno as presidential candidate on a "progressive" post-neoliberal platform that took him to victory at the polls with considerable popular support. However, the complex alliance of social and political forces woven together by Correa soon fell apart.

At first Moreno sought to initiate a democratic dialogue with all social and economic sectors, attempting to mark his distance from the strongly top-down politics of the Correa period. Given the accusations of electoral fraud in the second round, he was keen to show an openness to dialogue and remove some of the restrictions on social movements put in place by Correa, but this was really the mark of a weak government that lacked a political project of its own. Ostensibly a continuation of Correism, this new government in practice prioritized its negotiations with the dominant classes, in particular the primary goods export sector and the financial sector.

Moreno was able to garner the support of all the main chambers of commerce and business, the bankers, the export sector (more than the import sector), and the more reactionary wings of the Catholic and evangelical churches. The neoliberal economic measures agreed upon with the IMF and the drop in the price of primary goods left little room for maneuver for the economic elites and meant a steady decline in living standards for the majority of the population as the budget for social programs was steadily cut back. Thus, for example, the budget for dealing with gender-based violence was reduced from US$21 million in 2019 to US$11 million in 2020 in a country where a woman is murdered every three days. Conversely, in 2020 US$1.5 million was spent on "robocop" uniforms and shields for the national police.

The relationship between the government and the popular camp worsened. Correa had sought to monopolize the representation of the subaltern classes through the technocratic state (see Unda, 2017). The criminalization of protest was now stepped up and expanded. This was seen in the government reaction to the 2019 indigenous and union mobilization that resulted in the immediate jailing of leaders. This approach was also followed by the Lasso government in 2021. Correa had used the law to create a very broad definition of sabotage, rebellion, and terrorism, and this was now normalized and fully implemented.

CONJUNCTURE 1: OCTOBER 2019

At the start of October 2019, President Moreno announced a series of economic measures with a direct impact on the working and middle classes, among them a big fuel price hike. This led to an 11-day semi-insurrection of which Ecuador had not seen the like for 30 years (see Ponce et al., 2020, for an overview). Decree 883, which launched these neoliberal measures, responded to the interests of the Ecuadorian elite and also protected the interests of the global elites through an agreement signed by the government and the IMF in February. The IMF package of US$4,200 million opened the doors to an aggressive indebtedness strategy with the multilateral economic bodies. Thereafter the question of the debt and its interest became the dominant issue in the political economy. The fiscal deficit soon caused major disequilibrium, and to "correct" it the government decided to remove the subsidy on gasoline and diesel mainly used by the popular sectors and the middle class, public transportation, and small-and medium-scale industry. The freeing of prices on fuel led to an immediate rise in transportation costs and inflation of about 10–15 percent. An additional measure with an immediate impact on public sector unions and their members was the reduction of labor rights in the public sector, where employees were obliged to work an extra day per month and their vacation time was cut in half, from 30 days to 15. By contrast, the well-off benefited from the elimination of import duties on vehicles and cell phones and a large reduction of the tax on foreign remittances. The generalized rise in prices affected consumption and the cost of production while calling the actual survival of the popular classes into question. It was already expensive to produce in U.S. dollars and compete with the regional economy, and these measures made things even worse.

Employers sought to pass the increased cost of production on to the underprivileged and to public sector employees in particular, but the end result was to make life for the subaltern classes even more precarious. The aim of the government and the capitalist class was to reduce wages and dedicate all of the surplus value generated by workers to the payment of the foreign debt, even at the cost of the reproduction of social life.

The main union organization, the Frente Unitario de Trabajadores (United Workers' Front—FUT) and the indigenous Confederación de Nacionalidades Indígenas del Ecuador (Confederation of Indigenous Nationalities of Ecuador—CONAIE) immediately responded to Decree 883 by calling for an indefinite general strike with the sole demand of revoking it and ending the deal with the IMF. The massive mobilization, especially in areas with a dense indigenous population, included sustained road blockages and work stoppages that took many by surprise. As the protesters marched on the capital, the militancy of the base pushed the social movement leaders into more intransigent positions. The strike and roadblocks were turning into a veritable insurrection. Moreno and his cabinet retreated to the coastal city of Guayaquil, the home of the financial elite. The October 2019 mobilization and its success (the decree was withdrawn) represented a major reactivation of social movement organizations. The memory of the large-scale protests during the neoliberal era was revived, as was its success in overthrowing three presidents and in blocking the signing of a free-trade agreement. The period of seeming passivity during the 10 years of the Correa government was now a thing of the past.

Despite the insistence of the Moreno government and the mass media on portraying the events of October as a playing out of Correism versus anti-Correism, this was no longer the dominant contradiction. The authoritarianism and the extractivist economic model of Correism meant that few protesters were calling for a return of Correa. His followers did not play a dominant role in the insurrectional events. The transitional (toward open neoliberalism) regime of Moreno was now facing widespread popular repudiation of its policy of impoverishment and precarization of the people.

The appearance of President Moreno on national TV effectively surrendering to the representatives of the indigenous movement was a decisive turning point in the balance of class forces. This initial victory, particularly of the indigenous social movements, showed the importance of organization and mobilization in pursuit of the interests of the people. The streets were once again an area where popular organizations could construct a field of articulation of popular demands and find common objectives. The urgency of the need to construct a broad popular front was evident, but the divisions of the past, particularly those that emerged in the Correa period, hampered this effort. Nevertheless, the elections of 2021 saw the emergence of an indigenous movement candidate, Yaku Pérez, aimed at converting the social energy and politicization of the October days into an electoral victory for the social movements (see Parodi, 2021).

The repression of the October 2019 uprising was based on laws passed by President Correa after the confused events of September 2010, when elements of the national police force blocked highways and occupied the National Assembly in pursuit of a claim to reinstate benefits that the government had withdrawn. Correa went to police headquarters in Quito to confront the protesters, and a tense situation arose when he accused the police of treason. In the aftermath of these events, which Correa portrayed as an attempted coup, an interpretation disputed by the mainstream media (see Kurtenbach,

2014), he granted the armed forces funds to upgrade their equipment and carry out the professionalization and specialization they agreed were necessary and, defining the "internal enemy" in broad terms, criminalized protest, particularly against mega-mining projects (see Billo and Zukowski, 2015). From then until the 2021 elections, there was only a year and a half in which Ecuador was not under a state of exception. Not surprisingly, when it came to the 2021 elections there was little rapprochement between the candidate of Correism and that of the indigenous and environmental movements (one exception being the endorsement of Correa's candidate in the runoff presidential election by the CONAIE President Jaime Vargas, a decision that most of the organization's leadership repudiated).

CONJUNCTURE 2: PRESIDENTIAL ELECTIONS AND PANDEMIC 2021

In the first round of the presidential elections in February 2021, the three forces of the broad left—the Unión por la Esperanza (Union for Hope—UNES), Pachakutik, the political arm of the indigenous movement, and Izquierda Democrática (Democratic Left), a democratic socialist party—garnered 67 percent of the popular vote. Yet in the runoff elections in April the UNES candidate, Andrés Arauz, who had obtained 32 percent of the vote in the first round, added only 15 percent to this figure. The main reason was that Yaku Pérez and much of the indigenous movement called for a null vote, while Izquierda Democrática allowed its voters to choose even though its leader said that he would vote for the banker Lasso, the right-wing candidate. The result was an unprecedented 16 percent null vote that spelled victory for the right, whose candidate ended up just 5 percent ahead of Arauz. This outcome shows the depth of the divisions on the left among its political, social, and indigenous strands. There was an international debate around this at the time, with some observers calling for unity (see Santos, 2021) while others prioritized the independence of the indigenous movement and criticized the failings of Correism—a position also supported by certain currents of the international environmental movement that backed the antiextractivist message of the indigenous movement candidate.

The setting for this election was a complex and enduring crisis dating back to the loss of legitimacy resulting from the success of the October 2019 mobilizations and the government's disastrous performance in the face of the COVID pandemic. The Moreno government presided over the highest per capita death rate in the region (until Brazil overtook Ecuador) as the deficits in the health system became evident, with harrowing scenes particularly in Guayaquil, compounded by charges of corruption and negligence against health ministers. In the midst of the pandemic the government saw fit to deepen its economic adjustment policies and increase labor flexibilization measures that created more unemployment and precarity. As the state of exception was extended across the country, the electoral period began.

The electoral positioning of parties and social movements was inevitably dominated by proposals for dealing with the health and economic crises. With the memory of October 2019 still fresh, there were many radical and reformist proposals for managing the political process and some clearly ultraright propositions. Of the 16 electoral tickets presented, most were neoliberal in orientation, led by Guillermo Lasso, a banker from the Guayaquil elite who had twice unsuccessfully run for president. Andrés Arauz sought to present a "Correism without Correa" shorn of corruption and focused on efficient economic management. A third option emerged around the candidate of the indigenous movement, Yaku Pérez, who was widely seen as channeling the energies of the social movements (indigenous and environmental particularly) into the political arena. Despite its evident divisions and weaknesses, this campaign showed that the social movements could go beyond representing subaltern social groups and make a proposal for government. After a series of charges of fraud, however, it was announced that Yaku Pérez had come in third and that the second round would be between the old couple of neoliberalism (Lasso) and *progresismo* (Arauz).

This couple dominated the presidential race, but the broad forces of the left—UNES, Pachakutik, and Izquierda Democrática—obtained the most seats in the National Assembly and thus set the stage for another executive-legislature conflict. With Lasso's narrow win of the presidency, the austerity measures demanded by the IMF were implemented in the first six months. A labor reform led to a drastic destructuring of workers' lives, various decrees were passed deepening the extractivist development model, small-scale agriculture was decimated, and fuel prices and inflation increased. These measures can be seen as the mark of a weak government, bereft of social acceptance or broad hegemony. The state of exception, coupled with a discourse of security to mask ongoing repression, could not hide the fact that the government had largely lost control of the nation.

CONCLUSIONS

Ecuador, like many of its neighbors, is characterized by a rentier state that is incapable of containing social, political, and economic conflict and necessarily deploys a state of exception as the norm when dealing with a crisis. The current crisis goes back to the 1970s and 1980s and is characterized by a high degree of social inequality and minimum political legitimacy. This has led to a permanent fiscal crisis of the state, a tendency to return to primary sector production, low levels of education, a huge health deficit (evident in the COVID crisis), and endemic corruption of the political class. To manage the crisis exceptional measures have been taken, among them plebiscites and constituent assemblies, new laws, and the reduction of rights for those who criticize the dominant order and its use of violence. At the same time, Ecuador has since the early 1990s seen the emergence of an indigenous movement that has been able to overthrow governments, create a genuine social counterpower, and garner approximately 20 percent of the vote in the 2021 elections. Nevertheless, it is not yet a counterhegemonic force, at least partly because of its inability or unwillingness to engage with the Marxist and Correist left. The popular camp will, no doubt, build its strength on its control of the National Assembly and the ongoing discussions within and across the various sectors of the left.

Elections have not managed to overcome the crisis of hegemony that Ecuador has been experiencing since the 1990s. Institutional and constitutional change has left the state in charge of conflict resolution. This is a state that is beholden to international capital, and neither its neoliberal nor its progressive variant has changed the fundamentals for the subaltern classes. The ruling elite, while shaken by the 2019 uprising, has managed to regain control of government largely because a divided left was unable, even for pragmatic reasons, to work together. In the new conjuncture initiated after the 2021 elections we see a faltering neoliberal regime unable to establish hegemony and a broad social and political left reflecting on the period since Correa came to office in an effort to rebuild itself.

What many saw as an opportunity in the 2021 elections was also a reflection of the organizational and political limits of the organized popular camp. While this camp clearly captured the growing social discontent in the country, it lacked the capacity to construct and organize around sustainable and participatory proposals. For its part, Correism was unable to overcome the polarization that made the neoliberal right its main interlocutor and did not seek out other potential alliances within the organized popular camp. To this we must add the serious criticisms of the Correist project for criminalizing protest and for not engaging in the self-critical reflection that could call the extractivist model into question, incorporating the demands for a plurinational state, taking a stance against patriarchy, and, more broadly, showing a willingness to listen to the proposals of the popular organizations.

At the same time, it was difficult for the articulation between the indigenous movement, the labor movement, and the other popular organizations to take up the various problematics that dominated the conjuncture and open up a serious debate on the weaknesses of their attempts to establish an alternative strategy for power. No doubt the overarching problem was the absence of a strategy not only for accumulating forces for an anti-neoliberal mobilization but also for creating spaces in which proposals that went beyond the electoral domain could be debated. Advocating a vote for the openly neoliberal and proimperialist candidacy of Lasso showed the depth of the cul-de-sac in which they found themselves, notwithstanding the pragmatic argument that it would be easier to mobilize social discontent against a Lasso government than against a renewed Correist one. The case of Ecuador shows that the "creative tensions" between progressive governments and social movements that are the focus of this volume does not easily prevail when the leaders of two such different social and political forces fail to engage. The struggle for hegemony thus remains a task in Ecuador as, indeed, in the rest of Latin America.

NOTES

1. *Progresismo* is a term coined to describe collectively the left-of-center governments that came to power in Latin America from 1999 on (see Alaniz and Bruera, 2020). It is seen as amalgam of democratic socialism, social democracy, and social liberalism. Thus it supports the development of a welfare state, the defense of civil liberties, citizen participation, and some redistribution of wealth. It is seen as a pragmatic political discourse situated somewhere on the center-left. For Bolívar Echeverría (2001), however, it means simply the replacement of the old by the new, with innovation seen as an absolute positive that will lead inexorably to a better society.

2. Neoconstitutionalism represents a break with the rigid positivist norms of the past based on the assumption that the organization of the state and the protection of individual rights require more effort than the simple application of legal norms. The juridical term "neoconstitutionalism" denotes instead the need for the state to work proactively to ensure the maximum satisfaction of society's needs (see Celi, 2017, for its usage in the Ecuadorian context).

3. The "popular camp" is usually defined as the field of social, popular, and indigenous social movements. It may deploy various forms of struggle, from work stoppages, community mobilization, and insurrectional strikes to road closures. The popular camp may seek to articulate its struggles within the field and with social forces outside its immediate sphere of influence. It may also seek an articulation with political forces with a greater or lesser degree of convergence that is strategic or conjunctural.

REFERENCES

Acosta, Santiago
2021 "Leadership and opportunities for sustainable higher education vis-à-vis the pandemic," pp. 181–188 in Sjur Bergan, Tony Gallagher, Ira Harkavy, Ronaldo Munck, and Hilligje van't Land (eds.), *Higher Education's Response to the*

COVID-19 Pandemic: Building a More Sustainable and Democratic Future. Strasbourg: Council of Europe.

Alaniz, Maria and Rodrigo Bruera
2020 "Gobiernos progresistas en América Latina: agendas políticas y de comunicación." *Index.comunicación* 10 (2): 55–81.

Becker, Marc
2011 "Correa, indigenous movements, and the writing of a new constitution in Ecuador." *Latin American Perspectives* 38 (1): 47–62.

Billo, Emily and Isaiah Zukowski
2015 "Criminals or citizens? Mining and citizen protest." *NACLA*, November 2. https://nacla.org/news/2015/11/02/criminals-or-citizens-mining-and-citizen-protest-correa%E2%80%99s-ecuador.

CACES (Consejo de la Aseguramiento de la Calidad de la Educación Superior)
2019 *Modelo de evaluación externa de universidades y escuelas politécnicas 2019.* Quito: CACES.

Celi, Israel
2001. "La religión de los modernos." Congreso Nacional de Filosofía, Facultad de Filosofía y Letras, UNAM. https://www.flacsoandes.edu.ec/sites/default/files/agora/files/1262722400.la_religio_de_los_modernos_0.pdf.
2017 *Neoconstitucionalismo en Ecuador: ¿Judicialización de la política o politización de la justicia?* Quito: Universidad Andina Simón Bolívar
2019 "La educación superior pública puede cubrir solo el 51% de la demanda en Ecuador." June 16. https://www.eluniverso.com/noticias/2019/06/16/nota/7377747/educacion-superior-publica-puede-cubrir-solo-51-demanda-ecuador/.

Fernández-Savater, Amador
2020 *Habitar y gobernar: Inspiraciones para una nueva concepción política.* Madrid: Ned Ediciones.

Foucault, Michel
2002 "Governmentality," in James D. Faubion (ed.), *Power: The Essential Works of Michel Foucault 1954–1984.* Harmondsworth: Penguin.
https://www.15-15-15.org/webzine/2021/03/26/reply-to-the-open-letter-of-boaventura-de-sousa-santos-to-two-young-indigenous-ecuadorians/.

Galindo, Maria
2021 'Entrevista a Maria Galindo." https://letraslibres.com/politica/entrevista-a-maria-galindo-propongo-una-contracorriente-poetica-que-asuma-la-lucha-desde-el-goce/.

Kurtenbach, Ralph
2014 "Tough talk, tear gas, tragedy: the fight to frame one day's events in Ecuador." Theses from the College of Journalism and Mass Communications 41. http://digitalcommons.unl.edu/journalismdiss/41.

Mazzolini, Samuele
2021 "Rafael Correa and the Citizens' Revolution in Ecuador: a case of left-wing non-hegemonic populism," pp. 95–117 in P. Ostiguy, F. Panniza, and B. Moffitt (eds.), *Populism in Global Perspective: A Perfomative and Discursive Approach.* London: Routledge.

Minteguiaga, Analía
2010. "Los vaivenes en la regulación y evaluación de la educación superior en Ecuador: el caso del mandato 14 en el contexto constituyente," pp. 83–123 in René Ramírez (ed.), *Transformar la universidad para transformar la sociedad.* Quito: SENPLADES.

Munck, Ronaldo
2003 "Globalisation, neo-liberalism and the crisis in public sector management in Latin America," pp. 56–68 in G. Wood, P. Dibben, and I. Roper (eds.), *Contemporary Public Sector Management: A Comparative Perspective.* London: Palgrave.

Ospina, Pablo
2017 "La división de Alianza País: interpretación para las izquierdas latinoamericanas." https://www.rebelion.org/noticia.php?id=230801.

Parodi, Camila, Cesar Saravia, Ignacio Marchini, and Maru Waldhüter
2021 "Entrevista a Alejandra Santillana." https://www.marcha.org.ar/la-politica -ecuatoriana-no-esta-conectada-con-la-vida-entrevista-con-la-investigadora-social -alejandra-santillana/.

Ponce, Karina, Andres Vasquez, Pablo Vivanco,and Ronaldo Munck
2020 "The October 2019 indigenous and citizens' uprising in Ecuador." *Latin American Perspectives* 47 (5): 9–19.

Ramírez, René
2010 "Justicia distributiva en la universidad ecuatoriana, 1996–2006," pp. 27–56 in René Ramírez (ed.), *Transformar la universidad para transformar la sociedad.* Quito: SENPLADES.

Rodríguez López, Emmanuel
2018 *La política contra el Estado: Sobre la política de parte. Madrid: Traficantes de Sueños.*

Roth Deubel, André
2015 "Neo-institucionalismo y transformación democrática del Estado," pp. 13–60 in Gustavo Endara (ed.), *El rol del Estado: Contribuciones al debate.* Quito:FES/ILDIS/SENPLADES.

Santillana, Alejandra
2019 "Política de la delegación y tiempos de incertidumbre en Ecuador: forma estatal de pueblo y ambivalencias de la autonomía," pp. 257–278 in Gaya Makaran, Pavel López, and Juan Wahren (eds.), *Vuelta a la autonomía: Debates y experiencias para la emancipación social desde América Latina.* Mexico City: Bajo Tierra Ediciones/UNAM.

Santos, Boaventura de Sousa
2021 "Open letter to two young indigenous Ecuadorians." https://www.alainet.org/en /articulo/211406.

o, Rita and el Gutiérrez 2017 "Pensar en femenino." https://soundcloud.com/traficantesdesue-os/pensar-en -femenino-una-conversacion-con-rita-laura-segato-y-raquel-gutierrez/reposts.

Unda, Mario
2017 "Habemus populismo." https://lalineadefuego.info/habemus-populismo-por -mario-unda/.

PART 4

Social Movements in Mexico, Colombia, and Chile

Social movements played a key role in the rise to power of the Pink Tide governments at the outset of the new century. After a string of setbacks beginning in 2015, the left made a comeback, partly because of the militance of social movements. The following two chapters focus on these recent developments in three countries. In Mexico, the effervescence of social movements and protests catapulted Andrés Manuel López Obrador to center stage and paved the way for his election as president in 2018. In Chile mass anti-neoliberal protests led to the expansion of the Pink Tide bloc of nations with the presidential elections of December 2021, an outcome that repeated itself in the electoral contests held in June 2022 in Colombia.

Emelio Betances shows how the future president Andrés Manuel López Obrador (AMLO) contributed to the democratization of Mexico's closed political system through a strategy that united diverse social and political movements in a broad coalition against neoliberal policies. In addition, he examines mobilizations actively supported by AMLO that paved the way for the creation of the Movimiento Regeneración Nacional (National Regeneration Movement—MORENA) in 2011. Betances identifies three stages in the relationship between AMLO and social movements from his first presidential bid in 2006 until the present. In the first stage, AMLO played a leadership role and his followers actively participated in protests beginning with those in opposition to alleged fraud in the 2006 elections. In the second stage, MORENA leaders voiced support for protests while stopping short of participating in them as a party in order to preempt accusations of political manipulation. Since AMLO's election in 2018 the MORENA has entered a third stage in which the party has distanced itself from social mobilizations.

Nevertheless, AMLO has addressed some of the demands of the social movements, such as legislation that limits outsourcing and education reform that reverses the neoliberal measures of previous years. At the same time, Betances shows that AMLO's government failed to act decisively in response to mobilizations over the issue of femicide and the Maya Train project in southeastern Mexico.

In 2019 anti-neoliberal protests broke out throughout Latin America in which Pink Tide parties and social movements converged in challenging the existing order. Kyla Sankey and Aaron Tauss point out that Chile and Colombia "witnessed an insurrectional offensive by social movements, in the sense that the protesters [had begun] to envision a revolutionary horizon beyond the status quo." The protests in Chile, which were set off by a small subway fare increase, forced the government to accept elections for a constituent assembly in which "the big winners were new left-wing forces" and the old left in the form of Chile's Communist Party "made a surprising political comeback." Sankey and Tauss point out that "progressive political parties in Colombia are much weaker than many of their Latin American counterparts, which is why it was the social movements that initiated and largely led the protests." The takeaway from the events in both countries is that even when protests are not initiated or led by progressive political leaders, popular mobilizations can open a space for political leaders to push for more progressive demands and build coalitions. The contributors argue that the social movement experiences in Chile and Colombia hold a lesson for progressive governments and parties throughout the region. The left in Chile and Colombia "will be examining how, from the political arena, they can best recognize the diversity of the protesters and in particular the rights of women, LGBTQI and indigenous communities, students, and ecologists as part of a strategy for not only achieving power but retaining it and bringing about lasting social change."

Chapter 11

Social Movements, Political Linkages, and the Challenge to Democracy in Mexico

Emelio Betances

Mexico's President Andrés Manuel López Obrador (AMLO) brought together a coalition of social and political groupings that, despite a diversity of political views, opposed the implementation of neoliberal economic policies. The Obradorist sociopolitical movement contributed to the construction of participatory democracy by promoting mass participation at different levels. In doing so, it pushed hard to democratize Mexico's faltering liberal democracy, a closed political system with entrenched authoritarianism. The mobilizations that AMLO led and the social movement struggles that he supported paved the way for the creation of the Movimiento de Regeneración Nacional (National Regeneration Movement—MORENA) in 2011 and his contentious exit from the Partido de la Revolución Democrática—PRD), which he considered a spent force. The social movement struggles in the few years prior to 2018 contributed to his triumph by discrediting the existing system and questioning its legitimacy. Until then, the MORENA had had a close connection with social movements and popular mobilization, but once in power it abandoned the strategy of accompaniment and turned itself into an electoral machine.

AMLO's struggle to deepen democracy was part of new regional political developments in which social movements contributed significantly to the rise of Pink Tide governments. The Pink Tide began with the elections of Hugo Chávez in Venezuela (in 1998), Luiz Ignacio (Lula) da Silva in Brazil (in 2002), Néstor Kirchner in Argentina (in 2003), Tabaré Vázquez in Uruguay (in 2004), Evo Morales in Bolivia (in 2005), Rafael Correa in Ecuador (in 2006), and Mauricio Funes in El Salvador (in 2009). These governments had in common opposition to neoliberal policies and promised to bring the state back in a neodevelopmentalist reconfiguration to restore the citizens' rights curtailed by the neoliberal upsurge of the 1980s.

In contrast to their counterparts in South America, the anti-neoliberal forces in Mexico suffered electoral defeats in 2006 and 2012 but developed a powerful sociopolitical movement that transformed itself into a movement-party, the MORENA. AMLO had been a longtime militant and party leader and leading candidate of the PRD, which had a long-standing relationship with social movements and civil institutions at the state and federal levels. He rose to prominence as a result of the march to protest electoral fraud known as the Éxodo por la Dignidad (Exodus for Dignity), a cause/movement supported by the PRD in the mid-1990s. With AMLO as its presidential candidate, the MORENA won the national elections of July 1, 2018, receiving 53 percent of the votes while his opponents, Ricardo Anaya of the Partido de Acción Nacional (National Action Party—PAN) and José Antonio Mead of the Partido Revolucionario Institucional (Revolutionary Institutional Party—PRI), received 22 percent and 16 percent respectively. The MORENA's triumph in 2018 represented an important moment in the transition to a neodevelopmentalist state that sought control of the national economy, democratization, social equality, and sustainable development in a free-market framework.

AMLO went through a political metamorphosis from 2006 to 2018 in which his political project was made more acceptable to the dominant classes. He and his followers went from active participants in and organizers of protests (such as the protest against the electoral fraud of 2006 and the protests against proposed privatization of Petróleos Mexicanos (Mexican Petroleum—PEMEX) to supporters of protests without getting directly involved (such as the protests against the disappearance of 43 students in Ayotzinapa and the Yo Soy #132 students' protests). Since assuming the presidency, AMLO has had a mixed record with regard to social movements similar to the Pink Tide experiences with Evo Morales in Bolivia and the Kirchners in Argentina, but, even distanced from social and political mobilizations and protests, his government still has a far better track record than past PRI and PAN governments in terms of what it has delivered for the social movements.

In contrast to the Partido Revolucionario Institucional (Institutional Revolutionary Party—PRI) and its predecessor, the Partido de la Revolución Mexicana (Party of the Mexican Revolution—PRM), which was invigorated in the 1930s by mobilizations of the popular sectors, the peasantry, and organized labor, the MORENA emerged from below as a movement-party aiming to transform an entrenched authoritarian regime. Its growth from 2014 to 2018 as it became more moderate in an effort to attract both PRI and PAN followers was spectacular (Ellner, 2018). Will it go on to become another PRI?

Will AMLO go the way of the PRI and co-opt or neutralize the social movements? The fact that he does not propose socialist goals and limits himself to working within the legal framework of liberal democracy and the free-market economy could contribute to a tendency toward accommodation based on reformism as opposed to a struggle for structural change.

This chapter offers an overview of the role of social movements in the election of AMLO in 2018. First, it outlines social movement linkages with political parties and the state from 1985 to 2005. Second, it examines AMLO's active participation in major sociopolitical movements and mobilizations. Third, it analyzes social movement dynamics during the first two and half years of his administration and concludes that Mexican social movements have engaged with political parties and contributed to a process of "democratizing democracy" (Santos, 2005).

PERSPECTIVES ON SOCIAL MOVEMENTS

The social science debate on social movements has revolved around various approaches to the explanation of the dynamics of social transformation. One paradigm focuses on issues of culture and identity (Alvarez, Dagnino, and Escobar, 1998; Slater, 1985), while others are concerned with the political process (Tarrow, 1994; McAdam, Tilly, and Tarrow. 2001). Still others have stressed a horizontal approach to social change and rejected the strategy of taking state power as the primary goal of radical change (Holloway, 2002).

The premise of the horizontal approach is "the rejection of hierarchical relations of power that are created and reproduced through vanguardism, political and economic elitism, and the goal of seizing rather than transforming state power" (Stahler-Sholk, Vanden, and Becker, 2014: 8). This theory is "conceived of as both a project and a movement based on the notion of self-determination. It is a network-based participatory model of politics that rejects all the 'old' institutional politics, including representative democracy, and instead promotes direct democracy and self-governance" (Munck, 2020: 26). As such, it rejects all forms of engagement with the state, political parties, churches, and other institutions. The Zapatista movement that emerged in Mexico in the 1990s is a prime example of this approach (as Steve Ellner explains in his introduction to this book).

In contrast, another paradigm privileges the ties between resistance movements and the social construction of citizenship and democracy (Holston, 2008; Isin, 2008; Betances, 2016) and proposes engagement with political parties and the state while maintaining a degree of autonomy in the decision-making process. As noted by Munck (2020: 9), "the issue is not whether social movements have a relation with the state but the terms on which that relationship is conceived and negotiated." The next three sections are designed to shed light on the way these processes played out in Mexico.

HISTORICAL BACKGROUND OF
RECENT SOCIAL MOVEMENTS

The history of social movements in Mexico is one of constant struggle, co-optation, and repression. Throughout the twentieth and twenty-first centuries, the government prohibited any deviation by labor, peasant, and popular organizations from the status quo. The regime incorporated most of these organizations into the political system during the period of import-substitution industrialization of 1941–1970, but the implementation of neoliberal reforms from 1982 to 2018 led to their disincorporation and weakening, largely because of the privatization of numerous state-owned enterprises. Disincorporation exacerbated the unemployment generated by neoliberal reforms, leading to the creation of a large informal economy, severe social inequalities, and unprecedented degrees of out-migration (Silva and Rossi, 2018).

A wide range of social movements emerged during the neoliberal period—movements of workers, indigenous people, peasants, women, teachers, students, debtors, and LGBTQ people and movements against corruption, unfair urban land use, and mining. These movements were not just urban-based; for example, in rural areas the peasant movement El Campo No Aguanta Más (Peasants Can't Take It Anymore) joined forces with the Barzón, a debtors' movement, to protest the effects of the North American Free Trade Agreement. Though characterized by political and social fragmentation, some of these movements channeled their discontent through institutional means and were able to get some of their demands met (Mestries, 2015: 318–323).

Two social movement patterns are discernible for the period beginning in 1985: willingness to work with mainstream political parties and the state and rejection of co-optation and the top-down methods of the institutional political process. The Asamblea de Barrios (Neighborhood Assemblies—AB) illustrates the former pattern. It emerged in 1987 as a split-off from the Coordinadora Única de Damnificados (Coordinating Committee of Survivors—CUD), which was a response to the needs of the victims of an earthquake in Mexico City that left an estimated 250,000 people homeless and by November 1985 included more than 40 territorially based organizations. The AB supported Cuauhtémoc Cárdenas's presidential bid in 1988 in the hope of achieving its housing objectives. Cárdenas had left the PRI in 1986 and obtained the support of various leftist and nationalist organizations. The CUD rejected membership in Cárdenas's campaign and continued to pressure Miguel de la Madrid (1982–1988) to guarantee the implementation of the National Housing Program of 1987 (Haber, 2006: 173–212). When obvious electoral fraud prevented Cárdenas from reaching the presidency in 1988, AB members remained allied with him, joined his newly formed PRD, and held important positions on the party's national executive council and the executive council of the federal district when he headed the city government (1997–1999). Unquestionably, the AB skillfully engaged with a political party, but it ended up disappearing as a social movement.

In contrast with the AB, the Ejército Zapatista de Liberación Nacional (Zapatista Army of National Liberation—EZLN) is a territorial-based social movement organization that has avoided co-optation. When the Zapatistas first appeared as a guerrilla group in 1994, they enjoyed widespread support and became a promising voice for democratization. Their popularity forced the federal government to accept a cease-fire and negotiate the San Andrés Accords of 1996. According to the agreement, the government recognized the autonomy of indigenous people and promised to make the necessary constitutional reforms regarding political participation and political and cultural rights. In 2001 the Senate approved these constitutional rights, but the government refused to recognize indigenous autonomy. The state's reneging on the San Andrés Accords marked the end of negotiations for the EZLN (González Casanova, 2005: 80). It went on to establish *juntas de buen gobierno* (good government juntas) based on a participatory model of politics that eschewed engagement with the federal and state governments. Despite occasional harassment from federal troops, it has persisted for over a quarter of a century and exerted ideological influence on indigenous and nonindigenous movements in the region, but it remains confined to Chiapas and disengaged from institutional politics.

Another important social movement of the period, the Consejo General de Huelga (General Strike Council—CGH), enjoyed extensive support in 1998 when it declared a general strike at the Universidad Nacional Autónoma de México (National Autonomous University of Mexico—UNAM). In terms of its political significance, this movement was comparable to the 1968 mobilizations in which students demanded democratic freedoms and to the 1986 protests in which students rejected the dismantling of public education. It rejected all forms of exclusion: political, social, and educational (López, 2009:113–118). In December 1998, Rector Francisco Barnés announced a registration fee increase for new students, a policy that was seen as tantamount to the elimination of free education at the university, and in March 1999 the University Council approved it despite massive student protests. After three months the university authorities, without recognizing the CGH, replaced the fee requirement with voluntary registration fees. This measure led to the consolidation of factions including radicals, moderates, and those who favored returning to class, thus relieving the pressure on the university authorities. All attempts at mediation between the parties failed, and on February 6, a year after the strike began, the Policía Federal Preventiva (Federal Preventive Police—FPP) entered the university, arrested more than 1,000 students, and ended the longest strike in the university's history (Tamayo, 2009: 113–118). While the university authorities did not reimpose a registration fee, the UNAM community suffered a setback in that students and authorities were unable to reach a settlement to prevent its occupation by the FPP. The occupation strengthened the conservative sectors and weakened and demoralized the progressive forces.

The Asamblea Popular de los Pueblos de Oaxaca (Popular Assembly of the Peoples of Oaxaca—APPO) is another example of a movement intent on avoiding co-optation. Unlike the Zapatistas, the APPO is a front for a variety of organizations. It began with the occupation of Oaxaca's *zócalo* (main square) by the Oaxacan Section 22 of the Sindicato Nacional de Trabajadores de la Educación (National Union of Education Workers—SNTE) on June 14, 2006. The union advanced mostly labor grievances that neither the federal nor the state government had addressed. The state governor ordered the local police to evict the teachers and their supporters, but after about two hours the police were unable to do so. Thousands poured into the zócalo and the surrounding areas to support the teachers in their resistance to police repression. These supporters had their own grievances, which included dispossession from their land, failure to consult the public regarding the renovation of the city's traditional park, land use claims, and police refusal to engage in dialogue with the social movements. The APPO developed shortly after the zócalo was reoccupied and became the central actor in a second stage of protest. Its member organizations represented indigenous people, municipal governments, labor federations, civil institutions, women's rights groups, university students, political militants, artists, anarchists, neighborhoods, and academics. APPO groups took over the Oaxaca Radio Corporación, Radio Universidad, and the state television headquarters in an effort to inform the population about their activities. Until October 29, when the police retook the city, the APPO organized multiple marches, debated strategy in assemblies, and formed a virtual commune while life in the city went on without public authorities.

The APPO groups agreed on one issue, the demand for the governor's resignation. Ulises Ruiz was a PRIist with authoritarian tendencies and no tolerance for criticism. Snubbed by Ruiz, the APPO took its demand to the federal government, where the PRI persuaded President Vicente Fox (2000–2006) of the PAN to defend him. Subsequently the police took control of the city of Oaxaca, arresting 141, killing 3, and wounding 100, and banned all public demonstrations (Bolos, 2015).

The main lesson of the experiences of the Zapatistas, the UNAM student movement, and the APPO is that radical demands and unwillingness to negotiate with the authorities led to a dead end. The AB's experience suggests that social movement leaders need to balance their engagement with political parties carefully to avoid complete absorption by them. These experiences formed the backdrop for AMLO's channeling demands through institutional mechanisms and use of peaceful marches and demonstrations to further popular interests and democratization. He proposed a strategy of accompaniment, and despite its limitations it paved the way for his electoral victory in 2018.

THE OBRADORIST MOVEMENT AND ITS CHALLENGE TO LIBERAL DEMOCRACY

The rise of the Obradorist sociopolitical movement was a continuation of the struggle for democratization in a country that was characterized by one-party rule for most of the past century. The protests in the twenty-first century directly confronted the political, military, and economic elites, and meanwhile AMLO stood for democracy based on consultation and accompaniment as a corrective to the nation's "delegative democracy," in which the president had inordinate power. The struggle for democratization and demands around housing, health care, education, and pensions paved the way for the emergence of the MORENA in 2011.

AMLO left the PRI in 1986 along with Cuauhtémoc Cardenas, fought against two electoral frauds as the candidate of the PRD for governor of Tabasco (in 1988 and 1994), became president of the PRD (1996–1999), and then won the election to head the federal district (2000–2005). In the latter position, he implemented an austerity program for the management of the city budget, launched an anticorruption campaign, promoted large public works and housing development, and built new hospitals. In addition, he founded a new city university and implemented 13 social programs directed at low-income people (López Obrador, 2004). This social policy at the local level served as a laboratory for the implementation of similar programs nationwide after 2018.

AMLO's anticorruption campaign and the implementation of his social programs quickly caught the attention of the state's entrenched political elite. The push to discredit him manifested itself in 2005, when the city government that he headed was accused of disobeying a court order to stop the construction of a public road in the neighborhood of El Encino. Obedience to the order, however, was not the issue (Díaz Polanco, 2012: 27–29); this was a political plot engineered by the state to discredit and disqualify AMLO. The PRI, the PAN, and the Partido Verde Ecologista (Green Party) joined forces in the Chamber of Deputies to withdraw the constitutional immunity from prosecution that he enjoyed as mayor.

During the conflict, political tensions ran high in the city and the nation. Demonstrations of support for AMLO increased, and on April 24 more than a million citizens walked the 5 kilometers from the Museum of Anthropology to the zócalo in a March of Silence carrying banners that read "Fox: Assassin of Democracy," "We Speak in Silence to a Deaf Justice," and "AMLO Is Innocent." Dresdner Bank Lateinamerika and its associate Allianz Group cited a survey that gave AMLO 46.4 percent of the votes. According to this study, AMLO was 36 percent above the PAN and the PRI (with 26 and 25 percent respectively) (Díaz Polanco, 2012: 43). On April 27 Fox announced that he did not oppose the participation of any citizen in the next elections and ordered that charges against AMLO be dropped, thus allowing him to run for president (Díaz Polanco, 2012: 41–42; López Obrador, 2005).

The unintended consequence of the media campaigns to withdraw AMLO's immunity transformed him into an immensely popular politician determined to build a powerful sociopolitical movement to deepen the nation's democracy. He thus skillfully turned defeat into victory as he ran for president in the elections of 2006, having demonstrated that he was more than an election-oriented politician by mobilizing vast numbers of people around an issue of democratic principle.

Shortly after the elections, the president of the Instituto Federal Electoral (Federal Electoral Institute—IFE) declared Felipe Calderón of the PAN by a margin of less than 1 percent. This decision ignored the proof provided by AMLO and his team that there were 2.5 million inconsistencies in 13,000 ballot boxes that the IFE refused to review (Díaz Polanco, 2012:50). AMLO called for a box-by-box recount and urged people to demonstrate. Seeing no results after three massive mobilizations, he decided on July 30, 2006. to begin a sit-in that stretched from Chapultepec Park to the zócalo. The sit-in was peaceful throughout its 50-day duration. Daily assemblies were held that became a veritable school for their participants. Aware of the traffic jams created by the sit-in, organizers carried signs saying, "Excuse the inconvenience. We are building democracy." During this period, numerous marches and meetings were held. On August 30, AMLO led a demonstration with the reported participation of 2 million people. Despite these mobilizations, in the second week of September the IFE declared Calderón the winner.

AMLO never recognized Calderón as the winner and proceeded to organize the sociopolitical movement to fight for democracy that would culminate in the emergence of the MORENA in 2011. This campaign took him to the nation's 2,417 municipalities and included the founding of the Casas del Movimiento (Movement Houses), the Convención Nacional Democrática (National Democratic Convention—CND), and the Adelitas (named for the women who joined their husbands during the Mexican Revolution). The Casas del Movimiento and the Adelitas carried out a door-to-door campaign to raise awareness of the nation's problems and invite people to attend "information assemblies." The Adelitas organized around 10,000 women, and the information assemblies involved more than 100,000 supporters of the Obradorist sociopolitical movement (Figueroa-Ibarra, 2016: 124). Thus, the MORENA's origin was that of a movement more than a political party.

In 2008 Calderón sent a bill to Congress to privatize PEMEX. In response, AMLO shifted gears, and the Obradorist movement became the National Movement for the Popular Economy against the Oil Privatization and for National Sovereignty and created brigades for the defense of oil on a national scale. As part of this effort, the Adelitas blocked access to the Senate on the day it was slated to vote to privatize PEMEX (Combes, 2015: 424–427). Despite his success in securing support among the population and building a nationwide network, AMLO's campaign for the defense of PEMEX met resistance within his own party. A group called the Nueva Izquierda (New Left) led by Jesús "Chucho" Ortega held majority control of the PRD, and political and ideological differences weakened the battle against oil privatization. The Chuchos did not participate in the November 23, 2008 march that initiated the campaign. Differences with the Chuchos led AMLO to forge the Frente Amplio Progresista (Broad Progressive Front—FAP), made up of the Partido del Trabajo (Workers' Party—PT) and the Convergencia (Convergence), while continuing to build his own sociopolitical movement. At the same time, he remained in the PRD and competed favorably against Marcelo Ebrard for the party's presidential candidacy for the 2012 elections.

Fraud was again allegedly committed at AMLO's expense in the elections of 2012. The PRI manipulated electronic communications and bought votes for its candidate, Enrique Peña Nieto, with prepaid cards known as Monex and Soriana. Whereas campaign spending was capped by law at 336 million pesos, the PRI used this amount in just two weeks. An investigation by the Chamber of Deputies revealed that it spent 12 times this amount (Ackerman, 2015: 144–145). Despite enormous spending and publicity, Peña Nieto faced protests on the campaign trail. For example, when he visited the Universidad Iberoamericana in Mexico City in May 2012, the students yelled "Assassin!" and "Coward!" because of the repressive character of his administration as governor of the State of Mexico. His asking the university for the names of the students who had participated in the protest led to the formation of Yo Soy #132, a movement named in reference to the number of names he requested. Though brief, the movement spread to many private universities, tarnishing his image (Ackerman, 2015: 231–237). AMLO supported the students' demands but kept his distance from the movement. He received 32 percent of the votes against Peña Nieto's 38 percent.

Subsequently, PRD bureaucrats led by the Chuchos joined the PRI and the PAN in signing the Pacto por Mexico (Pact for Mexico), which affirmed the continuation of neoliberal policies. AMLO responded by leaving the party and converting the MORENA into a movement-party. In 2014 he registered it with the Instituto Nacional Electoral (National Electoral Institute—INE)[1] and organized 300 district assemblies that elected 2,500 district coordinators who voted to turn the movement into a party. Throughout this process of organization, the MORENA presented itself as a movement-party that accompanied and promoted social movements. It contrasted itself with electoral parties such as the PRI and the PAN in that it was internally democratic[2] but was intent on participating in elections to achieve the presidency. It held constituent assemblies in 31 Mexican states and the federal district of Mexico City and signed up three times the number required to qualify (Figueroa-Ibarra, 2016: 124–125). While it pursued power to ensure a transformation of the political regime within the constraints of liberal democracy, it promised to democratize democracy through mobilizations of its supporters and the social movements it supported.

Upon becoming president, AMLO took a leave of absence from the MORENA in an attempt to break with authoritarian practices of the past. This created a power vacuum in the party, leading to rivalry between competing factions in 2019 and 2020. Mario Delgado, the MORENA's coordinator in the Chamber of Deputies, emerged as its president in October 2020. In the 2021 midterm elections, despite a strong right-wing campaign, it retained control of the Chamber of Deputies and won 11 of the 15 governors' races but lost significant mayoral races. Undeniably, it remains the leading political party, but it has abandoned its strategy of accompaniment and promotion of social movements and thus has largely become an electoral party.

Though no longer a movement-party, the MORENA does promote referendums on diverse issues as an expression of participatory democracy. One referendum was held in August 2021 over a proposal to investigate corruption and human rights violations by former neoliberal presidents, among them Carlos Salinas (1988–1994), Ernesto Zedillo (1994–2000), Vicente Fox (2000–2006), Felipe Calderón (2006–2012), and Enrique Peña Nieto (2012–2018). The electoral law prohibits political parties from promoting referendums, and therefore it was up to the INE to do it, but as a rival of the AMLO government it failed to adequately publicize the event. The electoral law required a 40 percent turnout of registered voters for the referendum to be valid, but the turnout was only around 7 percent. AMLO called the referendum a success because it was the first one at the national level in the nation's history and promoted participatory democracy. A much bigger test for both the INE and the MORENA took place in April 2022, when a presidential recall election, another milestone, was held. Neoliberal parties have opposed this referendum on grounds that it is conducive to political instability, but AMLO defends it as the best way to democratize democracy.

PEÑA NIETO'S REFORMS AND THE DISAPPEARANCE OF 43 STUDENTS IN AYOTZINAPA

The disappearance of 43 students in Ayotzinapa in 2014 was a blow to the popularity of Peña Nieto, whose performance was already being questioned as a result of his energy policy. He was still celebrating the passage of legislation privatizing PEMEX and authorizing the president to decide, without a public bid or congressional participation, the distribution of oil camps among interested companies. In addition, the reform opened the possibilities for fracking for the extraction of oil and gas nationwide (Ackerman, 2015: 115–117). It also allowed private firms to generate electricity and enjoy preference over the state-owned Comisión Federal de Electricidad (Federal Commission of Electricity—CFE). Peña Nieto presented the privatization of PEMEX and his energy reform as his most important pieces of legislation, but the Mexican people did not perceive it that way; they had long seen oil as part of the nation's patrimony and identity. Peña Nieto's popularity began its sharp decline when news of the Ayotzinapa disappearances broke out. Mexicans were shocked by this event, and thousands went to the streets all over the country demanding, "Return them alive, just as they took them" (Gravante, 2020: 87–102; Ackerman, 2015: 230–231).

The 43 students had attended the Raúl Isidro Burgos Rural Teachers' College, which was a center of political activism. Peña Nieto blamed narco-traffickers for their disappearance and denied government involvement. The students' disappearance appeared to be a golden opportunity for AMLO to lead the struggle against a government that used repressive methods to deal with opponents. Nevertheless, he did not become directly involved in the protests any more than he had with the Yo Soy #132 student movement. He denounced the disappearance of the students and seconded the protesters' call for an impartial investigation, but he was obviously prioritizing the drive to organize the MORENA to compete in the 2018 presidential elections. Thus his distancing from social movements began prior to his winning the elections of 2018. The MORENA continued to call itself a movement-party, but its objectives had switched to political rather than social ones. This switch appears to be in contradiction with its founding document, "Proyecto Alternativo de la Nacion" (National Alternative Project), which went beyond narrow political issues to address the revolution of consciousness and critical thinking (Ramirez, 2011:27–98). Notwithstanding this distancing from social movements and its original ideological inspiration, when AMLO became president in 2018 he promised to investigate what was undeniably a massacre and invited international forensic experts to continue the investigation. Since then he has met numerous times with the parents of the victims to report on the findings of the investigation, but the issue remains unresolved.

SOCIAL MOVEMENTS UNDER THE AMLO GOVERNMENT

The AMLO presidency, like other Pink Tide governments, is the product of broad anti-neoliberal social and political movements. The momentum created by these movements led to his triumph in the elections of 2018. Shortly after his inauguration, AMLO kept his promises by increasing the federal minimum wage, which had remained frozen for 25 years, and creating 28 social programs to address the needs of low-income people. These programs include 11 million scholarships for impoverished children, pensions for more than 8 million older adults, the planting of a million hectares of trees, which employed more than 400,000 peasants, and free health care and medication in public hospitals. When the COVID-19 pandemic hit, his administration initiated a campaign to ensure protection for the population, and as of mid-2021 Mexico was ninth in the world in numbers vaccinated. As promised, there has been no increase in the prices of gasoline, gas, water, and electricity. The steadfast fight against government corruption and oil and gas theft and the termination of Calderón's failed war on narco-traffickers strengthened his popularity, which has hovered above 60 percent after two and a half years in office.

Despite the importance of AMLO's social programs in addressing the needs of poor people, they fail to promote active participation in the achievement of authentic social change (Silva, 2018: 47). This lack of inclusion explains the ongoing tensions in the government's dealings with the social movements. With the exception of the Zapatistas, all of them have sought to channel their demands through institutional mechanisms, but the process has been fraught with conflict. During the first few months in office, teachers affiliated with the Coordinadora Nacional de Trabajadores de la Educación (National Coordinator of Education Workers—CNTE), a dissident faction of the SNTE, protested in front of Congress for the reversal of Peña Nieto's neoliberal educational reform. After many demonstrations and demands to meet with the president, AMLO spoke with union leaders and reached an agreement to drop the most controversial aspects of the reform. The teachers' demands included elimination of obligatory evaluations pegged to job security, automatic assignment of jobs to graduates of teachers' colleges, creation of a tenure system to ensure job security, and tripartite negotiations with participation of labor and local and federal government. The AMLO government has met all these demands during its first three years in office.

Similarly, there have been tensions around the initiation of operations of a thermoelectric plant in Huexca, Morelos. Despite social movement opposition (represented by the Frente de Pueblos en Defensa del Agua y de la Tierra [Popular Front in Defense of Water and Land]), Calderón and Peña Nieto had proceeded to build the plant in an earthquake-prone area and close to population centers. At the time, AMLO supported the peasant protests against the two presidents and promised to address the issue if elected. Ejido spokespeople claimed that the plant would not only use their farming water source but also pollute it, an allegation denied by AMLO's government. AMLO requested an investigation by a United Nations technical team, which reported that the plant would not pollute agricultural water. Peasants also claimed that noise levels would be intolerable, an allegation that the AMLO government also rejected. Protests against the plant cost the life of an environmental activist, Samir Flores, shortly after AMLO took office. Activists blamed the federal government for his death, though it appears that the local authorities were responsible.

The AMLO government ordered a public opinion survey to determine local support for the plant. Although only 40 percent opposed the project, many claimed the government's proposal had won because people from unaffected areas were included in the poll. The plant is not yet in operation and remains a thorny issue because previous governments invested US$700 million in it and the government needs to pay private companies for unused pipelines. In the meantime, residents in the area and ejido members have sought court protection to block the plant's operation (Martínez and Muñoz, 2020). Peasant demands remain unresolved.

Likewise, ejido members, indigenous communities, and environmentalists (grouped in various social movement organizations) have opposed construction of sections of the Tren Maya (Maya Train) in the nation's Southeast because of its potential negative effects. It is one of the biggest public works projects of the AMLO administration, with 1,554 kilometers of rail, and will provide service for tourists and freight and local transportation in the area. In order to avoid the activation of court orders such as those requested by the social movements opposed to the construction of the Felipe Angeles Airport near Mexico City and the Morelos thermoelectric plant, the government ordered a survey to measure objections to the train. It also deployed considerable information for local residents in 15 planned assemblies and allegedly consulted over 100,000 people. The survey registered a 92 percent vote in favor and only 7 percent against (López Obrador, 2019).

Nevertheless, the United Nations High Commissioner for Human Rights/ Mexico, which sent observers to the regional assemblies, claimed that "the information presented only made reference to the possible benefits of the project and not the negative impacts that it could produce" (Langner, 2019). The government claimed that the statement was "lacking in any basis" (*La Jornada*, 2019). It also alleged that U.S.-based nongovernmental organizations have been behind the indigenous movements' efforts to seek court orders. Nevertheless, the issue is complex because ejido and other indigenous communities have credible grievances regarding the train's impact on landownership, the environment, and culture (Hernández Navarro, 2021; Núñez Rodríguez, 2021). Indisputably, if left unattended to, indigenous claims will cut into the AMLO government's popular support.

Tension also emerged with the demands of feminist organizations regarding femicide. Despite attempts at dialogue by Rosario Ibarra Piedra, director of the Comisión Nacional de Derechos Humanos (National Human Rights Commission), a small group of radical feminists demanded that the government implement measures to combat femicide, a national problem dating back to previous governments. In September 2019, a group of feminists (including the international grassroots feminist group Ni Una Menos) occupied the offices of the commission in protest of government inaction and in March 2021 threatened to enter the National Palace. The government shielded the National Palace with a fence and employed women police to prevent demonstrators from throwing paint or destroying doors. Nonetheless, protesters charged the women police and wounded a number of them. Minister of Interior Olga Sánchez Cordero joined Ibarra Piedra in an attempt to engage the protesters in dialogue.

The AMLO government has responded positively to organized labor's demand that outsourcing be restricted and regulated. Calderón had modified the federal labor law to allow for outsourcing, and by 2014 there were 3 million workers employed by companies providing outsourcing services. In 2020, the figure reached between 6 and 7 million of the nation's 23 million registered formal workers. Calderon's legislation was changed in 2021, and now outsourcing is restricted. Napoleón Gómez Urrutia, a mining labor leader and senator for the MORENA, led the fight to reform the law. The new legislation prohibits outsourcing for non-specialized work and provides mechanisms for regulation of specialized technical services. It creates a registry of firms that offer outsourcing services and ensures that they pay their taxes and worker compensation. It took Congress nearly a year to pass the legislation because of opposition from the Consejo Coordinador Empresarial (Business Council Coordinator—CCE), the Ministry of Labor, and even elements of the MORENA (Gómez Urrutia, 2021). Unquestionably, the new law is a major achievement for labor, but enforcing it remains a challenge.

CONCLUSIONS

This chapter has identified three important stages in the relations between AMLO and his party and the social movements. In the first stage, AMLO and his followers developed a direct relationship with social movements in the street protests against alleged fraud in the 2006 presidential elections and in the establishment of the Casas del Movimiento, the CND, the Adelitas, the information assemblies, and the brigades for the defense of oil. Broad popular participation laid the groundwork for the MORENA's founding. During the second stage the MORENA became more moderate. It supported student movements such Yo Soy #132, the Frente de Pueblos en Defensa del Agua y de la Tierra, and the CNTE, but it did not participate as a party in order to prevent accusations that the protests were organized for political purposes. The electoral results of 2012 demonstrated once more that AMLO had the capacity to win the presidency, but he needed to appeal to a broader audience. In short, at the time of AMLO's election in 2018, the MORENA was still closely linked to social movements and struggles.

Since achieving power, AMLO and the MORENA have ceased to be a force in favor of mobilization, and in fact the party has become largely an electoral machine. Nevertheless, they have sought to deliver on their promises to the social movements. As president AMLO has taken important steps to address the scourge of corruption and impunity and has implemented 28 social programs to combat poverty. He has also implemented a health care policy to mitigate the effects of the COVID pandemic and passed legislation to restrict outsourcing and an education reform that reversed Peña Nieto's reforms. At the same time, tensions remained concerning feminist demands regarding femicide, the Morelos power plant, and indigenous demands regarding the Maya Train and land issues. Undeniably, AMLO's policy addresses the issues of poverty and social inequality, but it aims only at a technical "incorporation" of citizens in which they passively receive aid rather than promoting the consolidation of popular organizations that could inject new energy into the MORENA and the government.

AMLO's relations with social movements will ultimately depend on his success in achieving a reduction of inequality, a goal that may be elusive in the context of a free-market economy. The MORENA, however, no longer maintains an intimate relationship with social movements, which will have to look for new allies if they are to continue to play a major role in the process of social change.

NOTES

1. The IFE changed its name to Instituto Nacional Electoral (INE) in 2014.

2. In contrast to the PAN and the PRI, the MORENA claimed that representative democracy, "while necessary, is not the essence of democracy. The essence of democracy is participative democracy, in which participation is daily, active, and permanent" (Figueroa-Ibarra, 2016: 125).

REFERENCES

Ackerman, John

2015 *El mito de la transición democrática: Nuevas coordenadas para la transformación del régimen mexicano*. Mexico City: Editorial Planeta.

Alvarez, S., E. Dagnino, and A. Escobar (eds.)

1998 *Culture of Politics, Politics of Culture: Re-Visioning Latin American Social Movements*. Boulder: Westview Press.

Betances, Emelio

2016 *En busca de la ciudadanía: Movimientos sociales y democratización en la República Dominicana*. Santo Domingo: Archivo General de la Nación.

Bolos, Silvia

2015 "El análisis de la complejidad de un movimiento social desde las múltiples dimensiones de análisis," pp. 339–380 in H. Combes, S. Tamayo, and M. Voegtli (eds.), *Pensar y mirar la protesta*. Mexico City: Universidad Autónoma Metropolitana.

Combes, Hélène

2015 "Repertorios de la movilización, estrategias políticas y reclutamiento militante," pp. 417–450 in H. Combes, S. Tamayo, and M. Voegtli (eds.). *Pensar y mirar la protesta*. Mexico City: Universidad Autónoma Metropolitana.

Díaz Polanco, Héctor

2012 *La cocina del diablo: El fraude de 2006 y los intelectuales*. Mexico City: Editorial Planeta Mexicana.

Ellner, Steve

2018 "López Obrador: third time´s the charm?" NACLA. https://doi.org/10.1080/10714839.2018.1479443.

Figueroa-Ibarra, Carlos

2016 "Participative democracy and the alternative national project of MORENA in Mexico," pp. 113–135 in E. Betances and C. Figueroa-Ibarra (eds.), *Popular Sovereignty and Constituent Power in Latin America: Democracy from Below*. New York: Palgrave Macmillan.

Gómez Urrutia, Napoleón

2021 "Outsourcing, impunidad y desigualdad." *La Jornada*. https://www.jornada.com.mx/2021/01/28/opinion/014a1pol.

González Casanova, Pablo

2005 "The Zapatista 'caracoles': networks of resistance and autonomy." *Socialism and Democracy* 19 (3): 79–92.

Gravante, Tommaso
2020 "Forced disappearance as a collective cultural trauma in the Ayotzinapa movement." *Latin American Perspectives* 47 (6): 87–102.

Haber, Paul Lawrence
2006 *Power from Experience: Urban Popular Movements in Late Twentieth-Century Mexico.* University Park: Pennsylvania State University Press.

Hernández Navarro, Luis
2021 "El amparo contra el Tren Maya," *La Jornada.* https://www.jornada.com.mx /2020/02/11/opinion/015a1pol.

Holloway, John
2002 *Change the World without Taking Power.* London: Pluto Press.

Holston, James
2008 *Insurgent Citizens: Disjunctions of Democracy and Modernity in Brazil.* Princeton: Princeton University Press.

Isin, Engin F.
2008 *Recasting the Social in Citizenship.* Toronto: University of Toronto Press.

Langner, Ana
2019 "Consulta por Tren Maya no cumple estándares internacionales: ONU," *La Jornada.* https://lajornadasanluis.com.mx/nacional/consulta-por-tren-maya-no -cumple-estandares-internacionales-onu/.

La Jornada
2019 "El gobierno descalifica críticas de la ONU-DH a consulta Tren Maya." https:// www.jornada.com.mx/2019/12/24/politica/006n1pol.

López, Luis
2009 "Actores movimientos y conflictos: ¿es posible la acción colectiva en un contexto de fragmentación sociocultural?" pp. 105–128 in F. Mestries, G. Pleyers and S. Zermeño (eds.), *Los movimientos sociales: De lo local a lo global.* Mexico City: Universidad Autónoma Metropolitana.

López Obrador, Andrés Manuel
2004 *Un proyecto alternativo de nación.* Mexico City: Editorial Grijalbo.
2005 *Contra el desafuero: Mi defensa jurídica.* Mexico City: Editorial Grijalbo.
2019 "Conferencia Mañanera." December 15.

Martinez, Fabiola and Alma Muñoz
2020 "La termoeléctrica en Morelos operara a finales de año: AMLO." *La Jornada.* https://www.jornada.com.mx/2020/09/11/politica/003n1pol.

McAdam, D., C. Tilly, and S. Tarrow
2001 *The Dynamics of Contention.* New York: Cambridge University Press.

Mestries, Francis
2015 "Las metamorfosis de una organización de deudores: El Barzón," pp. 305–338 in H. Combes, S. Tamayo, and M. Voegtli (eds.), *Pensar y mirar la protesta.* Mexico City: Universidad Autónoma Metropolitana.

Munck, Ronaldo

2020 "Social movements in Latin America: paradigms, people, and politics." *Latin American Perspectives* 47 (4): 20–39.

Núñez Rodriguez, Violeta

2021 "Fibra Tren Maya?" *La Jornada.* https://www.jornada.com.mx/2020/02/23/opinion/012a2pol.

Ramírez Cuevas, J., et al.

2011 *Nuevo proyecto de nación: Por el renacimiento de México.* Mexico City: Grijalbo.

Santos, Boaventura de Sousa (ed.)

2005 *Democratizar la democracia: Los caminos de la democracia participativa.* Mexico City: Fondo de Cultura Económica.

Silva, Eduardo

2018 "Social movements and the second incorporation in Bolivia and Ecuador," pp. 44–71 in E. Silva and F. Rossi (eds.), *Shaping the Political Arena in Latin America: From Resisting Neoliberalism to the Second Incorporation.* Pittsburgh: University of Pittsburgh Press.

Silva, Eduardo and Federico Rossi

2018 *Reshaping the Political Arena in Latin America: From Resisting Neoliberalism to the Second Incorporation.* Pittsburgh: University of Pittsburgh Press.

Slater, David

1985 *New Social Movements and the State in Latin America.* Amsterdam: CEDLA.

Stahler-Sholk, Richard, Harry E. Vanden, and Marc Becker

2014 "Introduction: New directions in Latin American social movements," pp. 1–18 in Richard Stahler-Sholk, Harry E. Vanden, and Marc Becker (eds.), *Rethinking Latin American Social Movements: Radical Action from Below.* Lanham, MD: Rowman and Littlefield.

Tamayo, Sergio

2009 "Participación ciudadana y movimientos sociales," pp. 79–103 in F. Mestries, G. Pleyers, and S. Zermeño (eds.), *Los movimientos sociales: De lo local a lo global.* Mexico City: Universidad Autónoma Metropolitana.

Tarrow, Sidney

1994 *Power in Movements: Social Movements, Collective Action and Politics.* Melbourne: Cambridge University Press.

Chapter 12

From Protest to Politics

Social Movements and Progressive Parties in Chile and Colombia

Kyla Sankey and Aaron Tauss

In the past two decades, while a Pink Tide of anti-neoliberal, progressive governments swept to power on the back of mass mobilizations across Latin America, Chile and Colombia continued along the path of neoliberal restructuring. In both countries, social movements and labor organizations were on the defensive. Chile's military dictatorship (1973–1990) and state and paramilitary violence in Colombia oversaw the violent decimation of organized labor and popular forces, while neoliberal reforms ushered in a new era of flexibilization and deregulation, undermining the power of working people to fight back. Seen in this light, it is no small feat that Chile and Colombia have witnessed some of the largest and most prolonged popular uprisings in Latin America in recent years. In Chile, a small increase of the Santiago subway fare in October 2019 triggered the largest wave of protests, riots, and strikes Chile had witnessed since the end of the Pinochet dictatorship. Shortly after, in November 2019, a package of neoliberal reforms introduced by Colombia's right-wing president Iván Duque sparked a national strike that spread across 550 of the country's 1,000 municipalities. Notably, the mobilizations have emerged not primarily from traditional agents of progressive change such as unions and leftist parties but from relatively new social forces. The most prominent protagonists have been young people, part of the increasingly precarious working and middle classes, along with social movements, feminist collectives, the unemployed, indigenous groups, and peasant and worker organizations.

More broadly, the social movements and popular organizations are the material expression of the hegemonic crisis of neoliberalism in the face of economic slowdown, state repression, and growing popular discontent. At the same time, they reflect the deepening crisis of the political establishment and the conventional forms of representation in both countries. In this respect, the situations in Chile and Colombia bear important resemblances to those of many Latin American countries in the 1990s and early 2000s, when mass mobilizations eventually gave rise to progressive Pink Tide governments. They also offer two of the most emblematic examples of the more recent waves of popular discontent that have swept the region and paved the way for the election of left-wing governments in Argentina (in 2019), Bolivia (in 2020), Peru (in 2021), and Honduras (in 2021). Gabriel Boric's election is the latest chapter in this trend of renewed Pink Tide advances throughout the region in recent years. At the time of writing, the progressive presidential candidate Gustavo Petro is the front-runner for Colombia's 2022 presidential election.

This chapter provides an account of the upsurge of popular resistance that has taken place in Chile and Colombia in the recent past, the diversity of its social composition, its specific demands, the protest strategies and tactics used and their relation to political projects. In different ways, the two experiences demonstrate that even in countries characterized by seemingly stable right-wing regimes and in the case of Colombia a weak political left, progressive, anti-neoliberal political projects can still be made viable through the power of mass mobilizations. Therefore both popular mobilizations raise important questions of strategy for anti-neoliberal mobilizations in a context where the traditional agents of the left have been weakened through neoliberal policies combined in Chile with the left's participation in Concertación governments, and in Colombia with repression. Finally, the chapter highlights the similarities and differences between the two cases and the lessons drawn about the relationship between social mobilizations and progressive parties, which have relevance for all countries in the region. The comparative methodological approach enables a better understanding of the complex and often contradictory interplay between leftist political parties and social movements in two political conjunctures marked by popular revolt and mass protest.

AUTONOMY, SOCIAL MOVEMENTS, AND POLITICAL POWER

The social movement upsurges that swept Chile and Colombia in recent years were not entirely independent from the traditional left infrastructure of political parties and unions, but their emergence, mobilization, and development followed a different logic. The prominence of new social actors, in particular young people, the tactics of carving out autonomous spaces in the barrios, the centrality of anti-neoliberal demands, and the rejection of the governing parties are in many ways reminiscent of the resistance that swept across other countries in the continent in the 1990s and early 2000s, led by movements such as the *piqueteros* in Argentina and the gas wars in Bolivia. As with these movements, the relevance of new social actors must be highlighted, although the following accounts demonstrate that these cannot be completely separated from unions and political parties. Notwithstanding the proclamations that the era of political parties had given way to the emergence of social movements, as captured in the slogan *¡Qué se vayan todos!*, the major development to come out of these movements was the return of progressive parties. Although the mobilizations in Chile and Colombia have emerged in countries marked by the stability of the right, the argument here is that the experience of these two countries offers fertile terrain for exploring one of the major controversies of the Pink Tide: the "autonomous" status of social movements and their relation to political parties.

Advocates of the so-called new social movement approach have defended social movements' need for absolute autonomy. Inspired by John Holloway's notion of changing the world without taking power, Zibechi's (2012: 15) account of new social movements argues that "they seek autonomy from the state as well as political parties." His criticism of political parties, adapting Lenin's famous phrase, is that when social movements engage in politics they become "transmission belts" subordinated to political parties and states (2017: 49). For Zibechi, any attempt to engage with progressive governments is a dead end, since governments will only impede their radical impetus through "the arts of governance and particularly of governing movements from below," serving merely "to extend the life of decrepit states" (Zibechi, 2012: 270).

According to Zibechi, the transformative processes created by the movements lie only within the movements themselves. The construction of "another world" is sought not for all members of society but for members of the social movement alone through their participation in projects of autonomous self-governance. Meanwhile, Marta Harnecker (2016: 8) argues that the task for social movements is not securing autonomy internally for their members only but "procuring the support of the masses and consensus in the majority of society." Zibechi's ideal of autonomy is made possible through self-organization and the creation of alternative administrative structures outside the state, structures that are directly democratic, horizontal, and built from below. Meanwhile, engagement with electoral politics will inevitably lead social movements to "become institutionalized and bureaucratized" (Oikonomakis, 2019: 16). This autonomist perspective, which draws a divide between the logic of social movements, on the one hand, and the logic of political parties, on the other, is premised on a vision of social change that is possible only on a small, localized scale, any attempt to achieve broader societal change through the capture of state power being strictly ruled out. To draw a clear dividing line between social and political movements in this way creates a distinction that, as Ronaldo Munck points out in this volume, "does not exist either in theory or in practice." As the two case studies presented here demonstrate, the divide between social and political is not reflected in the way movements themselves conceive of their activities. At certain times, social movements may engage in politics, at others in mobilization and movement building. Strategies may shift, and the strategy adopted at one moment may proceed to a different course in response to changing circumstances.

Social movements inevitably respond to and act in a very political context, whether they profess autonomy or not. Petras and Veltmeyer (2011) have highlighted that the new social movements of the 1990s and early 2000s were created in response to neoliberal state policies and sought to reverse those policies. The same may be said of the mobilizations in Chile and Colombia, which were created in response to a public transport fare hike and a neoliberal reform package, and both have at least partly engaged in political strategies, from negotiations to the project of a new constitution, seeking to counter the effects of neoliberal policies. Moreover, as Steve Ellner points out in this book's introduction, the impact of the broader political context on the capacity of social movements to mobilize, build, and act should not be underestimated. In contrast to Pink Tide governments, which frequently consulted social movements on issues that affected them, the neoliberal regimes in Chile and Colombia have negotiated with social movements only after protracted social conflicts. Moreover, the two cases presented here demonstrate that neoliberal governments have been far more repressive toward social movements than any Pink Tide government. While the actions of social movements are inevitably conditioned by political circumstances, left political parties also heavily rely on social movements. In a context where neoliberal governments not only control the instruments of the state but also enjoy the support of the mass media, left-wing political leaders rely on social movements to expose and bring to the fore the crisis of the right-wing regimes.

These case studies show that the strategies of social movements are far more complex and dynamic than any ideology of absolute autonomy would allow. In her political writing, Marta Harnecker (2016: 30) has argued for a strategy whereby political organizations show respect for the autonomous development of grassroots movements without seeing social movements as "conveyor belts for the party" or attempting to manipulate them. Social movements, for their part, may mobilize thousands, but to build the world they are demanding requires "a social and political force capable of changing the balance of forces in favor of the popular movement" (2015: 5) In practice, social movements are not fixated on an ideal of autonomy but adopt an array of strategies with both social and political dimensions and may change in response to changing contexts.

In both Chile and Colombia, the 2019–2021 uprisings resulted primarily from the struggles and the political activism of new social actors—young people, students, social movements, popular organizations, women's collectives, indigenous communities, and sectors of the middle class. The "traditional" left of unions and political parties, however, also played an important role in the organization of marches, mass gatherings, and strikes. In Chile one of the main reasons for the uprising was the deep-rooted discontent and the growing general frustration with the political parties that had governed the country for nearly three decades after the military dictatorship. The crisis of representation also affected the formerly progressive parties, which to some extent were seen as collaborators with the same corrupted system. It therefore came as no surprise that during the uprising social movements and popular organizations rejected co-optation by any political party and from the very beginning emphasized their autonomy. Nonetheless, the experience of Chile demonstrates how movements can build alliances with progressive political forces without necessarily compromising their autonomy. The election of the center-left candidate and former student leader Gabriel Boric, a member of the Convergencia Social (Social Convergence) and the Apruebo Dignidad (Approve Dignity) coalition, undoubtedly embodies the hopes of this generation of protesters. Even movements that did not belong to Apruebo Dignidad saw the vote for Boric as the best way to secure and advance the victories of the movements, most importantly through the constitutional process. Boric's victory showed that the 2011–2013 student protests and the 2019–2020 popular uprising had opened a space for left-wing political projects to build on. In Colombia, the social movements of the national strike have similarly sought to maintain their autonomy in order to avoid subordinating their objectives to those of political parties. In a country long characterized by not only stable right-wing governments but also, in contrast to Chile, a weak political left, the national strike highlights the role of mass mobilizations in bypassing the media to delegitimize right-wing Uribism and center the left-wing candidate Gustavo Petro as a viable political force. In contrast to Boric, Petro is a long-standing political figure who did not emerge as the candidate of social movements. Nonetheless, the protests have opened a space for progressive political projects such as this to advance. The cases of Chile and Colombia demonstrate how, to build a sustained alternative to the current status quo, political movements can recognize and respect the role of social mobilizations in building popularity and consensus beyond the electoral sphere.

CHILE

The October Uprising

The demonstrations of October 2019 were kicked off by hundreds of secondary school students, who resisted the subway fare increase by occupying subway stations and calling for fare evasion. The targeted actions came as no surprise, since secondary school students in 2006 and university students in 2011 had been at the forefront of weeks-long mass demonstrations against the country's neoliberal education system (Donoso, 2013; Bellei, Cabalin, and Orellana, 2014). This time around, the images of angry youths and police brutality spread rapidly on social media, and over the following days more people joined the actions. On October 18, thousands of people took to the streets in Santiago to protest against state repression and the conservative government of the billionaire President Sebastián Piñera (2018–2022). The demonstration provoked heavy clashes between protesters and the police. Dozens of subway stations, banks, hotels, pharmacies, and supermarkets were set on fire and in some cases looted. Within hours, the protests spread from the capital across the entire country. It soon became clear that the general discontent had to do not only with the subway fare increase but with Chile's neoliberal model and the country's corrupted and antidemocratic political system. That same night, the Piñera government declared a state of emergency in Santiago and other provinces and imposed nightly curfews, claiming that Chile was "at war" with a powerful internal enemy. For more than a week, 10,000 soldiers armed with tanks and war equipment patrolled the country. Such a measure had last been resorted to under the military dictatorship (Pérez, 2019; Tinsman, 2019; Palacios, 2020).

The government's brutal repression, however, helped the protesters' concerns gain even more support among the Chilean population. According to the Instituto Nacional de Derechos Humanos (National Institute of Human Rights—INDH), more than 30 people died, more than 3,700 were injured, and close to 10,000 were arrested (INDH, 2020). The United Nations (2019), Amnesty International (2019), and Human Rights Watch (2019) all criticized the serious human rights violations committed by the Chilean police and military, including murder, torture, mutilation, rape, and illegal arrest. A growing number of social movements, opposition parties, and human rights organizations called for Piñera's immediate resignation. When the military repression failed to produce the hoped-for results, the government presented a package of social measures, which included an increase of the minimum pension and the minimum wage, a higher tax rate for top incomes, and improvements in health care (Gobierno de Chile, 2019). In spite of the concessions, on October 25 over 1.2 million people took to the streets of Santiago. Secondary school and university students, workers, peasants, pensioners, unions, feminist collectives, and environmental and human rights organizations, the Mapuche indigenous movement, the LGBTQ community, and a multiplicity of social movements protested against the Piñera government, low pensions, precarious working conditions, ailing education and health systems, excessive highway tolls, and rampant police brutality (Lamadrid and Urrutia, 2019). They demanded women's rights, the protection of water resources and indigenous territories, social justice, and profound reforms of pensions, health care, and education. The renamed Plaza de la Dignidad (Dignity Square) in the center of Santiago became the epicenter and a symbol of the uprising. As the protests continued, the demand to replace Chile's neoliberal constitution—dating back to the Pinochet era—with a new democratically elected constitution became more and more prevalent. In mid-November, the Piñera government gave in and presented an agreement, signed by most political parties, to hold a referendum on a new constitution in April 2020.

Pinochet's Legacy and Deepening Crises

Chile's constitution, the legacy of the Pinochet regime, shapes the country's political economy to this day. Passed in 1980, it legally enshrined the military junta's comprehensive neoliberal reforms, which privatized state assets, social security (pensions, health, and education), and public services (water, electricity, telecommunications). It limited the state's socioeconomic role to a minimum and ensured elite control of the political system (Pizarro, 2020). Following the transition to formal democracy in the early 1990s, the consolidation of neoliberalism as a regime of political and economic normality unfolded under the aegis of the Concertación de Partidos por la Democracia, a coalition of center-left political parties that governed Chile for 20 years (Pérez, 2020; Sasse, 2021). The alliance included Chile's Socialist Party, whose historic leader, former President Salvador Allende (1970–1973), had been violently deposed in a coup d'état by Pinochet. Over the past three decades Chile has reported high growth rates, a decline in poverty, and rising levels of education. The flipside of the neoliberal model, however, is high levels of socioeconomic inequality and material insecurity, low wages and pensions, precarious working conditions, and extreme concentration of wealth and income (OECD, 2018; Sehnbruch and Donoso 2020; Fundación SOL, 2020).

Today, the richest 1 percent—consisting of about 400 families that dominate the Chilean economy—owns one-third of the country's wealth (UNDP, 2017; Fischer, 2017). At the same time, barely a third of the population can afford three meals a day. More than half of the working population earns US$500 a month (with a cost level comparable to that of the United States), and about 45 percent toil in the informal sector. Similar inequalities also exist in the health system. Approximately 85 percent of Chileans rely on the public health system, which provides slow and poor-quality services in run-down hospitals. While public spending on pensions remains low, 80 percent of Chilean pensioners receive less than the minimum wage (Mander, 2019). To compensate for the disparity between wages and the cost of living, three-quarters of Chilean households are now in debt—the highest figure in all of Latin America (Boddenberg, 2019).

Given these realities of a fractured society, it comes as no surprise that many Chileans eventually took their anger to the streets during the October uprising. It would be misleading, however, to reduce the protests to economic factors and the deepening hegemonic crisis of neoliberalism. Political motivations also play an important role. The massive protests of the recent past are certainly the expression of a profound crisis of political legitimacy and representation, which manifests itself in distrust of the political system, lack of identification with established parties, and declining voter turnouts (Rojas, 2021). The crisis of legitimacy is primarily rooted in the unwillingness and failure of the Concertacion (1990–2010, 2014–2018) and center-right coalitions (2010–2014, 2018–2022) to bring about real change over the past three decades, despite growing popular resistance (Jiménez, 2020).

The 1990s in Chile were marked not only by the continuation of Pinochet's legacy under democratic rule but also by the slow repoliticization of civil society and growing dissatisfaction with neoliberalism and Chilean oligarchic politics. During that decade students, contract workers, indigenous groups, and environmental activists began to organize small demonstrations calling for profound changes, but it was not until 2006 that a protest campaign initiated by secondary school students formed the first massive mobilization since military rule (Somma, 2012). In 2011 a second wave of demonstrations—this time spearheaded by university students—shook the country for weeks. Chile's leading national labor union, the Central Unitaria de Trabajadores (Workers' Unified Central—CUT), environmental activists, miners, workers, sectors of the indebted middle class, and the Mapuche indigenous movement joined forces and protested against unequal educational opportunities, police repression, elitist politics, precarious working conditions, environmental devastation, and low pensions. For the first time, the call for a new constitution became part of the political agenda. Chile's Communist Party, which had been part of the left-wing coalition Frente Popular (Popular Front) under the Allende presidency, was supportive of the student protests. One of the main leaders of the mobilizations, Camila Vallejo, later became a member of the Chamber of Deputies for the Communist Party. In 2017, other young leaders of the student demonstrations founded the Frente Amplio (Broad Front), a political coalition composed of left-wing parties and movements.

Transcending Heterogeneity

During the 2019 October rebellion, the resurfacing of the demand for a new constitution produced an integrative dynamic among the different protest groups, unifying their diverse concerns and reform proposals. The conviction increasingly prevailed that no structural socioeconomic and political transformation of Chile would be possible without overcoming Pinochet's legal legacy. This conviction played an essential role in the creation of a collective will and the definition of a common political denominator that transcended the particular interests (education, health care, social security, women's equality, environment protection, and indigenous rights) and opened a new horizon for a fundamental structural reorientation of the country's political economy. A collective will, however, emerged only as a product of the continuation of protest marches in the streets (Boos and Tauss, 2020).

Following Piñera's announcement of the constitutional referendum, hundreds of assemblies (*asambleas*) and neighborhood councils (*cabildos*) were formed in Santiago and other cities across the country (Guerrero and Cabezas, 2020). The objective was to discuss Chile's political and economic crisis, to identify social demands, and to elaborate bottom-up proposals for a new constitution (Gómez, 2019; Altamirano, Arroyo, and Maldonado, 2020). A social dialogue network called the Mesa de Unidad Social (Social Unity Roundtable), made up of unions and social movements, helped organize the activities, promote participation in protest marches, and strengthen solidarity among the participants. The different forms of democratic self-organization brought together a diversity of social and political expressions in a common space created for collective deliberation. At the same time, they were the material expressions of deep-rooted skepticism with regard to Chile's political parties and of the crisis of conventional forms of representation (Abufom, 2020; Garcés, 2020). Antiparty sentiment among activists was no longer restricted to Chile's center-left and center-right. For many protesters, large sectors of the Communist Party and the Frente Amplio were part of the problem. Above all, the proximity of some party members to the government of former President Michelle Bachelet (2014–2018), who had not kept her promise to bring about profound change, had an alienating effect on the protesters. For some, Chile's leftist parties were incompatible with the causes and motivations of the popular uprising. As in the past, however, Chile's unions played an important role in the organization of protest marches and the mobilization of their members in the events of 2019–2020 (Fundación Instituto de Estudios Laborales, 2021).

The call for a post-neoliberal constitution and the rejection of the political establishment were, however, not the only factors strengthening the ties between the different protest groups. Cultural expressions such as graffiti, wall paintings, dances, concerts, and sit-ins were also important. In addition, the protesters managed to develop unifying symbols such as the youths equipped with gas masks, goggles, and homemade shields on the fringe of the protests. Loosely made up of diverse political subjects, among them anarchists, football hooligans, and marginal adolescents, this *primera línea* (first line) defended demonstrators against the violent actions of the police. It swiftly became prominent in urban centers and developed an almost mythological symbolic place in the imaginary of the revolt. It was the main political-military innovation of the Chilean rebellion (Fernández, 2019). Another prominent symbol was the widespread protest gesture of covering one eye with the heel of the hand, referring to the more than 400 eye injuries caused by the police's rubber bullets. Digital communication channels such as Instagram, Facebook, or Twitter and newly founded alternative radio channels and online newspapers such as Chileokulto, El Desconcierto, and La Tercera were essential for spreading the unifying symbols, organizing protest activities, and denouncing police brutality.

Moving Ahead

The onset of the COVID-19 pandemic in March 2020 put an abrupt end to nationwide protests in Chile. In view of rapidly increasing infection, the government declared a state of emergency, banned mass gatherings, and postponed the constitutional referendum until October 2020. The pandemic not only weakened the protests and the democratic processes of self-empowerment set in motion but also significantly aggravated social inequality, indebtedness, unemployment, homelessness, and poverty (Reperger, 2021). The profound social and economic crisis laid bare the shortcomings of Chile's neoliberal model, and its partisan handling in favor of big capital and mismanagement by the Piñera government once again revealed the latter's oligarchic character (Atria, 2020).

In October 2020, 80 percent of Chileans voted for a new constitution written by a directly elected constituent assembly with gender parity. The delegate elections, held six months later, shattered Chile's old oligarchical political system and opened new avenues for a resurgent left. Of the 155 members elected to the assembly, 103 did not belong to any political party. However, as in past electoral contests, voter turnout was low (43 percent). More than half of the Chilean population was apparently not interested in casting a vote and participating in the democratic process that would determine the country's legal foundation for generations. The lived experience of many, which appeared to show that fundamental problems were not solved by elections, was certainly a decisive factor in this context. In addition, 40 years of neoliberal restructuring had fostered a culture of consumerist individual-ism that undoubtedly contributed to the depoliticization of many Chileans.

For Chile's left, it was not only the delegate elections for the constitutional convention that were a cause for celebration. Even more unexpected were the results of the municipal and gubernatorial elections that took place simul-taneously. Both the center-left coalition that had spearheaded the transition process from military dictatorship to formal democracy and the right-wing coalition built to defend Pinochet's legacy saw their votes collapse. The big winners were new left-wing forces. The coalition of the Frente Amplio and the Communist Party, which had played only a marginal role in Chilean politics in the recent past, made a surprising political comeback and won many iconic right-wing municipalities (Titelman, 2021). Nonparty candidates representing the concerns of the protest movement and feminist organizations also prevailed at the ballot box.

The results of the referendum and the elections revealed at least three trends. First, they reflected the widespread desire for state-guaranteed basic social and women's rights, the demands of indigenous peoples for greater recognition and inclusion, and the call of the environmental movement for an "ecological constitution" (Caviedes and Carvallo, 2021). Second, they showed that the majority of Chileans strongly rejected the two main political alliances (center-left and center-right) that had governed Chile in the post-Pinochet era. Third, they reflected the convergence of the criticisms and demands articulated by social movements in the most recent protest cycle and the concerns of political parties on the left. The newly formed alliances between Chile's political left and social movements also played a prominent role in the presidential elections, held in November and December 2021. Gabriel Boric, a former student leader and current congressperson for the Frente Amplio, defeated the ultraconservative and right-wing candidate José Antonio Kast and became Chile's youngest president. At age 35, Boric embodied Chile's younger generation, which was a major driving force behind the October uprising. His electoral coalition, Apruebo Dignidad, included the Frente Amplio, Chile's Communist Party, environmental movements, and feminist collectives. The presidential elections radicalized the trend toward political polarization that had already been evident in the lead-up to the constitutional referendum. Moreover, similar to past experi-ences in Pink Tide countries, the results in the presidential race showed the close, although not always aligned, relationship between social movements, popular organizations, and progressive political forces not only in the build-ing of revolts but also in the winning of elections. Some on the left supported Boric for tactical reasons—to prevent a presidency of the extreme right under Kast, whom they criticized for not radically calling into question Chile's neo-liberal accumulation model and its oligarchic and plutocratic political system

(Fauré, 2021). Other social movements saw his presidency as an opportunity to overcome Pinochet's legacy and as a step toward a more democratic and egalitarian society. Whatever the criticisms, Boric supported the demand for a new constitution from the beginning, and it is in this process that the hopes of the movements lie. His presidency will most likely have a positive influence on the struggle for a progressive post-neoliberal and feminist constitution. A referendum on the new constitution is scheduled for late 2022.

Chile's right, in contrast, aimed to preserve Pinochet's legacy and prevent the adoption of a new constitution. The country's dominant classes and transnational capital are unwilling to simply give up their privileges and profits. Both have benefited greatly from privatizations and the barely regulated exploitation of raw materials. Strong headwinds against the Boric government and the passage of a new constitution are therefore to be expected. In that confrontation, the strengthening of the interaction and collaboration between Chile's political left and social movements and the collective development of strategies of emancipatory transformation that go beyond elections and the institutions of the state will play a pivotal role. In the long run, the continuation and radicalization of protests, riots, strikes, neighborhood assemblies, popular educational programs, and the like will be key in the political struggle over a more democratic, egalitarian, feminist, plurinational, and ecologically sustainable future.

COLOMBIA

The Left's Resurgence

At the end of the 2000s, the Colombian left was in retreat. For the past two decades, paramilitary counterinsurgents tied to the drug trade, large landowners, cattle ranchers, agribusiness, the military, and conservative political parties had been conducting a campaign of terror that had wiped out most of its leaders or driven them into exile.[1] Meanwhile, the Democratic Security doctrine of right-wing President Álvaro Uribe (2002–2010) had effectively militarized all aspects of civic life in an effort to "remodel society into a militia and convert the citizen into a combatant with duties and obligations in the scenes of war" (Zibechi, 2005) In the countryside, Uribe's "scorched earth" strategy for defeating Colombia's decades-old guerrilla insurgency—the Fuerzas Armadas Revolucionarias de Colombia (Revolutionary Armed Forces of Colombia—FARC) and the Ejército de Liberación Nacional (National Liberation Army—ELN) saw millions of small-scale peasants displaced and their lands appropriated in a brutal process of agrarian counterreform. Nor was there much hope in the cities, where a combination of neoliberal structural adjustment and paramilitary terror had put labor on the defensive. The large and rapidly growing armies of precarious, unprotected workers found themselves unable to organize collectively and challenge the neoliberal policies that had decimated the urban and rural working classes (Gill, 2016). The rise of leftist governments in the region, brought to power on the back of mass mobilizations throughout the 2000s, only ignited Colombia's right, which became more belligerent and tightened its alliance with the United States.

Against this background, it is all the more remarkable that only a few years later Colombia was transformed into the epicenter of radical social protest in the region. The first wave of revolt broke out in the agrarian strike of 2013, when more than 1,000 protests predominantly in small rural towns brought the country to a standstill. In 2019 and 2021 a second protest wave hit the country that was very different in social base, character, and strategy from the first. The emergence of the latest cycle of mass mobilizations can be traced to a range of causes, not least of which were the devastating impacts of neoliberalism and militarization and the new space for political action opened by the peace negotiations between President Juan Manuel Santos (2010–2018) and the FARC. Yet, while the demonstrations brought new actors into the political sphere and challenged the hegemony of the neoliberal project in Colombia, the opposition did not initially succeed in creating an anti-neoliberal political movement strong enough to effectively challenge the power of the far-right and neoliberalism.

The year 2013 saw an unprecedented surge in social mobilization across the country, as mass civic strikes paralyzed towns and cities. With 1,027 protests, Colombia recorded the biggest upsurge in social activism since the civic strike of 1977 (CINEP, 2014). In contrast to that of 1977, however, the 2013 strike wave was predominantly rural. The main participants were various sectors of peasants from the traditional agricultural areas of the Andean and coffee regions, rural workers, and the more marginal peasants and landless workers of the peripheral frontier territories of the Southeast. The protesters were united in their opposition to the government's neoliberal policies in the countryside, not least of which were the free-trade agreements (over 40 have been signed in the past two decades, most recently with the United States and the European Union), volatile prices, and the unbridled expansion of natural-resource extraction.

Colombia's social movements, such as the Marcha Patriótica (Patriotic March)—closely tied to the Communist Party—and the autonomist Congreso de los Pueblos (Peoples' Congress), had not initiated the protests, but their leaders were key protagonists in organizing them and formulating their demands. This should hardly be surprising, considering that the main bases of both these movements are in the countryside. A coordinating committee was formed that successfully brought together some 4,000 activists from 12 social movements including the Organización Indígena de Colombia (Indigenous Organization of Colombia—ONIC), the Proceso de Comunidades Negras (Black Communities' Process—PCN), the Coordinador Nacional Agrario (National Agrarian Committee—CNA), and the Mesa Nacional de Interlocución Agraria (National Bureau of Agricultural Advocacy—MIA) for an agrarian summit. Participants in the discussions agreed on a petition with eight demands that focused on neoliberal agricultural policies, the militarization of the countryside, and the devastating impact of extractive industries on rural areas. However, the coalition ultimately disintegrated as the Santos government selectively negotiated with the organizations representing better-off peasants and neutralized the more radical sectors from the frontier regions with fierce police repression. Despite several days of protests and marches in Bogotá, the various movements were ultimately unable to unify their demands.

The 2019 National Strike

In 2019 Colombia was ignited by another wave of protests that was very different from the 2013 demonstrations in terms of both participants and aims. While in 2013 the mobilizations had been predominantly rural and had the left as key protagonists, the 2019–2021 national strike erupted in major cities and was led by young people. At the same time, it was also less cohesive and organized. While the tensions in 2013 had been more about colliding leaderships and organizational aims, in 2019–2021 the issue was that the protests lacked any clearly defined or recognized leadership.

The 2019 national strike was initially called by Colombia's main union confederations—the CUT, the Confederación General de Trabajadores (General Confederation of Workers—CGT), and the Federación Colombiana de Trabajadores de la Educación (Colombian Federation of Education Workers—FECODE), among others. Calls of this sort had often been made before, but no one, including those who called the strikes, was expecting the massive outburst that followed (Loingsigh, 2021). The protests spread far beyond the orbit of the organizations that would usually follow calls for a national demonstration, mobilizing more than 2.5 million people in 550 municipalities and paralyzing almost all the main cities. For the most part organized by public employees, teachers, university professors, and students, the scale and intensity of the mobilizations came as a surprise not only to the national government but also to the strike organizers themselves.

Even though political parties from the center (Alianza Verde [Green Alliance]) and center-left (Polo Democrático [Democratic Pole]) and the social movements supported the strike, it was not led by any movement or political party. Most notably, it was urban young people and women who ended up being the main protagonists in the mobilizations. The protesters were united in their opposition to the neoliberal reforms introduced by President Duque and their condemnation of repression against the protesters. The package included privatizations of Colombia's largest state-run oil company, Ecopetrol, telecommunications, electricity, the elimination of the state pension fund Colpensiones, a reduction of the minimum wage for young people, and an increase in energy prices (Dorado, 2019). The government refused to negotiate with the strikers, instead sending the riot police to crush the protests. Repression only galvanized the mobilizations, which escalated over months until the COVID-19 lockdown brought the process to a sudden halt in March 2020.

The arrival of the pandemic initially offered a respite for President Duque. It presented an opportunity for him to mobilize the country around a common enemy and reassert himself as a strong leader, curbing democracy and enforcing restrictions on economic and social activities. But the respite was short-lived. Income support packages were too small, reached too few people, and were unable to prevent poverty rates' soaring from 36 percent in 2015 to 43 percent in 2020 (*El Espectador*, 2021). In early 2021 Duque proposed tax reform, prioritizing the demands of international creditors and financial institutions to close the growing fiscal deficit (Ortiz, 2021). The reform proposed to maintain the tax exemptions given to large corporations while offloading the cost of the pandemic response onto the working and middle classes. The government hoped to pass the bill quickly through Congress, ignoring public pressure, but it failed to recognize that Colombia's political arena had changed dramatically since the signing of the peace agreement.

The 2021 National Strike

In late April 2021 fresh calls for a national strike exploded across 600 towns and cities all over Colombia. The protests were a spectacle the country had never seen before—fusing organized marches with orchestra concerts, theater, dancing, and participatory assemblies—profoundly transforming urban spaces. Autonomous territories were created, blockading parts of cities or major roads and rebaptizing them with names like Puerto Resistencia and El Puente de las Mil Luchas (Sánchez, 2021). Most of the blockades hosted communal soup kitchens led by women who called themselves "mothers of the frontline." The protesters demanded the withdrawal of the regressive tax reform, the dismantling of the Escuadrón Móvil Antidisturbios (Mobile Antiriot Squad—ESMAD), the rolling out of social welfare programs, greater regional autonomy, and the immediate resignation of President Duque.

With the continuation of the protests, it became increasingly clear that the seemingly disparate forces were united in their fight against Colombia's political and ruling class and that the energy of the protests was outside of the institutional structures of Colombia's traditional left. The 20-member national strike committee, predominantly consisting of unionists but also students and LGBTQ+ activists, had launched the protests, but within a few weeks it became evident that the strike was not under its control. Nor did the leaders of the blockades coordinate their actions with each other. Hernández (2021: 134) grouped the demands of the protesters into three categories: "(1) the national agenda led by the strike committee; (2) various sectorial agendas of teachers, women, indigenous people, peasants, artists, drivers, and other sectors, some at the national and some at the regional or local level; and (3) an agenda of young people from poor neighborhoods." While these groups differed in levels of coordination and acceptance of the national leadership, they were broadly unified around opposition to repressive state policies and the demand for basic guarantees and the right to protest.

Negotiations between the government and the committee initially made progress on a number of guarantees but quickly froze when the government retracted its agreement, demanding that all roadblocks be lifted immediately. The move essentially called the strike committee's bluff, since both sides knew that it did not enjoy sufficient representation among the disparate protest groups to make such a demand. Despite efforts by the strike committee to broaden its base by bringing in new activists from blockades across the country, the problems of leadership and representation became increasingly evident. At the blockade in Nuevo Resistir, protesters declared, "the strike committee doesn't represent us," instead signing on to the demands of the alternative "youth platform" (Hernández, 2021: 133). Thus, as the strike progressed, the young protesters, whose demands centered on unemployment and exclusion, came to see the strike committee as "part of the existing institutional fabric which has been shown to be anachronistic in the current climate of social upheaval" (Hawkins, 2021).

Notwithstanding claims by the Colombian right spearheaded by the former President Uribe, it was also not credible that the center-left leader and former member of the M-19 guerrilla organization Gustavo Petro was secretly directing the protests. While Petro expressed support for the protests, declaring that "this is not a strike but a social explosion caused by the government itself," he also called for the blockades to be lifted (Semana, 2021). In reality, Petro had no more power to call off the protests than perhaps the national strike committee itself did. Nonetheless, the lesson of the popular uprisings that paved the way for the electoral victory of Pink Tide governments was that mobilizations such as these could open a space for political leaders to push for a more progressive platform, even when they did not lead the process. Petro has been one of the most successful left-wing politicians in Colombia's recent history. He came in second in the 2018 presidential elections, with nearly 42 percent of the vote, and is the front-runner in the 2022 presidential election.

Within a few days, President Duque was forced to withdraw the tax reform, and Finance Minister Alberto Carrasquilla resigned. Meanwhile, police repression escalated. Within a month of the protests, human rights organizations reported 44 killings, 1,832 arbitrary detentions, and 28 cases of sexual assault, all committed by the police and the military (Indepaz, 2021). But neither reform nor repression could prevent the mobilizations from escalating. Devoid of legitimacy, the government retreated into right-wing conspiracy theories about the "Communist threat" or "Russian manipulation" (Hylton, 2021). However, since the signing of the peace deal, these scare tactics have not had the same demobilizing power and no longer shield the government from addressing the demands of ordinary Colombians faced with a crisis of reproduction and the collapse of the health system.

Political Crisis

Approval ratings have plummeted for President Duque, falling from 33 percent in 2020 to 18 percent in 2021 (Telesur, 2021a). The collapse of popular support has also infected the whole political establishment. Similarly, former President Santos's approval rating fell from 83 percent, when he was first elected in 2010, to 22 percent, when he left office in 2018 (BBC, 2018). Even former President Uribe, who is on trial for bribery and corruption, has seen a dramatic decline in popularity. Right-wing allies are rapidly distancing themselves from Uribe and his current protégé Duque, although they are still aligned with the agenda of *mano dura* (heavy-handed) law and order. This became very clear when a motion of censure for police violence against the minister for defense called for by the opposition failed 79–31 in Congress (Telesur, 2021b).

What Colombians commonly refer to as the "political and institutional crisis" (Valencia, 2021) is a powerful symptom of the hegemonic crisis of the neoliberal project predicated on the inability of the Colombian ruling elites to continue the strategy of militarized neoliberalism. The initial round of neoliberal restructuring in the 1990s led to the transnationalization of capital and class, which at first strengthened various factions of Colombia's ruling bloc—both the one linked to transnational capital and the local and regional blocs linked to land, agribusiness, paramilitarism, and narcotrafficking (Hylton and Tauss, 2016; Richani, 2020). Throughout the 2000s under the leadership of Uribe, an uneasy alliance between the two factions was cemented by rapid economic growth, propelled primarily by the commodities boom. Since 2013, however, the commodities bust and resulting economic slowdown have seen the alliance quickly unravel. This tendency has been most concretely evidenced in the tensions around the peace deal between Santos, who is more closely tied to the transnational elite, and the FARC. The deal was greeted with fierce opposition from the reactionary faction of the ruling class tied to land (represented in the presidencies of Uribe and Duque) (Richani, 2020). However, neither faction had foreseen that the restricted democratic opening created by the peace deal would open the way for the return not of the traditional "communist" threat of peasant guerrilla movements or even organized labor but of a new popular movement. A reconstituted left has regained a powerful street presence, defied police violence, and brought neoliberalism to the forefront of public debate. In building sizable power outside if not within the state, the insurrectionary process offers significant lessons for understanding the challenge of renewing Colombia's left.

CONCLUSION

The lessons of the Chilean and Colombian protests have broad implications for progressive political projects and their relation to social movements. Most important, the emancipatory subjects of social transformation, as discussed in this chapter, are heterogeneous and defend a diversity of demands (gender, environment, indigenous rights, pensions, health, education, pensions, peace, etc.) that progressive political parties have recognized the need to champion. The vibrancy and perseverance of the protest movements in Chile and Colombia demonstrate the role of social movements in opening the way for progressive political projects even when the relationship between the two is not direct.

The analysis of the protests in Chile and Colombia reveals similarities but also strong differences. The most obvious commonality of the revolts is their criticism of neoliberal policies, state violence, and environmental destruction and opposition to the government in power. The Chilean popular uprising and Colombia's national strike are thus the material expressions and political manifestations of the hegemonic crisis of both neoliberalism and the countries' conservative and right-wing party establishments. Whereas Colombia has long been characterized by a weak political left and stable conservative governments, in Chile the crisis of representation extends to political parties of the center and center-left. Both cases also show certain parallels in the heterogeneity of the protesters, who represent a wide variety of social and political backgrounds and experiences. In particular, the younger generation (secondary school and university students), women, and indigenous communities have played a key role in the mobilizations, and their heterogeneity is visible in their representations, symbols, and organizational forms. In both countries, however, the protesters managed to transcend their differences by uniting to confront the government, deemed the defender of an oligarchic system of multidimensional exclusion and discrimination. Moreover, they managed to envision post-neoliberal and partly postcapitalist horizons while simultaneously supporting social democratic political projects. In the Chilean case, especially, the call for a new constitution that would overcome Pinochet's legacy helped propel a powerful integrative dynamic.

In addition, social and political struggles of previous years such as those waged by secondary school and university students against a market-based education system or by environmental movements and indigenous organizations against extractivist megaprojects were essential for strengthening the protest capacities existing in Chile and Colombia today. In both countries, the demonstrators were confronted with extreme repression and state violence, resulting in many dead and wounded. In the Colombian case, paramilitary groups and right-wing civilians also participated in the attacks against protesters. Chile and Colombia have both witnessed an insurrectional offensive by social movements, in the sense that the protesters were not merely defending their political rights or their socioeconomic position. Instead, they began to challenge the social contract (in Chile in the form of the constitution) and in part the existing social order and to envision a revolutionary horizon beyond the status quo. Examples include the self-organized initiatives of direct democracy, territorial assemblies, neighborhood councils, and solidarity-based economic models, all of which are indispensable pillars of any emancipatory project that aims to transcend capitalism. At the same time, however, a reformist, center-left approach still dominates the political agenda in both countries.

The partial successes and collective experiences could, however, be important starting points for the formation of new processes of emancipatory movements and left electoral alliances. Nonetheless, progressive political parties in Colombia are much weaker than many of their Latin American counterparts, which is why it was the social movements that initiated and largely led the protests. In Chile, the constitutional referendum and the recent local elections showed that the mass mobilizations have already played an essential role in facilitating the convergence between the demands of the protesters in the streets and political parties on the left. That trend eventually culminated in the victory of Gabriel Boric in the presidential elections, which once again reflected the close interaction and interdependence of social movements, popular organizations, and progressive governments. Boric's triumph is reminiscent of past experiences in Pink Tide countries, and a similar scenario could unfold in Colombia. There, the months of protest have vehemently expressed the widely shared desire for a more democratic and peaceful country. The popular outcry and the demands of the protesters and social movements on the ground will certainly be a major factor in the 2022 presidential race, when for the first time in the country's history a left-leaning candidate has a real chance of winning. Regardless of the electoral outcome in Colombia, progressive political parties in both nations will be reflecting on the protest experiences of 2019. They will be examining how, from the political arena, they can best recognize the diversity of the protesters and in particular the rights of women, LGBTQI and indigenous communities, students, and ecologists as part of a strategy for not only achieving power but retaining it and bringing about lasting social change.

NOTE

1. One example of the paramilitary counterinsurgency campaign is the violent persecution and near-elimination of the left-wing parties Unión Patriótica, ¡A Luchar!, and Frente Popular in the 1980s and 1990s.

REFERENCES

Abufom, Pablo
2020 "Los seis meses que transformaron Chile." Rebellion, March 4. https://rebelion
    .org/los-seis-meses-que-transformaron-chile/.
Altamirano, Pedro, Javier Arroyo, and Claudia Maldonado
2020 "Cuadro de síntesis analítica del estallido social en concepción." ONG
    ECO, Educación y Comunicaciones. http://www.ongeco.cl/wpcontent/uploads
    /2020/10/CUADRO-DE-SINTESIS-ANALITICA-DEL-ESTALLIDOSOCIAL
    -EN-CONCEPCION.pdf.
Amnesty International
2019 "Chile: política deliberada para dañar a manifestantes apunta a responsabi-
    lidad de mando." https://www.amnesty.org/es/latest/press-release/2019/11/chile
    -responsable-politica-deliberada-para-danar-manifestantes/.
Atria, Fernando
2020 "Chileans finally have a chance to scrap Pinochet's constitution." *Jacobin*,
    October 10. https://www.jacobinmag.com/2020/10/chile-democracy-augusto
    -pinochet-constitution-referendum.
BBC
2018. "Toma de posesión en Colombia: por qué Juan Manuel Santos, el presidente
    que logró la paz con las FARC, se va como uno de los menos populares." August
    6. https://www.bbc.com/mundo/noticias-america-latina-45059911.
Bellei, Cristián, Cristián Cabalin, and Víctor Orellana
2014 "The 2011 Chilean student movement against neoliberal educational policies."
    Studies in Higher Education 39: 426–440.
Boddenberg, Sophia

2019 "Chile: Aufstand im Labor des Neoliberalismus." *Blätter für deutsche und internationale Politik* 12: 37–40.

Boos, Tobias and Aaron Tauss

2020 "Insurrektion und Protest: Die Mobilisierungen in Ecuador, Chile, Bolivien und Kolumbien." *PROKLA:Zeitschrift für kritische Sozialwissenschaft* 199: 373–393.

Caviedes, Sebastián and Fernando Carvallo

2021 "Orígenes socioeconómicos y trayectorias políticas en la convención constitucional chilena." November 4. https://rosalux-ba.org/2021/11/04/origenes-socioeconomicos-y-trayectorias-politicas-en-la-convencion-constitucional-chilena/.

CINEP (Centro de Investigación y Educación Popular)

2014 "Informe especial de luchas sociales de 2013." https://issuu.com/cinepppp/docs/informe_especial_luchas_sociales_en.

Donoso, Sofia

2013 "Dynamics and change in Chile." *Journal of Latin American Studies* 43 (1): 1–29.

Dorado, Fernando

2019 "El paro nacional, la protesta social auto-convocada y el precariado movilizado." https://viva.org.co/cajavirtual/svc0663/articulo04.html#_ftn1.

El Espectador

2021 "Pobreza monetaria en Colombia llegó a 42,5% en el año del coronavirus." elespectador.com/economia/pobreza-monetaria-en-colombia-llego-a-42–5-en-el-ano-del-coronavirus-article/.

Fauré, Daniel

2021 "¿Un voto para Boric o para frenar a la ultraderecha?" December 8. https://prensaopal.cl/2021/12/08/un-voto-para-boric-o-para-frenar-a-la-ultraderecha/.

Fernández, Roberto

2019 "Qué es y qué expresa la Primera Línea." December 20. https://www.eldesconcierto.cl/opinion/2019/12/20/que-es-y-que-expresa-la-primera-linea.html.

Fischer, Karin

2017 *Clases dominantes y desarrollo desigua:. Chile entre 1830 y 2010.* Santiago de Chile: Ediciones Universidad Alberto Hurtado.

Fundación Instituto de Estudios Laborales

2021 "Cronología sindical: el rol de la CUT durante el estallido social." April 13. https://fielchile.cl/v2/2021/04/13/cronologia-sindical.

Fundación SOL

2020 "La realidad del trabajo precario en Chile." May 4. https://rosalux-ba.org/2020/05/04/la-realidad-del-trabajo-precario-en-chile/.

Garcés, Mario Fernando

2020 *Estallido social y una nueva constitución para Chile.* Santiago de Chile: LOM Ediciones.

Gill, Lesley

2016 *A Century of Violence in a Red City: Popular Struggle, Counterinsurgency, and Human Rights in Colombia.* Durham, NC: Duke University Press.

Gobierno de Chile
2019 "Nueva agenda social." https://www.gob.cl/agendasocial/.
Gómez, Alfredo
2019 "Llenar las calles, llenar los cabildos, llenar de cabildos." *Izquierda,* no. 81. https://revistaizquierda.com/secciones/numero-81-diciembre-de-2019/llenar-las -calles-llenar-los-cabildos-llenar-de-cabildos.
Guerrero, Sebastián and Diego Cabezas
2020 "Revuelta popular, asambleas territoriales y educación popular." January 6. https://www.clacso.org/en/revuelta-popular-asambleas-territoriales-y-educacion -popular/.
Harnecker, Marta
2015 *A World to Build: New Paths toward Twenty-first-Century Socialism.* New York: NYU Press.
2016 *Ideas for the Struggle.* Broadway, NSW: Resistance Books.
Hawkins, Daniel
2021 "The national strike in Colombia: a trade union perspective." globallabour column.org/2021/07/01/the-national-strike-in-colombia-a-trade-union-perspective/.
Hernández, Jorge
2021 "De la marcha hacia el centro al bloqueo en los barrios: las luchas por recono-cimiento y oportunidades en Cali durante el paro nacional de abril-mayo de 2021," pp. 127–150 in Centro de Investigación y Documentación Socioeconómica (ed.), *Pensar la resistencia: Mayo del 2021 en Cali y Colombia.* Documentos Especiales CIDSE 6. Cali: CIDSE.
Human Rights Watch
2019 "Chile: eventos de 2019." https://www.hrw.org/es/world-report/2019/country -chapters/325503#.
Hylton, Forrest
2021 "La resistencia." *London Review of Books,* May 31. https://www.lrb.co.uk/blog /2021/may/la-resistencia.
Hylton, Forrest and Aaron Tauss
2016 "Peace in Colombia: a new growth strategy." *NACLA Report on the Americas* 48 (3): 253–259.
Indepaz
2021 "Cifras de la violencia en el marco del paro nacional 2021." https://www .doingbusiness.org/content/dam/doingBusiness/media/Annual-Reports/English/ DB2019-report_web-version.pdf.
INDH (Instituto Nacional de Derechos Humanos)
2020 "Hospitales: Reporte 18, febrero, 2020." https://www.indh.cl/bb/wp-content/ uploads/2020/02/Reporte-de-datos-18-febrero-de-2020.pdf.
Jiménez, César
2020 "#Chiledespertó: causas del estallido social en Chile." *Revista Mexicana de Sociología* 82: 949–957.
Lamadrid, Silvia and Miguel Urrutia
2019 "Un millón doscientos mil." November 6. https://www.clacso.org/en/un-millon -doscientos-mil/.

Loingsigh, Gearóid Ó.

2021 "Colombia: unions operating under an authoritarian regime," pp. 55–60 in Dario Azzellini (ed.), *If Not Us, Who? Global Workers against Authoritarianism, Fascism, and Dictatorships*. Hamburg: VSA.

Mander, Benedict

2019 "The death of Chile's pension promise." *Financial Times,* November 29. https://www.ft.com/content/4f8107f8-0fd4-11ea-a7e6-62bf4f9e548a.

OECD (Organisation of Economic Co-operation and Development)

2018 "OECD economic survey Chile." www.oecd.org/eco/surveys/economic-survey -chile.htm.

Oikonomakis, Leonidas

2019 *Political Strategies and Social Movements in Latin America: The Zapatistas and Bolivian Cocaleros*. London: Palgrave Macmillan.

Ortiz, Carlos

2021 "La codicia de las élites en la pandemia," pp. 41–52 in Centro de Investigación y Documentación Socioeconómica (ed.) *Pensar la resistencia: Mayo del 2021 en Cali y Colombia*: Documentos Especiales CIDSE 6. Cali: CIDSE.

Palacios, Indira

2020 "Chile's 2019 October protests and the student movement: eventful mobilization?" *Revista de Ciencia Política*.40 (2): 214–234.

Pérez, Carlos

2019 "De la revolución de la chaucha a la guerra de Piñera." November 8. https://www.clacso.org/en/de-la-revolucion-de-la-chaucha-a-la-guerra-de-pinera/.

2020 "Vierzig Jahre Neoliberalismus in Chile." https://www.medico.de/fileadmin/_migrated_/document_media/1/carlos-prez-soto-40-jahre-neoliberalismus-in-c.pdf.

Petras, James and Henry Veltmeyer

2011 *Social Movements in Latin America: Neoliberalism and Popular Resistance*. New York: Springer.

Pizarro, Roberto

2020 "Chile: rebelión contra el Estado subsidiario." *El Trimestre Económico* 87 (346): 333–365.

Reperger, Simone

2021 "Corona in Chile: Das Ende des Neoliberalismus?" *Blätter für deutsche und internationale Politik* 6: 37–40.

Richani, Nazih

2020 "Fragmented hegemony and the dismantling of the war system in Colombia." *Studies in Conflict and Terrorism* 43: 325–350.

Rojas, René

2021 "Will neoliberalism finally end in Chile?" *Jacobin*, June 7. https://www.jacobinmag.com/2021/06/rene-rojas-interview-democracy-new-constitution -constituent-assembly-plebiscite-left-chile.

Sánchez Salcedo, José Fernando

2021 "Reflexiones sobre prácticas y culturas políticas en el paro del 2021," pp. 53–66 in Centro de Investigación y Documentación Socioeconómica (ed.), *Pensar la resistencia: Mayo del 2021 en Cali y Colombia*: Documentos Especiales CIDSE 6. Cali: CIDSE.

Sasse, Lea

2021 *Chile despertó: The Reasons for the Mass Protests in Chile 2019/2020.* Working Paper 166. Berlin: Hochschule für Wirtschaft und Recht Berlin/Institute for International Political Economy.

Sehnbruch, Kirsten and Sofia Donoso

2020 "Social protests in Chile: inequalities and other inconvenient truths about Latin America's poster child." *Global Labour Journal* 1 (1): 52–58.

Semana

2021 "Gustavo Petro vuelve a hablar de alocución: 'hoy ya no estamos ante un paro, sino ante un estallido social.'" semana.com/nacion/articulo/gustavo-petro-vuelve-a-hablar-de-alocucion-hoy-ya-no-estamos-ante-un-paro-sino-ante-un-estallido-social/202157/.

Somma, Nicolás

2012 "The Chilean student movement of 2011–2012." *Interface: A Journal for and about Social Movements* 4 (2): 296–309.

Telesur

2021a "Desaprobación de Iván Duque alcanza el 75% en Colombia." September 2. https://www.telesurtv.net/news/colombia-desaprobacion-ivan-duque-encuesta-invamer-20210902-0026.html.

2021b "Cámara colombiana niega moción de censura contra el Ministro de Defensa." June 1. https://www.telesurtv.net/news/colombia-camara-niega-mocion-de-censura-ministro-defensa-20210601-0030.html.

Tinsman, Heidi

2019 "La democracia chilena: las protestas y las herencias de la dictadura." NACLA. November 19. https://nacla.org/news/2019/11/19/la-democracia-chilena-las-protestas-y-las-herencias-de-la-dictadura.

Titelman, Noam

2021 "What does Chile's new left want?" NACLA. May 25. https://nacla.org/chile-new-left-frente-amplio.

United Nations

2019 "Informe ONU sobre la crisis en Chile describe múltiples violaciones de derechos humanos y hace un llamado a reformas." December 19. https://acnudh.org/chile-informe-describe-multiples-violaciones-de-derechos-humanos-y-llama-a-reformas/.

UNDP (United Nations Development Program)

2017 "Desiguales: orígenes, cambios y desafíos de la brecha social en Chile." https://www.cl.undp.org/content/chile/es/home/library/poverty/desiguales--origenes--cambios-y-desafios-de-la-brecha-social-en-.html.

Valencia, Alberto

2021 "¿Qué está pasando en Colombia?," pp. 15–40 in Centro de Investigación y Documentación Socioeconómica (ed.), *Pensar la resistencia: Mayo del 2021 en Cali y Colombia*: Documentos Especiales CIDSE 6. Cali: CIDSE.

Zibechi, Raúl

2005 "Militarism and social movements.*"* https://www.counterpunch.org/2005/03/05/militarism-and-social-movements/.

2012 *Territories in Resistance: A Cartography of Latin American Social Movements.* Chico, CA: AK Press.

2017 *Movimientos sociales en América Latina: El "otro mundo" en movimiento.* Bogotá: Desde Abajo.

Conclusion

The State, Social Movements, and Political Strategy in Latin America

Ronaldo Munck

Taking a retrospective view of the various national case studies contained in this volume in light of the issues framed in the introduction, I will try to pull together some of the main conclusions and lessons learned. This effort is intended not to close the debate but to open up a new research agenda that might help us in the period to come. We need to start, though, with certain theoretico-political clarifications that are essential to decoding the case studies' sometimes dense empirical material. First, it is important to understand that the capitalist state is not simply an instrument that can be "captured," as it were, by progressive or left-of-center governments and turned into a lever to usher in socialism. As is capital itself, the capitalist state is a social relation that reflects the dominant power in society, a "material condensation of a relationship of forces amongst classes" (Poulantzas, 1980: 128). Second, it is important to understand that the term "autonomy" as applied to social movements has at least two meanings, one of which is independence from bourgeois forces and another, derived from classical anarchist thought, is independence even from left-wing parties and, in some variants, from any politics whatsoever—a far more problematic proposition. To put it bluntly, "political independence" and "independence from politics" are not the same thing.

At this point, I will seek to weave in the findings of the various national case studies in terms of two overarching themes. One of these is social movements as at once within and against the state, with all the contradictions that entails. This helps us analyze the fraught but also productive engagement of some social movements with the post-2000 progressive governments of Latin America (as addressed by the editors of this volume in Ellner 2020; Munck, 2020; and Sankey and Munck, 2020). The other is the way in which radical social movements can work with reformist structures/forces while also seeking to outflank them. This dialectic, suitably updated, can serve to illuminate current debates around the state, social movements, and political strategy.

THE STATE AS A SOCIAL RELATION

In a recent overview of the challenges faced by the left-of-center governments in Latin America, Juan Carlos Monedero (2019: 5) noted that "the question of state power is one of the most complex issues for emancipatory politics." One of the most creative writers in the critical Marxist tradition on state power was Nicos Poulantzas, who had considerable influence in Latin America (see De Ipola, 1983) and is now making something of a comeback in radical political sociology (see Gallas et al., 2006). Poulantzas, writing in the late 1970s, when socialism appeared on the agenda after the 1974 Carnation Revolution in Portugal, was asking whether there was a path other than the classical Leninist "dual power" strategy and the reformist strategy encapsulated in the notion of a "long march through the institutions." He moved beyond his early Althusserian structuralism to embrace the microphysics of power articulated by Foucault and the emerging Gramscian problematic, but, above all, he engaged in practical politics and "learned on the job," as it were (see Jessop, 1985). His basic conclusion was that while building socialism did not end with the gaining of state power, contrary to anarchist belief it did include that step.

For socialist challenges to the capitalist state, the question of political strategy is crucial, and our analysis therefore needs to be fluid and adaptable to the circumstances. It needs to develop mediating concepts—such as hegemony, power bloc, and the people—between the abstract determinants of state power and the actual developments in political struggle as articulated in this volume. As noted above, the state cannot be seen as a neutral tool that provides equal opportunities to all social actors and political forces. This does not mean that a negative outcome is inevitable when transformative politics and social movements engage with the state. As Poulantzas (1980: 153) puts it, "whether or not one plays the game of existing power and becomes integrated into the state depends on the *political strategy* that is followed." That strategy under democratic conditions (and that includes contemporary Latin America) necessarily involves "creative tensions" (Poulantzas, 1983: 22) between social movements and left parties or, expressed differently, between direct democracy and representative democracy.

As for social movements, there is a long-standing debate on how they might fit in with a state-oriented strategy for political transformation. Against Foucault, Poulantzas did not see the adoption of a strategy for power as necessarily leading to the "integration of the plebs" into hypostatized power, though he did argue that "political strategy must be grounded in the autonomy of the organizations of the popular masses" (Poulantzas, 1980: 153). However, he was not consistent on this point; as a proponent of what was then known as left Eurocommunism, he still had faith in the ability of the communist parties to steer between maximalism and reformism. At the end of his life he moved beyond the strategy of state-driven transformation, taking a position more open to social movements as he moved closer to the revolutionary Marxism of Henri Weber. Previously, Weber had criticized Poulantzas for not taking into account the cyclical nature of popular mobilization and the dangers of demoralization and demobilization if all emphasis were placed on the transformation of state power (Weber, 1983).

POST-NEOLIBERALISM

The progressive governments across Latin America of the 2000s did not appear as a wave or a rising tide. Much writing takes this period as somehow self-contained, and the enthusiasm it awakened, though understandable in a global era characterized by defeat and demoralization, detracts from a cold analysis of its achievements and limitations. I would go back to postwar Latin America for a comparable continental wave of subaltern upsurge overflowing the boundaries of the existing order and its capacity to co-opt and divert the energy from below. From the 1950s to the 1970s we witnessed a wide range of social and political upheavals expressed in the "populist" governments, anti-imperialism, and developmental alliances. The main actors were the organized working class and its organizations, on the one hand, and the movements for land reform, on the other. This period closed with the military dictatorships that began in Chile in 1973. The 1980s were widely seen as a "lost decade" because neoliberal economic policies decimated the national development model and the working classes alike. There were just hints of the way widespread popular discontent could explode such as the semi-insurrectional Caracazo of 1989.

However, the 1990s were largely characterized as the long night of neoliberalism represented well by the Menem decade in Argentina, where a national-popular movement put itself at the head of an imperialist plan to recolonize Latin America. It was an era of severe economic crises: Mexico in 1994, Brazil in 1999, and Argentina in 2001–2002. The latter marked the end of the era of neoliberal hegemony as the collapse of the economic model led to a semi-insurrectional situation and the glimmer of dual power. Uprisings in Ecuador (in 1990) and Bolivia (in 1999) highlighted a pattern of revolt against the privatizations and other measures imposed by neoliberalism. The social movements of this era, for example, around water and gender issues, were not the class-based ones of the 1970s, and it is well to recall how class movements such as unions were weakened by militarism and monetarism. Emblematic of the new social movements leading this new phase of plebeian resistance were the Confederación de Nacionalidades Indígenas of Ecuador (Ecuadorian Confederation of Indigenous Nationalities—CONAIE), formed in 1986, and the Movimento dos Trabalhadores Rurais Sem Terra of Brazil (Landless Workers' Movement—MST), formed in 1985, both of which came to fruition in the 1990s as they extended their reach. There was a sea change under way as traditional forms of sociality returned and civil society began to rearticulate itself. This period closed and a new one opened with the election of the unique and contradictory figure of Hugo Chávez in Venezuela in 1998.

The 2000s are of course the era of the progressive governments that spread across the continent on the back of the social movement upsurges. These were not so much class-based as based on territory, including the barrio, and were centered around anti-neoliberal demands. There was an illusion in 2002 in Argentina that the era of politics was over and that the social movements would now be in command. The popular slogan *¡Que se vayan todos!,* referring to politicians, sought to mirror the Zapatista experience that began in 1994. In Argentina and elsewhere, national-popular movements returned to politics as part of a left turn. The social domain was not sufficient to achieve the demands of the social movements; politics was once again the terrain of engagement. The feminist movement perhaps captured best the way in which social movements could work in this new era, with a strong commitment to its own autonomy while engaging with the political domain to achieve feminist objectives.

By the mid-2000s the contradictions of the left-of-center post-neoliberal governments were beginning to show. There was an impetus, inevitable with the passing of time, to institutionalize these regimes that often led to continual reelection of political leaders. The struggle with the right-wing restorationist forces, notably in the case of Venezuela, led to an authoritarian turn after the death of Chávez in 2013. The relationships of progressive governments with social movements, though varied, were always characterized by tensions, as was predictable given their competing priorities. It would be an exaggeration to think of Bolivia under Morales as a "government of social movements" as its supporters portrayed it, but neither was it a continuation of neoliberalism by other means or a "passive revolution" in which restoration of the capitalist order was the true underlying objective (see, for example, Modonesi, 2013). What we do see generally during this phase is a prevalence of a social movement political grammar as against the earlier class grammar or the autonomist one that flourished briefly in Argentina in 2002.

The years 2013 to 2018 saw the unraveling of many of these left-of-center governments as the international conditions (the end of the commodities boom) and national ones (a natural disillusionment) set in. In Brazil, for instance, the Partido dos Trabalhadores (Workers' Party—PT), which held power for over a decade in a situation of relative stability, succumbed to corruption at the same time that it failed to continue delivering to its constituents and refrained from threatening the existing order. In Argentina, the openly promarket Mauricio Macri gained power on a wave of resentment against the left-Peronist movement. In Bolivia the long-lasting Morales government was swept from office after Morales's dubious decision to stand yet again even after losing a referendum. However, politics is a process, of course, and movements can learn and reconfigure themselves. Thus, the left-Peronist candidate swept Macri's market democracy from office in 2019, the movement led by Morales achieved an unprecedented victory in Bolivia in 2020 with the support of some of the social movements that had distanced themselves, such as the labor unions, and Correa's Citizens' Revolution nearly won the presidential elections of 2021 in Ecuador.

The removal from office of the Morales government in 2019 in a police/army operation backed by a reactionary uprising in the East of the country and legitimized by the Organization of American States was at least not opposed by some prominent indigenous and feminist leaders in a campaign that had international repercussions. Essentially, they argued that Morales had brought the coup on himself with his authoritarianism and his policy of controlling the social movements. Thus, Silvia Cusicanqui (2019) launched a fierce attack on Morales and the MAS government even as the reactionary forces were repressing the social movements with great violence:

> We are accused by an archaic left, a left that would represent the indigenous without knowing it, a male-centered left that has led everyone to be ashamed of critical thinking, I call it the new only one way to think [as neoliberalism presented itself]. It is part of a continental left coalition linked to the so-called progressive governments who have a guilty conscience because they are procapitalist.

Similarly, some members of the feminist and indigenous movements, who had been part of the Morales government or advisers to it, turned their refusal to call what took place a "coup" into a wider critique of the progressive governments in general.

This all-out attack on the progressive governments and the lack of will to defend them against the conservative/imperialist backlash that ensued was quite common in some quarters. Thus, Raúl Zibechi (2012: 270) argued that it would have been better for the social movements if the progressive governments had never happened; they would have continued radicalizing autonomously and would not have become entangled with the state. For Zibechi the purpose of the progressive governments was simply to "govern the movements and cancel their anti-systemic effects." These governments were exercising new forms of domination aimed at integrating the poor and disempowering the social movements through a concerted "offensive against autonomy" (305) and through social welfare programs. Only by "overcoming their offensive against autonomy . . . will the movements be able to get back on their feet and resume their march toward emancipation" (306).

For Zibechi (2017: 202) matters were quite simple: we "cannot construct another world through the state, that is a new iron law of revolution confirmed by a century of nefarious experiences." Underlying these proclamations are an essentialist conception of the state that fails to take into account its nature as a social relation and a simplistic opposition between a bad state and virtuous social movements based on the liberal duality between state and civil society. Nor is there an "iron law of revolution" akin to Michels's iron law of oligarchy with regard to unions or political parties. While Zibechi's journalistic accounts of social mobilization have been seriously questioned in Latin America for their lack of analytical and empirical rigor (see, for example, Cruz Rodriguez, 2019), he has been lauded as a leading theorist by "antipolitics" groups much as "antidevelopment" groups have taken up a particular version of *buen vivir*.

This maximalist or separatist perspective—which sees progressive governments as the main enemy—relies heavily on neoliberal thinking that demonizes the state and builds up a mythical civil society. It ignores the fact that in Latin America the left has been strongest when there were strong links between political activity and mass mobilizations. It takes literally the divide between reform and revolution when in practice there is no absolute division between the two. Above all, it pits the social against the political domain, a conflict that does not exist either in theory or in practice (see Baño, 1985). There has been a sophisticated debate in recent decades on precisely how the social and the political aspects of hegemony construction can be articulated (see, for example, Sader, 2011; García Linera, 2014). It is not a question of supporting all the actions of actually existing progressive governments but one of at least starting from the premise that they are not the main enemy of social movements. For Sader (2011: 125), the discourse of the World Social Forum is partly responsible for these positions in that it crystallized the separation between social struggle and the political sphere and thus "froze the strategy of the popular movements in the phase of resistance." This virtually spelled the end of strategy for much of the left, especially the international left, which could not move beyond the notion that "another world is possible" without spelling out the transitional measures for achieving this and dealing with the reality of state power. Instead, some members of this camp took refuge in a neoliberal vision of an always worthy civil society.

SOCIAL MOVEMENTS AND AUTONOMY

The question of autonomy with regard to social movements has been part of a key strategic debate in Latin America in recent decades. For some analysts/activists, autonomy is a negation of the world of capital and of political domination. This can lead to a certain apoliticism or even antipolitics such as the position of John Holloway (2002) in *How to Change the World without Taking Power,* which ignores all the crucial national and international issues of the day and rapidly descends into an impotent "scream." The project of autonomy also has as a central driver the rejection of any engagement with state power. It seeks to wrest from the state the political spaces and legitimacy dating back to the colonial era. It rejects all forms of domination and calls for an increase in social self-determination outside the boundaries of representative democracy. Best expressed by the Zapatistas and the *piqueteros* (or romanticized images of them), it refuses to engage with the state or with political parties, including those of the left.

The term "autonomy" also has a more specific and limited meaning in social movement discourse and left strategizing more broadly. The women's movement and the indigenous movements have always advocated autonomy in the sense of not subordinating themselves or their objectives to established political parties. In doing so, they have rejected Lenin's dictum that unions serve as "transmission belts" for delivering party directives to the working masses. Nevertheless, as Ana Dinerstein (2014: 5) notes from a critical autonomist perspective, the "autonomy of social movements vis-à-vis the state is both possible and impossible" in the sense that both capital and the state will always seek to capture or co-opt the movements. This does not mean, however, that social movements can ignore the state (most of their demands are in fact directed at it) or the political parties that seek to advance the project of radical social transformation.

Whereas political autonomy reflects a spirit of independence and self-reliance, autonomy from politics seeks to insulate social movements, as it were, from the hurly-burly of the political world. Social movements clearly do need to maintain their autonomy from political parties, even when they may share a general political outlook with them, to avoid the subordination of their objectives. But an assertion of autonomy that is not cast in the frame of the struggle to achieve hegemony can very rapidly lead to an apoliticism that disarms the movements politically and prevents them from making the necessary social and political alliances. The alternative notion of political autonomy that I pose, working within a hegemony-building frame, is about self-determination and creating the conditions for emancipation. It is thus not a question of creating a "fetishism of autonomy" (Hellman, 1992: 54) but one of focusing on the role it plays in the construction of the sociopolitical subject.

WITHIN AND AGAINST THE STATE

Those who work within the state may also take political action against it, given the fact that the state is social and not a thing, complex and contradictory rather than simple and unitary. As one research/action group studying how we might work within and against the state at the same time put it, "The struggle against the state—against the social relations it perpetuates—goes on all the time" (CSE, 1979: 5). The conception of the state as an arena for political contestation is very different from a conception of it as an instrument for domination. As Bob Jessop (1985) and others have shown, it is not that "the state" acts autonomously on the political stage but rather that its powers are activated by state officials and political leaders who exercise political will in specific ways. The state is heterogeneous—a complex institutional matrix— and subject to various pressures and change, albeit with a constant tendency to revert to its role as defender of the established order.

The chapters in this book demonstrate the complexity and contradictory nature of the relations between social movements and progressive governments and add a much-needed grounding to these theoretical assertions. Thus we see how feminism in Latin America, as an example of a "new social movement," has shown a remarkable ability to navigate between the state and terrains of autonomous mobilization. As Eduardo Moreira da Silva and Clarisse Goulart Paradis show in their chapter, there have always been complex interactions between feminists and the state in Latin America. Feminism has sought to influence public policy directly through participation and inclusion in the state apparatus, not least during periods of left-of-center governments since 2000. This has not necessarily spelled incorporation, and protest continues to function as an interaction in the cycle of negotiations with the state. In his chapter, Daniel Burridge focuses specifically on feminist cogovernance and movement-state negotiations in El Salvador in the context of Frente Farabundo Martí para Liberación Nacional (Farabundo Martí National Liberation Front—FMLN)–controlled state institutions. Feminist organizations have worked within and against the state in a way that has transformed the bureaucratic and authoritarian tendencies of the state itself. Cogovernment is no panacea and is certainly not devoid of contradictions, but critical collaboration between movements and the political order can advance basic social demands.

The longest period of social movement engagement with a progressive political party took place in Brazil with the PT in office, first at the regional level after 1988 and then at the national level from 2002 to 2016. In his chapter Gabriel Funari shows that the party was torn between its commitment to abide by the constitutional distribution of power and meeting the demands of its marginalized constituencies and their social movements. Ultimately the implementation of social reforms did not curb the political system's dependency on graft and patronage. Land reform was one of the main challenges facing these governments when, as described by Anthony Pahnke in this book, they came into conflict with the MST. The influential MST always tempered its autonomous orientation with support for the PT, especially at election times. External conditions, not least its conflictual/cooperative relationship with the PT, provided it with some opportunities but also foreclosed others. In the period since the removal of the last PT government in 2016, the MST has been forced to rely on its own resources without the umbrella of a friendly government.

THE DIALECTIC OF UNITY AND OUTFLANKING

The dialectic of unity and outflanking was a common meme in revolutionary Marxist circles in the 1970s. It meant that one could join forces with social democratic or reformist parties in pursuit of shared common goals while at the same time maintaining autonomy to address more radical objectives. This was a somewhat instrumental application of the united-front strategy, but in practice social movements may adopt similar strategies. Political strategy is crucial here, and it speaks against all forms of structuralism by placing agency at the heart of the analysis. The outcome of social movement engagement with progressive governments should not be seen as predetermined. After the apparent collapse of the first wave of left-of-center governments in Latin America—associated with the period between the death of Chávez in 2013 and the election of Macri in 2017—many "autonomist" commentators went so far as to say that the social movements would have been better off if they had never engaged with these governments—a notion that most movement leaders would undoubtedly not agree with. The case studies above provide rich evidence that the outcome of this engagement was never predetermined, with the state absorbing and neutralizing challenges. Rather, these case studies open up a wide range of possibilities, with advances and retreats that are part of the creative tensions involved. In some cases, social movements were able to carry out a dialectic of unity and outflanking that allowed for joint work with reformist forces without sacrificing the autonomous interests of more radical movements.

The theorists of new social movements have considered unions part of the bourgeois state (an ideological state apparatus, as it were), but in Latin America they were key actors in the defeat of the military dictatorships in the 1980s and in the rise of the left-of-center governments at the turn of century. In their chapter, Fabricio Carneiro, Guillermo Fuentes, and Carmen Midaglia describe the conflictual but also cooperative relationship between progressive parties and labor unions in the Southern Cone. The picture that emerges is a mixed one and cannot simply be described as co-optation. Where there is a unified union movement, the electoral strategies of progressive parties can lead to a fruitful alliance in pursuit of post-neoliberal economic policies. Focusing on Argentina, Leandro Gamallo discusses social conflict in a wide array of sites and its impact on the deepening of democracy. While some social movements were brought under the sway of progressive Peronist governments, others continue to mobilize on the streets to press their demands.

The dialectic of unity and outflanking was seen in the informal workers' movements and in the women's movement as with Ni Una Menos. In various countries organizations representing informal workers have pressured the established unions to represent their concerns and even form close alliances. The Latin American feminist movements for their part have managed to balance a wide appeal to democratic forces with a strong antipatriarchal orientation. It is thus possible to promote broad-based unity while maintaining a radical orientation. The alternative "purist" approach advocated by some autonomist currents would condemn these movements to splendid isolation without advancing their objectives. In practice, a rich diversity of experiences illustrates the viability of the dialectic of unity and outflanking (see Klachco and Arkonada, 2016; and Gaudichot, 2019) and belies any simplistic reading based on autonomist preconceptions.

Bolivia has undoubtedly been the leading example of intense social movement and progressive government interaction since 2006. There has been a rather polarized international debate around this experience, with some accusing the progressive government of betraying the social movements that were instrumental in its rise to power. In his chapter, John Brown examines in detail the interactions between the social movements and the progressive government and points to a complex and nuanced outcome that is not reducible to a betrayal narrative. Far from being a "reconstituted neoliberalism" (Webber, 2017), the Morales government changed the balance of forces in Bolivia in significant ways until its overthrow by a right-wing coup in 2019. Its roots in the popular classes were demonstrated by its decisive victory in the 2021 elections, which showed a unified social movement/progressive party front, albeit with significant tensions within it. Nevertheless, there were lessons to be learned from earlier attempts by the governing party to control the social movements that led to divisions in the popular organization leaderships and provided opportunities for the right-wing opposition. Seeking to control social movements in this way leads to social mobilizations' being stymied (they cannot be easily switched on and off). A social movement emphasis on "relative autonomy" may well ensue in the upcoming period, after the first wave of progressive governments and the early illusions it inspired.

THE RETURN OF POLITICS

One influential interpretation of the Zapatista experience is Holloway's (2002) thesis on changing the world without taking power. In many ways it bears a relationship to the Zapatista experience similar to that of Regis Debray's *Revolution in the Revolution* (1970) to the Cuban Revolution: it systematizes the lessons learned from an idealized reading of a complex historical experience, and it has resonance internationally without having a major impact in Latin America. After a brief flourishing in Argentina in 2002 and in the experience of the *piqueteros,* its impact faded (Almeyra, 2004). Indeed, the "scream" that Holloway idealized—*¡basta ya!*—did not change the world at all. While the right-wing utopia of a market-dominated society disappeared at the end of the 1990s, an autonomist utopia and the end of politics did not even last that long. Politics was returning center-stage toward the end of the 1980s and the "social illusion" that society could resolve its own problems was no longer seen as plausible by more than a few. With the return of politics, we saw the return of strategic thinking on the left (see Bensaid, 2020) as the setbacks of the past were absorbed and superseded by a new nondogmatic strategic debate.

The debate on the left on a strategy for power had largely vanished by the 1980s. Earlier debates had focused on the likes of Chile in 1973 and Portugal in 1974. How could the left "seize power" when it was no longer "storming the Winter Palace"? What was the relationship between progressive (often reformist) political forces and the aspirations of the revolutionary left? The 1980s and 1990s were by and large a period of defeat and demoralization, and accordingly these discussions disappeared from view. They were revived at the end of the 1990s with the Seattle antiglobalization movement of 1999 and the launching of the World Social Forum in 2001 as a social movement counter to capitalist globalization. These movements, as reflected in Hardt and Negri's (2000) *Empire,* saw an unmediated revolt by the "multitude" against the new global order. From this perspective political strategy faded from view. What the experience of the Latin American progressive governments and their complex relationship with social movements provided us with was a laboratory for studying the strategic and conflictual dimensions of state power, political parties, and social movements.

Just proclaiming the "autonomy" of social movements raised the need for political independence to a complete rejection of the political. Those who championed "autonomist" social movements said nothing about the way in which the experiences of resistance could be articulated politically. It was as if the multitude could spontaneously aggregate the plurality of its actions without the mediation of politics. As for the notion of autonomy taken as a political strategy, the conclusion presented by Gustavo Oliveira and Monika Dowbor (2020: 51–52) is relevant: "We cannot think of autonomy as a category that can explain what a particular social movement is. Movements are fluid and in many situations unpredictable because they are subject to diverse social dynamics." This element of fluidity and constant change cannot be captured outside a strategic power frame. Movements are not constantly mobilized; they ebb and flow, as the case studies above all show. Nor are social movements always progressive; the protests in Brazil in 2013 that began as anti-neoliberal but then gained an anti-PT dynamic, and there were mass mobilizations in Argentina against the legalization of abortion in 2021. In short, we cannot glorify all mobilizations and demonize all politicians.

With the waning of the Pink Tide governments beginning in 2015, the illusion of a simple global struggle against capitalist globalization faded almost completely. The question of the state was again central. The hope of a left utopia was as vain as the reformist Keynesian or Polanyian dreams of reining in the new rampant capitalism through state or social action, respectively. The Latin American experience since 2000 demonstrates that there is no unmediated path to social transformation—that all paths necessarily pass through the national state. On the sliding scale of strategic places in which power is contested, the national is still a decisive position, as the reemergence of nationalism and populism shows. Not even a strategy of dual power can be posed outside of the existing political institutions. Strategic left thinking has advanced considerably during this phase of complex political struggle and change at local, national, and regional levels in Latin America. We are now back in the era of strategic reason.

In the strategic debate now under way, the question of power has again come to the fore. We should recall, with Foucault (1996: 86–87), that power has no essence; it is not a substance but a relation. We need to bear in mind the "web of microscopic, capillary political power . . . the whole set of little powers, of little institutions situated at the lowest level." Social movements do not just respond simply to state power or the class that dominates but most often engage with these infrapowers, the direct forms of oppression they experience. We have seen in the country case studies above that this power is fragile and that electoral results can fundamentally change the balance of class forces in a country. Thus freedom is not the absence of power but realized only through its relation to power. What is vital is the "decisive will not to be governed" (Foucault, 1997: 35) that we witness in the political arena around elections and in the ongoing struggles of social movements.

We need to reject the inevitability of any particular outcome of the tense relation between progressive governments and social movements and instead develop a better understanding based on the kind of empirical data contained in the case studies above on what Foucault would see as the contingent nature of rupture. In Venezuela, where the rupture with the established order was most marked, we saw how contingent and contradictory that was with regard to the Chávez government's relationship with the militant peasant movement. Thus, in response to mass rural mobilizations in 2005–2006, as Lucas Koerner's chapter illustrates, the radical government was unable to meet their demands for a full agrarian reform, for this would have entailed a dismantling of the existing judiciary structures under the influence of the opposition. In Mexico, after the election of Andrés Manuel López Obrador in 2018, there were far fewer expectations of radical change from above, as it were, but we do see a close relationship between social movements and political parties. The engagement in which this resulted, as Emelio Betances shows in his chapter, has contributed in a tangible way to democracy even though it has not resulted in the fundamental social change advocated, for example, by the Zapatistas. In Ecuador, as Alejandra Santillana and Sebastián Terán Ávalos show, a long history of uprisings and revolts has questioned the stability of the established order. The 2021 election brought to the fore the frontal opposition between the progressive political movement associated with Correa and the ambitions of the indigenous and environmental movements, which went far beyond the "creative tensions" referred to above.

In conclusion, neither an obsession with an impossible autonomy or a focus on the state that ignores the deep transformations in civil society is adequate for understanding the complex dialectical relations between the social and the political dimension. The demonization of politics (*¡Que se vayan todos!*) and of "populist" or authoritarian leaders cannot be answered by a pure autonomy that condemns social movements to an inability to make the social and political alliances necessary to ensure that their objectives are met. Of course, in practice we observe a continuum between these two strategies. To move forward, the discursive construction of "the people" at times of elections that was achieved by progressive political/social movements needs to be matched by the construction of hegemony (including on the cultural terrain) by all left-of-center forces across society and its institutions. Without this, progressive governments will come and go without building a durable alternative to the established order.

While this is not the place for hasty conclusions, the resounding victory of the left candidate Gabriel Boric in the second round of the 2021 Chilean presidential elections, where he gained 56 percent of the popular vote, seems to validate some of the points made above and will provide a fascinating laboratory for the study of social change and political conflict in the years to come. It would be facile to see his victory as a simple culmination of the 2011–2013 student-led protests (of which he was a leader) and the wider citizen revolts of 2019–2021 and the constitutional process. There is a dialectic between social and political processes, and one cannot be read from the other. The message of the right wing is not an aberration, and José Antonio Kast, who is an open admirer of General Pinochet and whose father was a member of the German Nazi party, did achieve 44 percent of the vote. In the first round he won handsomely in the North of country, whipping up anti-immigrant feelings, and in the South, where the Mapuche question polarized political opinion. His message of order and stability was widely heard, and the accusation of "communism" (or just "Venezuela") had considerable resonance. The Boric campaign turned this around with a massive door-to-door campaign that gave it a 20 percent advantage in the northern province of Antofagasta. Boric openly appealed to the center and muted some of his earlier radical positions, for example, forming an explicitly "antifascist" alliance that drew in many of the Christian Democrats. The issue is not whether this was correct; he could have gone after the 52 percent of the population who did not vote in the first round with a more radical message. The point is, as noted above, that it is politics that prevails at certain points in the complex interplay between the social and political wings of the movement for social transformation.

REFERENCES

Almeyra, Guillermo
2004 *La protesta social en la Argentina (1990–2004): Fabricas recuperadas, piquetes, cacerolazos, asambleas populares*. Buenos Aires: Ediciones Continente.
Baño, Rodrigo
1985 *Lo social y lo político: Un dilema clave del movimiento popular*. Santiago: FLACSO.
Bensaid, Daniel
2020 "Sur le retour de la question politico-stratégique," *Contretemps: Revue de Critique Communiste*, January 11.
CSE (Conference of Socialist Economists)
1979 *In and Against the State*. London: CSE.
Cruz Rodríguez, Edwin

2019 "Pensar los movimientos sociales en y desde América Latina: una mirada crítica a la contribución de Raúl Zibechi." *Estudios Políticos* (Universidad de Antioquia) 56: 175–197.

Cusicanqui, Silvia

2019 "La sociedad boliviana no ha renunciado a su derecho, a su memoria y a su autonomía."
https://desinformemonos.org/la-sociedad-boliviana-no-ha-renunciado-a-su-derecho-a-su-memoria-y-a-su-autonomia-silvia-rivera-cusicanqui/.

Debray, Regis

1970 *Revolution in the Revolution.* Harmondsworth: Penguin.

De Ipola, Emilio

1983 "Présence de Nicos Poulantzas en Amérique Latine," p. 368 in Christine Buci-Glucksmann (ed.), *La gauche, le pouvoir, le socialisme: Hommage à Nicos Poulantzas.* Paris: PUF.

Dinerstein, Ana

2014 *The Politics of Autonomy in Latin America: The Art of Organising Hope.* London: Pluto Press.

Ellner, Steve (ed.)

2020 *Latin America's Pink Tide: Breakthrough and Shortcomings.* Lanham, MD: Rowman and Littlefield.

Foucault, Michel

1996 "Truth and juridical forms." *Social Identities* 2: 327–342.

1997 "What is critique?" in Sylvère Lotringer and Lysa Hochroth (eds.), *The Politics of Truth.* New York: Semiotext(e).

Gallas, Alexander, L. Brethhauer, J. Kannankulam, and I. Stulze (eds.)

2006 *Reading Poulantzas.* London: Merlin Press.

García Linera, Alvaro

2014 *Plebeian Power, Collective Action, and Indigenous Working-Class and Popular Identities in Bolivia.* Chicago: Haymarket.

Gaudichaud, Franck

2019 "Conflictos, sangre y esperanzas: progresismos y movimientos populares en el torbellino de la lucha de clases latinoamericana," pp. 13–96 in Franck Gaudichaud, Jeffery Webber, and Massimo Modonesi (eds.), *Los gobiernos progresistas latinoamericanos del siglo XXI: Ensayos de interpretación histórica.* Mexico City: UNAM Ediciones.

Hart, Michael and Antonio Negri

2000 *Empire.* Cambridge: Harvard University Press.

Hellman, Judith

1992 'The study of new social movements in Latin America and the question of autonomy," pp. 52–61 in Arturo Escobar and Sonia Alvarez (eds.), *The Making of Social Movements in Latin America.* Boulder: Westview Press.

Holloway, John

2002 *How to Change the World Without Taking Power.* London: Pluto Press.

Jessop, Bob

1985 *Nicos Poulantzas: Marxist Theory and Political Sociology.* Basingstoke: Macmillan.

Klachko, Paula and Katu Arkonada

2016 *Desde abajo desde arriba: De la resistencia a los gobiernos populares, escenarios y horizontes del cambio de época en América Latina.* Buenos Aires: Prometeo.

Modonesi, Massimo

2013 *Subalternity, Antagonism, Autonomy: Constructing the Political Subject.* London: Pluto Press.

Monedero, Juan Carlos

2019 "Snipers in the kitchen: state theory and Latin America's left cycle." *New Left Review* 120: 5–32.

Munck, Ronaldo

2020 *Social Movements in Latin America: Mapping the Mosaic.* Newcastle: Agenda Publishing.

Oliveira, Gustavo Moura de and Monika Weronika Dowbor

2020 "Dynamics of autonomous action in social movements: from rejection to construction." *Latin American Perspectives* 47 (5): 49–61.

Poulantzas, Nicos

1980 *State, Power, Socialism.* London: Verso.

1983 "Une révolution copernicienne dans la politique," pp. 37–41 in Christine Buci-Glucksmann (ed.), *La gauche, le pouvoir, le socialisme: Hommage à Nicos Poulantzas.* Paris: PUF.

Sader, Emir

2011 *The New Mole: Paths of the Latin America Left.* London: Verso.

Sankey, Kyla and Ronaldo Munck

2020 "Social movements, progressive governments, and the question of strategy." *Latin American Perspectives* 47 (4): 4–19.

Webber, Jeffery

2017 *The Last Day of Oppression and the First Day of the Same: The Politics and Economics of the New Latin American Left.* London: Pluto Press.

Weber, Henri

1983 "Une nouvelle strategie democratique?" pp. 51–61 in Christine Buci-Glucksmann (ed.), *La gauche, le pouvoir, le socialisme: Hommage à Nicos Poulantzas.* Paris: PUF.

Zibechi, Raúl

2012 *Territories in Resistance: A Cartography of Latin American Social Movements.* Translated by Ramor Ryan. Oakland, CA, and Edinburgh: AK Press.

2017 *Movimientos sociales en América Latina: El "otro mundo" en movimiento.* Bogotá: Desde Abajo.

Index

Index

About the Contributors

Emelio Betances teaches sociology at Gettysburg College. His publications include *State and Society in the Dominican Republic* (1995), *The Catholic Church and Power Politics in Latin America: The Dominican Case in Comparative Perspective* (2007), and *Busca de la ciudadanía: Los movimientos sociales y la democratización en la República Dominicana* (2016).

John Brown is a lecturer at the Centre for the Study of Politics, Maynooth University, Ireland. He is the author of *Deepening Democracy in Post-Neoliberal Bolivia and Venezuela: Advances and Setbacks* (2022) and "Neoliberalization, De-democratization, and Populist Responses in Western Europe, the US, and Latin America" (*Critical Sociology* 46 [7–8], 2020).

Daniel Burridge is a Ph.D. candidate in sociology at the University of Pittsburgh. He is also the youth development program director for Santa Maria Community Services in Cincinnati, Ohio, and secretary of the board of Voices on the Border. His dissertation is titled "Reinventing the Left(s) in El Salvador and Nicaragua: Revolutionary Legacies, Movement-State Negotiations, and Competing Projects of Governance."

Fabricio Carneiro is a professor in the Political Economy and Welfare research group at the Universidad de la República de Uruguay. His recent publications include (with Guillermo Fuentes and Martin Freigedo) "Health Care Reform in Latin America: Not All Roads Lead to Rome," in Satyro, del Pino, and Midaglia (eds.), *Latin American Social Policy Developments in the Twenty-first Century* (2020).

Susan Eckstein is a professor in the Pardee School of Global Studies and the Department of the Sociology at Boston University. She is the author of *Cuban Privilege: The Making of Immigrant Inequality in America* (2022) and coeditor (with Adil Najam) of *How Immigrants Impact Their Homelands* (2013).

Steve Ellner is a retired professor of the Universidad de Oriente in Venezuela and associate managing editor of *Latin American Perspectives*. He is the author or editor of over a dozen books on Latin American politics and history, among them the recent collections *Latin America's Pink Tide: Breakthroughs and Shortcomings* (2020) and *Latin American Extractivism: Dependency, Resource Nationalism, and Resistance in Broad Perspective* (2021).

Guillermo Fuentes is a professor in the Political Economy and Welfare research group at the Universidad de la República de Uruguay. His recent publications are (with Fabricio Carneiro and Martin Freigedo) "Health Care Reform in Latin America: Not All Roads Lead to Rome," in Satyro, del Pino, and Midaglia (eds.), *Latin American Social Policy Developments in the Twenty-first Century* (2020), and (with Xavier Ballart) "Gaining Public Control on Health Policy: The Politics of Scaling Up to Universal Health Coverage in Uruguay" (*Social Theory and Health* 17 [1], 2019).

Gabriel Funari is a Ph.D. candidate in the University of Oxford's Department of Sociology. He is the author of "Family, God, Brazil, Guns … : The State of Criminal Governance in Contemporary Brazil" (*Bulletin of Latin American Research* 40, 2021).

Leandro Gamallo is a postdoctoral fellow of the Instituto de Investigaciones Gino Germani at the Universidad de Buenos Aires and co-coordinator of the CLACSO research group Vigilantism and Collective Violence. He is the author of *De la furia a la acción colectiva: Las represalias violentas en Argentina* (2020), *Violencias colectivas: Linchamientos en México* (2014), and "Collective Violence and Politics in Argentina" (*New Global Studies* 14 [2], 2020).

Lucas Koerner is a Ph.D. student in Latin American and Caribbean history at Harvard University and a contributing editor of Venezuelanalysis.

Carmen Midaglia is a professor of political science and dean of the Faculty of Social Sciences at the Universidad de la República de Uruguay. She is co-coordinator of the CLACSO Poverty and Social Policy research group and the Public Policy research group of the Asociación Latinoamericana de Ciencia Política and coeditor of *Latin American Social Policy Developments in the Twenty-first Century* (2021).

Ronaldo Munck is a professor of sociology and director of the Centre for Engaged Research at Dublin City University and a senior researcher at the Instituto Interdisciplinario de Estudios e Investigaciones de América

Latina of the Universidad de Buenos Aires. He is the author of *Rethinking Global Labour: After Neoliberalism* (2020) and *Social Movements in Latin America: Mapping the Mosaic* (2020) and a lead author of Amartya Sen's International Panel on Social Progress report *Rethinking Society for the 21st Century* (2018).

Anthony Pahnke is an associate professor in the Department of International Relations at San Francisco State University. He is the author of *Brazil's Long Revolution: Radical Achievements of the Landless Workers Movement* (2018). His work on social movements, Brazilian politics, and development has appeared in the *Journal of Peasant Studies*, *Latin American Politics and Society, Monthly Review*, and *New Politics*.

Clarisse Goulart Paradis is a professor at the Universidade da Integração Internacional da Lusofonia Afro-Brasileira in Bahia, Brazil. She holds a Ph.D. in political science from the Universidade Federal de Minas Gerais and focuses on feminist political theory, state feminism, and women's activisms in Latin America.

Federico M. Rossi is a Humboldt Senior Fellow at the German Institute for Global and Area Studies in Hamburg and a professor and researcher of the Consejo Nacional de Investigaciones Científicas y Técnicas at the Universidad Nacional de San Martín in Buenos Aires. He is the author of *The Poor's Struggle for Political Incorporation: The Piquetero Movement in Argentina* (2017) and coeditor (with Marisa von Bülow) of *Social Movement Dynamics* (2015) and (with Eduardo Silva) of *Reshaping the Political Arena in Latin America* (2018).

Kyla Sankey teaches in the School of Business and Management at Queen Mary, University of London. Her work focuses on the history and politics of land struggles in Colombia, Latin American development, and social and labor movements in Latin America. Her publications include articles in the *Journal of Agrarian Change, Journal of Developing Societies, Critical Sociology,* and *Latin American Perspectives*.

Alejandra Santillana Ortiz is a feminist and a researcher at the Instituto de Estudios Ecuatorianos and the Observatorio del Cambio Rural and teaches at the Universidad Andina Simón Bolívar. She is a member of the CLACSO research group Estudios Críticos al Desarrollo Rural and of its Red de Género, Feminismos y Memoria en América Latina y el Caribe and also of a number of feminist collectives including the Ruda Colectiva Feminista,

Feministas del Abya Yala, and the Confluencia Feminista del Foro Social Mundial de Economías Transformadoras.

Eduardo Moreira da Silva teaches political science at the Universidade Federal de Minas Gerais. He is the author of *Ressignificações da representação política na contemporaneidade: Atores e conectores da rede estadual de Direitos Humanos em Minas Gerais* (2021) and articles in the *Revista Opinião Pública* and *Revista do Serviço Público*.

Aaron Tauss is an associate professor of international relations at the Universidad Nacional de Colombia, Medellín. He is the editor of *Marx: Crítica radical y praxis emancipadora en el siglo XXI* (2022) and *Sozial-ökologische Transformationen: Das Ende des Kapitalismus denken* (2016), the coauthor of *¿Pensar el fin del capitalismo?* (2015), and a coeditor of *Paramilitary Groups and the State under Globalization* (2022).

Sebastián Terán Ávalos teaches in the Facultad de Ciencias Humanas of the Pontificia Universidad Católica del Ecuador. His research is in the area of political sociology and sociology.

www.ingramcontent.com/pod-product-compliance
Lightning Source LLC
Chambersburg PA
CBHW021809270326
41932CB00007B/108